Understanding Delinquency

HUGH D. BARLOW
Southern Illinois University, Edwardsville

THEODORE N. FERDINAND
Southern Illinois University, Carbondale

 HarperCollins*Publishers*

Sponsoring Editor: Alan McClare
Project Coordination and Cover Design: York Production Services
Production Manager: Michael Weinstein
Compositor: York Production Services
Printer and Binder: R.R. Donnelley & Sons Company
Cover Printer: New England Book Components

Understanding Delinquency

Library of Congress Cataloging-in-Publication Data

Barlow, Hugh D.
    Understanding delinquency / Hugh D. Barlow, Theodore N. Ferdinand.
        p.   cm.
    Includes index.
    ISBN 0-06-042028-6
    1. Juvenile delinquency.   2. Juvenile delinquency—United States.
    I. Ferdinand, Theodore N.   II. Title.
    HV9069.B297   1992
    364.3'6'0973—dc20   91-32657
                                                                    CIP

91   92   93   94   9   8   7   6   5   4   3   2   1

Contents

Preface

This book is intended for advanced undergraduate and graduate students interested in understanding the misbehavior of youth and official reactions to it. We draw upon a rich heritage of theory and research stretching back more than a century. The main thrust of the work, however, is a review and analysis of contemporary scholarship.

Despite the political nature of our subject—delinquency—we have tried to avoid ideological debate. There is much to be learned from perspectives stretching clear across the political spectrum, and indeed, this textbook collaboration has drawn together two criminologists who are not of one ideological mind. On numerous occasions we have had to confront our differences head on. Value neutrality is inconceivable when considering such topics as drug use, gangs, delinquency in relation to race, class, and gender, and the overarching issue of societal reactions. We believe the final manuscript was enhanced by our willingness to explore issues from positions that initially at least we disagreed with.

Judging from media accounts, public opinion surveys, and the actions of government officials, these are times of pessimism about crime and delinquency. People see things getting worse, not better. As a result policies and practices flourish that tip the balance in favor of sterner law enforcement, harsher penalties, and more funds for the hard end of the justice process.

To be sure, there is little positive that can be said about the spread of crack cocaine, the upsurge in gang violence, and the growing core of chronic delinquents. But important and worrisome as they are, these problems are not the whole story. The bulk of juvenile offenders are still sporadic offenders who commit in the main minor offenses and are shaped more by situational opportunities and adolescent identity issues than any deep-seated criminal disposition. We therefore give serious attention to sporadic delinquents (no other text that we are aware of does this), the characteristics and correlates of status offending, and the nature of cliques and gangs.

For science, however, the problem of delinquency demands not only an understanding of adolescent misbehavior but also an explanation of why particular activities, people, and events come to be defined as delinquent, and why reactions to them are patterned as they are. Though we give in this book an emphasis to adolescent misbehavior, we also consider the problems of juvenile justice. Overall, we adopt a perspective that joins structure and process and that deals with delinquency on both a macro and micro level.

Finally, we attempt to find merit in each of the several theoretical viewpoints generally followed in studying delinquency—social controls, strain, conflict, and cultural deviance. We have discovered certain harmonies among them though each has its particular domain, scope, and utility. The student who reads and digests this book will come away seeing that each conceptual model answers questions that only it can handle effectively. The challenge lies in finding the right conceptual model for the right question.

Even though we have written the book for upper level students, we do not assume an extensive exposure to delinquency research or the theories that guide it. We therefore devote Chapter 2 to a description of how data on delinquency are generated and the principle methods of doing research in this area. In other chapters we demonstrate how particular methods are applied to the analysis of specific issues, for example, the prevalence and incidence of offending or the nature of the chronic delinquent. Theory is fundamental to an understanding of delinquency, and for this reason theory permeates the book, though specific theoretical issues and viewpoints are addressed in Chapters 11 and 12. In this way readers will be able to see how theory is applied to specific issues such as drugs and delinquency, gangs, or female delinquency. They will also see how the dimensions of theory—its domain, scope, testability, and even its political implications—affect its usefulness in explaining delinquency.

We believe it is vital for students of crime and delinquency to understand the historical and comparative dimensions of offending as well. How can current practices and patterns be explained without comprehending how they originated and developed? From time to time we invite readers to consider how we got to where we are and to apply the experiences of other societies when thinking about the problems of our own. For example, though proceeding from a much lower level of delinquency than in the United States, the Japanese have also experienced a slow but steady rise in recent years. Can we learn something about delinquency from the experience of the Japanese? Probably. Can we learn something about methods of controlling delinquency from the Japanese? See Chapter 10.

Many people helped us produce this book. Alan McClare, our editor, gave steady and helpful encouragement, keeping the project moving. Many colleagues made helpful suggestions:

Victor Burke, *University of Michigan*
Paul Holdeman, *Colorado State University*
David M. Horton, *University of Texas at Austin*
John A. Humphrey, *University of North Carolina at Greensboro*
Walter Shirley, *Sinclair Community College*
Ronald Tait, *University of Maryland*

Needless to say, they bear no responsibility for any of the book's shortcomings. We have done nothing here that both of us do not fully endorse. We are also grateful to our colleagues at the Carbondale and Edwardsville campuses of Southern Illinois University who spurred us on by their commitment to scholarship and who also understood the need for isolation from time to time.

Finally, we are most grateful to our families for their support. One of the memorable outcomes of this collaboration was the opportunities it afforded to bring our two families together. Our wives, Lynne Schmidt Barlow and Carolyn Baker Ferdinand, were a constant and much appreciated source of warmth and diplomatic criticism. The second author's two sons, Lorrin and Van, also made many very valuable suggestions regarding clarity and phrasing. Although our names are listed alphabetically in authorship, as nearly as we can determine we contributed equally to the volume.

Hugh D. Barlow
Theodore N. Ferdinand

Chapter

1

The Nature of Delinquency

*I*n August, 1990, an apparent double murder occurred in a middle-class midwestern suburb, leaving residents horrified and frightened. The crime was the talk of the city for two weeks. Detectives of the elite Major Case Squad, composed of investigators from different police departments in the region, spent hundreds of hours gathering evidence and interviewing all sorts of people, including many possible suspects. Not quite two weeks after the crime, the police announced the case was solved, and many residents were even more horrified and alarmed as the details came to light.

The murder victims were two young boys aged 7 and 9. They had not returned home after going off to play. A frantic search was made by relatives, neighbors, and police. Several hours later their nude bodies were found in a nearby wooded area. The boys had been strangled with their own shoelaces.

Everyone had a theory of what had happened, most people linking the crime to a killing that had occurred in the same woods two years earlier. The favorite theory was that an adult child-molesting serial killer was on the loose, and no child was safe. Some residents called for bulldozing the woods; most called for more police protection, while many neighborhood parents ordered their children to stay indoors. But few people were prepared for the story that eventually emerged. It turned out the boys had been in the woods with two older brothers of one of the boys, and all four had been engaged in an autoerotic "sex game" in which the blood supply to the brain is restricted in order to heighten the pleasure of masturbation. Apparently—(the details will probably never be made public)—the older boys (aged 10 and 13) had held the shoelaces around the younger boys' necks, and the younger boys died from lack of oxygen. The older boys were taken into custody by juvenile authorities, the 13-year-old charged with second degree murder, the 10-year-old with helping to conceal a crime.

Reactions were predictable. The news media scurried around interviewing children and parents in the neighborhood, finding out about the victims and their families, but most of all about the suspects and the goings on in the nearby woods. Characterizations of the older suspect ranged from "A nice, quiet boy" to "He was mature for his age and thought he was real cool," but no one described him as a "delinquent." As for the woods, everyone agreed it was a favorite hangout for neighborhood kids. Some youths reported that sexual activities among children were commonplace in the woods, others claimed never to have seen any, and parents generally denied that any such things went on there, especially not the sort engaged in by the boys in question. Shaken by the bizarre nature of the crime, some people called for the 13-year-old to be tried as an adult even though state law set the limit at 14 or older. Even if convicted of murder he would have to be released from custody at age 18, and many people could be heard objecting to this. No one pointed out how unfortunate it was that the suspects' identities were made public, in clear violation of the juvenile code, by an "unnamed police source."

This case is certainly not the everyday fare of juvenile authorities. In an extreme way, however, it illustrates some things that much crime and delinquency have in common: short-term pleasure, risk taking, and victims (sometimes the participants themselves). It also illustrates the group context of much delinquency: The fun and risky adventures take place in the company of others. The case also points to the importance of opportunity and freedom from supervision in facilitating and shaping crime and delinquency. It illustrates, furthermore, the role of the authorities and the public in shaping conceptions of proper conduct, including the definition of offenses and offenders, and the appropriateness of reactions to them. The case also illustrates that violent crimes are not confined to inner-city ghettos or to hardened delinquents with long rap sheets, and it shows as well that behavior is sometimes explained not by underlying motives but by situational contingencies. These issues are some of the most important in the field of juvenile delinquency and are among the topics we examine in the chapters that follow.

In this chapter we explore the meaning of delinquency and consider how acts and people come to be labeled delinquent. We will also consider how scientific interest in the problems of crime and delinquency developed and look briefly at some of the theoretical issues involved in the study of delinquency.

THE MEANING OF JUVENILE DELINQUENCY

As Robert Mennel (1973) observes, children have always misbehaved. Yet the notion of juvenile delinquency was unheard of until the eighteenth century, when organized state responses to adolescent crime and deviance first took shape. For centuries, problem children had been handled mainly in a family setting, with little or no involvement of the state. But the system of familial control began to weaken during the sixteenth and seventeenth centuries as more and more unpropertied people migrated to the cities in search of work and shelter.

In the overburdened cities, poor and immigrant families were prone to collapse, and more and more children could be found wandering the streets and getting into trouble. Industrialization hastened the process, and by the late eighteenth century "juvenile delinquency" was recognized everywhere as a major urban problem (see Box 1-1).

One response of European authorities to the growing delinquency among youth (which by most accounts was mainly petty and mischievous) was to reinvent family controls through a system of apprenticeships. Poor, neglected, idle, and mischievous children were farmed out to private households where they worked under the strict discipline of the householder at tasks considered suitable to their sex. On the other hand, children convicted of murder, armed robbery, and other serious felonies were subject to

---

Box 1-1   # Delinquency in London in the Early 1800s

There are, probably, 70,000 persons in the metropolis who regularly live by theft and fraud; most of these have women, with whom they cohabit, and their offspring, as a matter of course, follow the example of their parents, and recruit the general mass of mendicancy [begging], prostitution, and delinquency. This is the chief source of juvenile delinquents, who are also augmented by children, abandoned by the profligate among the working classes, by those of poor debtors confined, of paupers without settlement, and by a few wayward spirits from reputable families, who leave their homes without cause, either from the neglect or misfortune of their natural protectors. Children of this description are found in every part of the metropolis, especially in the vacinity of the theatres, the marketplaces, the parks, fields, and outskirts of town. Many of them belong to organized gangs of depredators, and are in the regular employ and training of older thieves; others obtain a precarious subsistence by begging, running errands, selling play-bills, picking pockets, pilfering from shops and stalls. Some of them never knew what it is to be in a bed, taking refuge in sheds, under stalls, piazzas, and about brick-kilns; they have no homes; others have homes, either with their parents or in obscure lodging-houses, but to which they cannot return unless the day's industry or crime has produced a stipulated sum.

It is from the thousands of children so situated that the chief mass of criminals is derived, who fill our prisons, the hulks, and convict-settlements. It is a most extraordinary fact, that half the number of persons convicted of crime have not attained the age of discretion. During the last seven years, out of 16,427 commitments in the county of Surray, 7,292 were under twenty years of age, and 370 under twelve years of age, and several of these not more than eight or ten years of age. . . .

Source: John Wade (1829), "A Treatise on the Police and Crimes of the Metropolis; especially Juvenile Delinquency, Female Prostitution, Mendicity, Gaming . . .", cited in Sanders, 1970: 135.

many of the same punishments meted out to adults: execution, transportation, prison , branding, and mutilation.

Exceptions to these general practices existed but were not widespread. Throughout Europe and colonial America, institutions for children emerged here and there, most of them small, privately financed, and unregulated. Contemporary social historians point out that these charitable "homes," "houses," "schools," and "hospitals" often ended up captives of the emerging capitalistic ethos, which stressed the economic value of children along with the virtues of profitability (see Platt, 1969; Mennel, 1973). As a result, philanthropy often had the hallmarks of exploitation, many children being forced to work long hours on a meager diet and under abusive conditions. The pervasive attitude among philanthropists and other do-gooders was one of promoting "virtuous industry" among the poor and delinquent, a euphemism for hard work under harsh conditions (see Sanders, 1970: 70–90).

Mennel (1973: xxvi) observes that organized responses to the misbehavior and deviance of youth grew partly as a result of this "calculated philanthropy," partly because of a "rising distrust of the ability of poor families to raise their own children," and partly through the failure of existing state efforts to deal effectively with the problem (see also Donzelot, 1979). The term *juvenile delinquency* began to be used as a euphemism for the crimes and misbehaviors of poor and lower-class children (see Platt, 1969). In the minds of many influential people, the problem called for a special response:

> The key to the solution of delinquency seemed to lie in the development of more institutions. A system of social control would have to be developed apart from the family which would discipline homeless, vagrant, and destitute children—the offspring of the poor. Ideally, this system would avoid the cruelty of sending children to jail, but it would nonetheless ensure that they were suitably corrected and reformed. [Mennel, 1973: xxii]

Given the assumption of failed familial control, the state was encouraged to take on the role of parent under the doctrine of *parens patriae*. In America, the jurisdictional complexity of the United States meant there was no national strategy, and individual states proceeded pretty much at their own pace. Yet a general movement beginning early in the nineteenth century can be discerned: from "houses of refuge" in New York, Boston, and Philadelphia; to the widely used but soon disreputable "reform schools"; and finally to the juvenile court. The juvenile court appeared first in Chicago, with the enactment of an 1899 Illinois law titled "An Act to Regulate the Treatment and Control of Dependent, Neglected, and Delinquent Children." A specialized state apparatus for dealing with problem children was thus established, and other jurisdictions quickly followed suit.

Under the 1899 Illinois act, delinquency was defined as a violation of "any law in this State or any City or Village ordinance." Dependency and neglect covered a multitude of conditions, including but not restricted to being destitute, homeless, or abandoned; being in need of public support; being deprived of "proper" parental care or guardianship; living with "vicious" or "disreputable" people or in an unfit place; or being a habitual beggar (Mennel, 1973: 130–131).

Lumping delinquency, dependency, and neglect together in the same statutory bundle appears to reflect three related notions: (1) the idea that children committing crimes and children suffering hardship and neglect come from the same barrel (i.e., the lower class); (2) the idea they could therefore be dealt with in essentially the same way; and (3) the idea that problem children could be "saved" through intervention, care, and treatment rather than through punishment. The ostensible purpose of the juvenile court, then, was to offer problem children specialized help and protection (as any good parent would), administered and regulated by the state. Under the Illinois act, delinquent children were not to be treated as criminals, meaning that the procedures for handling them and the dispositions available would be different from those used for "real" criminals.

In theory, the main thrust of the dispositional reforms was to keep children out of custodial institutions. In practice, the number of children detained in public and private reformatories and other "benevolent" institutions in the United States grew significantly during the period 1890 to 1923. John Sutton (1990: 1369) observes that the "institutional capacity expanded 112% in absolute numbers, and 44% as a ratio to the juvenile population." Additionally, Sutton notes, far from private custodial institutions withering in the face of expansion in the public sector, their growth outpaced that of public institutions. Thus, a period of much-publicized benevolence and reform actually resulted in more children being confined, the bulk of them in private institutions. Apparently, the reformers "were persuasive enough to create a perception of crisis in the child-saving system but not sufficiently united or powerful to mobilize support for comprehensive reform" (Sutton, 1990: 1394).

Conceptions of Juvenile Delinquency Today

The creation of the juvenile court stands as a major accomplishment of the so-called Progressive Era, despite the lack of comprehensive dispositional reforms. Over the past fifty years, the language of juvenile court statutes has changed in various ways. Many of the most significant changes however, are procedural rather than substantive. Thus, contemporary statutes contain much more about the rights of children and the procedures designed to protect their interests. The Illinois Juvenile Court Act of 1987 is a good example (see Box 1-2 on page 6). These issues were the basis of many appellate court battles over the rights of children versus those of adults, and over the balancing of the public's need to know what the state is doing on its behalf and the need to protect the privacy of children. For example, only since the 1960s have children had an automatic right to an attorney to represent them before the court.

A long-standing criticism of juvenile codes has been the broad range of behaviors that could result in a child being adjudicated delinquent. Commenting on the situation in the late 1940s, Sol Rubin (1949: 2) noted that "*no* juvenile court law confines its definition of delinquency to violations of laws and ordinances." In addition to such violations, all states included some of the following behaviors under the rubric of delinquency:

- growing up in idleness or crime
- wandering the streets at night
- habitually using vile, obscene, or vulgar language
- being incorrigible or otherwise beyond parental control
- jumping trains or entering them without authority
- visiting a house of ill repute

- habitually consuming alcohol
- engaging in promiscuous sexual behavior
- running away
- being habitually truant from school
- patronizing a poolroom
- habitually gambling

Box 1-2   **Excerpts from the Illinois Juvenile Court Act of 1987**

PURPOSE AND POLICY

The purpose of this Act is to secure for each minor subject hereto such care and guidance, preferably in his or her own home, as will serve the moral, emotional, mental, and physical welfare of the minor and the best interests of the community; to preserve and strengthen the minor's family ties whenever possible, removing him or her from the custody of his or her parents only when his or her welfare or safety or the protection of the public cannot be adequately safeguarded without removal; and, when the minor is removed from his or her own family, to secure for him or her custody, care, and discipline as nearly as possible equivalent to that which should be given by his or her parents, and in cases where it should and can properly be done to place the minor in a family home so that he or she may become a member of the family by legal adoption or otherwise. . . .

In all procedures under this Act, the following shall apply:

(a) The procedural rights assured to the minor shall be the rights of adults unless specifically precluded by laws which enhance the protection of such minors [for example, protecting confidentiality and restricting accessibility to records].

(b) Every child has a right to services necessary to his or her proper development including health, education and social services.

(c) The parent's right to the custody of their child shall not prevail when the court determines that it is contrary to the best interests of the child. . . .

OTHER PROVISIONS

[Most juvenile codes do not use words such as *prosecution, trial,* and *sentencing* when referring to juvenile court. Thus:]

"Adjudicatory hearing" means a hearing to determine whether . . . allegations that a minor under 18 years of age is abused, neglected or dependent, or requires authoritative intervention, or addicted, respectively, are supported by a preponderance of the evidence or whether the allegations . . . that a minor is delinquent are proved beyond a reasonable doubt. . . .

[Inspection and copying of the police records of minors arrested or taken into custody before their 17th birthday is restricted to specified parties, namely, law enforcement officers (when necessary for official duties), prosecutors, probations officers, social workers or others assigned by the court when it is essential to their duties, authorized military personnel, and persons engaged in bona fide research (when authorized by court and when the confidentiality of the juvenile is assured). In addition, there are restrictions on what can be reported to the media:]

Law enforcement officers may not disclose the identity of any minor in releasing information to the general public as to the arrest, investigation or disposition of any case involving a minor.

[Court records are similarly restricted.]

DELINQUENT MINORS

Those who are delinquent include any minor who prior to his 17th birthday has violated or attempted to violate, regardless of where the act occurred, any federal or state law or municipal ordinance.

[However, criminal prosecutions are limited:]

Except as provided in this Section, no minor who was under 17 years of age at the time of the alleged offense may be prosecuted under the criminal laws of this State or for violation of an ordinance of any political subdivision thereof.

[Thus:]

The definition of delinquent minor . . . shall not apply to any minor who at the time of an offense was at least 15 years of age and who is charged with first degree murder, aggravated criminal sexual assault, armed robbery, when the armed robbery was committed with a firearm, [and certain other firearms offenses]. These charges and all other charges arising out of the same incident shall be prosecuted pursuant to the Criminal Code. . . .

[In other words, such minors as well as all minors 17 to 21 years of age will be tried as if they were adults (i.e., at least 21 years of age).]

[The Act also treats drug law violations by a minor at least 15 years of age on any primary, elementary, secondary school, or college property as a prosecutable offense under the state's Controlled Substance Act or Criminal Code.]

[The Act permits any minor 13 years of age or older to be tried as an adult under the provisions of the Criminal Code, provided the act committed constitutes a crime under state law, and provided a motion to that effect is filed by the state's attorney and approved by a juvenile judge before any adjudicatory hearing commences. In such hearings the Act requires that the minor be represented by counsel. However:]

In making its determination on a motion to permit prosecution under the criminal laws, the Juvenile Judge shall consider among other matters: (1) whether there is sufficient evidence upon which a grand jury may be expected to return an indictment; (2) whether there is evidence that the alleged offense was committed in an aggressive and premeditated manner; (3) the age of the minor; (4) the previous history of the minor; (5) whether there are facilities particularly available to the Juvenile Court for the treatment and rehabilitation of the minor; and (6) whether the best interest of the minor and the security of the public may require that the minor continue in custody or under supervision for a period extending beyond his minority. . . .

DISPOSITIONAL ORDERS

[A variety of dispositions are available to the juvenile court, including probation; conditional discharge to parent(s) or guardian; protective (i.e., monitored) supervision by probation officers; drug or alcohol treatment; commitment to the care of the Department of Children and Family Services; or commitment to the Department of Corrections, Juvenile Division, to be detained in secure public facilities such as a juvenile detention home.]

"Juvenile Detention Home" means a public facility which provides for the safety, medical, educational, recreational, religious and other needs of youth held in a secure setting and may be either a free-standing structure or in the same building as an adult jail or lock-up as long as, in the latter case, the two are separate such that there would be no contact between juvenile and adult residents in the respective facilities. . . .

[Special procedures and dispositions are set out for "habitual juvenile offenders." Habitual juvenile offenders are minors who for a third time have been adjudicated guilty of an offense that would be a felony crime if committed by an adult, *and* the third offense was one of the following: murder or involuntary manslaughter, criminal sexual assault, aggravated or heinous battery involving permanent disability, disfigurement or great bodily harm to the victim, burglary of home or residence, home invasion, robbery or armed robbery, or arson. The state's attorney must file a petition to have the child adjudicated as a habitual juvenile offender, and the minor has a right to trial by jury. If the court decides that the minor is a habitual juvenile offender, the *mandatory* disposition is confinement until age 21 without possibility of parole, furlough, or nonemergency authorized absence (but good time may be earned at the rate of 1 day for 1 day served).]

Source: Illinois Revised Statutes, 1987.

Because these offenses would not be crimes even if they could be committed by adults (a few obviously cannot be), they are conventionally referred to as "status offenses," that is, illegal by virtue of the offender's age. As Rubin (1949: 4) points out, the juvenile code is broader in its restrictions than is the penal code governing the behavior of adults. The broad conception of delinquent behavior also reinforces the long-standing notion that the delinquency *problem* is essentially one of unsavory children from unsavory backgrounds.

During the 1960s, rates of crime and delinquency began to rise dramatically, as shown in Figures 1.1 and 1.2. In the case of property crime, arrest rates per 100,000 children under age 18 rose from 336.6 in 1960 to 1172.2 in 1979; for violent crimes, arrest rates rose from 26.6 in 1960 to 147.6 in 1979. These are increases of 248 and 455 percent, respectively. This alarming fact was worsened by the discovery that *middle-class* children from prosperous suburbs were by no means immune from delinquency. Not only were middle-class children being arrested in increasing numbers on charges of theft, drug use, and running away, but also the growing use of data collection techniques based on self-reports of offending (see Chapter 2) demonstrated that children from all walks of life could be considered delinquent. "Affluent parents have come to realize that they can no longer guarantee their children immunity from the system of justice so long reserved for children of the less favored" (Mennel, 1973: 198).

In our view, these developments help explain two trends: on the one hand, the procedural changes protecting the rights and reputations of children who get into trou-

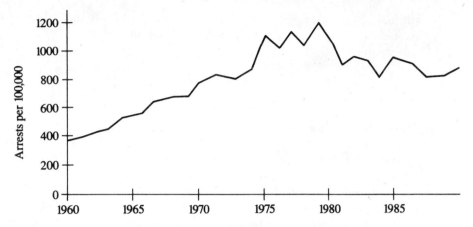

Source: FBI, *Uniform Crime Reports*, Washington, D.C.: U.S. Dept. of Justice, various dates.

*"Property Index Crimes" are burglary, breaking or entering, larceny-theft, and auto theft.

Figure 1.1 Juvenile arrests for property index crimes.

ble; and on the other hand, the increasing intolerance toward juveniles who most closely fit the conventional image of "real" criminals and who are most likely to come from lower-class or minority backgrounds (on this point, see Cicourel, 1968: 120). Examples of the latter include "habitual juvenile offender" provisions, often stipulating mandatory incarceration; an upscaling in the penalties for violent predatory crimes and for certain drug offenses; and the easing of restrictions on the ability of states to try such offenders as adults. (See Box 1-2 for examples of these provisions.) Given the political and social

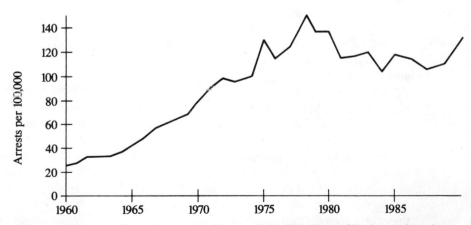

Source: FBI *Uniform Crime Reports*, Washington, D.C.: U.S. Dept. of Justice, various dates.

*"Violent Index Crimes" are criminal homicide, robbery, aggravated assault and forcible rape.

Figure 1.2 Juvenile arrests for violent index crimes.

history of juvenile delinquency, we believe it is less likely that either of these trends would have emerged had they conflicted with the interests of middle- and upper-middle class parents.

Law in Action: The Imposition of Delinquent Labels

No matter what the law books say, it is the *application* of law that really determines what and who is delinquent. Roscoe Pound (1923) called this "law in action," and his term is certainly apt. It draws attention to the decision making of legal actors, to the forces that shape their decisions, and to the consequences of those decisions for individuals affected by them and for society as a whole.

The importance of law in action becomes clear when we think of the term delinquent as a *label* attached to behavior and people rather than simply an act in violation of the law. Only when that label is actually applied is an act or person singled out for special treatment (arrest, prosecution, adjudication, trial, punishment). In effect, the person's status is transformed from "good" citizen to "delinquent" or "criminal." The social significance of a given act or person, then, lies in the reactions it calls forth. Children become official delinquents through a process in which that identity is socially constructed. (See Cicourel, 1968, for a detailed examination of this process.)

This is not meant to imply that delinquent children do not deserve the label. Most probably do, at least in the sense that they have behaved in violation of the juvenile code. However, the construction of that code (as we have seen) and its application in everyday enforcement may lead to children being labeled delinquent because of who they are rather than because of what they have done. It turns out that people in some groups are more likely to be singled out as delinquents and criminals than are other people.

A classic study of the differential imposition of delinquent labels is by William Chambliss (1973). Chambliss followed the experiences of two small-town juvenile gangs whose members were students at Hannibal High. The youths regularly broke the law. However, only the members of one gang, the Roughnecks, were considered delinquent by officials and repeatedly arrested. The other gang, named the Saints by Chambliss, largely escaped criminalization, and no members were ever arrested. Why the difference?

According to Chambliss, four factors played an important role in the differential response, and all related to the class position of the gang members: The Roughnecks came from lower-class families, whereas the Saints came from "respectable" upper-middle-class families. First, the Roughnecks were more *visible*. Unlike the Saints, whose members had access to cars and could escape the local community, the Roughnecks had little choice but to hang out under the surveillance of neighbors and local authorities. Second, the outward *demeanor* of the Saints deceived parents and officials. Around authority figures they wore masks of courtesy and obedience, and if accused of misbehavior they were apologetic. The Roughnecks, on the other hand, made no pretense at penitence when accused, and they made no effort to hide their hostile feelings. They were commonly rude to passersby, and they engaged in disturbances and fights, which the Saints avoided. In short, the Roughnecks misbehaved openly and showed little regard for social customs or the feelings of others; the Saints largely kept their misbehavior hidden. (For more on hostile and unpenitent demeanor as an affront to authority, see Black, 1980).

Third, in responding to the gangs' misbehavior, authorities and community members displayed a reactive *bias* that favored the Saints. The Roughnecks were labeled as "troublemakers" and "delinquents," while the Saints were characterized as typical adolescents who were merely sowing their wild oats as normal boys do. Chambliss (1973: 29) writes that

> in the eyes of the police and school officials, a boy who drinks in an alley or stands intoxicated on the street corner is committing a more serious offense than is a boy who drinks to inebriation in a nightclub or a tavern and drives around afterwards in a car. Similarly, a boy who steals a wallet from a store will be viewed as having committed a more serious offense than a boy who steals a lantern from a construction site.

Fourth, in defining the Roughnecks as boys who get into trouble, the community *reinforced* the "deviance" of gang members and helped produce a self-fulfilling prophecy: Deviant self-images promoted further deviance, and the Roughnecks found themselves seeking out, and being sought by, friends with similar self-images. As time went by, the escalating delinquency of the Roughnecks was matched and reinforced by escalating community disapproval and punishment. The Saints, in the meantime, remained respectable in the eyes of the community although in fact they continued to maintain a high level of delinquency. Chambliss (1973: 31) concludes his analysis as follows:

> Selective perception and labeling—finding, processing and punishing some kinds of criminality and not others—means that visible, poor, nonmobile, outspoken, undiplomatic "tough" kids will be noticed, whether their actions are seriously delinquent or not. Other kids, who have established a reputation for being bright (even though underachieving), disciplined and involved in respectable activities, who are mobile and monied, will be invisible when they deviate from sanctioned activities. They'll sow their wild oats—perhaps even wider and thicker than their lower-class cohorts—but they won't be noticed.

Aaron Cicourel's (1968) study of juvenile justice in two California cities confirms the downward skew of delinquency labeling. (For more recent literature, see Brooks, 1989.) Cicourel found that most official delinquents came from semiskilled and unskilled backgrounds, especially those delinquents recommended for prosecution (called "petitioning") and detention. Cicourel shows that these decisions are *routine* constructions influenced by what officials perceive to be the real causes of delinquency (e.g., disorganized families, a defiant attitude) and by the need to "get the job done." In addition, in the less likely event that a child from a middle- or upper-class family is caught up in the enforcement net, the family's greater resources are mobilized routinely to reduce the likelihood that the child's homelife will be tagged as "bad," which would explain the delinquency in the eyes of the authorities and warrant the child's removal from the home.

Differential enforcement of law is experienced by juveniles in another way: They are subject to more surveillance, harassment, degradation, and violence than adults, and police (especially juvenile officers) tend to be moralistic toward them (see Black, 1980: 24–28). On the other hand, the eventual disposition of juveniles stopped or arrested by police tends to be *less* severe than that experienced by adults. Donald Black (1980: 27–28) explains the enforcement response to juveniles as follows:

This seeming contradiction, a blend of unusual severity with unusual leniency, reflects the peculiar world of social control that juveniles inhabit. On the one hand, when abroad in public places young people are largely free of adult authority. On the other hand, for the rest of the day, at home and at school, they are subject to an enormous amount of social control by their parents and teachers. . . . In public places, the police effectively fill the normative vacuum created by the absence of parents and teachers. . . . Once in the police station, however, juveniles are most likely to be spared further action, since they can simply be returned to the jurisdiction of home and school. . . . Juveniles of all kinds . . . are subject to greater amounts of nonlegal social control than are adults—especially adult men—and this explains the leniency they generally enjoy at the police station. But when they are on the streets, they have no such immunity. To the contrary . . . , few people are more vulnerable to the police.

SCIENCE AND DELINQUENCY

The scientific study of delinquency is relatively young. Its origins are usually traced to the early nineteenth century, around the same time that authorities were expressing grave concern over rising rates of crime and delinquency. This was no coincidence, of course, but the timing was also influenced by the emergence of new disciplines we now take for granted: biology, sociology, and statistics. These disciplines applied the positivistic methods of science to the study of human beings and their activities.

The great insight of the early positivists was that theories could (and should) be tested against a body of facts. When applied to individuals and to society, the methods of science (observation, measurement, experimentation) would enable students of human behavior to move beyond the armchair and into the real world. Today, there is considerable debate over the benefits of positivism, some scholars arguing that facts are not concrete, objective things but, rather, are "constructed meanings produced within specific cultural, political, and economic contexts" (Michalowski, 1988: 18). Others have suggested that positivism has actually impeded the development of general theories of crime and delinquency by producing a "chaos" of narrow, discipline-bound definitions and theories (Gottfredson and Hirschi, 1990: 82–83; see also Matza, 1964). It is unlikely that the debate will be resolved anytime soon (see Gibbs, 1988; Nettler, 1988), but it is certainly worth noting that while the bulk of criminological work falls in the positivistic camp, important contributions have also come from scholars identifying with the social constructionist perspective, for example, the work of Cicourel (1968) cited above.

One of the most enduring arguments found in the scientific literature on crime and delinquency is that criminals (delinquents) are different from noncriminals (nondelinquents). One of the first to claim proof of this was Cesare Lombroso (1911). An Italian physician, Lombroso was attached to the army and later to prisons and asylums, which gave him a unique opportunity to examine thousands of individuals in search of the criminal type. Profoundly influenced by the evolutionary doctrine advanced by Charles Darwin, Lombroso claimed a triumphant discovery in 1870: the existence of a "born criminal," a sort of atavistic throwback to a more primitive evolutionary human state. According to Lombroso's research, the born criminal possessed five or more physical stigmata, or anomalies, for example, an asymmetrical cranium, a receding chin, a low forehead, large ears, too many fingers, protruding lips, low sensitivity to pain, and overly large or small eyes.

No one has subsequently confirmed Lombroso's apparent discovery, although interest in biological correlates of criminality remains strong to this day (see Wilson and Herrnstein, 1985; Daly and Wilson, 1988). Actually, the biological perspective most prominent in modern criminology combines biological with social variables, something that Lombroso himself eventually did. He mentioned poverty, emigration, high food prices, police corruption, and changes in the law itself as nonbiological codeterminants of criminal behavior. Modern sociobiologists have moved well beyond Lombroso in the sophistication of their theory and research, and yet no theory so far proposed seems adequate to the task of explaining just *how* biological differences produce differences in delinquency or crime, or any kind of deviance for that matter (see Fishbein, 1990).

According to Gottfredson and Hirschi (1990), two things are responsible for more confusion than enlightenment over the years since Lombroso embarked on his positivistic journey to uncover the cause of crime. One is the notion that delinquents or criminals are different from nondelinquents and noncriminals in ways other than their offending and that these differences *explain* the offending. In their view, the *tendency* to commit deviance (of any sort) is universal, individuals and groups differing only in their propensity to do so. Furthermore, the likelihood of any particular deviant act occurring varies independently of variations in the propensity of individuals to do it. The crimes that occur most often are the simplest and easiest to commit.

The second is the tendency of positivists to look for causes of crime within their own disciplines.

> The disciplines routinely begin by asking "What causes crime?" Not surprisingly, each discipline answers the question by pointing to its own central concepts. Thus sociology looks to social class, culture, and organization; psychology looks to personality; biology looks to inheritance; and economics looks to employment or work. [Gottfredson and Hirschi, 1990: xiv]

Gottfredson and Hirschi do not argue that positivistic research has failed to produce important knowledge about crime and delinquency. Instead, their position is that "much of the research generated by these disciplines is beyond the reach of their own explanations of crime" (Gottfredson and Hirschi, 1990: 274). We will have more to say on the Gottfredson–Hirschi perspective in later chapters.

TYPES OF THEORIES

Theories explain something. Unfortunately, some theories are written in such a way that it is difficult to pinpoint exactly what the explanation is. This makes it extremely difficult to test the theory (a major goal of science), a problem that is exacerbated when the theorist fails to link concepts to data or to suggest the appropriate strategies for doing so. To avoid these difficulties, some scholars insist that theories be *formally constructed.* According to Jack Gibbs (1972: 7–8),

> . . . a mode of formal theory construction stipulates: (1) major divisions or parts of a theory, (2) basic units of a theory (for example, statements in the form of empirical assertions),

(3) criteria by which basic units are distinguished as to type and identified, (4) rules by which statements are derived from other statements, (5) the procedure for tests of statements derived from the theory, (6) rules for the interpretation of tests, and (7) criteria for assessing theories.

Unfortunately, few if any criminological theories meet Gibbs's conceptualization of a formal theory, and this may explain why testing them has proved so elusive. It may also explain why many students in crime and delinquency courses (and in the social sciences generally) have such a difficult time with theory.

As if difficulties in assessing theories were not enough, theories also differ in other ways that complicate the landscape. One way theories differ is in level of analysis. For example, some are called *macrotheories,* while others are *microtheories.* Macrotheories deal mainly with large-scale phenomena such as social change or the social, economic, and political organization of society. Within this framework, crime and deviance are viewed as the properties of whole groups of people rather than of individuals. Because they focus on how societies are organized, such *macrosociological* theories usually relate crime to social structure. This does not mean they lack relevance for the everyday lives of individuals. On the contrary, such theories attempt to make sense of the everyday behavior of people in relation to forces that transcend individuals and even the immediate groups to which they belong.

Microtheories, on the other hand, focus on the ways individuals interact with others and with their immediate groups. *Microsociological* theories focus on the ways in which social interaction creates and transmits meanings. They emphasize the social processes by which people and events become delinquent or criminal. For example, as people move from situation to situation they are confronted with all sorts of messages, rules, and expectations, some of which may not be at all obvious. Through a process of sending, receiving, and interpreting messages, individuals help construct the social reality of which they are a part. This book finds the contributions of both types of theories useful in unraveling juvenile delinquency.

Another way theories differ is in their scope. Scope refers to the range of phenomena a theory purports to explain. *General theories* are meant to explain a broad array of facts and are generally not restricted to time or place. A general theory of crime will explain many (if not all) types of crime and can be applied to many (if not all) social and historical settings. Such a general theory also would subsume more *restricted* theories. Restricted theories explain a narrower range of facts or apply to a limited set of circumstances. Most modern theories of delinquency are regarded as restricted, a fact which reflects the boundaries of disciplines as well as the long-standing belief that crimes and criminals differ in significant ways and therefore require different theories to account for them. (Criminologists are seeing, however, signs of renewed interest in general theory; the most recent example is Gottfredson and Hirschi, 1990).

THE CHOICE OF THEORETICAL PERSPECTIVE

One of the most important decisions students of delinquency must make concerns the choice of theoretical perspective from which to analyze their subject. This decision is influenced, first, by the definition of the subject itself. Definitions that focus on delinquency as *behavior* invite perspectives that address the causes of delinquent behavior, that distinguish among different types of delinquent behaviors, and that shed light on the contexts and situations in which delinquent behaviors occur and on the opportunity structures that facilitate them. Definitions that focus on delinquency as *status,* on the other hand, invite perspectives that address the circumstances under which individuals and activities come to be labeled delinquent, and the effects those labels have on the people, activities, and events subject to them.

A second consideration in choosing a perspective from which to analyze delinquency is whether the subject matter is conceptualized as a phenomenon *sui generis,* something unique and distinctive in its own right. If it is, the models developed to explain delinquency will address its distinctive nature and therefore may not be directly transferable to other realms. Such an approach may borrow from the different scientific disciplines, but must inevitably supplant them with a perspective unique to its subject matter. In other words, this approach seeks to overcome the limitations of discipline-bound perspectives (see Gottfredson and Hirschi, 1990, Chapter 5).

The authors of this text view delinquency as both a status and a behavior. We also believe that no single discipline provides *the* perspective from which to study it. While we see delinquency largely as a social phenomenon, we also agree that biological, psychological, moral, and legal perspectives provide crucial insights into its nature, causes, and consequences. Periodically throughout the book we draw on these perspectives to help in our analysis of particular problems, but in the main our approach is sociological. Our concentration on the social dimensions of delinquency reflects our academic training and to some extent the realities of contemporary delinquency research, most of which has focused on four theories whose key concepts are sociological: control, strain, differential association, and cultural deviance (for a discussion of these theories, see Chapter 12).

In this work we shall present social scientific perspectives on delinquency as faithfully and respectfully as we can. We have not been governed by fadish enthusiasm in our selection of points of view. Rather, we emphasize those theories that the facts seem to fit best and that have proven useful in our own understanding of delinquency. We have not consciously sought to advance any particular ideological agenda, though no doubt our political views have seeped into our conclusions and colored them. But we are not of one mind on politics, and to a certain extent our differences have led to a better balance in the viewpoints presented here. We have been guided primarily by the evidence for and against a particular argument about delinquency. We have not endorsed a viewpoint or theory on political or moral grounds.

SUMMARY

In this chapter we explored the meaning of delinquency and how and why some activities, people, and events come to be labeled delinquent. We also looked briefly at the scientific study of delinquency and outlined the perspective taken in this book.

The problem of juvenile delinquency was born in the late eighteenth century when changing conditions brought on by the Industrial Revolution finally overwhelmed traditional forms of social control. The societal response to the growing numbers of poor, unsupervised, undisciplined, often homeless children wandering city streets was a hodge-podge of private and public endeavors under the guise of benevolence with correction. A spate of reforms designed to promote order and protect property while ostensibly saving children from the horrors of crime, dependency and neglect culminated in America with the establishment of the juvenile court in Illinois in 1899.

These reforms of the Progressive Era actually resulted in more children being confined, and the control net continued to widen well into the twentieth century. By the 1960s, rising crime rates and procedural reforms designed to shore up constitutional protections resulted in two trends: on the one hand, greater sensitivity to the rights and reputations of children who get into trouble, and on the other hand, increasing intolerance of forms of delinquency most often associated with lower-class and minority youths, especially gang activity, drug sales, and predatory street crimes. The historical downward skew of delinquency labeling continued, with disproportionate numbers of official delinquents coming from families at the lower end of the socio-economic scale.

Seeking to apply the methods of science to the analysis of social behavior, the nineteenth century positivists looked for the causes of crime and delinquency in the differences between delinquents and non-delinquents and between different types of delinquents and delinquencies. This strategy continues today but not without opposition. Some question such basic positivist assumptions as the objective nature of facts, while others point to the limitation of explanations rooted in individual disciplines.

This book takes a social scientific perspective on crime and delinquency that borrows from a variety of different disciplines and examines its subject at both micro and macro levels of analysis. Delinquency is conceptualized, first, as behavior that subjects a child to the possibility of intervention by the police and courts, and, second, as a status conferred through that intervention. Doing delinquent behavior and acquiring delinquent status might be thought of as two sides of the same coin. Even though they are connected, a satisfactory explanation of one does not mean we have an adequate understanding of the other, and vice versa.

PLAN OF THE BOOK

The remainder of the book is organized as follows: First we consider how the "facts" about delinquency and crime are created. Facts are not simply out there but are produced through the actions of researchers, data gatherers, and all those who participate in crime and delinquency as offenders and reactors. The picture we form of delinquency, then, depends on who produces the facts and on how and why they do it. The production of data on crime and delinquency is not something we can take for granted, and research is designed with this in mind. Research designs are influenced by the training of the investigator; by the goals of the project; by considerations of complexity, convenience, and cost; and, if relevant, by the particular theory being tested. We consider all these issues as we investigate how delinquency research is carried out and try to describe the contours and patterns of delinquency.

Next we explore various delinquency patterns. We take the position that delinquency involvement is a matter of degree. Accordingly, we examine two major patterns of involvement, sporadic and chronic. We also examine delinquency involvement in relation to special groups, offenses, and contexts: gangs, gender (women especially), status offending, drugs and alcohol, family, peers, and schools. Although delinquency theories are discussed periodically throughout these chapters, we reserve detailed discussion of theory until chapters 11 and 12.

Finally we explore the question of justice. The issue has already come up in this chapter and will be addressed again at various points in following chapters. However, in the final chapter we take a more detailed look at juvenile justice, including an extensive discussion of strategies designed to control and prevent delinquency.

REFERENCES

Black, Donald. 1980. *The Manners and Customs of the Police.* New York: Academic Press.

Brooks, Laure Weber. 1989. "Police discretionary behavior: A study of style." In *Critical Issues in Policing.* Edited by Roger G. Dunham and Geoffrey P. Alpert. Prospect Heights, Ill.: Waveland Press.

Chambliss, William J. 1973. "The Saints and the Roughnecks." *Society* 11:24–31.

Cicourel, Aaron V. 1968. *The Social Organization of Juvenile Justice.* New York: John Wiley & Sons.

Daly, Martin, and Margo Wilson. 1988. *Homicide.* New York: Aldine de Gruyter.

Donzelot, Jacques. 1979. *The Policing of Families.* New York: Pantheon Books.

Fishbein, Diana H. 1990. "Biological Perspectives in Criminology." *Criminology* 28:27–72.

Gibbs, Jack P. 1972. *Sociological Theory Construction.* Hinsdale, Ill.: Dryden Press.

———. 1988. "Reply to Michalowski." *The Criminologist* 13, no. 4: 4–5.

Gottfredson, Michael R., and Travis Hirschi. 1990. *A General Theory of Crime.* Stanford: Stanford University Press.

Lombroso, Cesare. 1911. *Crime, Its Causes and Remedies.* Boston: Little, Brown.

Matza, David. 1964. *Delinquency and Drift.* New York: John Wiley and Sons.

Mennel, Robert M. 1973. *Thorns and Thistles.* Hanover, N.H.: University Press of New England.

Michalowski, Ray. 1988. "Response to Nettler." *The Criminologist* 13, no. 4: 4, 18.

Nettler, Gwynne. 1988. "Christian Science vs. Social Science: Michalowski vs. Gibbs." *The Criminologist* 13, no. 2: 4–5.

Platt, Anthony. 1969. *The Child Savers: The Invention of Delinquency.* Chicago: University of Chicago Press.

Pound, Roscoe. 1923. *Interpretations of Legal History.* New York: Macmillan.

Rubin, Sol. 1949. "The legal character of juvenile delinquency." *The Annals* 261:1–8.

Sanders, Wiley B. 1970. *Juvenile Offenders for a Thousand Years.* Chapel Hill: University of North Carolina.

Sutton, John R. 1990. "Bureaucrats and entrepreneurs: Institutional responses to deviant children in the United States, 1890–1920s." *American Journal of Sociology* 95:1367–1400.

Wilson, James Q., and Richard J. Herrnstein. 1985. *Crime and Human Nature.* New York: Simon and Schuster.

Chapter
2

Finding Out About Delinquency

*I*n this chapter we will consider how researchers find out about delinquency. We will also discuss the major research strategies used to test theories about crime and delinquency. Our space is limited, however, so readers wishing a more comprehensive and detailed discussion can consult relevant research methodology texts (e.g., Hirschi and Selvin, 1967; Hagan, 1982; Binder and Geis, 1983).

SOURCES OF DELINQUENCY DATA

There are three main sources of information about the nature and extent of delinquency and crime: (1) police and court records, usually called "official data"; (2) victimization surveys; and (3) self-report surveys. This section of the chapter briefly describes each source and considers its benefits and limitations.

Official Data

Students of crime and delinquency rely heavily on published data taken from official records. These data are readily available, and they are relatively inexpensive to secure. Today, they are often available in "machine-readable" format, which means that they can be accessed and manipulated directly by computer. Official records of delinquency are of two sorts: those pertaining to delinquent *acts,* and those pertaining to delinquent *people.* They are called official records because they are compiled and disseminated by local, state, or federal authorities. These authorities compile information on offenses and offenders that come to their attention; therefore the kind of data they collect reflects their particular role in the criminal justice system. The further removed an agency is from the actual offense, the less useful its information is as an indicator of the nature or extent of delinquency. Thus, information on delinquency compiled through the juvenile court system tells us only about those offenders and offenses that make it to court; most do not. Even arrest data are a poor approximation to the real numbers of offenses and offenders (see Dunford and Elliott, 1984; Huizinga and Elliott, 1987).

The police are closest to offenses (and offenders) since they are usually the first official agency to come in contact with them. The primary source of published police data on crime and delinquency is the FBI's annual publication of the *Uniform Crime Reports (UCR).* The *UCR* contain information on offenses and arrests, but only the arrest data distinguish suspects by age. In 1987, an estimated 12,711,600 people were arrested in the United States; 21.1 percent of these were under age 18. The most common offenses were larceny-theft (including shoplifting, pocket picking, and any kind of stealing that does not involve force or fraud), runaway, burglary, liquor law violations, assaults, vandalism, and disorderly conduct, in that order. There were four times as many arrests for larceny-theft as there were for disorderly conduct (FBI, 1988: 168).

Despite the large numbers, the police only uncover the tip of the iceberg of crime and delinquency. This is because the vast majority of offenses remains hidden, the so-called dark figure of crime. Crimes remain hidden for various reasons (see Barlow, 1990: 120–130). Many are unknown to anyone but the offenders themselves, and in some cases even the offenders may not realize a crime has been committed. For example, did you know that it is a federal offense to open someone else's mail? Many offenses are hidden because witnesses or victims fail to report them to authorities. The most common reasons given for nonreporting are that the crime was unsuccessful, that it was not important enough, or that nothing could be done. Even violent crimes often go unreported, the most frequent reason being that people feel it is a private or personal matter (Bureau of Justice Statistics, 1989: 88–89). Information compiled through victimization surveys (discussed later) indicates that over 60 percent of offenses are not reported, a situation that has remained unchanged for many years (see Barlow, 1990: 122). This does not include status offenses, which are even less likely to be reported.

The official crime picture is shaped by the activities of the police themselves. Indeed, the police have the last word on which offenses get into their official record books. Only if the police decide to report an event as a crime is it eligible for the official record. That decision is far from inevitable even if the offense occurs in their presence and the offender is caught red-handed. Some offenses are simply dismissed as "unfounded," which means the police regard the incident as noncriminal or at least could not verify that an offense had occurred. Such decisions are certainly welcome when no crime has been committed, but evidence indicates that "founding" decisions are quite often in error. For example, an internal audit of the Chicago police department discovered that 18 percent of 377 rape cases, 36 percent of 649 robberies, and 50 percent of 708 burglaries had been incorrectly dismissed as unfounded (*Chicago Sun Times,* April, 1983). Similar findings have been reported elsewhere (e.g., Schneider, 1977; Maxfield, Lewis, and Szoc, 1980).

The police decision not to report a complaint may be influenced by what happens during encounters with victims, witnesses, and suspects. Researchers who rode around with the police in three U.S. cities discovered that although the legal seriousness of an alleged offense was the primary criterion guiding police reporting decisions, other things were also taken into consideration: The police were more likely to take formal action if the complainant showed respect and deference, if the complainant requested that such action be taken, or if the complainant and suspect were strangers (Black, 1970; Reiss, 1971). A nine-month observational study of police encounters with juvenile suspects found that police were more likely to take formal action (including making arrests) if suspects were cocky, argumentative, or uncooperative (Piliavin and Briar, 1964).

If a formal arrest is made, then a crime has been "cleared," and a suspect can be added to official police record books. Arrested individuals are the people officially doing official crime, even though they have not yet been convicted of the offense(s) in question. Again, only the tip of the iceberg is visible in police arrest records. Nevertheless, it is the only official count we have. Among the things we can learn from it are the typical age, race, and sex of suspects, and the relationship of these factors to the offenses committed. For example, police arrest data indicate that *age-specific arrest rates* (that is, the proportion of people of a given age who are arrested) tend to increase rapidly throughout adolescence, peaking at around 18 to 20 years of age and then falling off in a continual decline thereafter. This so-called age curve of crime has been observed for many different types of offenses, for males as well as females (though female rates rise to a much lower peak and taper off more gradually) and for whites as well as blacks. Indeed, some criminologists have claimed that the relationship between age and crime is *invariant,* holding across different countries as well as across history (Hirschi and Gottfredson, 1983; Gottfredson and Hirschi, 1987). (For commentaries, see Greenberg, 1985; Blumstein, Cohen, and Farrington, 1988a, 1988b; Tittle, 1988).

Police arrest data chronicle police activity as much, if not more, than they do the activities of criminals, and this fact is not lost on some critics who argue that poor and minority neighborhoods are overpoliced when compared with other parts of the city (Hagan, Gillis, and Chan, 1978; Smith, 1986). Some of these neighborhoods may well have more robberies, aggravated assaults, and murders than other areas, but the concentration of police enforcement also produces more official drunks, loiterers, vandals, petty offenders, and delinquents. The result is that official arrest data are composed disproportionately of poor and minority individuals. For example, although black Americans constitute only 12 percent of the U.S. population, in 1983 they constituted 48 percent of the people arrested for serious violent crime and 43 percent of those arrested for property crime. Looking deeper into the criminal justice system, blacks constituted almost 40 percent of those serving jail sentences and 47 percent of those serving state prison terms (Bureau of Justice Statistics, 1988: 41).

Just as there is evidence that poor and minority neighborhoods are overpoliced, there is also evidence that systematic underrecording of crimes occurs there as well. Such underrecording appears to be related to the type of crime involved and the people against whom it is directed. Kinsey, Lea, and Young (1986: 60–61) observe that English police disparagingly refer to some offenses as "rubbish" crimes, meaning that they are not "real" crimes in the police perspective. Rubbish crimes typically involve lower-class, minority, or female victims who are assaulted in a domestic setting by a friend, lover, or relative, or by an offender whom police regard as an amateur. Similar observations of police stereotyping and the resulting underrecording of crime have been made in U.S. and Canadian cities (see Shearing, 1979; Elias, 1986). The upshot of this is the prospect that the dark figure of crime will grow. When people feel the police will not help them, the flow of crime information to the police is reduced, thus further distorting the picture of crime that is drawn from official sources.

The researcher who is interested in information on juvenile offenders beyond the point of arrest will find that official records are often poorly maintained, and differences in legal definitions and administrative practice make comparisons across jurisdictions extremely difficult. To further complicate matters, the administration of juvenile justice is different and largely separate from the adult system. In many states, juvenile justice is a loose network of separate agencies that have different responsibilities. Illinois is a good example. The various agencies with jurisdiction in juvenile matters include

- local, county, and state police agencies
- juvenile and criminal courts, juvenile probation services, and other court service agencies
- Juvenile Division of the Illinois Department of Corrections
- Illinois Department of Children and Family Services
- Illinois Department of Mental Health and Developmental Disabilities
- Illinois Department of Alcoholism and Substance Abuse
- private social service agencies providing foster care, crisis intervention, residential care, various kinds of treatment, counseling, and other services
- schools

Considering this list, it should come as no surprise that good national data on juvenile offenders have been virtually nonexistent, and this has been especially true of data on status offenders (Smith et al., 1980: 197; Snyder and Finnegan, 1987: ix–x). However, modern electronics and widespread use of management information systems have dramatically improved data collection efforts within states and nationwide. Recent publications by the National Center for Juvenile Justice (e.g., Snyder et al., 1989) and by the justice information agencies of various individual states (e.g., Illinois Criminal Justice Information Authority, 1989) attest to these improvements. Nevertheless, it should always be remembered that the further away one moves from the criminal event itself, the more selective and unrepresentative of actual delinquencies the data become.

Victimization Surveys

One way researchers attempt to uncover the dark figure of crime is through *victimization surveys*. A victimization survey is designed to determine whether people have been victims of crime. The most well-known and extensive survey is the annual National Crime Survey (NCS), conducted by the Census Bureau on behalf of the Bureau of Justice Statistics, a unit of the Justice Department. The NCS has been conducted every year since 1972. Approximately 49,000 households (not individuals) are contacted each year, and members 12 years of age and older are interviewed. In 1987 roughly 93,000 people were interviewed (Bureau of Justice Statistics, 1989: iii). The housing unit *address* is kept on file for three years, and interviewers go back every six months even if the family originally interviewed there has moved. Once a household address has been in the sample for three years it is replaced by another. The sample is so constructed that in effect the interviewing and rotation are continuous.

The NCS interview is composed of two parts. The first determines whether respondents have been victims of crime "during the past 6 months." If they have, the second part elicits detailed information about the incidents that respondents recall. Recent revisions to the NCS survey instrument have extended the range of information collected. Among other things, one can learn about the protective measures victims took when they were assaulted, robbed, or raped; about relationships between victims and offenders involved in those crimes; about the family circumstances of crime victims; about the spatial distribution of crimes; and about the nature and timeliness of the police response.

NCS data are not without limitations, however. First of all—and this is true of most surveys—they rely on recall. Unfortunately, people's memories are often flawed. Second, respondents may purposely deceive interviewers, though carefully constructed questionnaires and well-trained interviewers can reduce the risks of this. Embarrassment or fear may be common reasons for deception in the case of crimes that victimize women or children. The simple expedient of using female interviewers in a nonthreatening setting has been shown to uncover more domestic violence (Kinsey, Lea, and Young, 1986: 63). Third, the NCS data are not comparable with the *Uniform Crime Reports*. Offense definitions, data collection methods, scope, and the kinds of information solicited differ in various ways from one to the other (see Barlow, 1990: 136). Fourth, information about *offenders* is dependant upon the victim seeing the perpetrator or subsequently finding out who it was. Fifth, victims' perceptions about many things—what actually happened, for example, or an offender's age—may be inaccurate.

These difficulties mean that NCS data are imperfect, yet they are without question the best and most convenient data to use for many research projects, especially those dealing with the circumstances surrounding criminal victimization. On the other hand, their use in delinquency research is likely to be more limited precisely because of the fourth and fifth problems just mentioned.

Self-Report Surveys

A different way that researchers explore the dark figure of crime is through the use of *self-report* surveys. These surveys ask people to recount their own involvement in delinquency and crime. The usual technique employs a questionnaire listing a variety of "deviant," illegal, or criminal activities. Respondents are asked how often they have engaged in any of the acts during a specified period of time, usually the year preceding the survey.

Self-report surveys have been most widely used to explore the nature and extent of juvenile delinquency. There are three reasons for this: First, most juvenile crime is hidden from official records, especially at the level of individual cases; second, relatively easy access to representative samples of juveniles can be secured through the school system; and third, adults are more likely to balk at admitting to criminal activities.

With adolescents as their target, self-report questionnaires can be constructed to include status offenses, things that would not be crimes if committed by adults. On the other hand, there are scholars who believe that some widely used self-report instruments have tended to trivialize juvenile crime because they have been heavily weighted in favor of status offenses and otherwise minor crimes. It is precisely because of this, they argue, that the prevalence of self-reported delinquency is similar across class, race, and sex lines (see Hindelang, Hirschi, and Weis, 1979).

More recent self-report surveys of adolescent crime have sought to avoid the problem of trivialization. This is done by including a more extensive and varied list of predatory crimes (such as robbery, burglary, and sexual assault) along with the standard list of status offenses. This is illustrated in Figure 2.1. This list of 47 items was developed for use in the National Youth Survey (NYS). The survey was conducted with a representative sample of American youth born between 1959 and 1965. The initial survey was conducted in 1977, and the same sample was reinterviewed annually over a period of five years. The NYS has produced a wealth of information about the delinquency involvement of youth. One of the first things it confirmed was that while most delinquency is sporadic and minor in nature, a small group of "chronic" delinquents is responsible for a disproportionate amount of all types of self-reported delinquency (Dunford and Elliott, 1984). We will make use of the National Youth Survey when we discuss sporadic and chronic delinquency in later chapters.

Over the past thirty years many smaller-scale self-report studies have been done, often in a single school or city. One great advantage of the instrument is that it can be easily tailored to specific research questions. On the other hand, critics of the technique point out that self-report research has tended to underrepresent people at greater risk of delinquency, for example, urban residents, youths with police records, and school dropouts (see Kleck, 1982). Regardless of how carefully the self-report study is constructed and carried out, all single-school or single-city studies face the problem of *generalizability:* The results simply may not be applicable elsewhere.

To recapitulate, we have reviewed the three primary sources of data on delinquency: official records, victimization surveys, and self-report surveys. Together, they provide a wealth of information, but none is without its limitations and drawbacks. Self-report techniques are clearly best for tapping the prevalence and incidence of juvenile crime and status offenses. However, when one moves into the realms of serious and chronic delinquency, official police records may identify many of the same offenses and offenders. Victimization data give a different view of crime, seeing things from the perspective of victims. They help researchers construct images of the circumstances surrounding criminal events, but they, too, have their limitations. Let us turn, now, to the major research strategies criminologists use to examine crime and delinquency and to test their theories.

METHODS OF DELINQUENCY RESEARCH

A variety of methodologies is available to the delinquency researcher. Some are more commonly used than others, often because of cost, time, and convenience rather than inherent superiority. The choice of a particular research strategy is also influenced by the

[The following behavior items were designed to tap delinquent or criminal behavior as reported by interview respondents. It should be noted that the National Youth Survey items cover a more extensive list of behaviors than have most previous questionnaires. The researchers wanted a set of items that was both comprehensive and representative of the range of delinquent acts. This list of forty-seven acts may well become the standard for future self-report measures.]

Self-Reported Delinquency and Drug-Use Items As Employed in the National Youth Survey

How many times in the last year have you:

1. Purposely damaged or destroyed property belonging to your parents or other family members.
2. Purposely damaged or destroyed property belonging to a school.
3. Purposely damaged or destroyed other property that did not belong to you (not counting family or school property).
4. Stolen (or tried to steal) a motor vehicle, such as a car or motorcycle.
5. Stolen (or tried to steal) something worth more than $50.
6. Knowingly bought, sold, or held stolen goods (or tried to do any of these things).
7. Thrown objects (such as rocks, snowballs, or bottles) at cars or people.
8. Run away from home.
9. Lied about your age to gain entrance or to purchase something; for example, lying about your age to buy liquor or get into a movie.
10. Carried a hidden weapon other than a plain pocket knife.
11. Stolen (or tried to steal) items worth $5 or less.
12. Attacked someone with the idea of seriously hurting or killing him/her.
13. Been paid for having sexual relations with someone.
14. Had sexual intercourse with a person of the opposite sex other than your wife/husband.
15. Been involved in gang fights.
16. Sold marijuana or hashish ("pot," "grass," "hash").
17. Cheated on school tests.
18. Hitchhiked where it was illegal to do so.
19. Stolen money or other things from your parents or from other members of your family.
20. Hit (or threatened to hit) a teacher or other adult at school.
21. Hit (or threatened to hit) one of your parents.
22. Hit (or threatened to hit) other students.
23. Been loud, rowdy, or unruly in a public place (disorderly conduct).
24. Sold hard drugs, such as heroin, cocaine, and LSD.
25. Taken a vehicle for a ride (drive) without the owner's permission.
26. Bought or provided liquor for a minor.
27. Had (or tried to have) sexual relations with persons against their will.
28. Used force (strong-arm methods) to get money or things from other students.
29. Used force (strong-arm methods) to get money or things from a teacher or other adult at school.
30. Used force (strong-arm methods) to get money or things from other people (not students or teachers).
31. Avoided paying for such things as movies, bus or subway rides, and food.
32. Been drunk in a public place.
33. Stolen (or tried to steal) things worth between $5 and $50.
34. Stolen (or tried to steal) something at school, such as someone's coat from a classroom, locker, or cafeteria, or a book from the library.
35. Broken into a building or vehicle (or tried to break in) to steal something or just to look around.

36. Begged for money or things from strangers.
37. Skipped classes without an excuse.
38. Failed to return extra change that a cashier gave you by mistake.
39. Been suspended from school.
40. Made obscene telephone calls, such as calling someone and saying dirty things.

How often in the last year have you used:

41. Alcoholic beverages (beer, wine, and hard liquor).
42. Marijuana-hashish ("grass," "pot," "hash").
43. Hallucinogens ("LSD," "Mescaline," "Peyote," "Acid").
44. Amphetamines ("Uppers," "Speed," "Whites").
45. Barbiturates ("Downers," "Reds").
46. Heroin ("Horse," "Smack").
47. Cocaine ("Coke").

Figure 2.1 Self-reported delinquency items from the 1977 National Youth Survey. *Source:* Delbert S. Elliott and Suzanne S. Ageton. 1980. "Reconciling Race and Class Differences in Self-Reported and Official Estimates of Delinquency." *American Sociological Review* 45(7), February 1980. Reprinted by permission of the American Sociological Association.

purpose of a study; the availability of alternative strategies; the nature and findings of prior research (if any); and by the knowledge, skills, and training of the researcher.

Not surprisingly, most delinquency research deals with the beliefs, attitudes, experiences, and behaviors of young people. The main way to study these things is through direct contact with the individuals concerned. There are various difficulties in doing this, some of which have already been mentioned. However, a word ought to be said about three recurring problems: *ethics, reactivity,* and *attrition.*

Ethics   Any research with human subjects involves ethical dilemmas. Since what is ethical is a matter of judgment and is relative, people do not always agree on what the dilemmas are, let alone on their resolutions. The risks of being charged with unethical conduct are lessened, however, if delinquency researchers follow these practices:

1. Avoid procedures that inflict physical or mental anguish, or otherwise threaten the well-being of subjects.
2. Secure the voluntary, informed consent of participants, which means that they are told of possible dangers or risks associated with their participation and that they agree to participate without being pressured to do so.
3. Allow participants to withdraw from the research at any time.
4. Protect the anonymity of participants—especially important when the behavior in question is illegal and punishable.
5. Debrief participants after the research—especially important if the researcher has had to deceive participants as to the real purpose of the research. Deception may be the only way a researcher can protect results from being contaminated if subjects know what is going on.
6. Avoid practices that invite or encourage participants to break the law. Moral issues aside, when researchers participate in gang activities in order to study

them, for example, their role as objective scientists may become confused with their role as participants.

Reactivity People who are being studied may behave differently because of it. This is the problem of *reactivity*. Any researcher who intends to interview, experiment with, or observe other people must try to minimize reactivity. One answer is deception. Another is to conduct the research over a relatively long period of time in the hope that subjects have adjusted to, or forgotten, the fact that they are being studied. A third is for the researcher to be as unobtrusive as possible. A fourth—mainly appropriate in experimental research—is to use a control group (discussed later).

Attrition This problem generally surfaces in projects that require subjects to participate over an extended period of time. Attrition occurs when people drop out of a research study. Sometimes they move away, sometimes they decide not to participate after initially agreeing to do so, sometimes they cannot be found by researchers, and sometimes they simply forget. Attrition only becomes a serious problem if it distorts the representativeness of a sample or reduces its size significantly.

The remainder of the chapter discusses the main research strategies employed in the study of crime and delinquency. The survey method has already been discussed, but we will encounter further examples of its use in some of the studies described below.

Cross-Sectional Studies

Much criminological research is *cross-sectional,* meaning that data are collected at a single point in time or over a short period of time. For example, a researcher interested in the relationship between family life and self-reported delinquency might interview a sample of youths about conditions and relationships at home to see if any differences there are associated with differences in reported delinquency. A simple but well-designed cross-sectional study can be an effective way to test specific hypotheses about family factors and delinquency. Sometimes the results are unexpected.

Two studies illustrate this point. In one, a sample of 824 male and female adolescents residing in private households in an urban area were interviewed about their family situation and their relationships with parents (Cernkovich and Giordano, 1987). They were also asked about their involvement in delinquency and their relationships with friends. In the other study (Johnson, 1986), over 700 male and female high-school sophomores were interviewed about family conditions and delinquency. In addition, data were gathered on the official trouble experienced by the sample, that is, contacts with police, school officials, and other authorities.

The methods used in these two studies were conventional enough, but their findings have challenged conventional wisdom as well as some earlier delinquency research. For example, both studies found that children from broken homes (i.e., single parent) were not more prone to delinquency than other kids, nor were children with stepparents. The studies also found that girls and boys differ not only in the frequency and seriousness of their delinquency (boys are more delinquent in both ways) but also in the family factors that appear to influence their behavior. For example, Cernkovich and Giordano found that females were more strongly influenced by the belief that parents respected, supported, and accepted them and by parental disapproval of their friends, whereas boys were more strongly influenced by parental control and supervision of their behavior and by the frequency with which they talked with their parents about their feelings, ideas, and future plans.

In the Johnson study, regardless of levels of self-reported delinquency, girls living in female-headed households had more official trouble than children living in intact, in male-headed, or in stepparent homes. This finding could not be accounted for by differences in race, class, quality of parent-child relations, or quality of school experiences. This suggests that "police and school and court officials . . . find it easier or more appropriate to officially respond to the behavior of daughters of single mothers. . . ." (Johnson, 1986: 73).

The fundamental limitation to most cross-sectional research is the lack of a temporal dimension other than what can be created through questions about past events. Apart from the fact that people may not remember past events accurately even if they want to, the behavioral links between past and present can only be inferred. If researchers wish to move beyond such inferences, or are interested in direct tests of causality, there are other strategies to consider. One is the experiment.

Experiments

When researchers wish to establish whether one variable causes another, they will think first of constructing an *experiment*. The experimental method is generally considered the ideal way to measure causation because the experimenter can control the research process. The "true" or "classic" experiment examines causation in the following way:

1. It establishes whether there is, in fact, a relationship or association between the key variables. The variable that is believed to cause the effect is usually called the *independent* or *treatment* variable, and is conventionally denoted by the letter X. The variable that X affects or causes is called the *dependent* or *outcome* variable, and is designated Y. The first step in establishing causality is to show that a change in X is associated with a change in Y.

2. However, because two variables are associated does not necessarily mean that one causes the other. The design of a true experiment allows the researcher to establish that the change in X occurs *before* the change in Y. This is conventionally referred to as establishing the "temporal (or causal) order" of a relationship.

3. Showing that X and Y are related and that a change in Y followed rather than preceded a change in X still does not establish that X causes Y. This is because the change in Y might have been caused by something other than X. A true experiment allows the researcher to rule out "rival" causes. This is arguably the most difficult thing to do in social science research if for no other reason than there are often many variables, some probably unknown, that could affect Y directly or the relationship between X and Y.

To satisfy the three criteria of causation—association, temporal order, and exclusion of rival causes—the true experiment is usually conducted in a controlled laboratory setting, with people ("subjects") *randomly* assigned to either *experimental* or *control* groups. Those subjects assigned to the experimental (or "treatment") group will be exposed to manipulation of the independent variable, X, while those assigned to the control group will not. In both groups, the dependent variable, Y, will be measured before and after the manipulation of X. If Y changes in the experimental group but not in the control group, or changes more in the former than in the latter, the experimenter is reasonably confident that the change in Y was caused by the change in X. However, the experiment ought to be repeated with other subjects, just to make sure.

In the true experiment, then, the use of a control group helps ensure that any change in Y is due to the manipulation of X and not something else. The before-and-after measurements establish the temporal order, and the random assignment helps ensure that there are no preexisting differences between subjects in the two groups that might account for the experimental outcome. Even so, when only a few subjects are used in an experiment, it is hard to ensure that the experimental and control groups are alike even with random assignment. In this event, the researcher will try to limit differences among his subjects beforehand by using only people who are of the same sex, say, or the same race, age, or economic or educational background.

This is just one way in which researchers performing experiments with human beings often have less than full control over possible rival causes. In many cases it is simply not plausible to bring representative samples of people into a laboratory for experimentation. In crime and delinquency research, the difficulties of carrying out true experiments are exacerbated by the very nature of the subject: Not only is it often not possible to isolate or manipulate important variables in a laboratory setting, but there are also many kinds of crime that one would certainly not wish to experiment with in the laboratory or anywhere else.

Field Experiments   True experiments are rare in delinquency research, as they are in the social sciences generally. Aside from the difficulties just mentioned, the more control researchers exercise over the experimental environment, the less that environment approximates the real world. Laboratory findings or experiments conducted in other controlled settings such as prisons, halfway houses, and boarding schools may have little validity outside those environments. (Of course, this objection would not apply if the findings were to be used only within the setting where the experiment took place.)

An alternative is to conduct experiments in the field, where the environment more closely approximates the natural settings in which social behavior occurs. What they lack in researcher control, field experiments may gain in generalizability, that is, applicability beyond the experimental situation. And it should be pointed out that researchers usually try to construct field experiments so that they approximate as closely as possible the characteristics of true experiments.

The Provo Experiment   A classic experiment in delinquency research is the Provo (Utah) experiment designed to study the effectiveness of a community treatment program for youths who had committed serious offenses and/or were repeat offenders (Empey and Erickson, 1972; also see Lundman, 1984: 157–172). All 326 boys first went through an adjudicatory hearing in which the judge assigned them to either probation or incarceration. At that point in each boy's hearing, the judge opened an envelope containing a randomly selected piece of paper saying "experimental" or "control" group and announced the placement decision. In this manner each boy was randomly assigned to one of four groups: the probation experimental group, the probation control group, the incarceration experimental group, and the incarceration control group.

Those boys assigned to the experimental probation group were placed in a special community treatment program, while their control counterparts were placed on regular probation. Those boys assigned to experimental incarceration were also placed into the special community treatment program, while their control counterparts were placed in a state training school.

The experimental treatment program included daily guided group interaction in which the boys described and discussed their delinquent activities, debated their futures, and came to terms with their fears and emotions and considered how they might deal with them in nondelinquent ways. In addition, the boys in this group went home each evening and on the weekend. "On the street they had to choose between delinquent and conforming behavior. Moreover, they were making visible choices. Group members generally knew one another directly or by reputation, and were thus aware of what a member was doing apart from the group" (Lundman, 1984: 166). Through the group sessions, some of the boys gradually learned that they could gain recognition and prestige by avoiding delinquent activities; they became informal leaders who looked after new arrivals and thus furthered their own involvement in and commitment to the process of treatment.

The results of the experiment for delinquency prevention were mixed. In terms of future trouble with the law, the boys sentenced to experimental probation could not be distinguished from the boys who had been placed on regular probation. On the other hand, those placed on probation had fewer future arrests than those sentenced to incarceration in the state training school. The boys initially sentenced to incarceration but then diverted into the community treatment program also had fewer future arrests than the boys actually incarcerated. Together, these findings suggested that community-based, group-centered treatment was more beneficial as an alternative to incarceration than as an alternative to regular supervised probation.

A variety of practical problems affected the actual carrying out of the Provo experiment, and compromised its design as a result. The most important of these surfaced when the juvenile court judge proved reluctant to sentence youths to incarceration. It was soon apparent that there were too few boys to permit meaningful comparisons between the control and experimental groups among boys sentenced to incarceration. To solve the problem, Empey and Erickson sent all the incarcerated local boys to the experimental treatment program and compared this group with boys sent to the state training school from other parts of Utah. This provided better numbers for purposes of comparison but violated the criterion of random assignment and therefore compromised the effort to rule out rival causes.

Practical problems reflect the operations of the real world, and most field experiments have to contend with them sooner or later. There is nevertheless a growing consensus in criminological circles that even with their problems, field experiments deserve more attention than they have received. Even scholars at odds on major methodological issues can be found in agreement on this point (see Gottfredson and Hirschi, 1987; Blumstein, Cohen, and Farrington, 1988b).

Longitudinal Research: Cohort Studies

Experimental research is sometimes longitudinal, and some longitudinal studies have included experiments along with other methodologies. A *longitudinal* study is conducted over time and is often designed to establish if and when changes occur in the variables under investigation. Some researchers believe that longitudinal designs are a good way to address questions of causality, especially the temporal ordering of key variables. Others select longitudinal designs because they provide the only effective way of tracking developmental and historical changes in the same population or sample.

A variety of different longitudinal designs have been used in delinquency research. One of the most common is the panel study. A panel study involves gathering information about a group (panel) of people at two or more points in time. In order to avoid problems such as subject reactivity and attrition, some panel designs rotate people into and out of the sample as the study continues. The National Crime Survey, described earlier, is an example of a panel study that uses this sort of rotation. However, most panel studies are done with much more limited samples and are designed to address specific research questions, for example, whether youths' perceptions of the risks of being punished for illegal behavior influence their subsequent conduct (see Bishop, 1984; Paternoster, 1987), or whether adolescent drinking influences delinquency involvement, or vice versa (see Temple and Ladoucer, 1986).

One of the most interesting and controversial types of longitudinal research is the *cohort study*. A cohort study measures changes that occur over time among people who are in common circumstances or share a similar characteristic. Because cohort studies are usually complex, time consuming, and expensive, they are relatively rare. This is especially true of *prospective* cohort studies, which are also long-term. In this type of study, delinquency researchers measure changes in circumstances, experiences, and behavior as the children under study grow up. In some prospective cohort studies the measurements begin at birth; in others the cohort is composed of school aged children. Such studies may take twenty-five years or even longer to complete.

The theoretical value of prospective cohort studies in delinquency research lies in their ability to examine how and why some youngsters become delinquent whereas other youngsters in similar circumstances do not. They are also valued for what they can tell us about the development of so-called delinquent and criminal "careers." For example, a rare consensus in criminological circles is that experienced adult criminals usually began their careers in crime as juveniles, and the likelihood of such a career developing is greater the earlier the child gets in trouble with the law. On the other hand, many juveniles mature out of crime before they reach adulthood, and some youngsters dabble in delinquency without ever getting seriously involved. By repeatedly gathering information on an individual's family, school, health, economic circumstances, contacts with the criminal justice system, and other behavior patterns and comparing it with information on the rest of the group, cohort researchers hope to pinpoint the crucial factors that explain the emergence, character, and duration of delinquency involvement.

In the cohort research of interest here, the dependent variable is delinquent or criminal involvement, which can be measured in various ways, as we have seen. The independent measurements vary from study to study, depending mostly on the specific research problem being addressed and on the training of the researchers. However, prospective cohort studies are generally broad in the range of variables they measure because the time, effort, and cost hardly justify anything less. Following are brief descriptions of three well-known prospective cohort studies.

The Cambridge Study in Delinquent Development   Begun in 1961, this study has become a classic. Led by Donald West, researchers in England contacted 411 boys aged 8 to 9 years, all of whom were attending one of six local primary schools in a working-class district of London (West, 1967). The sample was designed to be representative of the male population of the area. The boys were interviewed and given psychological tests at ages 8, 10, and 14, and were interviewed again at ages 16, 18, and 21. In addition, parents, teachers, and some of the boys' peers were also interviewed periodically. Questions dealt with a range of issues, from family circumstances, child-rearing practices, school behavior and performance, and truancy; to other boys' perceptions of their honesty, daring, and popularity, among other things. Delinquency involvement was measured by self-reports and also by official records of convictions.

Reports from the study have documented the emergence of delinquent careers in some of the boys, and further followups (at ages 24 and 31 to 32) have examined the transition from juvenile to adult criminal involvement (see West and Farrington, 1977; West, 1982; Farrington, 1988). Findings from this important study will be cited at various places in the chapters that follow. One of the most significant is simply this: The minority of boys with self-reports of early delinquency involvement and early criminal convictions differed significantly from the rest on most measurements used throughout the study, and were significantly more likely to continue their criminal activity into adulthood and to be involved in life-styles considered deviant by conventional standards (Farrington, 1988: 71–72).

The Cambridge-Somerville Youth Study   If not the first, then certainly the most famous American prospective cohort study is the Cambridge-Somerville Youth Study. First brought to national attention by Edwin Powers and Helen Witmer (1951), then followed up by William and Joan McCord (1959) and later by Joan McCord herself (1978, 1986), this study followed 750 boys judged to be at risk of delinquency. Because the study was designed to provide a longitudinal *experimental* test of various treatment methods, the boys were divided into experimental and control groups. The experimental group received various "services," such as medical care, counseling, recreational opportunities, and tutoring, while the control group did not.

Two notable findings from this study were (1) that the child most often involved in persistent delinquency was one who experienced maternal rejection and whose parents provided little supervision, were harsh in their disciplining methods, and were in conflict with each other; and (2) that thirty years after the original measurements were taken, the boys (now men) who had received treatment services turned out to have fared worse than the control group—they showed more alcohol use, more mental illness, more crime, and more premature deaths. McCord (1978, 1980) cannot explain this but speculates that the experimental subjects may have had unrealistic expectations about the effects of treatment, and when their lives seemed to be unraveling, they experienced heightened frustration and feelings of failure. The failure of the Cambridge-Somerville Youth Study to find any reduction in crime or delinquency for the youth who received extensive services was surprising to say the least. But with the benefit of hindsight, several other reasons for the failure can be proposed. To begin, the children were selected on the basis of several pre-delinquency measures, but subsequently other "non-difficult" children were included as well. Therefore, the experimental and control groups included not only pre-delinquent children but non-delinquent children as well. The non-delinquent children could hardly be expected to show reduction in delinquency in response to services.

In addition, some of the pre-delinquents may have been influenced by factors unresponsive to counseling or beyond its scope (for example, dyslexia, or the influence of older siblings). Furthermore, the counseling itself was applied quite infrequently, and the other services, while wide-ranging, were not intensive (see Lundman, 1984: 33). On the average, a family was contacted for counseling less than 12 times per year, and social agencies and schools combined received on average only one contact per month. The social services were thus applied very thinly, and to a portion of children (the nondelinquents) who could not show much benefit in any case. Small wonder the results were not more positive!

The Kauai Longitudinal Study   This study began even before its subjects were born and is remarkable because of the scope of its biological, cognitive, medical, behavioral, and social measurements (see Werner, Bierman, and French, 1971; Werner and Smith, 1977). All pregnant women on the island of Kauai (population 32,000), Hawaii, were screened in 1954 on a variety of medical and psychological variables, and the 698 children subsequently born in 1955 were followed into their 25th year (Werner, 1987).

Half the children lived in chronic poverty, but even so, marked variations were found in the risks of delinquency even among the poorer children. Different combinations of factors were identified as delinquency predictors at different ages. For example, a child's health and temperament and its mother's health and age were found to be significant factors during infancy, but during adolescence the composition and coherence of the family and the presence of chronic family conflict were important predictors of a child's trouble with the law. Werner (1987: 39–40) describes a major conclusion of the study as follows:

> Although most of the children who became delinquent were poor, it needs to be kept in mind that *poverty alone* was not a sufficient condition for the development of antisocial behavior. A low standard of living increased the likelihood of exposure of the child to *both* biological and psychological risk factors. But it was the joint impact of constitutional vulnerabilities and early family instability that led to serious and repeated delinquencies in *both* middle-class as well as lower-class children on Kauai. . . .
>
> Regardless of social class standing, children with "difficult temperaments" who interacted with distressed caretakers in disorganized, unstable families had a greater chance of developing delinquent behavior than children who were perceived as rewarding by their caretakers and who grew up in supportive homes.

The three cohort studies we have reviewed meet four conditions that are considered desirable in longitudinal research (Farrington, Ohlin, and Wilson, 1986): (1) They are prospective, following the subjects as they grow up; (2) they involve collection of material from various sources—for example, self-reports as well as police and court data—and additional information from parents, teachers, and others; (3) the sample size is relatively large (over 100 subjects), thereby producing larger subcategories of subjects (e.g., chronic, sporadic, and nondelinquents) for analysis and enabling researchers to generalize the findings to similar groups in other places; and finally, (4) they cover an extensive period of time, at least five years, in the lives of the subjects.

For all this, prospective cohort studies are not without their critics (see Esbensen and Menard, 1990), and not all researchers agree that these four conditions necessarily characterize good longitudinal research. For example, much can be learned from qualitative research in which single individuals or small groups of subjects describe and interpret their experiences and activities as they live or recall them. Examples of this sort of research include Parker's (1974) study of the Roundhouse Boys in Liverpool, England, and the autobiographical account of Stanley, the Jack-Roller, introduced to the public by Clifford Shaw (1930) over sixty years ago.

Recently, two prominent criminologists have argued that longitudinal research may be overrated. Travis Hirschi and Michael Gottfredson (1983; also see Gottfredson and Hirschi, 1987, 1990) direct their criticism primarily at longitudinal research on criminal careers, but in doing so they challenge various beliefs about the benefits of longitudinal research, including this one: that longitudinal research is superior to standard cross-sectional, one-point-in-time designs as a means to establishing temporal or causal order among variables (see Gottfredson and Hirschi, 1987: 586–606).

The heart of the Hirschi-Gottfredson critique is that longitudinal research has not in fact advanced our understanding of the causes of crime or delinquency beyond that already established through cross-sectional studies. Furthermore, they argue that the real reason some researchers (e.g., Farrington, Ohlin, and Wilson, 1986; Blumstein et al., 1986) advocate prospective longitudinal studies may be that the method fits their theories of crime causation, not because it contains inherent methodological virtues (Gottfredson and Hirschi, 1987: 608). Thus, the desirability of following individuals over time is grounded in the theory that crime results from changes in the characteristics, conditions, or experiences of individuals as they grow up. The upshot, according to Gottfredson and Hirschi (1987: 610), is a blurring of the distinction between theory and method.

The debate sparked by Hirschi and Gottfredson (see also Blumstein, Cohen, and Farrington, 1988a and 1988b; Gottfredson and Hirschi, 1988; Tittle, 1988; Hagan and Palloni, 1988) is unlikely to be resolved in the near future, nor is it likely to dampen enthusiasm for longitudinal research. Indeed, in April, 1990, the National Institute of Justice and the MacArthur Foundation announced a grant of $2.5 *million* for a new cohort study described as "one of the most complete and interdisciplinary studies in the history of criminology" (*NIJ Research in Action,* May-June, 1990: 2).

Hirschi and Gottfredson appear to hold the minority position on the question of longitudinal research. As they themselves argue (1987: 608), the use of any particular research design is guided by the theory being tested, and when the theory (whatever it is) purports to explain a crime in temporal terms, a longitudinal design is defensible where a cross-sectional design often is not. Blumstein, Cohen, and Farrington (1988b: 72) undoubtedly spoke for many of their colleagues when they defended longitudinal surveys (such as the Cambridge Study in Delinquent Development) as "markedly superior to cross-sectional surveys in describing the natural history and course of development of a phenomenon, in studying developmental sequences, and in drawing causal inferences."

Observational Research

Some major advances in understanding delinquency and crime have come through careful and systematic observation of behavior *as it occurs*. Observational studies are especially useful if we don't know what to expect—usually because theory is weak or nonexistent. They are also helpful in providing researchers with firsthand knowledge of behavior in the rich, often complex contexts in which it occurs.

The use of observational research in the study of social deviance is controversial (and difficult) partly because people usually don't want to be watched by outsiders when they are doing something for which they could be punished. When people know they are being watched, they might try to fool the researcher by doing something quite different from what they would otherwise do. Observational research is also controversial because of abuses that have occurred. Although not everyone agrees on exactly what constitutes abuse, the famous study by Laud Humphreys (1975), cited in almost every introductory sociology text, comes to mind. Humphreys observed homosexual encounters as they occurred in public restrooms in a St. Louis park. In itself this might have raised eyebrows, but Humphreys also recorded the license plates of participants and had a contact in the police department provide names and addresses so Humphreys could later interview the participants as part of the study. Clearly, this strategy entailed risks for the subjects and today would probably not be approved because of right to privacy statutes and tighter federal controls over research.

Because much crime and delinquency occurs when there are no witnesses—at least no official ones—the usual observational strategy is for the researcher to become a *participant observer*. Participant observers do not have to commit offenses but are usually present or nearby when offenses occur, or they participate in talk and other activities related to the crimes of the people they are studying. A wide range of delinquent and criminal behaviors have been studied in this way, from organized crime (Ianni, 1972) to drug dealing (Adler, 1985), juvenile gangs (Spergel, 1964; Campbell, 1984), and less "formal" delinquent networks (Parker, 1974). Participant observation has also been used in the study of the interaction between police and suspects on the street (Piliavin and Briar, 1964; Reiss, 1971) and between defendants and others in the judicial process (Maynard, 1984).

Participant observation puts the researcher close to the people and activities that are being studied and as a result provides insights that would often be missed through other methods of research. A classic example is the work of William Foote Whyte (1943). Whyte spent over three years hanging around with a streetcorner group in Boston of ethnic Italian youths dubbed the Corner Boys. Whyte noted that sociologists using conventional measurements of the neighborhood's social and economic character—including rates of crime and delinquency—would have written it off as a "disorganized slum." But through Whyte's participant observation he was able to show that the neighborhood was far from disorganized, though it was certainly poor. He discovered that the residents worked hard, took care of one another, and that even among the boys there were clearly demarcated responsibilities, lines of authority, and mechanisms of social control to ensure conformity.

Whyte's study also showed some of the difficulties associated with participant observation. One important issue the researcher must decide is whether to reveal his or her identity. If people realize they are being studied, they may behave differently (the question of reactivity); on the other hand, if they know they are being studied from the start, and are given time to adjust to the presence of an outsider and to establish trust, people may act as they normally would. To complicate matters further, ethical questions may be raised, for example, whether people have a right to know they are being studied. Whyte struggled with these issues, initially choosing not to reveal his true purpose. He told the boys he was writing a book about the history and customs of the neighborhood. Once his presence was accepted by most of the boys, he became more open about his research.

Sometimes it is difficult to establish trust, especially when activities being observed are illegal and there is uncertainty about the researcher's true role. Irving Spergel (1964: 190–198) documents this difficulty in his book about delinquent subcultures in the three ethnic neighborhoods he dubbed Racketville, Slumtown, and Haulberg. Spergel found that he had to define and redefine his role continuously, both to new people he met and to those he already knew who were still uncertain or uneasy. Some youths were openly suspicious, if not hostile.

> Little Augie raised a question about what I was doing in the neighborhood. He wondered whether I was a cop, a "stool pigeon," or a Youth Board worker. I tried to clarify my role as a researcher. Little Augie said that what I was saying to him wasn't clear and that he suspected my real motives. . . . He then said that he did not want to become a guinea pig for me. [Spergel, 1964: 191–192]

On other occasions, Spergel found that the boys were testing him, which included "attempts to frighten me, 'baiting' or 'ranking' me, and . . . minor acts of physical violence." Spergel (1964: 193) goes on to say that

> the testing behavior appeared to serve several functions: to demonstrate the group's uncertainty in the face of a new and strange relationship, to discover whether or not I was a "right guy," and to determine my areas of personal weakness and of personal strength.

A researcher must show sensitivity, perseverance, and tolerance if uncertainties and fears are to be overcome. The payoff can be substantial: The works of Whyte, Spergel, and the other participant observers mentioned above have provided knowledge about delinquency and crime that could not have been secured in any other way.

Biographical Research: Oral Histories

Participant observation is commonly referred to as a *qualitative* research strategy. Rather than measuring things that can be expressed as numbers—for example, how much Y changes when there is a change in X, or how many times people have been arrested, or the strength of association between delinquency rates and certain family or neighborhood characteristics—qualitative studies construct and interpret images of reality based on direct observation in the field and on the first-person accounts of participants. Because qualitative methods are more subjective and exploratory than quantitative forms of measurement, some scholars believe they are of limited value in scientific research and are useful mainly in suggesting ideas that can be subsequently tested with "hard" (i.e., quantitative) data. In criminology and delinquency research the debate has clearly been running in favor of quantitative techniques. One has only to consult methodology texts in the field to see that this is so (e.g., Hagan, 1982; Binder and Geis, 1983).

This is in sharp contrast to the situation in the 1920s and 1930s, when *both* research strategies were widely used, often by the same investigators. A case in point is the work of Clifford Shaw. Shaw headed the Institute for Juvenile Research at the University of Chicago, and with his colleague Henry McKay embarked on an ecological study of delinquency in Chicago. Based on the geographic mapping of crime and delinquency, certain areas of the city were labeled "delinquency areas," and these areas shared various features besides high crime rates: They were close to the central business district, they had high concentrations of minority and foreign born residents, they were overcrowded and physically rundown, most of the residents were poor and unskilled, and there were few locally supported community organizations to which people belonged. Shaw and McKay believed that these conditions "combine to render difficult the development of a stable and efficient neighborhood for the education and control of the child and the suppression of lawlessness" (Shaw, 1931a: 387). The term *social disorganization* was used to describe the inability of these neighborhoods to regulate themselves (Bursik, 1988: 542).

Despite the voluminous quantitative data, Shaw and his colleagues could not tell what it all meant from the standpoint of individual youths growing up in delinquency areas. They believed, for example, that delinquency values were transmitted from one generation or group of residents to the next; but how was this accomplished? The answer could be gained, in their view, only be delving into the life histories of individual delinquents. So, Shaw turned to qualitative research, eventually compiling over 200 life histories.

A life history (sometimes called an "own story") is a first-person account of behavior and experiences, usually given orally under the guidance of the researcher (see Bennett, 1981). Depending on the researcher's interest and the age of the subject, life histories can run to a few pages or to volumes. Many of Shaw's histories were short; however, three of the longer histories were turned into books: *The Jack-Roller: A Delinquent Boy's Own Story* (Shaw, 1930), *The Natural History of a Delinquent Career* (Shaw, 1931b), and *Brothers in Crime* (Shaw, McKay, and McDonald, 1938). Together, the life histories "enable a reader to *see* the process of transmission of delinquent practices from one person or group to another and the gradual evolution of those practices through further participation in delinquent groups" (Bennett, 1981: 189).

Jack-Roller has become a classic in criminology and in sociological field research (Snodgrass, 1982: 3). It is the story of Stanley, who was 12 when he first met Shaw in 1921. Stanley had already run up an extensive arrest history and had spent almost half his life in institutions. By the time he was 17, Stanley had 38 arrests, most for petty offenses but also for more serious crimes such as assaulting and robbing drunks or homosexuals—so-called jack-rolling. In Stanley's own words, "We sometimes stunned the drunks by 'giving them the club' in a dark place near a lonely alley. It was bloody work, but necessity demanded it—we had to live" (Shaw, 1930: 85).

Through Stanley's story (and those of other delinquent youths), Shaw shows how delinquent attitudes and practices develop and are transmitted from boy to boy, and also how individual delinquent "careers" evolve. The acquisition of delinquent attitudes and practices is encouraged through friendships, by neighborhood traditions, and by the breakdown of parental controls, evidenced, for example, by Stanley's constant battles with his stepmother, who never displayed any affection for Stanley (see Snodgrass, 1982:

79). Additionally, Shaw used life histories to suggest appropriate treatment programs. In Stanley's case, this included finding a "sympathetic and informal" foster home, obtaining employment as a salesman (which did not last), helping him develop contacts with new, nondelinquent friends, and maintaining weekly contact with him. As Stanley later reported when he was 70 years old (see Snodgrass, 1982), Shaw's efforts helped turn him away from crime despite occasional relapses (one when he was 23 that resulted in yet another prison term). On a larger scale, Shaw's oral histories helped him construct the delinquency prevention program known as the Chicago Area Project, which focused on changing the delinquent child's social environment through neighborhood reconstruction organized via community self-help projects.

The Chicago work with life histories has not gone without criticism (see especially Bennett, 1981: 179–210). The criticisms include Shaw's failure to include oral histories of *non*delinquent youths living in high delinquency neighborhoods, the lack of comprehensive details about family and neighborhood characteristics, and the lack of information about the *non*delinquent activities and associations of delinquents. Nevertheless, the life history research of Shaw and his colleagues at the Institute for Juvenile Research helped establish a form of qualitative research that has periodically produced very informative and influential studies of crime (e.g., Sutherland, 1937; Chambliss, 1972; Klockars, 1974; Steffensmeier, 1986).

Comparative and Historical Research

A century ago, French sociologist Emile Durkheim ([1893] 1964: 65) observed that there is no known society without crime. "Its form changes," he went on, "but, everywhere and always, there have been men who have behaved in such a way as to draw upon themselves penal repression." In order to find out whether and how crime varies from place to place, or from time to time, criminologists use *comparative* or *historical* research. Ideally, comparative research compares different societies at the same point in time; historical research examines the same society at different periods in its history. The methodologies can be combined, though this strategy also combines their difficulties and limitations.

These difficulties and limitations include the costs and time involved, which are usually considerable, language barriers, political obstacles, lack or poor quality of available data, noncomparable definitions of crime and delinquency, and the ethnocentric tendency of researchers living in one society or time period to see their own as the standard against which to measure others. The last point is illustrated by the assumption, apparently held by some prominent criminologists, that American views of crime and delinquency can be applied everywhere (see Barak-Glantz and Johnson, 1983; Gottfredson and Hirschi, 1990: 171–178). At the very least, researchers must be sensitive to the fact that in other societies and time periods the actions and meanings associated with crime are likely to differ from their own (Beirne, 1983).

If these difficulties can be overcome, the benefits of comparative and historical research are considerable. Not only does this sort of research provide a way to measure the scope of theories—for example, does a theory developed to explain delinquency involvement in America also apply to, say, Germany, Israel, and India?—but it also places our own experiences with crime and delinquency in a larger perspective. Researchers today may learn from historical and comparative research about problems with crime and delinquency that have not yet surfaced, and perhaps how to avoid them. For example, the Communist bloc countries currently undergoing rapid social, economic, and political change may be able to learn important lessons in delinquency prevention from studying nineteenth-century Britain and America or contemporary Japan.

SUMMARY

This review of sources of data and research methods hardly does justice to a complicated topic. However, it is our hope that readers will better understand the strengths, weaknesses, and utility of the information about delinquency presented in the chapters that follow. It is important to remember that no one research strategy or type of data stands above all the rest; each has its drawbacks, and each has its benefits. In the final analysis, the appropriateness of a given methodology or body of data depends on the research question being addressed.

One of the main points of this chapter is that information on crime and delinquency is generated in many different ways and by many different people. Although it is customary to think of the police and courts as authoritative sources of information, we have seen that official data are not without their limitations. And the limitations grow the further removed the information source is from the delinquent event itself. Attempts to uncover the dark figure of crime through self-report and victimization studies bring researchers closer to the event, but these methods also turn out to have their limitations and deficiencies. In the end, data on crime and delinquency are produced through a process that requires individuals to assign and interpret meanings in the absence of agreed-upon rules for doing so. Small wonder the data cannot be taken for granted or at face value.

REFERENCES

Adler, Patricia A. 1985. *Wheeling and Dealing: An Ethnography of an Upper-Level Drug Dealing and Smuggling Community.* New York: Columbia University Press.

Barak-Glantz, Israel L., and Elmer H. Johnson. 1983. *Comparative Criminology.* Beverly Hills: Sage Publications.

Barlow, Hugh D. 1990. *Introduction to Criminology.* 5th edition. Glenview, Ill.: Scott, Foresman/ Little, Brown.

Beirne, Piers. 1983. "Generalization and Its Discontents: The Comparative Study of Crime." In *Comparative Criminology.* Edited by Israel L. Barak-Glantz and Elmer H. Johnson. Beverly Hills: Sage Publications.

Bennett, James. 1981. *Oral History and Delinquency.* Chicago: University of Chicago Press.

Binder, Arnold, and Gilbert Geis. 1983. *Methods of Research in Criminology and Criminal Justice.* New York: McGraw-Hill.

Bishop, Donna. 1984. "Deterrence: A Panel Analysis." *Justice Quarterly* 1:311–328.

Black, Donald J. 1970. "Production of Crime Rates." *American Sociological Review* 35:733–748.

Blumstein, Alfred, Jacqueline Cohen, Jeffrey Roth, and Christy A Visher, eds. 1986. *Criminal Careers and Career Criminals.* Vol 1. Washington, D.C.: National Academy Press.

Blumstein, Alfred, Jacqueline Cohen, and David P. Farrington. 1988a. "Criminal Career Research: Its Value for Criminology." *Criminology* 26:1–35.

———. 1988b. "Longitudinal and Criminal Career Research: Further Clarifications." *Criminology* 26:57–74.

Bureau of Justice Statistics. 1988. *BJS Data Report, 1987.* Washington, D.C.: U.S. Department of Justice.

Bureau of Justice Statistics. 1989. *Criminal Victimization in the United States, 1987.* Washington, D.C.: U.S. Department of Justice.

Bursik, Robert J., Jr. 1988. "Social Disorganization and Theories of Crime and Delinquency: Problems and Prospects." *Criminology* 26:519–551.

Campbell, Anne. 1984. *The Girls in the Gang.* Oxford: Basil Blackwell.

Cernkovich, Stephen A., and Peggy C. Giordano. 1987. "Family Relationships and Delinquency." *Criminology* 25:295–319.

Chambliss, William J., ed. 1972. *Box Man: A Professional Thief's Journey.* New York: Harper and Row.

Dunford, Franklyn W., and Delbert S. Elliott. 1984. "Identifying Career Offenders Using Self-Report Data." *Journal of Research in Crime and Delinquency* 21:57–86.

Durkheim, Emile. 1964. *The Rules of Sociological Method.* New York: The Free Press.

Elias, Robert. 1986. *The Politics of Victimization.* New York: Oxford University Press.

Empey, LaMar T., and Maynard L. Erickson. 1972. *The Provo Experiment: Evaluating Community Control of Delinquency.* Lexington, Mass.: Lexington Books.

Esbensen, Finn, and Scott Menard. 1990. "Is Longitudinal Research Worth the Price?" *The Criminologist* 15:1, 3, 5, 6.

Farrington, David P. 1988. "Social, Psychological and Biological Influences on Juvenile Delinquency and Adult Crime." In *Explaining Criminal Behaviour.* Edited by Wouter Buikhuisen and Sarnoff A. Mednick. Leiden, Netherlands: E. J. Brill.

Farrington, David P., Lloyd Ohlin, and James Q. Wilson. 1986. *Understanding and Controlling Crime: Toward a New Research Strategy.* New York: Springer-Verlag.

Federal Bureau of Investigation. 1988. *Crime in the United States, 1987.* Washington, D.C.: U.S. Department of Justice.

Gottfredson, Michael R., and Travis Hirschi. 1987. "The Methodological Adequacy of Longitudinal Research on Crime." *Criminology* 26:581–614.

———. 1988. "Science, Public Policy, and the Career Paradigm." *Criminology* 26:37–55.

———. 1990. *A General Theory of Crime.* Stanford: Stanford University Press.

Greenberg, David F. 1985. "Age, Crime, and Social Explanation." *American Journal of Sociology* 91:1–21.

Hagan, Frank E. 1982. *Research Methods in Criminal Justice and Criminology.* New York: Macmillan.

Hagan, John, A. R. Gillis, and J. Chan. 1978. "Explaining Official Delinquency: A Spatial Study of Class, Conflict, and Control." *Sociological Quarterly* 19:386–398.

Hagan, John, and Alberto Palloni. 1988. "Crimes as Social Events in the Life Course: Reconceiving a Criminological Controversy." *Criminology* 26:87–100.

Hindelang, Michael J., Travis Hirschi, and Joseph G. Weis. 1979. "Correlates of Delinquency:

The Illusion of Discrepancy Between Self-Report and Official Measures." *American Sociological Review* 44:995–1014.

Hirschi, Travis, and Michael R. Gottfredson. 1983. "Age and the Explanation of Crime." *American Journal of Sociology* 89:552–584.

Hirschi, Travis, and Hanan C. Selvin. 1967. *Delinquency Research.* New York: The Free Press.

Huizinga, David, and Delbert S. Elliott. 1987. "Juvenile Offenders: Prevalence, Incidence, and Arrest Rates by Race." *Crime and Delinquency* 33:206–223.

Humphreys, Laud. 1975. *Tearoom Trade: Impersonal Sex in Public Places.* Chicago: Aldine.

Ianni, Francis A. J., with Elizabeth Reuss-Ianni. 1972. *A Family Business: Kinship and Social Control in Organized Crime.* New York: Russell Sage.

Illinois Criminal Justice Information Authority. 1989. *Trends and Issues 89: Criminal and Juvenile Justice in Illinois.* Chicago: ICJIA.

Johnson, Richard E. 1986. "Family Structure and Delinquency: General Patterns and Gender Differences." *Criminology* 24:65–84.

Kinsey, Richard, John Lea, and Jock Young. 1986. *Losing the Fight Against Crime.* Oxford: Basil Blackwell.

Kleck, Gary. 1982. "On the Use of Self-Report Data to Determine the Class Distribution of Criminal and Delinquent Behavior." *American Sociological Review* 47:427–448.

Klockars, Carl B. 1974. *The Professional Fence.* New York: Free Press.

Lundman, Richard J. 1984. *Prevention and Control of Juvenile Delinquency.* New York: Oxford University Press.

Maxfield, Michael A., Dan A. Lewis, and Ron Szoc. 1980. "Producing Official Crimes: Verified Crime Reports as Measures of Police Output." *Social Science Quarterly* 61:221–236.

Maynard, Douglas W. 1984. *Inside Plea Bargaining.* New York: Plenum Press.

McCord, Joan. 1978. "A Thirty-Year Follow-up of Treatment Effects." *American Psychologist* 33:284–289

———. 1980. "The Treatment that Did Not Help." *Social Action and Law* 5:85–87.

———. 1986. "Instigation and Insulation: How Families Affect Antisocial Behavior." In *Development of Antisocial and Prosocial Behavior.* Edited by D. Olweus, J. Block, and M. Radke-Yarrow. Orlando, Fla.: Academic Press.

McCord, William, and Joan McCord. 1959. *Origins of Crime: A New Evaluation of the Cambridge-Somerville Youth Study.* New York: Columbia University Press.

Parker, Howard J. 1974. *View From The Boys.* London: David and Charles.

Paternoster, Raymond. 1987. "The Deterrent Effect of the Perceived Certainty and Severity of Punishment: A Review of the Evidence and Issues." *Justice Quarterly* 4:173–217.

Piliavin, Irving, and Scott Briar. 1964. "Police Encounters with Juveniles." *American Journal of Sociology* 70:206–214.

Powers, Edwin, and Helen L. Witmer. 1951. *An Experiment in the Prevention of Delinquency: The Cambridge-Somerville Study.* New York: Columbia University Press.

Reiss, Albert J., Jr. 1971. *The Police and the Public.* New Haven, Conn.: Yale University Press.

Schneider, Anne L. 1977. *The Portland Forward Check of Crime Victims: Final Report.* Eugene, Oreg.: Oregon Research Institute.

Shaw, Clifford R. 1930. *The Jack-Roller: A Delinquent Boy's Own Story.* Chicago: University of Chicago Press.

————. 1931a. *Delinquency Areas.* Chicago: University of Chicago Press.

————. 1931b. *The Natural History of a Delinquent Career.* Chicago: University of Chicago Press.

Shaw, Clifford R., Henry D. McKay, and James F. McDonald. 1938. *Brothers in Crime.* Chicago: University of Chicago Press.

Shearing, Clifford D. 1979. "Subterranean Processes, the Maintenance of Power: An Examination of the Mechanisms Coordinating Police Action." Paper presented to the annual meeting of the American Sociological Association, August 17-21, New York.

Smith, Charles P., David J. Berkman, Warren M. Fraser, and John Sutton. 1980. *Reports of the National Juvenile Justice Assessment Centers: The Status Offender.* Washington, D.C.: U.S. Department of Justice.

Smith, Douglas A. 1986. "The Neighborhood Context of Police Behavior." In *Communities and Crime.* Edited by Albert J. Reiss, Jr., and Michael Tonry. Chicago: University of Chicago Press.

Snodgrass, Jon. 1982. *The Jack-Roller at Seventy.* Lexington, Mass.: Lexington Books.

Snyder, Howard N., and Terrence A. Finnegan. 1987. *Delinquency in the United States.* Washington, D.C.: U.S. Department of Justice.

Snyder, Howard N., Terrence A. Finnegan, Ellen H. Nimick, Melissa H. Sickmund, Dennis P. Sullivan, and Nancy J. Tierney. 1989. *Juvenile Court Statistics 1985.* Pittsburgh: National Center for Juvenile Justice.

Spergel, Irving. 1964. *Racketville, Slumtown, Haulberg: An Exploratory Study of Delinquent Subcultures.* Chicago: University of Chicago Press.

Steffensmeier, Darrell J. 1986. *The Fence: In the Shadow of Two Worlds.* Totowa, N.J.: Rowman and Littlefield.

Sutherland, Edwin H. 1937. *The Professional Thief.* Chicago: University of Chicago Press.

Temple, Mark, and Patricia Ladouceur. 1986. "The Alcohol-Crime Relationship as an Age-Specific Phenomenon: A Longitudinal Study." *Contemporary Drug Problems* 86:89–115.

Tittle, Charles R. 1988. "Two Empirical Regularities (Maybe) in Search of an Explanation: Commentary on the Age/Crime Debate." *Criminology* 26:75–85.

Werner, Emmy E. 1987. "Vulnerability and Resiliency in Children at Risk for Delinquency: A Longitudinal Study from Birth to Young Adulthood." In *Prevention of Delinquent Behavior.* Edited by John D. Burchard and Sara N. Burchard. Beverly Hills: Sage Publications.

Werner, E. E., J. M. Bierman, and F. E. French. 1971. *The Children of Kauai: A Longitudinal Study from the Prenatal Period to Age Ten.* Honolulu: University of Hawaii Press.

Werner, E. E., and R. S. Smith. 1977. *Kauai's Children Come of Age.* Honolulu: University of Hawaii Press.

West, Donald J. 1967. *The Young Offender.* Harmondsworth, England: Penguin Books.

West, Donald J. 1982. *Delinquency: Its Roots, Careers, and Prospects.* London: Heinemann.

West, Donald J., and David P. Farrington. 1973. *Who Becomes Delinquent?* London: Heinemann.

————. 1977. *The Delinquent Way of Life.* London: Heinemann.

Whyte, William Foote. 1943. *Streetcorner Society.* Chicago: University of Chicago Press.

Chapter
3

The Sporadic Delinquent

As we have already seen, delinquency is widespread. There are probably very few youths who will not commit a delinquent act at some point during adolescence. This raises a question: Can we draw a meaningful distinction between delinquents and nondelinquents? The answer is probably no. Self-report studies show that the small minority who never admit to committing a delinquent act share many social and personal characteristics with the majority who do.

The position taken by many researchers today is that delinquency is a matter of *degree*. It is not so much that there are delinquents and nondelinquents but, rather, that there are youths who commit more or less serious offenses, more or less frequently, over a longer or shorter period of time. Delinquency can thus be visualized in terms of three continua, as shown in Figure 3.1. The first continuum represents the frequency with which delinquent acts are committed, the second represents the severity or seriousness of transgressions, and the third represents the time period over which offending takes place (duration). Any given individual may fall at different points on the three continua, but we believe consistency is more likely than inconsistency, especially at the extremes. For example, youths who are the most frequent offenders are also the offenders most likely to commit serious crimes and most likely to have a long history of delinquency involvement. In contrast, youths who rarely commit an offense are most likely to commit minor offenses, and their involvement in delinquency will be short lived.

Over the years, delinquency research has tended to emphasize the extremes of the continua, often comparing youths who commit many felony crimes over many years with those who rarely, if ever, commit even petty offenses. Travis Hirschi (1969: 48–53) believes this tendency stems from the popularity of certain definitions of delinquency. For example, *role* definitions emphasize a person's adoption of self-images and life-styles consistent with a sustained and often escalating involvement in delinquent activities. Such definitions are consistent with the idea of "criminal careers." *Syndrome* definitions,

A. Frequency of offending

Low ——————————————————————————————— High

Once or twice   (Occasionally)   (Many times)

B. Seriousness of offending

Low ——————————————————————————————— High

(Status offenses)   (Misdemeanor crimes)   (Felony crimes)

C. Duration of offending

Short ——————————————————————————————— Long

(Days or weeks)   (A few months)   (A year or two)   (Many years)

Figure 3.1 The continua of delinquency

on the other hand, emphasize the repetition of certain (usually serious) delinquent acts. Hirschi believes that both sorts of definitions "tend to lead to the 'delinquent-nondelinquent' dichotomization of subjects because . . . it is difficult to rank cases other than those at the extremes" (53, note 15). The contention is that a lot of delinquency (and delinquents) between the extremes thus escapes serious study. This may be called the grey area of delinquency research.

THE SPORADIC DELINQUENT

We think this grey area is important enough to warrant closer examination. We use the term *sporadic delinquent* to refer to the youth who occasionally commits delinquent acts in the course of growing up. We do not specify that the delinquencies committed are all petty, nor that they all take place over a short period of time. We leave open the possibility that there are different kinds of sporadic delinquents, some who occasionally commit only status offenses, for example, and others who occasionally commit more serious offenses. We also recognize that some sporadics may commit their offenses over a relatively short period of time, whereas others may space them out over many years. Only good research will establish whether these distinctions are important enough to justify incorporating them into a typology of sporadic delinquents.

We should note that other authors have spoken of *occasional* offenders. Cesare Lombroso (1911) was one of the first. Lombroso's nineteenth century research with soldiers, prisoners, and mental patients led him to distinguish the so-called born criminal from those who were insane, those who committed crimes under great emotional stress ("criminals by passion," he called them), and the "criminaloid." It is the criminaloid who Lombroso believed is drawn into occasional crime by situational or environmental factors. But Lombroso's passionate criminal is also an occasional offender.

Psychologists have also written of occasional delinquents and criminals, though the term commonly used is *acute* offender. David Abrahamsen (1960) identifies three types of acute offenders: *situational offenders*, who have succumbed to acute provocation or temptation; *associational offenders,* whose reference groups (family, peers) display strong criminal or delinquent tendencies; and *accidental offenders,* whose crimes occur as a result of chance or mistake. In a typology similar to Abrahamsen's, Alexander and Staub (1956) also write of situational and accidental offenders.

Among the sociologists who have written about occasional offenders are Donald Gibbons (1965), and Marshall Clinard and Richard Quinney (1973). Occasional offenders are seen as committing crimes or delinquencies sporadically, when incentive and opportunity fortuitously combine. Prominent among the types of offenses committed in this fashion are vandalism, joyriding, shoplifting, and brawling. Occasional offenders do not develop images of themselves as delinquents or criminals, nor are their crimes generally sophisticated or technical. Such offenders generally subscribe to conventional values and rarely progress into delinquent or criminal careers.

Mention should be made also of the distinction between occasional and *casual* delinquency introduced by the late Stephen Schafer and Richard Knudten (1970). In their view, occasional delinquency is episodic, committed by largely conventional (prosocial) youths who act "in accordance with the pressure of circumstances at particular moments" (113). Casual delinquency, on the other hand, may occur frequently and is committed by youths whose commitment to conventional values is weaker. The latter point seems to be the crucial distinction. Schafer and Knudten go on to say that

> the occasional delinquent deviates on occasion; the casual delinquent deviates spontaneously and irregularly, whenever he has the chance. In occasional delinquency "the opportunity uses the child," but in casual delinquency "the child uses the opportunity." [116]

Examples of occasional delinquency given by the authors include the boy who shoots someone for attacking his mother, the girl who steals a loaf of bread to ease the hunger of her "penniless widowed mother," or the boy who fiddles his way into a football game (109). Casual delinquencies include early drinking, sexual aberrations, petty theft, periodic shoplifting, minor fraud, and periodic truancy (116).

There may be value to this distinction, but little evidence is brought to bear on the differences, and it is unclear how they represent alternative "personality types" as claimed by the authors (110). Indeed, Schafer and Knudten acknowledge that the occasional delinquent may periodically be a casual delinquent. Furthermore, the examples given of the delinquent *activities* corresponding to each type are improbably petty for the casual offender and (mostly) implausibly altruistic for the occasional delinquent.

To summarize, it has long been recognized that there is a sporadic, or episodic, character to much delinquency and therefore that the youths who do delinquent acts should not all be lumped together. The terms used to identify sporadic delinquency and delinquents vary from author to author, and some have suggested that sporadic delinquents may not comprise a homogeneous category. There seems to be agreement that sporadic delinquency reflects the impact of opportunity and other situational factors, something we will explore in more detail later. First, however, we need to establish the extent of sporadic delinquency, or more correctly, the size of the sporadic delinquent population.

How Many Sporadic Delinquents?

Although there is wide agreement that sporadic delinquents far outnumber chronic offenders, estimates of their actual proportion are rarely given. In general, authors seem content to say simply that most juvenile delinquents are occasional offenders. Until recently, no national data were available on which to base such estimates, and one can see why: The task would be monumental. For one thing, we would need to survey the youthful population *every* year, to say nothing of accumulating the yearly offense totals for all subjects over the course of their childhood. Only in this way could we uncover the *incidence* of offending, that is, the number of delinquent acts committed by a particular individual while a juvenile. Time and money tend to work against such large-scale endeavors.

However, the National Youth Survey (NYS), conducted by the Behavioral Research Institute at the University of Colorado, has now made available just the kind of information we need. Directed by Delbert Elliott, the NYS was based on a national sample of adolescents considered representative of American youths born between 1959 and 1965. The initial survey was conducted in 1977 with 1725 subjects and covered delinquency involvement during the preceding year. During each of the next five years the same subjects were interviewed again and were asked to recall their delinquency involvement during the calender year that just ended. Because some of the initial subjects refused to be interviewed again or could not be located, the sample size for the final (1981) interviews was 1494. However, in the authors' view the "lost" respondents did not seriously effect the representativeness of the sample over the five years (Elliott et al., 1983).

During the interviews, respondents were asked how many times they had participated in a variety of delinquent acts "from Christmas a year ago to the Christmas just past." These self-reported delinquency (SRD) items are shown in Figure 2.1 on page 24. It should be noted that almost all the items are violations of criminal statutes. For this reason, the NYS delinquency measure avoids trivializing delinquency, a charge leveled at some other self-report studies (see Hindelang, Hirschi, and Weis, 1979). Room is left, however, for some common status offenses—skipping classes, running away, sexual intercourse, lying about one's age. Figure 2.1 shows the full set of self-report delinquency items.

There are at least five ways that delinquency involvement can be depicted using the NYS data. One method is to look at the annual self-reported delinquency activity of each respondent in the sample without regard to the type of acts committed. Another way is to look at the number of acts committed by each individual over some combination of years, or the entire five-year period, but again without regard to the offense. A third method brings in the type of offense committed so that annual delinquency activity can be described in terms of the frequency with which different crimes and delinquencies are committed. A fourth does the same thing for combinations of years, or for the entire five-year period. The fifth method brings in the duration of offending; it is the most complex form, incorporating both frequency and seriousness of *annual* offending over the entire five-year period. In this way, all three of the delinquency dimensions shown earlier in Figure 3.1 can be analyzed, something which most other studies have been unable to do.

Our interest lies in estimating the proportion of juvenile delinquents who are sporadic offenders. In a report using the National Youth Survey data, Franklyn Dunford and Delbert Elliott (1984) provide two sorts of evidence on this. The first is based on a typology of delinquents, which combines offense frequency and seriousness and uses the *annual* incidence of offending (the third method outlined above). The second is an application of the fifth method.

Dunford and Elliott (1984: 64–65) first distinguish between four types of delinquents (see Table 3.1). Although the words *sporadic* and *occasional* are not used, it is evident that as we move down the table, the categories would be more and more to the high end of the frequency and seriousness continua discussed earlier. But what about "serious patterned delinquents"? No mention is made of the frequency of offending. The authors explain their decision to ignore frequency in the definition of this type of delinquent as follows:

> First, all of the alternative definitions explored resulted in either too many delinquent types or some inequity that was worse than the one existing here. Second, the vast majority of the youth identified as serious patterned delinquents, given this definition, reported committing delinquent acts at a rate *far exceeding 12 offenses per year*. For example, in the first year of the study, those in this classification reported an average of 117 criminal offenses (excluding status offenses). [1984: 67, italics added]

Dunford and Elliott show that for the years 1976 through 1978, around 30 percent of the NYS sample were either exploratory or nonserious patterned delinquents *in any given year*. Over 60 percent were classified as nondelinquents (but could have committed up to three relatively nonserious offenses), leaving less than 10 percent classified as serious patterned delinquents. Keeping in mind that an annual offense rate of less than 2 offenses per month, with only two serious crimes for the entire year, would place a person in the nonserious patterned delinquent category, then as many as 90 percent of all juveniles might conceivably be called sporadic offenders (i.e., all but the serious patterned delinquents).

Table 3.1   DELINQUENT TYPES AS CLASSIFIED BY THE NATIONAL YOUTH SURVEY

Nondelinquents	Youths engaging in fewer than four self-reported delinquent offenses (i.e., 0 to 3 offenses) and no UCR part 1 offenses* during any given calendar year
Exploratory delinquents	Youths engaging in four to eleven self-reported delinquent behaviors and no more than one UCR part 1 offense in any given year
Nonserious patterned delinquents	Youths engaging in twelve or more self-reported delinquent behaviors and no more than two UCR part 1 offenses in any given calendar year
Serious patterned delinquents	Youths committing at least three UCR part 1 offenses in a given year . . . irrespective of the frequency of any other offenses

*UCR (FBI Uniform Crime Report) part 1 (or index) offenses means homicide, robbery, forcible rape, burglary, aggravated assault, larceny-theft, motor vehicle theft, and arson; homicide and arson were excluded in this study (Dunford and Elliott, 1984: 62–63).

Source: Dunford and Elliott, "Identifying Career Offenders Using Self-Reported Data". *Journal of Research in Crime and Delinquency*, p. 64–65. Copyright© 1984 by Sage Publications, Inc. Reprinted by permission of Sage Publications, Inc.

Dunford and Elliott then looked over the entire five-year history of their sample and brought in *duration* of offending. The authors took all youths classified as "patterned delinquents" in two or more consecutive years and called them "career offenders." Those career offenders who committed at least three serious crimes in two consecutive years were called "serious career offenders"; those who had not, were considered "nonserious career offenders." Noncareer offenders were then identified as those who had earlier been classified as exploratory or patterned (but never in consecutive years). Finally, those who had been defined as nondelinquents *in all five years* were classified as "nonoffenders." Using this method, 37.5 percent of the sample were nonoffenders, 43.2 percent were classified as noncareer offenders, and 19.3 percent as career offenders. Of the latter 242 offenders, 172 were classified as nonserious, and 70 as serious career delinquents (Dunford and Elliott, 1984: 79).

We believe that the noncareer offender in the Dunford and Elliott study best approximates what we are calling the sporadic delinquent. This juvenile commits delinquencies and crimes relatively infrequently in the course of adolescence but often enough to suggest that it is more than just a momentary lapse. On the other hand, there is no hint of chronic involvement as is clearly the case with the career offenders.

How Different Is the Sporadic Offender?

A valuable feature of the Dunford and Elliott study is the authors' attempt to validate their offender types with comparisons involving various social-psychological and demographic variables, as well as the nature of the self-reported offenses. In all, some 31 different comparisons were made, and in almost all cases the authors discovered a clear progression in scores as they moved from nonoffender to noncareer offender to nonserious career offender and, finally, to serious career offender. Thus, the noncareer offenders were more likely than nonoffenders to report having committed all manner of crimes, but less likely than career offenders, and much less likely than serious career offenders (Dunford and Elliott, 1984: table 5).

So it was with many other variables, as Table 3.2 shows. The delinquents we are calling sporadic (i.e., noncareer) were more likely than career offenders to be involved in conventional activities in school, or with family and friends, but were less likely to be so involved than nonoffenders; on the other hand, they were more likely than nonoffenders to receive negative labeling from family, teachers, or peers, but less so than career delinquents. One of the most substantial differences across the types was observed in questions dealing with *delinquent peers*. Scale values for serious career delinquents were almost double those for nonoffenders for both association with delinquent peers and expressions of commitment to them. In between, however, noncareer offenders fell closer to nonoffenders than they did to nonserious career offenders. This points to the importance of delinquent peers in chronic delinquency, something we consider in detail in the next chapter.

The Dunford and Elliott (1984: 77) study provides self-reported rates for different types of criminal (i.e., non*status*) offending and thus permits inferences about the nature of the illegal activities committed by sporadic offenders. Their criminal behavior is dominated by occasional illicit drug use and minor assaults on fellow students, parents, or teachers, with property damage coming in third. However, the fact that some sporadic

TABLE 3.2　Comparison of Offender Types on Self-Reported Delinquency Rates and Selected Social-Psychological Variables, National Youth Survey

Variables	Nonoffender	Noncareer*	Nonserious career	Serious career
Self-report delinquency**				
Felony assault	.00	1.12	1.07	6.89
Minor assault	.28	4.13	10.06	22.23
Robbery	.00	.32	.30	2.20
Illegal services	.02	.56	11.34	27.14
Index offenses	.00	1.58	3.76	13.80
Social-psychological factors				
Involved in school	7.69	6.54	5.42	4.68
Involved with family	10.69	9.83	8.26	8.40
Negative labeling from				
Family	23.38	25.69	28.68	31.86
School	23.30	25.03	28.98	31.12
Peers	21.45	23.50	26.52	28.20
Exposure to delinquent peers	14.48	18.30	23.77	27.05
Commitment to delinquent peers	3.85	4.37	5.26	6.03

*This category approximates our notion of the sporadic offender.

**Offenses are as follows: *felony assault* (gang fights, aggravated assault, sexual assault), *minor assault* (hit teacher, parent, or students), *robbery* (strong-armed, against students, teachers, or others), *illegal service* (prostitution, sold drugs), *index offenses* (felony assault, robbery, stealing motor vehicle, stealing something worth over $50, and breaking into a building or vehicle).

Source: Dunford and Elliott, "Identifying Career Offenders Using Self-Reported Data". *Journal of Research in Crime and Delinquency*, p. 77. Copyright© 1984 by Sage Publications, Inc. Reprinted by permission of Sage Publications, Inc.

delinquents will occasionally commit such serious offenses as sexual assault or strong-arm robbery suggests that it would be inappropriate to trivialize the consequences of their behavior.

Compared with career delinquents, the sporadic offenders in the Dunford and Elliott study had much lower rates of theft than chronic offenders and rarely participated in the provision of illegal services such as selling drugs or prostitution. Sporadic delinquents apparently remain on the periphery of illegal market activity, and are thus prevented from transforming their activities into the sort of serious financial enterprise that would inevitably deepen their involvement in crime (compare Schwendinger and Schwendinger, 1985: 186).

THE DEMOGRAPHICS OF SPORADIC DELINQUENCY

Dunford and Elliott (1984) found no significant race or class differences among their four delinquent types: Career delinquents were no more likely to come from lower-status backgrounds or to be members of minority groups than noncareer offenders or nonoffenders. This finding appears to contradict a cohort study in Philadelphia, which found that recidivists were more likely to come from low socioeconomic backgrounds and to be black (Wolfgang, Figlio, and Sellin, 1972). The difference may be due to the fact that the Philadelphia study used official police records as its data source on delinquent activity rather than self-reported accounts. For one thing, official records skew offenses toward the more serious forms of crime, in part because they reflect what the authorities *react* to rather than what is actually going on. And it is more likely to be the lower-class juvenile whose delinquent behavior is reacted to (Chambliss, 1973). Secondly, when Dunford and Elliott looked at the arrest records of NYS samples, they found that the probability of arrest was low even for serious crimes and for highly recidivistic individuals. For example, among a subgroup of youths who reported 20 or more index crimes over a two-year period, "for every 1 arrest for any offense, an average of 40 index offenses were reported" by the youths themselves (Dunford and Elliott, 1984: 81). Incredible as it sounds, so much delinquency and crime remained hidden to the official record that Dunford and Elliott could identify only 2 percent of the self-reported career delinquents using police records.

It is possible that other factors contribute to the inconsistent findings on class and race. The Wolfgang study, pioneering as it was, looked at youths in only one city, whereas the National Youth Survey monitored the entire country. What happens in Philadelphia may not happen elsewhere to the same degree, or at all. In addition, the Wolfgang study covered the arrest experiences of youths living during the late fifties and early sixties; some of the difference between the two studies may therefore be explained by the fact that the NYS research looked at the delinquency of youths living almost 20 years later.

Other reports using the NYS data do show, nonetheless, that youths from lower-class families show higher overall incidence rates *for serious offenses* than do youths with middle-class backgrounds (e.g., Elliott and Huizinga, 1983). It appears more likely that it will be the lower-class youth who will progress out of sporadic delinquency into chronic involvement in serious crimes. But as we shall see in the next chapter, whether this happens for any given juvenile depends considerably on when the first involvement in serious crime occurs and on the age at first arrest. The younger juveniles are when they commit their first serious offense and when they are first arrested, the greater their chances of progressing beyond sporadic delinquency.

THE RESPECTABILITY OF SPORADIC OFFENDERS

It is commonly argued that sporadic offenders do not think of themselves as delinquents or criminals (Sykes and Matza, 1957; Gibbons, 1965; Clinard and Quinney, 1973; Peterson and Braiker, 1981). They see themselves as normal, that is, relatively respectable and law abiding. They recognize that their periodic crimes and delinquencies are wrong but dissociate themselves from real criminals. Their orientation, if not commitment, is more to convention than to crime.

Yet if this is true, how do we explain their periodic involvement in delinquency and crime? A variety of factors may be at work. One possibility is that situation-inspired *techniques of neutralization* are employed that redefine an act as acceptable, if not right. Faced with situational pressures to violate the law, generally conforming individuals may find themselves on the horns of a dilemma: whether to resist the pressures and thus act consistently with their self-image of respectability, or to enjoy the potential benefits of the crime, whatever these may be, at the risk of undermining that self-image and becoming the sort of person they ordinarily condemn. A solution that promises the best of both worlds justifies the act in terms that are acceptable to conventional morality. Thus, techniques of neutralization permit transgressors to remain respectable in their own minds, and *after the fact* they become a means of convincing others—parents, authorities, and delinquency researchers—of their continuing respectability!

Gresham Sykes and David Matza (1957) have identified five techniques of neutralization.

1. *Denial of responsibility*   Here, offenders blame the contemplated act on circumstances beyond their control. The boy who steals sees his friends making him do it; the girl who runs away says her parents forced it on her; the juvenile who joyrides blames it on being high. In each of these cases culpability is shifted away from the offender.

2. *Denial of injury*   With this technique a delinquent act is justified on the grounds that it won't hurt anyone. Stealing is borrowing, the intended victim can afford it, or "I'm not going to *really* hurt him."

3. *Denial of the victim*   Here, the moral import of an offense is neutralized by claims that the intended victim has it coming, or even that there is no victim at all (the lost or abandoned money, building, or car doesn't belong to anyone). At the very least, the victim is transformed into an understandable target. Thus, someone who leaves his car unlocked, who charges inflated prices, or whose behavior is considered deviant is fair game.

   To deny that some victims are real implies that there are others who are. Apparently, even chronic delinquents identify undeserving victims and considered them off-limits. George, a 24-year-old with a long history of delinquency and crime, tells how to avoid being burglarized:

   Being friendly helps a lot. . . . I don't think that no one would want to break into a person's house if he or she is a friendly type of person, because thieves are people and they like people too, and if a person is really kind and nice to them, it really bothers them about stealing things from them. [Merry, 1981: 90]

4. *Condemnation of the condemners*   Sometimes crime is justified on the grounds that everyone is doing it. This technique may be invoked for specific offenses—"Don't tell me about doing drugs when you're smoking and drinking booze!"—or used in a general way to point up the moral deficiencies of authority figures. A former leader of Chicago's Black Gangster Disciples illustrates this technique in his comments about the police:

   Some of them are involved in crime. They gyp people out of money, stick up people and sell some of the drugs they take from people.

   Don't you ever wonder why it is that you can have lots of police in an area and they know most of the gang members by name, yet crime keeps going up? [Recktenwald and Sheppard, 1984, Jan. 8: 14]

5. *Appeal to higher loyalties*   The final technique of neutralization identified by Sykes and Matza is illustrated by the adolescent who commits his crime be-

cause (he tells himself) his gang's survival depends on it or, at an older and higher plane, by the president who justifies illegal activities in terms of national security.

The importance of neutralization techniques in lessening the effectiveness of constraints associated with conventional self-images is by no means established. Indeed, research on neutralization theory has been limited, and the results have been inconsistent. This is partly explained by the difficulty of establishing how people think *before* they violate the law. Most of the research has looked at what people say after the fact, and this provides only inferential evidence at best (Matza, 1964; Ball, 1966; Hirschi, 1969; Hindelang, 1973)

One study that looks at neutralizing behavior and *subsequent* delinquency is by William Minor (1980, 1981). Minor found that youths who accepted excuses for delinquent acts were more likely to commit subsequent misdeeds. However, even though the relationship was strongest for those who expressed moral disapproval of the acts in question, the relationship was also found among youths who did not disapprove of the acts and had committed them in the past. This finding led Minor (1981: 313) to suggest that neutralization "may not only *allow* deviance, but also *encourage* it." (see also, Hirschi, 1969: 208.)

While trying to shore up a conventional self-image in the face of episodic pressures to be delinquent, some adolescents may succumb to the accumulative impact of past rationalizations and social reinforcements. The reinforcements may come in various forms, depending on what is valued at the time, but they remind individuals that certain behaviors *are* rewarding. Over time, these challenges to conventional attitudes and behaviors may chip away at a "respectable" child's resistance to delinquent pressures.

It is important to point out that some theorists reject the idea that rationalizations are used primarily to neutralize moral responsibility and guilt. Thus, Schwendinger and Schwendinger (1985: 137–140) describe the rhetoric of adolescents they studied as "instrumental," without moral substance. "The rationalizations overwhelmingly appealed to minimizing risks or other tactical considerations; therefore they could not be understood on the basis of 'techniques of neutralization' " (138–139). Even when it appears that a gang leader is making an appeal to higher loyalties when exhorting his members to fight in defense of the gang, the appeal may imply no subscription to convention or legal norms: "They may make this appeal simply because the members are afraid to fight or because they promised their parents or girlfriends that they would not" (139). In his autobiography, John Allen (1977: 40) also alludes to the instrumental character of seemingly moral rhetoric. He remembers that during his youth he and his friends would not rob stores whose owners had good reputations. Why? Not because the store owner didn't deserve it but because "we naturally wouldn't go into his place for fear that somebody might see us and call the police or describe us for the people that own the store."

Despite doubts as to the validity of the neutralization hypothesis, one essential point should be borne in mind: The use of rationalizations for guilt reduction *before* an offense is committed presupposes a troublesome measure of moral inhibition regarding the behavior in question. Those most likely to feel the pangs of conscience, and most likely to need and recognize a way to remove them, are surely those whose delinquent experiences are sporadic rather than recurring.

DELINQUENT OCCASIONS

The view that most juveniles drift in and out of delinquent episodes has been developed most systematically by David Matza (1964) in his book *Delinquency and Drift*. Matza believes that most people are neither totally free nor totally restrained. This version of soft determinism contends that juveniles "drift" from conformity to deviance and back again, and that movement either way is partly a matter of choice and partly a matter of external influence. Most adolescents (males especially) lie in a sort of limbo between the demands of middle-class convention and law, on the one hand, and the demands of male adolescent subculture, with its emphasis on acting out, on the other. Delinquent episodes may arise when adolescents are free to respond to the law-violating cues and incentives around them.

William Sanders (1981: 81–95) suggests that delinquent episodes may be encouraged by certain types of situations. Borrowing some ideas from the late Erving Goffman (1959, 1963, 1967) Sanders distinguishes between social occasions that are "tight" and those that are "loose." A social occasion is "an affair, undertaking, or event bounded by time and place within which many situations and gatherings form, dissolve, and reform" (Goffman, 1963: 18). They differ, however, by what goes on in them, by how they structure and control behavior, and by the expectations participants bring to them. A classroom occasion differs from a party occasion; a work occasion differs from a family occasion.

Some occasions are relatively loose, and some are relatively tight. Loose occasions are more informal, they permit a diversity of activities and multiple involvements, and the normative boundaries constraining behavior are more flexible, less well defined. Party and family occasions are generally loose occasions. Tight occasions have strict boundaries defining appropriate behavior, and the timing and ordering of events is precise; involvements are limited and limiting. Work and classroom occasions are generally tight occasions. However, Sanders (1981: 83) points out that "there are, of course, continuums of looseness and tightness, and many normally tight occasions may display features of informality, such as certain avant-garde, unstructured educational programs, and many parties are so formal that they can be considered tight occasions."

Juveniles generally spend more time in loose occasions than adults, especially if the latter are employed full time and raising a family (Werthman, 1967). Even when adults find themselves in relatively loose situations (for example, at lunch meetings, shopping, making repairs around the house), the compelling nature of the activities and the fact that they often occur between other tight occasions means their time is not really free (Sanders, 1981: 83, 89).

The more involved people are in tight occasions, the less time they have for loose occasions. Juveniles differ in the amount of free time they have, for some have part-time jobs, some are members of school athletic teams, some are involved in scouting or other structured group activities after school, and some have demanding family responsibilities. These are more or less tight occasions, and the more time they consume outside the classroom, the less time there is left for loose associations.

Because juveniles are less likely to feel constrained in loose situations, they are more likely to behave in ways that violate the law. But whether free time is turned into delinquent time depends also on the people present in the occasion, and on the opportunities and incentives it provides for displaying valued adolescent attributes *in ways that violate the law*. If those present in a loose situation are not inclined or equipped to break the law, delinquency is unlikely, and if a loose occasion provides plenty of opportunities for displaying character in *legal* ways, there is less incentive to do so illegally. Let us consider these issues in more detail.

"Hanging Out"

A favorite loose occasion for juveniles with free time is "hanging out." Hanging out with friends is an occasion in which boredom can be turned into fun, and sometimes the fun is illegal. Hermann and Julia Schwendinger spent many years studying youth cliques and gatherings, and in their view being an adolescent is not a particularly exciting time:

> Typically, a day in the life of an adolescent "hangs," and the adolescent "hangs" with it; he or she is suspended in a meaningless and often suffocating limbo. Countless hours are spent literally just "hanging around" and complaining about it. These youth can at least depend on the company of their peers to provide some stimulation and enjoyment. [Schwendinger and Schwendinger, 1985: 191]

Hanging out can take place at a friend's house, at the local baseball diamond or basketball court, in a parking lot, or simply in the street. Generally, the location will be dictated by convention and by activity choices, but these are both dependent to a certain extent on resources. Places to hang out are unlikely to be far afield if youth have to walk there. In addition, territorial considerations may come into play: Youths generally hang out on their own turf. Finally, hanging out is structured by the physical characteristics of places as well as by the routine activities of the people who live and work there. These days, shopping malls are desirable places for youths to hang out, especially if they have a video arcade. But such malls are usually found in suburbs, not inner-city neighborhoods, and they differ substantially in design (open air, strip, enclosed), volume of traffic, types of stores, and security. These facts not only influence who hangs out where but also what goes on and the rewards, costs, and risks attached to it.

Youths with after-school commitments or summer employment have less time to hang out, and therefore are less likely to be involved in the delinquent activities that such loose occasions often produce. Indeed, they not only have less opportunity to hang out, but they probably have less *need* to hang out. For one thing, they are not as bored (which does not mean they necessarily *like* what they are doing), and for another, their after-school activities often will provide them with routine, identity-building opportunities not available to kids with lots of free time.

Taking the perspective of symbolic interaction, Sanders (1981: 90–92) points out that "identities are made (and unmade) in social situations." How we perform in a given situation largely determines how others judge our character, who we *really* are, and, ultimately, how we judge ourselves. In tight situations, tests of character are formalized and standardized, and usually under the control of others—teachers, coaches, supervisors. In loose situations, character building can occur more or less at any time and may be entirely opportunistic. It is important to remember, however, that the same individual who comes over poorly in one situation may be regarded highly in another.

> For example, a juvenile may be seen in school and classroom situations as "dull," "slow," or, in the parlance of educational newspeak, "educationally handicapped." The same juvenile, however, may be a gang leader in his neighborhood, and when he's with his gang, engaging in gang activities, he is seen as "tough," "brave," full of "heart." His appearance and even his general performance may not be substantially different in the two situations, but the different audiences and contexts dictate the sense that is to be made of the performance. [Sanders, 1981: 90]

In our society, adolescent males value competitiveness and like to show that they are tough and cool in potentially dangerous situations. They also like to show that they are smart, which is sometimes displayed by verbal aggression and dexterity, at other times by putting it over on others, especially authority figures. But how does one demonstrate these qualities? How does one prove oneself?

One must find the right situation. For some that quest is relatively easy; for others it is much harder. Conventional middle-class society provides lots of opportunities for middle-class youths to show character—in the classroom, in organized sports, in fraternities and sororities, on the tennis courts and ski slopes, and in scouting and in surfing. Taking risks is expected, even encouraged, but always within the framework of conventional (i.e., approved) activities. Validation comes from both adults and peers, and if a child shows signs of failing, there are "absorption mechanisms" to cushion the effect—psychiatric counseling, boarding school, vacation trips, and so on (Schwendinger and Schwendinger, 1985: 39).

Lower-class adolescents, especially the urban poor, often have neither the opportunity nor the inclination to participate in middle-class identity-building exercises. Relegated to the streets, these youths must demonstrate character by using the relatively meager resources at hand. The skills and popularity of breakdancing show that the exercise need not violate the law, but demonstrations of toughness and coolness invariably will. It is risky and exciting to fight, to steal cars, to do what authority frowns on (Werthman, 1967).

It can be a test of character to defeat the controls of others' tight occasions, thereby making them loose. How often have we seen kids (of all kinds, we might add) disrupt the classroom, takeover the McDonald's parking lot, or interfere with the orderly flow of traffic. Boredom is turned into adventure in the search for "something to do" (Sanders, 1981: 88), and the riskier and more creative the activity, the more it demonstrates both cool and superior ability. The Schwendingers (1985: 156–157) describe one such caper by a group of boys involved in tire stealing:

> One night, a "competition" was held in which four teams of two partners each raced to steal a top-grade automobile tire in the shortest time. Speed was essential in this task, and partners were chosen primarily on the basis of their ability to work fast. On the night of the competition, four teams of boys rolled stolen tires down the middle of the street in a race to reach the time-keeper.

Character validation occurs immediately in such situations "because the capable thief or fighter is amply rewarded by the admiring glances of his friends" (Schwendinger and Schwendinger, 1985: 156; see also Werthman, 1967).

The preceding exercise could just as well have been carried out by boys from wealthy backgrounds as by those living in poverty. Indeed, the periodic demonstration of character through competition and risk taking is the hallmark of adolescence in general. However, where lower-class children are likely to spend more time hanging out on street corners or vacant lots, middle- and upper-class juveniles are likely to spend more time in tighter situations, under adult supervision and constraint. The Schwendingers (1985: 208–209) suggest that advantaged ("socialite") adolescent groups put up with these constraints in exchange for the benefits they receive—cars, spending money, vacations, and comfortable living. They may even try to keep "wild" members under control. But hair is let down on trips to the beach, during vacation time, and at rented cottages away from adult supervision. It is on loose occasions like these that socialite youth engage in periodic fights, drunken brawls, hazings, and property damage.

But where the sporadic violence of middle-class youths is less visible and more easily excused by authorities (just kids letting their hair down), that of street-corner groups is public and what "real" delinquents do. The police are on the lookout for it, and citizens (especially the business community) are quick to report trouble. It is, thus, the street-corner youth whose sporadic forays into delinquency and crime are likely to bring contact with the police relatively early on. As we shall see in the next chapter, that contact may contribute to turning a sporadic delinquent into a chronic delinquent.

Delinquency as Play

The situational aspects of delinquency have been emphasized in a study by Pamela Richards and her colleagues, Richard Berk and Brenda Forster (1979). These authors surveyed nearly 3000 students living in "an affluent middle-class suburb of a large midwestern city." Their research was guided by a "decision-making framework," in which environmental influences—family, peers, school—limit but "do not rigidly force individuals into deviance" (40). Rather, individuals "choose from a mix of both deviant and nondeviant options whose outcomes can be predicted with varying degrees of certainty" (40). Richards and her colleagues argue that adolescence is heavily *leisure based,* and delinquency reflects the investment of leisure time in play activities that are illegal or potentially deviant (i.e., peer conflict or running away from home). Taking a rationalist perspective, the authors believe that purposive decision making occurs in which choices are guided by an assessment of benefits and costs and influenced by established preferences, or "tastes," and situational opportunities (184).

While arguing that their leisure framework might well be applied to the delinquency of most lower-class youths (198–199), Richards and her colleagues decided to explore middle-class delinquency, hoping to improve our knowledge of this neglected area. Using self-report data, they found not only that sporadic delinquency was widespread among their student respondents but also that it was primarily petty from the point of view of criminal law. For grades 5 through 12, the bulk of delinquency consisted of alcohol use, fighting with fellow students, minor theft, vandalism, and cheating on tests. Nevertheless, many students admitted committing such offenses more than twice during the six months preceding the survey, and 30 percent of the high school students said they had been taken down to the police station at least once during their lifetime.

Not surprisingly, the authors found also that forms of delinquency intercorrelate; that is, students reporting a serious offense are more likely than other students to report other serious offenses. It appears that most students who admit to minor delinquencies tend to remain at that level, a finding confirmed in other studies (e.g., Kobrin, Hellym, and Peterson, 1980).

Vandalism is among the most commonly reported offenses for all student age groups, and the authors believe students invest considerable leisure time in it because its potential costs are offset by its varied rewards. Among these are its thrill or excitement value; its potential for spoils or trophies, which may be more symbolic than real (for example, defacement and destruction imply power, for disgruntled youths the power to take revenge); and its contribution to the development of "human capital," including information and skills. For example, participation in vandalism may teach "techniques for effective use of a BB gun, knowledge of the risks involved in breaking into school after hours, or the best way to coordinate group action during a series of Halloween pranks" (Richards, Berk, and Forster, 1979: 81). Indeed, the authors believe that the group processes involved in the commission of most juvenile crimes help refine an individual's understanding of social roles and develop leadership and other interaction skills.

Drug use also demonstrates the importance of peer involvement. For these students, as indeed for most people, alcohol and drug use is preeminently a *social* activity. They choose to drink or take drugs in the company of others, most often at parties or dances, at small gatherings of friends, at concerts or movies, and, significantly, when there is nothing else to do (Richards, Berk, and Forster, 1979: 121). Not only are the benefits direct, in the form of such psychic rewards as "feeling good," "relaxing," and so forth, but they may contribute to an adolescent's standing and general sociability.

In short, the Richards study tends to confirm the "normality" of occasional adolescent delinquency, its group and situational contexts, and its relatively petty nature. The free time, and potential boredom, that accompanies adolescent years presents both the opportunity and the incentive for juveniles to explore their environment as well as themselves. Growing up is a time of testing, of searching for self-worth and meaning, and while on occasion this search may lead to trouble with the law, most often it does not. The sporadic delinquency and crime of most adolescents remains a temporary feature of their lives, from which they emerge largely no worse for wear. The picture is rather different for the chronic delinquent, to whom the next chapter is devoted.

The passage from child to adult brings new responsibilities and, despite what many children believe, decreasing free time. It is a time of settling down: making plans for the future, choosing (and succeeding in) a college or a job, and for some, starting a family. All these activities cut down on loose occasions and increase the young adult's stake in conformity. What is more, many of the activities that previously brought mild censure, if not tolerance, are no longer delinquencies but crimes, punishable publicly and often with hard time.

If their behavior is anything to go by, most juveniles seem to appreciate their changing status and new obligations, for by age 17 rates of misbehavior begin to drop off markedly. The change is obviously easier for those whose delinquency has been petty, opportunistic, and motivated by adventure. Many sporadic delinquents fit this picture. But even those sporadic offenders who have had periodic contacts with the police, perhaps even a spell in detention, seem quite ready to go straight when they reach adulthood. A study of working-class British delinquents found that by age 17 many were abandoning the large, male-dominated peer groups of their delinquent past in favor of fewer, closer friends, and earlier brushes with the law were often cited in discussions of the need to go straight.

> It made me conscious I've been in trouble with the police and it makes me more careful not to get done again for anything, even driving. I make sure I don't buy or sell drugs and I make sure nobody shoves any drugs on me. I have all my pockets buttoned up. . . . I've always been a mug all my life and I'm trying to turn the other way now. I'm going to let all the rest be mugs. [Knight and West, 1975: 48]

It seems, then, that youths who mature out of delinquency do so because the opportunities and incentives for it become less favorable, while new responsibilities encourage commitment to conformity.

SUMMARY

We began this chapter by observing that delinquency involvement is a matter of degree. We consider it fruitful to distinguish three dimensions along which that involvement varies: frequency, seriousness, and duration. The bulk of delinquents are sporadic offenders who occasionally commit delinquent acts, sometimes serious ones, over the course of adolescence. Yet sporadic delinquents have been largely ignored in traditional research, and the recent rush to understand the relatively small core of chronic (sometimes called "career") delinquents has not improved matters.

Our attempt to identify the sporadic delinquent led us to rely heavily on the ambitious research effort of the National Youth Survey. The NYS "noncareer" offender best approximates our sense of the sporadic delinquent, and almost half of the 1,494 subjects interviewed fell into this category.

Sporadic delinquents are essentially law-abiding youths who drift in and out of delinquent episodes as incentive and opportunity come together in the absence of overwhelming moral objections. The situations most conducive to sporadic offending are a typical feature of many youths' lives: loose occasions where "hanging out" with friends, opportunistic identity-building activities, and risk-taking play bring youths into conflict with adult rules and, sometimes, with the law. The normalcy of it all is reflected perhaps best of all in the fact that most sporadic delinquents escape the trouble that helps turn a small minority of youths into chronic offenders.

REFERENCES

Abrahamsen, David. 1960. *The Psychology of Crime.* New York: Columbia University Press.

Alexander, Franz, and Hugo Staub. 1956. *The Criminal, the Judge, and the Public.* Glencoe, Ill.: Free Press.

Allen, John. 1977. *Assault with a Deadly Weapon: The Autobiography of a Street Criminal.* New York: Pantheon Books.

Ball, Robert A. 1966. "An Empirical Exploration of Neutralization Theory." *Criminologica* 4:22–32.

Chambliss, William J. 1973. "The Saints and the Roughnecks." *Society* 11:24–31.

Clinard, Marshall, and Richard Quinney. 1973. *Criminal Behavior Systems—A Typology.* Revised Edition. New York: Holt, Rinehart, and Winston.

Dunford, Franklyn W., and Delbert S. Elliott. 1984. "Identifying Career Offenders Using Self-Reported Data." *Journal of Research in Crime and Delinquency* 21:57–86.

Elliott, Delbert S., Suzanne Ageton, David Huizinga, B. A. Knowles, and R. J. Canter. 1983. *The Prevalence and Incidence of Delinquent Behavior: 1976–1980.* Boulder, Col.: Behavioral Research Institute.

Elliott, Delbert S., and David Huizinga. 1983. "Social Class and Delinquent Behavior in a National Youth Panel: 1976–1980." *Criminology* 21:149–177.

Gibbons, Don C. 1965. *Changing the Lawbreaker.* New York: Prentice-Hall.

Goffman, Erving. 1959. *The Presentation of Self in Everyday Life.* New York: Doubleday.

———. 1963. *Behavior in Public Places.* New York: Free Press.

———. 1967. *Interaction Ritual.* New York: Doubleday.

Hagan, John, A. R. Gillis, and John Simpson. 1985. "The Class Structure of Gender and Delinquency: Toward a Power-Control Theory of Common Delinquent Behavior." *American Journal of Sociology* 90:1151–1177.

Hindelang, Michael J. 1973. "Causes of Delinquency: A Partial Replication." *Social Problems* 20:471–487.

Hindelang, Michael J., Travis Hirschi, and Joseph G. Weis. 1979. "Correlates of Delinquency: The Illusion of Discrepancy Between Self-Report and Official Measures." *American Sociological Review* 44:995–1014.

Hirschi, Travis. 1969. *Causes of Delinquency.* Berkeley: University of California Press.

Knight, B. J., and D. J. West. 1975. "Temporary and Continuing Delinquency." *British Journal of Criminology* 15:43–50.

Kobrin, Soloman, Frank R. Hellym, and John W. Peterson. 1980. "Offense Patterns of Status Offenders." In *Critical Issues in Juvenile Delinquency.* Edited by David Shichor and Delos H. Kelly. Lexington, Mass.: Lexington Books.

Lombroso, Cesare. 1911. *Crime, Its Causes and Remedies.* London: Stevens.

Matza, David. 1964. *Delinquency and Drift.* New York: John Wiley and Sons.

Merry, Sally Engle. 1981. *Urban Danger: Life in a Neighborhood of Strangers.* Philadelphia: Temple University Press.

Minor, William W. 1980. "The Neutralization of Criminal Offense." *Criminology* 18:103–120.

———. 1981. "Techniques of Neutralization: A Reconceptualization and Empirical Examination." *Journal of Research in Crime and Delinquency* 18:295–318.

Peterson, Mark A., and Harriet B. Braiker. 1981. *Who Commits Crime. A Survey of Prison Inmates.* Santa Monica: Rand.

Rechtenwald, William, and Nathaniel Sheppard. 1984. "Gangs." *Chicago Tribune,* January, 8–12.

Richards, Pamela, Richard A. Berk, and Brenda Forster. 1979. *Crime as Play: Delinquency in a Middle Class Suburb.* Cambridge, Mass.: Ballinger.

Sanders, William. 1981. *Juvenile Delinquency: Causes, Patterns, and Reactions.* New York: Holt, Rinehart, and Winston.

Schafer, Stephen, and Richard Knudten. 1970. *Juvenile Delinquency—An Introduction.* New York: Random House.

Schwendinger, Herman, and Julia Siegel Schwendinger. 1985. *Adolescent Subcultures and Delinquency.* New York: Praeger.

Sykes, Gresham, and David Matza. 1957. "Techniques of Neutralization: A Theory of Delinquency." *American Sociological Review* 22:664–70.

Werthman, Carl. 1967. "The Function of Social Definitions in the Development of Delinquent Careers." In *Task Force Report: A Report of the President's Commission on Law Enforcement and the Administration of Justice.* Washington, D.C.: U.S. Government Printing Office.

Wolfgang, Marvin E., Robert M. Figlio, and Thorsten Sellin. 1972. *Delinquency in a Birth Cohort.* Chicago: University of Chicago Press.

Chapter
4

The Chronic
Delinquent

Not long ago, a committee of 15 citizens from around the country recommended to the president and Congress that "the task of highest priority in the field of juvenile delinquency is to deal directly and decisively with [the] small core of youth who are responsible for much of the nation's crime" (National Advisory Committee, 1984: 1). This small core is made up primarily of repeat offenders, youths who commit crimes and delinquencies over and over again in the course of growing up. These youths are the subject of this chapter.

DEFINING THE CHRONIC DELINQUENT

Apart from the notion of repetitive offending, there is little consensus on exactly who the chronic delinquent is. It is not clear, for example, how many offenses a juvenile must commit to be classified as a chronic delinquent, nor whether the offenses must be of a certain type. To add to the confusion, the words *chronic* and *career* are often used interchangeably, but clearly the latter denotes more than repetitive offending. A career implies that a person has a recognizable identity, and special perspectives and behaviors related to a core activity. This may be true of some persistent recidivists but is surely less likely true of those who commit relatively minor offenses or those who never get caught.

Finally, there is little consensus on the duration of offending: Some authors apply the term *chronic* to juveniles whose criminal activity spans three or four years; others specify a minimum number of offenses (or arrests) but make no mention of duration.

We use a broad definition of chronic delinquency, one that allows us to pull together research findings from studies that have used different definitions and methods. For purposes of this chapter, think of the chronic delinquent as a juvenile whose offending behavior lies at the right end of the three continua presented in Figure 3.1 on page 43. In comparison with other delinquents, chronic delinquents commit more serious offenses, more often, and over a longer period of time.

THE EXTENT AND SCOPE OF CHRONIC DELINQUENCY

Marvin Wolfgang and his colleagues at the University of Pennsylvania first drew attention to the chronic delinquent (Wolfgang, Figlio, and Sellin, 1972). They studied 9,945 boys, all born in 1945 and all residents of Philadelphia, from their 10th to their 18th birthdays. Data on the cohort's delinquent activities were gathered from three sources: school, police, and juvenile court. Delinquency was defined as any official "police contact." A police contact did not mean a boy was arrested, because the officer in question might have chosen an informal (remedial) response. Nevertheless, the contact counted as an offense if it was officially filed as part of a boy's rap sheet. The authors felt they would catch more delinquency this way than if they had used merely arrest or court data. In addition, their measurements would be less subject to *selection biases*, which may distort measurements based on arrests or convictions. When selection biases operate, some people are processed differently than others, perhaps because of age, sex, or race. If certain offenders avoid arrest because they are female, for example, a count of arrests would not reflect the correct proportions of males and females who were actually suspected of the offenses in question.

Over a third (3,475) of the 1945 Philadelphia cohort had a record of delinquency, and these boys had a total of 10,214 police contacts. However, just 627 boys (6.3 percent) accounted for more than half those contacts. These boys averaged 8.46 police contacts per person, and *all* had had at least 5 contacts.

A second study, using a 1958 birth cohort consisting of 13,160 boys, also residents of Philadelphia, again found that a small group of juveniles accounted for more than half the official police contacts (Tracy, Wolfgang, and Figlio, 1990). This study identified 982 boys with five or more police contacts. These boys made up only 7.5 percent of the cohort and only 23 percent of those with records of delinquency.

Other studies, often using different methods, generally confirm that there is a small core of delinquents who commit a disproportionate share of offenses (e.g., Gold, 1970; Shannon, 1982; Cernkovich, Giordano, and Pugh, 1985), and studies from abroad paint a similar picture. For example, using self-reports of delinquency involvement among 900 school children in Stockholm, Sweden, Elmhorn (1965) discovered that persistent delinquency was characteristic of less than 10 percent of the sample, and even fewer children when more serious offenses were considered.

In England, the Cambridge Study of Delinquency Development (see Chapter 2) also confirmed the existence of a small minority of chronic delinquents. For 14 years,

West and Farrington (1977) followed a cohort of 411 boys born in a working-class area of London during the years 1951 to 1954. Extensive interviews were supplemented by police and court records. Of the original youths, 389 were reinterviewed at age 18 to 19, and among these boys, 82 had been convicted of a juvenile offense. However, among those convicted, only 17 percent had been convicted four or more times.

The use of conviction records to identify chronic offenders may not be the best approach since doing so ignores those juvenile offenders who are arrested but not convicted, those who are questioned by the police but not arrested, and those who are never discovered. In this sense, conviction records are like a fishing net with large holes. Self-reports of delinquency involvement help researchers plug some of the holes. For example, West and Farrington asked the boys about their delinquent activities during the three years preceding the interviews. Twenty-four boys admitted to at least 22 offenses, and three boys admitted to at least 39. West and Farrington describe one of the most actively delinquent boys this way:

> . . . The descriptions he gave of his undetected crimes . . . revealed a serious commitment to delinquent activities. He not only admitted 20 taking and driving [joyriding] offences, but explained that he had prepared himself by stealing in advance a set of master keys for a common make of car. He also admitted stealing from slot machines on 29 occasions, usually to get money, sometimes to get cigarettes. As for the 4 burglaries he had committed in the last 3 years, he said, "We done a couple of houses, and we done a shop. I worked with someone else, usually for the money. We don't bother with goods—except for the shop where we got cigarettes and sold them. . . ."
>
> In contrast his 15 shop-lifting exploits appeared frivolous. He said he stole "a load of rubbish—bangles and beads. I do it for kicks, you know, with my mates." He displayed no guilt, regret or concern when describing his numerous delinquencies. Shortly after the interview he was convicted again, this time for unlawful possession of lead. [West and Farrington, 1977: 29–30]

The National Youth Survey   In the preceding chapter we discussed the findings of the National Youth Survey (NYS). Recall that this survey involved interviews with a national sample of adolescents born in the years 1959 through 1965. Each year, from 1977 through 1981, subjects were asked how many times they had participated in a variety of delinquent acts during the preceding year.

Of the 1494 youths interviewed during all five years, 784 (52 percent) were defined as delinquent. However, of these, less than a third (242) had persisted in frequent delinquent activity over the course of two or more consecutive years, and even fewer (70) had persisted in serious criminal activity (e.g., felony crimes of theft, violence, and sale of narcotics). Taken together, however, these career offenders accounted for a disproportionate amount of *all types* of reported delinquency (Dunford and Elliott, 1984).

Another interesting finding is that very few (2 percent) of the career offenders could be identified on the basis of official arrest records showing five or more arrests (a common standard of chronicity). According to Dunford and Elliott (1984: 79), "this means that all but a tiny fraction of youth engaged in frequent and serious offending will be overlooked" if chronic offenders are defined in terms of five or more arrests. The authors go on to show that the probability of an arrest is in fact uniformly low for all levels of self-reported delinquency. Even when the number of self-reported offenses exceeded

200 (per person), only 19 of every 100 offenders had an arrest record. Although sheer number of offenses does raise the probability of an arrest, a review of the arrest records of 23 of the youths who reported 20 or more index crimes in a two-year period showed that only one had actually been arrested for an index offense during the same period. The authors concluded that the probability of an arrest was "very low" until the rate of self-reported offending exceeded 100 offenses (Elliott, Dunford, and Huizinga, 1987: 111).

If these data are to be believed, most chronic offenders get away with their crimes for months, if not years on end. But what of the few who are caught and punished? Are they any different? A recent study suggests that indeed they are: The frequency and seriousness of their offending is much worse than those whose crimes remain hidden (or at least unpunished).

Cernkovich, Giordano, and Pugh (1985) believe that general youth surveys such as the NYS underrepresent the truly serious chronic offenders, "youths involved in serious and repeated violations of the law who are most visible to the police and courts, and who are feared most by the community itself" (706). When they compared a sample of incarcerated offenders with subjects from a neighborhood sample, they found the former to be uniformly more delinquent in both frequency and seriousness of offending. Even when the 128 worst subjects from the neighborhood sample, those responsible for 95 percent of all major crimes (i.e., motor vehicle theft, aggravated assault, robbery, breaking and entering, rape, and sale of hard drugs), were compared with the incarcerated offenders, their level of criminal involvement paled in comparison (730).

To illustrate, we have borrowed some of the findings presented by Cernkovich, Giordano, and Pugh (1985). Table 4.1 shows the percent of neighborhood and institutional *chronic* male offenders (those responsible for at least five major offenses during the year preceding the interviews) who reported "never" having committed a given offense, and those who admit to having done it at least two or three times a week. The neighborhood chronics were more likely to report never having committed the offenses in question and were less likely to admit having committed them two or three times a week.

It appears that those who persist in committing serious offenses over an extended period of time stand the best chance of landing in jail, but one could hardly argue from this that current penal practice protects the community from the chronic delinquent. As we have said, most of the offenses of most chronic delinquents are undetected and unpunished.

SPECIALIZATION AND VIOLENCE

Experience in an activity tends to improve the skills of participants and helps identify the things they do best. Experience in crime is no exception, and it is reasonable to ask whether chronic offenders show evidence of specialization. A prevalent fear is that some will specialize in crimes of violence. These "child monsters" are pictured roaming the streets in search of defenseless victims to assault, rob, or rape. This imagery is fanned by well-publicized cases of brutality against the elderly, the infirm, or the very young, and

Table 4.1   DELINQUENCY INVOLVEMENT OF
             CHRONIC OFFENDERS*

Delinquent act	Percent reporting	
	Never	2–3 Times or more a week
Grand theft		
Neighborhood sample	68.8	3.8
Institution sample	8.8	28.9
Fencing stolen goods		
Neighborhood	46.3	7.5
Institution	11.4	26.3
Vandalism		
Neighborhood	46.3	3.8
Institution	25.4	19.3
Concealed weapon		
Neighborhood	43.8	20.0
Institution	28.1	44.7
Gang fight		
Neighborhood	46.3	7.5
Institution	29.8	21.1
Sold marijuana		
Neighborhood	67.5	11.3
Institution	16.7	52.6
Sold hard drugs		
Neighborhood	91.3	1.3
Institution	58.8	17.5
Public drunkenness		
Neighborhood	61.3	6.3
Institution	24.8	37.2
Theft $5–$50		
Neighborhood	66.3	2.5
Institution	14.0	24.6
Breaking and entering		
Neighborhood	62.5	—
Institution	17.5	23.7

*Differences significant at p = < .001

Source: Cernkovich, Giordano, and Pugh. *Journal of Criminal Law and Criminology,* 76:705–32, 1985. Reprinted by permission of Northwestern University School of Law.

by growing awareness that as much as half of all police-blotter violent crime is committed by juveniles, who appear to be getting away with it.

Do chronic delinquents specialize, and if so, in what kind(s) of delinquent activity? The evidence on specialization is sparse and rather mixed. According to some studies, chronic delinquents pursue all kinds of crime, mostly as the occasion and the opportunity arise. Other studies suggest that some specialization exists, that it is more common among chronics than among other offenders, and that it is especially so as a person's delinquency involvement increases.

The Philadelphia cohort studies fall in the latter camp. Evidence of specialization was found for theft and robbery in both cohorts. It was especially marked in the 1958 cohort among nonwhite offenders with nine or more police contacts (Tracy, Wolfgang, and Figlio, 1990: 172–173). Examining only *violent* offenders from the same cohort, Piper (1985) also found that the likelihood of specialization increased with the number of police contacts, but there was less specialization in violent offenses than in other criminal activities. Another study that examined the 1958 cohort suggests that in the course of their careers some chronic offenders specialize for a time, then become generalists for a while, and later resume a more specialized focus (Kempf, 1987).

Using a sample of 750 Cook County, Illinois, youths with court convictions for delinquency, Bursik (1980) found that specialization was not a dominant feature of offense histories. However, some evidence of specialization in robbery-type offenses was found among both white and black youths, and blacks were much more likely than whites to specialize in personal injury offenses. A study that examined 70,000 juvenile court records also found evidence of specialization in certain offenses, for example, runaway, burglary, and motor vehicle theft (Farrington, Snyder, and Finnegan, 1988). The authors concluded that nearly 20 percent of the offenders showed signs of specialization.

Unfortunately, all these studies relied on official data in describing delinquency patterns. Even though the analyses are highly sophisticated, it is inconceivable that they tapped the actual offense behavior of the juveniles studied. Remember that self-report studies show that chronic delinquents commit scores, if not hundreds, of offenses, so the idea that offense patterns based on police rap sheets or court convictions somehow describe the presence or absence of specialization is questionable.

Case studies and surveys using self-report data indicate that offense specialization is the exception rather than the rule, even among persistent recidivists. Hartstone and Hansen (1984) examined 114 juveniles with extensive records of delinquency, including violent crimes, and found no evidence of crime specialization. Offenses varied from occurrence to occurrence. Merry (1981: 111) observed that even the most criminally active street-corner youths in Dover Square spread their delinquencies broadly: hustling, prostitution, drug pushing, burglary, robbery, purse snatching, and picking pockets.

On the question of violence, the evidence is less controversial. There is general agreement that chronic offenders are more likely than others to commit violent crimes, but most do so rarely, and many not at all.

The best-known study of the issue is by Donna Hamparian and her associates in Columbus, Ohio. Their Dangerous Offender Project examined the delinquent careers of all juveniles born during 1956 to 1960 and arrested at least once for a violent crime (Hamparian et al., 1978). In all, 1,138 juveniles were identified from police files. Collectively, they accounted for 4,499 crimes (i.e., arrests), most of which were nonviolent. The records of 811 subjects were examined closely. One-third of these 811 juveniles had been arrested at least five times and were identified as chronic offenders. They accounted for 40 percent of the cohort's aggravated offenses (i.e., murder, rape, armed robbery, and aggravated assault) and nearly 45 percent of all index crimes against the person. However, only 22 youths had been arrested for two or more aggravated crimes, and none seemed to fit the "child monster" image. The violent crimes of these youths appeared "clumsy and inadvertent" (Dinitz and Conrad, 1980: 145): "One of the monsters stabbed a tormentor who was taunting him about his obesity. The wound was in the shoulder; the victim needlessly bled to death." The bulk of the violence occurred during apparently impulsive robberies. In all, the Columbus study found no evidence of repeated acts of violence among most of its chronic offenders. While larger, more heterogeneous, less economically stable cities may show more juvenile violence, nobody has yet suggested that chronic delinquents are by and large chronically violent (see also Hartstone and Hansen, 1984).

PROGRESSION

It is assumed by many people that young offenders do not start out committing serious crimes but, rather, that they move (progress) from minor to major offenses as their involvement in delinquency grows. What does the evidence say?

It is mixed. Findings in support of progression come from the National Youth Survey (Elliott, Huizinga, and Morse, 1985). Some youths who admitted persistent offending over the five years of the study moved upward in both frequency and seriousness of offending. Although the majority of youths in any given state at the beginning of the survey tended to remain that way or to reduce their delinquent activity, the minority who increased their involvement moved to a higher level of seriousness, and once they reached that level, almost half (44 percent) remained that way from year to year.

Both of the Philadelphia cohort studies found evidence of progression, but the movement from less to more serious crime was most pronounced *within* offense types (Tracy, Wolfgang, and Figlio, 1985: 15–19). Thus, if earlier police contacts had been for offenses involving injury, future police contacts for injury offenses involved crimes that ranked higher in seriousness. Similar, but less pronounced, progression was observed for property damage offenses and robbery.

A pattern of progression among chronic delinquents is not inevitable. The Columbus study found more of a yo-yo effect: Chronic offenders often committed their violent offenses during the first third of their careers and then moved up and down in the seriousness of their offenses. Cernknovich, Giordano, and Pugh (1985) found a total of 222 youths in their neighborhood sample who reported frequent (48 or more) minor crimes "during the past year" but no major crimes.

DEMOGRAPHICS OF CHRONIC OFFENDERS: GENDER, CLASS, AND RACE

We have seen that a small minority of juvenile delinquents become chronic offenders. But is anything else special about this minority?

Chronic delinquents, especially those with histories of violent crime, are more likely to be *male* than female, to be of *low socioeconomic status* rather than high, and to be *nonwhite* rather than white.

Gender   Even though self-report studies show far more delinquency among females than official statistics indicate, when it comes to serious offending, males far outrank females in both self-report and police-based measurements of delinquency. In Philadelphia, only the 1958 cohort study had information on females. But when compared with their male counterparts, the 14,000 females where 2.5 times *less* likely to have had contact with the police, and those that had had contact were 3 times *less* likely to be designated chronic offenders. The female share of offending "did not represent either the volume or the severity of delinquency as was the case for their male counterparts" (Tracy, Wolfgang, and Figlio, 1985: 11).

The rarity of female offenders with arrests for violent crimes is confirmed by the Columbus cohort (Hamparian et al., 1978: 70). Females comprised only 15.6 percent of the violent cohort, and only 24 girls had five or more arrests (compared with 329 males). Even less frequent is the female delinquent with multiple court referrals for violent crime: Shelden's (1987) study of 1,000 youths first referred to juvenile court in 1980 found only three girls with five or more referrals on "mostly" serious charges. The ratio of males to females was 20 to 1. Almost all the chronic females were "nuisance" offenders—charged with status offenses, petty theft, drunk and disorderly conduct, or drug and/or alcohol possession. A study of 69,504 youths referred to court in two western states found that males were twice as likely as females to have two or more court referrals (Snyder, 1986).

Self-report studies confirm that chronic offenders are disproportionately male, especially when serious offenses are considered (Dunford and Elliott, 1984; Cernkovich, Giordano, and Pugh, 1985). But when female delinquents do achieve chronic status and admit to serious offending, their rates of serious crime are not consistently lower than their male counterparts. In the study by Cernkovich, Giordano, and Pugh, although females were more likely to report that they had never carried a concealed weapon, never robbed, and never broke into anyone's home or business, they were as likely as males to admit that they had stolen relatively expensive items, had committed aggravated assault, had sold marijuana or hard drugs, or had fenced stolen goods. We will have more to say on female delinquency in Chapter 8.

Social Class   The relationship between socioeconomic status (or social class) and delinquency has been a matter of debate for decades and will probably remain so as long as legal and social definitions of crime and delinquency favor the upper classes over the lower. Put simply, the everyday activities of lower-class people are more likely to be defined as delinquent or criminal than are the everyday activities of upper-class people.

To a large extent, this fact explains why far fewer middle- and upper-class juveniles appear in official statistics than appear in self-report studies. But what about the high end of delinquency and crime? Are children from middle and upper classes as likely as others to be chronic offenders?

The answer is no. A review of 90 different studies found only 21 that did not confirm a negative relationship between rates of delinquency and socioeconomic status (Braithwaite, 1981). More importantly, crimes of violence and personal theft were much more likely to be committed by persons from lower-class backgrounds.

The familiar studies of chronic delinquency confirm this finding. Elliott and Ageton's (1980) analysis of National Youth Survey data found that lower-class youths (those in families whose principle wage earner is unskilled, semiskilled, or a service worker) are more likely than others to be high-frequency offenders, and they admitted to four times as many predatory crimes against persons than did middle-class youths (children in families whose principle wage earner holds a professional or managerial occupation). Later analysis of the complete NYS data confirmed this relationship (Elliott and Huizinga, 1984).

The Philadelphia and Columbus cohort studies also found a substantial class effect. In Columbus, less than 10 percent of the chronic offenders came from neighborhoods with average or above average incomes, and the authors point out that the geographical location of chronic offenders "does not assure that their families enjoyed incomes equal to the average for their neighbors" (Hamparian et al., 1978: 128). In both the 1945 and the 1958 Philadelphia cohorts, the low socioeconomic-status juveniles were more delinquent and more involved in serious offenses (Tracy, Wolfgang, and Figlio, 1990).

It would be a mistake to leave the impression that there is no controversy surrounding the association of social class with chronic delinquency. For one thing, the notion of social class itself is a matter of controversy, there being no consensus on how to define, let alone measure, the concept. Secondly, some theories of delinquency and crime predict that rates of offending will be greater among higher-class individuals than among those at the bottom of the class hierarchy. Power-control theory is an example (see Chapter 8). According to this theory, factors associated with deviance such as risk taking and freedom from the supervision of others increase as one moves up the class ladder. Finally, there is the argument that preoccupation with lower-class criminality diverts attention away from the crimes of the powerful, which may be equally victimizing even though some are not technically illegal.

There is no simple response to these points. The research that supports the conclusion that chronic delinquents are more likely to be found among lower-class youths is not uniform in its definitions and methods, nor has it generally focused on crimes associated with power and privilege. On the other hand, if one looks at criminal victimization from the standpoint of those most likely to be the victims of serious street crimes—robbery, assault, and burglary, for example—then the urban lower class stands out not only because it is disproportionately victimized but also because its youth are identified most often as the chronic offenders largely responsible for it.

Race   In the United States, many studies have compared the delinquency of white children with that of black children. As with socioeconomic status, race emerges as a factor in delinquency only at the high end of the frequency and severity continua.

Strasburg's (1984) review of over 500 New York City court records, as well as numerous interviews with officials and juvenile offenders, showed disproportionate numbers of blacks among a small number of chronic offenders. In Philadelphia, nonwhite delinquents were more likely than whites to have five or more police contacts, and for the 1958 cohort this was true regardless of gender. The Columbus study, on the other hand, found that while blacks were "vastly overrepresented" in the violent offender cohort, the probability of having had five or more arrests did *not* vary by race (Hamparian et al., 1978: 132). In both Philadelphia and Columbus, however, black juveniles more often had police contacts for robbery than did white juveniles.

It needs to be said that blacks are no more prone to breaking rules than are whites. But black juveniles are more likely to show up in official and self-report statistics on predatory crimes against the person. Putting race and gender together, the rank order among serious chronic offenders in American studies is almost universally nonwhite male, first, followed by white males, nonwhite females, and then white females.

EXPLAINING CHRONIC DELINQUENCY

In Chapter 3, we considered why many youngsters occasionally commit delinquent or criminal acts during the course of growing up. The answer was couched in terms of guilt neutralization, loose occasions, opportunities, boredom, and play. But there seemed to be nothing extraordinary in the backgrounds, personalities, or experiences of sporadic delinquents.

Chronic delinquents are a different story. When compared with less delinquent children, chronic offenders stand out in a number of ways. (For reviews of the literature, see Buikhuisen, 1988; Burchard and Burchard, 1987; Greenwood and Zimring, 1985; Rutter and Giller, 1984.)

1. They are more likely to suffer from minor birth defects, to have abnormal electrical activity in the brain, or to have various other neurological deficits.
2. They are more likely to come from families with low income, a criminal father, a mother with mental illness, many siblings, or siblings with records of delinquency and crime.
3. They are more likely to have experienced inconsistent parental discipline, lack of parental love and affection, or lack of parental attention.
4. They are more likely to have a history of antisocial and aggressive behaviors; to have engaged in heavy smoking, drinking, and drug use; and to have a history of truancy and low academic achievement.
5. They are more likely to have committed a serious crime, and to have been arrested and incarcerated, at an early age.
6. They are more likely to associate with and be friends of other kids with histories of delinquency and crime.

Impediments to Effective Socialization

Many of the correlates of chronic delinquency listed above are believed to influence behavior through their impact on the socialization process. Some are thought to impede a child's ability to learn and to develop attitudes and behaviors consistent with self-control, deferred gratification, and moral restraint.

In this vein, renewed interest in biological explanations of behavior has drawn attention to the impact of various genetic and constitutional factors (number 1 in the list above). (The best review of this biological renaissance is by Wilson and Herrnstein, 1985; but see also Gottfredson and Hirschi, 1990: 47–63.) According to this perspective, children with aggressive and impulsive temperaments, with low intelligence and poor information-processing skills, with a less responsive autonomic nervous system, with suppressed fear sensitivity (a result of hormonal imbalance), with an attention deficit disorder (A.D.D.), or with minor birth defects begin the developmental process at a disadvantage. The fact that these characteristics are found disproportionately among chronic delinquents suggests there is a place for biology in the explanation of chronic misbehavior.

Unfortunately, it is difficult to disentangle biological influences in the socialization process from the actions of the primary socializing agents themselves—parents, siblings, teachers—and from other early childhood experiences. Poor parental supervision and inconsistent discipline; lack of love and emotional support; parental perception that a child is incorrigible, neurotic, or simply refuses to learn; and an inequitable distribution of familial resources may all hinder effective socialization in the absence of any underlying biological impediment. The same can be said of negative labeling by teachers and peers. All of these conditions show correlations with chronic delinquency (Buikhuisen, 1988; Werner, 1987; Loeber and Dishion, 1983).

The same is true of family characteristics such as large size and low income, and these may even help *produce* some of the biological impediments mentioned above. Low income and large family size may result in malnutrition, poor prenatal and postnatal care, and inadequate parental monitoring of a child's behavior and welfare. Poverty exacerbates the developmental impact of biological impairments and negative family or school experiences with authority because it makes the search for socially acceptable solutions more difficult. Options available to middle- and upper-class families are often not open to the lower classes, if they are even thought of at all. In short, the behavior and circumstances of socializing agents may exacerbate or blunt the impact of biological impediments to successful socialization.

Signs of Failure

Children who begin life with disadvantages need more support from others and must work harder to attain the rewards and avoid the penalties handed out on behalf of conventional society. Unfortunately, the signs and symptoms of failure are commonplace. Early and repeated difficulties with authorities—parents, school officials, police—are one of the signs, and they seem to be a characteristic experience of children who become chronic delinquents (Gold, 1970; West and Farrington, 1977; Dinitz and Conrad, 1980; Shannon, 1982; Denno, 1984). In the study by Cernkovich, Giordano, and Pugh (1985), high-frequency serious offenders had more contact with official sanctions both inside and outside of school when compared with other youths.

Poor academic scores and discipline problems are signs of failure in school, and they reinforce each other (see also Thornberry, et al., 1991). In the view of parents, teachers, and even a child's peers, these difficulties are often taken as proof of social maladjustment—a personality out of sync with convention—and, at the extreme, even mental illness or retardation. Maladjusted children are then vulnerable to the hostility, ridicule, and ostracism of those around them. They are tagged as losers (even by people who should know better—see Ahlstrom and Havighurst, 1971), and their failure leads to isolation and further undermines their attachment to conventional society and their adoption of attitudes and beliefs consistent with conformity.

Early arrest (and punishment) by criminal justice authorities is another sign of failure and is also associated with chronic delinquency (e.g., Wolfgang, Figlio, and Sellin, 1972; Dinitz and Conrad, 1980; Dunford and Elliott, 1984; Cernkovich, Giordano, and Pugh, 1985; Tontodonato, 1988). A controlled study of 400 Kansas City youths who were followed for six years showed that those with arrests before eighth grade had a higher than average number of arrests over the study period as well as above average arrests for serious crime (Ahlstrom and Havighurst, 1971). Joan McCord's (1981) followup study of 208 boys into adulthood found that those still committing offenses *as adults* were much more likely than desisters to have been arrested before age 16. Similar results turned up in West and Farrington's (1977) study of lower-class London youths.

While early trouble with the authorities may nip delinquency in the bud, or at least turn potential delinquents away from serious crime, there are others for whom the experience seems to increase the risks of future offending. Gold (1970) speculates that there are four pressures to continued delinquency: (1) To stop means the offender agrees that she or he is "bad," an idea that is rejected; (2) to stop in the face of risks and threats means she or he is "chicken"; (3) the motives for committing the act in the first place are rarely removed by being caught (if it's for excitement, juveniles may even be encouraged); and (4) further crime is a way of venting anger, of striking back.

Some theorists claim that a child's self-concept is seriously battered by repeated confrontations with authorities and other signs of failure. In the search for a positive identity, for good feelings about self, the child may find socially accepted activities (sports or music, for example) in which is it possible to do well. If this occurs, a "loser" may become a "winner," and as success in the endeavor grows, more is to be lost by nonconformity (Buikhuisen, 1988, following Hirschi, 1969). On the other hand, if the child is unable to find (or does not look for) socially acceptable ways of countering a battered ego, a sense of being someone, of counting, of having "smarts," may still be achieved through activities and associations that are frowned upon by conventional society—gang involvement, drug use, or other crimes and delinquencies.

Firsthand accounts of incarceration in juvenile institutions suggest that the experience has a hardening effect on some boys. While imprisoned, they learn more of the values and techniques of crime and often come away embittered toward authorities. Even the relatively open institutions can be tough places, and kids learn that survival, symbolically if not literally, means fighting, hustling, and stealing. Allen (1977: 10) describes his experience when held in an institution without walls in his early teens:

> I learned a lot of things at Junior Village—mostly more bad than good. Kids from all over town were sent to Junior Village. It was a tough little place; it was a place where you fought almost every day because everybody trying to be tougher than the next person. Before I got to the place I knew all about it—what you supposed to do, how you supposed to act. That was the advantage I had hanging around with older kids. So the first thing I did . . . was to see who had the biggest mouth . . . and I proceeded to hit him right in his mouth. He was kind of head of the cottage, and I was showing the others "I'm not gonna take no shit off none of y'all, and I'm not even going to take none from him 'cause he all y'all's boss. . . ." So you just walk right in and fight, two or three times a day, and then you'd wake up the next morning and fight some more.
>
> I also learned how to shoot crap pretty good. . . . I learned the right way to go about housebreaking, the right way to get away from the truant officers, the right way to steal from

the Safeway. And I learned about drop-pockets. You make a small tear in the lining of your coat, big enough for whatever you want to put in there; then you steal cigarettes. . . .

My fighting became much better because I did it more often. Lying. I used to lie, but before then I wasn't no expert at lying. I became an expert liar. I learned how to hot-wire cars right there in the place—on the superintendent's car.

Allen acknowledges that he knew what to expect and how to establish a reputation; one suspects that he welcomed every opportunity to improve his skills in crime, and probably showed his fellow inmates a trick or two. He came from a neighborhood where "we ran wild, and the adults were wild. It would be nothing for us to be on the front steps playing hide-and-seek and all of a sudden you hear bang, bang, bang, and people are shooting at each other in the street. . . . In Southeast, everybody did the same thing, and it was a struggle just to get along" (Allen, 1977: 3). The institution simply exposed Allen to more concentrated doses of the same sorts of things he was experiencing on the street. Hardening probably would have happened there, too, but more slowly.

Boys with more innocent backgrounds are likely to be unprepared for the rigors of institutional life, and some will be easy prey for the gangs that frequently inhabit juvenile and adult facilities. Many inner-city boys find it hard to escape the influence of neighborhood gangs; it is even more difficult when locked up with them. Gypsy describes his initiation when first detained in a juvenile facility at age 12 and a half:

When I went to Warwick, particularly, you know I was beat up because I was not a member of the Chaplains, I was not a member of the Viceroys, I was not a member of the Enchanters, so when I went in, this was total a new thing to me. The most serious crime that I had committed was playing hookey, and maybe snatching a banana from the fruit stand on the corner. [Vachss and Bakal, 1979: 276]

So when Gypsy got out he promptly joined a gang, the Junior Knights, of which he became president.

Association with Other Delinquents

Whether the rejects of conventional society seek out others like them or whether their association with rejected youths helps make them failures (rejects) is open to debate. It is probably a bit of both; that is, rejected youths gravitate toward each other, and the experience enhances everyone's chance of being rejected by conventional society.

But for some youths, the opportunities and incentives for crime are present long before there is failure or rejection at school. This occurs when parents (usually the father) and older siblings are themselves involved in criminal activity. When a child's primary socializing agents are committing delinquencies and crimes, the role model presented, the activities observed, and the techniques that can be learned are not those of conventional society. The fact that criminal activity and arrests of other family members correlates significantly with chronic delinquency suggests that these early experiences are important. Yet criminal activities are commonplace in many families (Lincoln and Straus, 1985), and most children of criminal families do not become chronic delinquents. Thus, parental and sibling crime is not a sufficient cause of chronic delinquency, but it can be another impediment to a child's adoption of, and commitment to, conventional norms. Early familiarity with crime may increase the chance that such behavior will be viewed as an acceptable, and profitable, alternative to conventional activities when (or if) a child experiences failure at school or work.

Experience with crime and delinquency in the home is often complemented by direct or vicarious experience of it at school and among peers. Fagan and Wexler (1987) interviewed 98 chronically violent delinquents with an average of 10.5 prior arrests. These youths generally saw their own families as violent, but they had also experienced or seen serious crimes in school and among their friends. In fact, the youths' frequency of serious offending correlated most strongly with delinquency among their friends. A similar finding emerged in a recent study of 588 adolescents in two Boston communities (Morash, 1986).

The finding that association with friends who are delinquent is associated with high rates of offending is not new (see Glueck and Glueck, 1950; Knight and West, 1975), but its confirmation by the National Youth Survey lent it considerable weight (see Elliott and Ageton, 1980; Elliott, Huizinga, and Ageton, 1985). The conventional argument is that when youths are involved with delinquent friends, the association produces further delinquency. *How* it does it is a matter of debate, but various mechanisms are suggested: the group's power to sanction behavior of members, the social rituals that confirm membership and confer status, the role models provided by the group's leader(s), and the facilitation of activities that are not easily (or successfully) performed alone. The essential idea is that the delinquency of the group rubs off on its members, and vice versa.

It all sounds simple enough, but the issue of peer influence remains controversial. In the first place, some studies have found that chronic delinquents are *weakly* attached to delinquent peers (e.g., Chapman, 1986). They are loners rather than team players. Second, a study of incarcerated offenders found that group members who conformed to conventional standards were *more* popular than less conforming members (Osgood et al., 1986). Third, at least two observational studies, one in the United States (Schwendinger and Schwendinger, 1985) and one in England (Parker, 1974), have shown that sporadic and chronic delinquents participate *side by side* in the same street-corner networks, and the sporadics remain occasional offenders.

There is also a methodological problem that needs to be resolved: It is entirely possible that when chronic offenders are asked to identify their friends, they select individuals they know to be like themselves; or, when asked to identify other chronic offenders among their peers, they project their own levels of offending onto those they pick. In either case, chronic offenders would tend to show up in associations with delinquent peers.

Conventional analyses of the peer association factor in delinquency have been criticized as too simplistic. Robert Agnew (1991: 47) observes that in "most studies, researchers simply measure the number of the adolescent's friends who are delinquent and/or the frequency with which friends commit delinquent acts. No effort is made to examine other dimensions of peer interaction." Such things as duration, intensity, frequency and other dynamics of peer associations are largely ignored in the research or they are lumped together in an undiscriminating manner.

Using National Youth Survey data, Agnew (1991) examined a model of the delinquency-peer association relationship that included four measures of peer interaction: *attachment to peers* (for example, whether youths feel they fit in well with their friends, feel close to their friends, and have friends who listen to their problems); *time spent with peers* (for example, how many afternoons and evenings subjects spend with their friends during the school week); *peer approval for delinquency* (for example, friends' likely reaction if subject stole, sold drugs, or committed certain other crimes); *peer pressure for deviance* (for example, willingness to break rules or commit offenses in order to be popular with or gain respect of one's friends). Agnew discovered that having close friends known to have committed serious offenses (burglary, sale of hard drugs, or theft over $50.00) was strongly related to subjects' self-reported delinquency, but generally *only* when the peer interaction variables were at above-average levels. Subjects with seriously delinquent friends who reported high levels of peer approval for their delinquency, for example, also had relatively high levels of self-reported delinquency; having seriously delinquent friends appeared to have no effect on the delinquency of subjects who reported average or below average levels of peer approval.

There is another issue that further complicates what appeared to be a simple matter. Rather than influencing a youth's *propensity* to commit crimes, it has been suggested that delinquent peer groups merely *facilitate* crime among individuals whose tendencies are already compatible with it (Hirschi, 1969; Linden and Hackler, 1973; Gottfredson and Hirschi, 1988, 1990). This view is summarized by the old adage "Birds of a feather flock together." A network (it is rarely a formal looking group) of delinquency-prone individuals creates and responds to criminal opportunities in its milieu. The type and frequency of criminal acts will be determined largely by that milieu. A chronic delinquent is most often a lower-class, street-corner male who keeps company with other lower-class, street-corner males, and this suggests that the milieu of lower-class, street-corner society is itself conducive to high rates of serious crime.

THE MILIEU OF CHRONIC DELINQUENCY

We have pictured the chronic delinquent as beginning life with various impediments to effective socialization and subsequently experiencing conditions, events, and interactions that encourage antisocial behavior. These childhood experiences are cumulative in their influence, and the earlier, more frequent, and more varied the criminal response, the more likely the child will end up a chronic delinquent (Loeber and Dishion, 1987).

But we need to say more about the *milieu* of chronic delinquency, and the actions of delinquents within that milieu, to fully understand persistent recidivism. The term *milieu* refers to the environment within which people act, to which their actions respond, and which their actions, in turn, affect. The milieu of chronic delinquency is primarily a lower-class, street-corner milieu. It is a milieu of blocked opportunities for conventional success, of meager economic, health, educational, and social resources; it is a milieu of unemployment and underemployment; it is a milieu of single parent families; it is (often, but not always) a milieu of neighborhood blight and decay; it is a milieu in which there is little to lose by crime and potentially a lot to gain; it is a milieu in which *rational* solutions to the ever-present disadvantage, deprivation, and danger often involve breaking the law; it is a milieu with a heavy police presence—even in schools—and yet everyone knows the real risks of being caught and punished are low, and can be minimized with skill, planning, and organization.

The various elements of this milieu change little from year to year, and when they do, conditions are more likely to worsen than improve. About the most variable element is the actions of the police and courts, in the form of periodic maneuvers aimed at doing something about the crime problem. But this is all taken into account and accommodated by street-corner networks, so that the frequency and type of offenses committed shift in response to changing enforcement. Here is an illustration from Howard Parker's (1974) observational study of a network of Liverpool adolescents, almost all of whom qualify as chronic delinquents.

The Boys from Roundhouse, a run-down inner-city neighborhood, had been taking advantage of growing opportunities to steal "catseyes" (car radios with shiney knobs) as more and more of the better cars parked downtown came equipped with them. As word spread of the "action," more and more youths got involved. Catseye theft became an almost daily routine for boys in this and other local networks. Needless to say, the police did not sit still (you can be sure that the well-heeled victims complained loudly). One day, the following conversation ensued (Parker, 1974: 91):

> *Joey:*   There's so many on the cars now that someone's getting caught every day.
> *Colly:*   It's not The Boys though as much as Ritz's lot, they're out every night now like we were.
> *Jimbo:*   Yes but they don't even wait til it's dark and they're not doing it properly, that's why they're getting caught. If you see them with a radio you can tell straight away by just looking at them, and they're walking dead fast and that. They'll all get caught, that lot.
> *Colly:*   That's it, if you're careless like you will get caught, but if you rob properly you've got a good chance of getting away with it.

Colly, Jimbo, and Joey were more experienced in crime (and punishment) than some other boys in the network, and their response to the increased risk of arrest was not to give up crime but, rather, to be more covert, devious, and inventive. For a while, they shifted operations outside the area, enlisting the willing help of neighborhood fences whose profits were now threatened by the increased police presence. This move brought the boys more experiences and new connections (both of which they could share with others), and it expanded their criminal repertoire and their criminal opportunities.

They and their friends also stopped carrying the "punches" used for breaking a car's small quarter-light in order to gain entry. The boys reasoned that possession of such a tool would invite arrest if stopped by the police. This accommodation had various unintended consequences (Parker, 1974: 92).

> For the unhappy car-owner . . . it was no longer his . . . quarter-light that was broken: now The Boys simply put the boot into the main front-door window causing extensive and expensive damage. . . . Cars nearer [The Boys' own neighborhood] became prime targets, as the "carriers" [the person holding the stolen radio] had more cover and the "attackers" more confidence. Cars were increasingly screwed late at night under cover of darkness.

This account shows the boys' rational, problem-solving approach to changing risks and opportunities in their street-corner milieu. It also shows how crime may actually increase and become more serious, as a result of increased police activity.

Illegal Markets

An important element of the inner-city street-corner milieu and one of the principle facilitators of criminal activity is the *illegal market*—economic relationships through which illegal goods and services are exchanged, usually for cash. Fences, drug dealers, pimps, and loan sharks are pivotal figures. Their roles provide incentives and opportunities for crime, and they exemplify the *instrumental* and *entrepreneurial* aspects of illegal markets.

When crimes (e.g., theft, robbery, drug sales) are committed in order to achieve some other goal (e.g., money, status), they are said to be instrumental. But achieving the desired goal often requires planning, organization, and management—the hallmarks of entrepreneurship. Illegal markets are born and flourish when entrepreneurship and instrumental crime come together. Distinct positions and roles emerge with organization, and the connections between them provide pathways for the flow of goods, services, cash, and, most importantly, information. When all works well, the profits are considerable, the risks minimal. But the market rarely succumbs when things go badly, for its location, mode of operations, or personnel are easily changed.

Many kids, from all walks of life, are drawn into this highly rational enterprise, for such markets flourish anywhere illegal goods and services are in sufficient demand to warrant the costs and risks of doing business. On the other hand, the participation of most kids is sporadic, an adjunct to loose occasions, perhaps, or squeezed in among other structured activities. They are the buyers of goods and services rather than the sellers; their involvement in the enterprise is transitory, reflecting a temporary need or circumstance (a "hot" typewriter has "mysteriously" come into their possession and they want to sell it quickly) rather than a long-term relationship. The illegal market thus facilitates some sporadic crime.

For a minority of kids, illegal markets facilitate and encourage chronic participation in crime. These are the kids for whom instrumental crime is a rational alternative to "putting up with a bad deal" (Parker, 1974: 107), as well as an outgrowth of the mutual reinforcement that occurs in friendship groups of like-minded peers (Giordano, 1986). Indeed, participation in illegal markets both reflects and encourages a gradual shift in the motivations for delinquency and crime: from an interest in largely expressive activities to a more adult interest in material payoff (see Werthman, 1967). Interviews of adult offenders with long histories of delinquency and crime suggest that this shift in motivation is uniform and often occurs early in the biographies of chronic delinquents (Knight and West, 1975; Peterson and Braiker, 1981).

The illegal market facilitates instrumental crime primarily by providing people (and things) to steal for and to sell to. It also acts as an organizational model for street-corner youths who recognize the need for a system to take proper advantage of criminal opportunities. The Schwendingers (1985: 272) point out that when stabilized, "divisions of labor encourage the development of roles such as those of burglar, prostitute, narcotics connection, and fence." The autobiography of John Allen, a street criminal, illustrates both points. Consider this account of Allen and his friends at 10 to 11 years old:

> We weren't real organized, but we did have our own little system. My job was getting into places 'cause I was small. . . . We knew most of the time what we was going after when we went in these little places. Different guys would request different things. My main thing was

carrying cigarettes and edible stuff. Most of the places we broke into was just little corner stores that didn't have much that was really valuable aside from food. [Allen, 1977: 38]

In summary, illegal markets "promote the transition of some delinquents to so-called 'criminal careers' " (Schwendinger and Schwendinger, 1985: 272) partly because they provide opportunities for continued participation in crime, but most importantly because they encourage the development of organized instrumental crime among juveniles who feel they have little to lose and much to gain.

TRANSITION TO ADULTHOOD

Not all (perhaps not even most) chronic delinquents become adult criminals, but if we wanted to predict who would carry on their criminal activities into adulthood, the chronic delinquent with a history of arrests would be our best bet.

A retrospective account of their juvenile histories by 624 California inmates showed that those who began their juvenile crime before age 13, and who committed serious crimes frequently as juveniles, reported the most serious and varied criminal involvement as adults (Peterson and Braiker, 1981). Those who began crime early in life were more likely than others to see it as a normal part of their way of life ("everyone they knew was involved in crime"), more likely to have developed criminal attitudes and identities, and more likely to have been arrested and incarcerated as a juvenile.

Followup studies of delinquent boys also confirm a strong association between high rates of serious juvenile offending and subsequent crime as an adult (West and Farrington, 1977; West, 1982; Jesness, 1987). One of the consistent findings in these followup studies is the importance of juvenile convictions: Boys who escape official labeling and punishment as juvenile offenders are less likely to continue their offending into adulthood, and this is especially true if the prior convictions had been for serious property crime (Knight and West, 1975; McCord, 1981; see also Shannon, 1982).

Because the more intrusive forms of intervention (such as incarceration) show strong association with recidivism in many studies (Gabor, 1986), it is convenient to blame future crime on the experience of being punished. Indeed, we have already seen how incarceration (and other enforcement practices) may fuel criminal enterprise. But it is possible that many of the juveniles punished early and harshly are "a more hardened lot to begin with" (Gabor, 1986: 58). In addition, punishment hardly ever addresses the problems and conditions that gave rise to crime and delinquency in the first place, and they *continue to operate* once the punishment is over.

This may well explain why largely nonpunitive, helping programs often fail to turn chronic delinquents around. Joan McCord (1978, 1980) evaluated 506 men in a followup study that began when the men were young teenagers. Those who had received a variety of "services" (e.g., medical care, counseling, recreational opportunities, tutoring) showed more crime (and other problems) as adults than did boys in a control group. McCord's speculation is that those who were "treated" developed unrealistic expectations about their futures and experienced feelings of relative deprivation when their expectations were not fulfilled (see also our comments in Chapter Two, pages 31–32). (Of course, an alternative interpretation is possible: The mere passage of time erased any of the benefits that might have initially accrued from the "treatment.") Ahlstrom and Havighurst (1971: 219) use a similar interpretation to explain why "maladjusted" inner-city black boys profited less from an extensive work-study program than similarly situated white boys: When the program was over, the black boys still faced less attractive employment opportunities.

We are a long way from fully understanding why some chronic delinquents become adult criminals and others do not. Given that most start out with disadvantages of one sort or another, the hope for these children lies with experiences that lessen the impediments to effective socialization and promote full and rewarding participation in conventional society. Since the incentive and opportunity for serious crime seem to be permanent elements of lower-class street-corner society, this requires social change on a grand, and probably impossible, scale.

What does the National Advisory Committee recommend we do about the chronic delinquent? Its recommendations are uninspiring: There should be more federal initiatives (but states should identify problems and find solutions); there should be more research and training; there should be more cooperation between juvenile and adult justice systems (National Advisory Committee, 1984: 11–15). In the meantime, lock 'em up: "Our urban society cannot continue to suffer at the hands of the vicious juvenile" (8). The monster myth prevails.

The current publicity surrounding delinquent gangs and the spreading use of crack cocaine certainly suggests that there is every reason to be concerned about this nation's youths. We will investigate these topics in more detail in Chapters 5 and 6. Suffice it to say that there need be no increase in the number or proportion of chronic delinquents for there to be an increase in the overall rates of crime: Some chronic delinquents may simply commit more crimes. The data are ambiguous on this issue, but this does not lessen the concern. If chronic delinquents are getting out of hand, it is unlikely that repressive countermeasures will have any effect, for unless they are initiated at a very young age, say 5 or 6, they are probably too late. And even then, such measures do not address the environmental forces that affect the experiences and life chances of inner-city youths who make up the bulk of those chronic delinquents whose crimes (rightly or wrongly) cause the most concern.

SUMMARY

Chronic delinquents commit offenses repeatedly over the course of adolescence, and they are far more likely than sporadic offenders to commit serious crimes. Even though only a small minority of youths become chronic delinquents, they are responsible for a disproportionately large share of the serious delinquency that is reported by authorities or discovered through survey research. It is not unusual for chronic delinquents to commit hundreds of offenses before they reach adulthood, and they get away with most of them. There is little evidence of offense specialization among chronic delinquents, although chronic offenders are far more likely to commit violent crimes than are sporadic delinquents.

Not surprisingly, therefore, much research has been directed at understanding chronic delinquency. Birth and elementary school cohort studies, and retrospective accounts by adult offenders, have consistently shown that chronic delinquents tend to get into trouble with the law at an early age, and that those troubles escalate as they move through the teenage years. The signs and symptoms of failure are commonplace, and problems in the home, at school, and with legal authorities tend to reinforce each other. Gangs may offer some boys the opportunity to "be someone," but they also facilitate and encourage continued involvement in delinquent activities. Although the impact on delinquency of association with delinquent peers is the subject of considerable debate, there is general agreement that such associations are strongly correlated with high rates of offending.

The milieu of chronic delinquency is perhaps the best tip to its causes. It is a milieu of meager resources and blocked opportunities for conventional success; of inadequate familial support and supervision; of street crime, truancy, gangs, and drugs; of flourishing illegal markets that draw on and facilitate criminal activity; and of a heavy, but largely ineffective, police presence. All youths are susceptible to the "seductions of crime" (Katz, 1988), but youths who have experienced failure, who face dim prospects, and who lack access to supportive adults who will supervise, teach, and discipline them, find little in this milieu to turn them away from crime and much to make it attractive.

REFERENCES

Agnew, Robert. 1991. "The Interactive Effects of Peer Variables and Delinquency." *Criminology* 29:47–42.

Ahlstrom, Winton M., and Robert J. Havighurst. 1971. *400 Losers.* San Francisco: Jossey-Bass.

Allen, John. 1977. *Assault with a Deadly Weapon: The Autobiography of a Street Criminal.* New York: Pantheon Books.

Braithwaite, John. 1981. "The Myth of Social Class and Criminality Reconsidered." *American Sociological Review* 46:36–57.

Buikhuisen, Wouter. 1988. "Chronic Juvenile Delinquency: A Theory." In Buikhuisen and Mednick, 1988.

Buikhuisen, Wouter, and Sarnoff A. Mednick, eds. 1988. *Explaining Criminal Behaviour: Interdisciplinary Approaches.* Linden, Netherlands: E. J. Brill.

Burchard, John D., and Sara N. Burchard, eds. 1987. *Prevention of Delinquent Behavior.* Beverly Hills: Sage.

Bursik, Robert J. 1980. "The Dynamics of Specialization in Juvenile Offenses." *Social Forces* 59:851–864.

Cernkovich, Stephen A., Peggy C. Giordano, and Meredith D. Pugh. 1985. "Chronic Offenders: The Missing Cases in Self-Report Delinquency Research." *Journal of Criminal Law and Criminology* 76:705–732.

Chapman, William R. 1986. "The Role of Peers in Strain Models of Delinquency." Paper presented at the annual meeting of the American Society of Criminology, Atlanta, Georgia.

Chesney-Lind, Meda. 1987. "Girls and Violence: An Exploration of the Gender Gap in Serious Delinquent Behavior." In Crowell, Evans, and O'Connell, 1987.

Crowell, David H., Ian M. Evans, and Clifford R. O'Connell, eds. 1987. *Childhood Aggression.* New York: Plenum Press.

Denno, Deborah J. 1984. "Family Income, Ability, and Crime: Implications for Youth Unemployment." Paper presented at the annual meeting of the American Society of Criminology, Cincinnati, Ohio.

Dinitz, Simon, and John P. Conrad. 1980. "The Dangerous Two Percent." In Shichor and Kelly, 1980.

Dunford, Franklyn W., and Delbert S. Elliott. 1984. "Identifying Career Offenders Using Self-Report Data." *Journal of Research in Crime and Delinquency* 21:57–85.

Elliott, Delbert S., and Suzanne Ageton. 1980. "Reconciling Race and Class Differences in Self-Reported and Official Estimates of Delinquency." *American Sociological Review* 45:95–110.

Elliott, Delbert S., and David Huizinga. 1984. "The Relationship Between Delinquent Behavior and ADM Problems." Unpublished report prepared for the Behavioral Research Institute, Boulder, Colorado.

Elliott, Delbert S., David Huizinga, and Suzanne S. Ageton. 1985. *Explaining Delinquency and Drug Abuse.* Beverly Hills: Sage.

Elliott, Delbert S., David Huizinga, and Barbara J. Morse. 1985. "The Dynamics of Deviant Behavior: A National Survey." *Progress Report.* Boulder, Colo.: Behavioral Research Institute.

Elliott, Delbert S., Franklyn W. Dunford, and David Huizinga. 1987. "The Identification and Prediction of Career Offenders Utilizing Self-Reported and Official Data." In Burchard and Burchard, 1987.

Elmhorn, K. 1965. "Study in Self-Reported Delinquency Among School-Children in Stockholm." In *Scandinavian Studies in Criminology,* Volume 1. London, England: Tavistock Publishers.

Fagan, Jeffrey, and Sandra Wexler. 1987. "Family Origins of Violent Delinquents." *Criminology* 25:643–669.

Farrington, David P., Howard N. Snyder, and Terrence A. Finnegan. 1988. "Specialization in Juvenile Court Careers." *Criminology* 26:461–487.

Gabor, Thomas. 1986. *The Prediction of Criminal Behaviour.* Toronto: University of Toronto Press.

Giordano, Peggy C. 1986. "Friendships and Delinquency." *American Journal of Sociology* 91:1170–1202.

Glueck, Sheldon, and Eleanor Glueck. 1950. *Unraveling Juvenile Delinquency.* Cambridge: Harvard University Press.

Gold, Martin. 1970. *Delinquent Behavior in an American City.* Belmont, Calif.: Brooks-Cole.

Gottfredson, Michael R., and Travis Hirschi. 1990. *A General Theory of Crime.* Stanford: Stanford University Press.

Greenwood, Peter W., and Franklin E. Zimring. 1985. *One More Chance.* Santa Monica: Rand.

Hamparian, Donna M., Richard Schuster, Simon Dinitz, and John P. Conrad. 1978. *The Dangerous Few: A Study of Dangerous Juvenile Offenders.* Lexington, Mass.: Lexington Books.

Hartstone, Eliot, and Karen V. Hansen. 1984. "The Violent Juvenile Offender: An Empirical Portrait." In Mathias, DeMuro, and Allinson, 1984.

Hirschi, Travis. 1969. *Causes of Delinquency.* Berkeley: University of California Press.

Hirschi, Travis, and Michael Gottfredson. 1988. "Toward a General Theory of Crime." In Buikhuisen and Mednick, 1988.

Jesness, Carl F. 1987. "Early Identification of Delinquent-Prone Children: An Overview." In Burchard and Burchard, 1987.

Katz, Jack. 1988. *The Seductions of Crime: Moral and Sensual Attractions of Doing Evil.* N.Y.: Basic Books, Inc.

Kempf, Kimberly L. 1987. "Specialization and Criminal Career." *Criminology* 25:399–420.

Knight, B. J., and D. J. West. 1975. "Temporary and Continuing Delinquency." *British Journal of Criminology* 15:43–50.

Lincoln, Alan J., and Murray A. Straus. 1985. *Crime and the Family.* Springfield: Charles C. Thomas.

Linden, E., and J. C. Hackler. 1973. "Affective Ties and Delinquency." *Pacific Sociological Review* 16:27–47.

Loeber, Rolf, and Thomas J. Dishion. 1983. "Early Predictors of Male Delinquency." *Psychological Bulletin* 94:68–99.

——— . 1987. "Antisocial and Delinquent Youths: Models for Their Early Identification." In Burchard and Burchard, 1987.

Mathias, Robert A., Paul DeMuro, and Richard S. Allinson, eds. 1984. *Violent Juvenile Offenders: An Anthology.* San Francisco: NCCD.

McCord, Joan. 1978. "A Thirty-Year Follow-up of Treatment Effects." *American Psychologist* 33:284–289.

——— . 1980. "The Treatment That Did Not Help." *Social Action and Law* 5:85–87.

——— . 1981. "A Longitudinal Perspective on Patterns of Crime." *Criminology* 19:211–218.

Merry, Sally Engle. 1981. *Urban Danger: Life in a Neighborhood of Strangers.* Philadelphia: Temple University Press.

Morash, Merry. 1986. "Gender, Peer Group Experiences, and Seriousness of Delinquency." *Journal of Research in Crime and Delinquency* 23:43–67.

National Advisory Committee. 1984. *Serious Juvenile Crime: A Redirected Federal Effort.* Washington, D.C.: U.S. Department of Justice.

Osgood, D. Wayne, Martin Gold, and Carolyn Miller. 1986. "For Better or Worse? Peer Attachments and Peer Influence Among Incarcerated Adolescents." Paper presented at the annual meeting of the American Society of Criminology, Atlanta, Georgia.

Parker, Howard J. 1974. *View from The Boys.* London: David and Charles.

Peterson, Mark A., and Harriet B. Braiker. 1981. *Who Commits Crime? A Survey of Prison Inmates.* Santa Monica: Rand.

Piper, Elizabeth S. 1985. "Violent Recidivism and Chronicity in the 1958 Philadelphia Cohort." *Journal of Criminal Law and Criminology* 75:319–344.

Rutter, Michael, and Henri Giller. 1984. *Juvenile Delinquency: Trends and Perspectives.* New York: Guilford Press.

Schwendinger, Herman, and Julia Siegel Schwendinger. 1985. *Adolescent Subcultures and Delinquency.* New York: Praeger.

Shannon, Lyle. 1982. *Assessing the Relationship of Adult Criminal Careers to Juvenile Careers.* Washington, D.C.: U.S. Department of Justice.

Shelden, Randall G. 1987. "The Chronic Delinquent: Gender and Racial Differences." Paper presented at the annual meeting of the American Society of Criminology, Montreal, Canada.

Shichor, David, and Delos H. Kelly, eds. 1980. *Critical Issues in Juvenile Delinquency.* Lexington, Mass.: Lexington Books.

Snyder, Howard. 1986. *Court Careers of Juvenile Offenders.* Pittsburgh: National Center for Juvenile Justice.

Strasburg, Paul A. 1984. "Recent National Trends in Serious Juvenile Crime." In Mathias, De-Muro, and Allinson, 1984.

Thornberry, Terence P., Alan J. Lizotte, Marvin D. Krohn, Margaret Farnworth, and Sung Joon Jang. 1991. "Testing Interactional Theory: An Examination of Reciprocal Casual Relationships among Family, School, and Delinquency." *Journal of Criminal Law and Criminology* 82:3–35.

Tontodonato, Pamela. 1988. "Explaining Rate Changes in Delinquent Arrest Transitions Using Event History Analysis." *Criminology* 26:439–459.

Tracy, Paul E., Marvin E. Wolfgang, and Robert M. Figlio. 1985. *Delinquency in Two Birth Cohorts: Executive Summary.* Washington, D.C.: U.S. Government Printing Office.

Tracy, Paul E., Marvin E. Wolfgang, and Robert M. Figlio. 1990. *Delinquency Careers in Two Birth Cohorts.* New York: Plenum Press.

Vachss, Andrew H., and Yitzhak Bakal. 1979. *The Life-style Violent Juvenile.* Lexington, Mass.: Lexington Books.

Werner, Emmy E. 1987. "Vulnerability and Resiliency in Children at Risk for Delinquency: A Longitudinal Study from Birth to Young Adulthood." In Burchard and Burchard, 1987.

Werthman, Carl. 1967. "The Function of Social Definitions in the Development of Delinquent Careers." In *Task Force Report: A Report of the President's Commission on Law Enforcement and the Administration of Justice.* Washington, D.C.: U.S. Government Printing Office.

West, Donald J. 1982. *Delinquency: Its Roots, Careers and Prospects.* London, England: Heinemann.

West, Donald J., and David P. Farrington. 1977. *The Delinquent Way of Life.* London: Heinemann.

Wilson, James Q., and Richard J. Herrnstein. 1985. *Crime and Human Nature.* New York: Simon and Schuster.

Wolfgang, Marvin E., Robert M. Figlio, and Thorsten Sellin. 1973. *Delinquency in a Birth Cohort.* Chicago: University of Chicago Press.

Chapter
5

Gang Delinquency

Gangs are a key part of the delinquency problem. Scarcely a week goes by in America without newspaper headlines reporting marauding teenage gangs somewhere, and Sarnechi's research in Sweden shows that gangs aggravate the problem there as well (see Box 5.1). Gangs play a major part in urban delinquency in many ways.

First, they serve as a vigorous incubator of delinquency in their immediate vicinity. Drive-by shootings of gang rivals and innocent bystanders, gang invasions of dances and parties, gang trafficking in drugs and automatic weapons, and pitched battles among rival gangs—all are commonplace in Los Angeles, Chicago, Philadelphia, Washington, Miami, and Detroit. Delinquents who would otherwise be committing property crimes, vandalism, or minor assaults become in gangs violent offenders who use deadly weapons and are a serious threat to their neighborhoods.

A longtime observer of Los Angeles gangs, Joan Moore (1988a) notes that between the 1950s and 1970s recruitment rituals came to include violent tests of courage and strength, gang members increasingly described themselves as loving violence, and deadly weapons became much more common. The picture today in Los Angeles is even worse. Gangs intensify any delinquency problem the neighborhood already presents, and as the gangs become more sophisticated, their delinquency becomes more serious.

Second, gangs widen the horizons of delinquents in their neighborhoods. Nongang delinquents commit mainly status offenses, property crimes (shoplifting, auto theft, or burglary), minor assaults, drug offenses, or vandalism. But gang members intimidate witnesses, extort "insurance" payments from storeowners, traffic in drugs, and use automatic weaponry in conflicts with rival gangs and the police. According to a *Wall Street Journal* report (September 30, 1988: 1, 12), in Chicago on occasion the Black Gangster Disciples have taken control of several high rise apartment buildings in the city's low-income Robert Taylor Homes. They use apartments in these buildings to store weapons and drugs, and at night they sell them in the corridors and stairwells after breaking out the lights. After dark the residents can only huddle in fear in their apartments.

A resident in Rockwell Gardens (another low-income housing complex on Chicago's west side) lived next door to a gang member. One dark night a molotov cocktail came

Box 5-1   # Research on Swedish Gangs

Jerzy Sarnecki, a Swedish criminologist of Polish heritage, has undertaken an ambitious study of gang delinquency in Borlänge, Sweden, an industrial town of 50,000 about 155 miles north of Stockholm (see Sarnecki, 1988). Although Sarnecki uses the term *gangs* to describe his delinquents, he admits that his groups do not correspond to the gangs that have emerged in America's inner cities in the post–World War II period. His gangs are cliques or at best emerging gangs and not the well-established gangs that are found in Los Angeles, Chicago, or New York.

He used police crime blotters dealing with juveniles in Borlänge for 1975 to 1977, 1978 to 1980, and 1982 to 1984. These blotters included all information known to the police regarding the offense, the victim, and the suspects. Although the relationship between police data and actual criminality is admittedly problematic, Sarnecki believed that arrests were accurate enough in describing the juvenile's criminality to warrant proceeding with the study. Some 575 juveniles who were suspected of offending during 1975 to 1977 and 611 juveniles who were suspected during 1982 to 1984 formed the basis of his study.

Both groups closely resembled one another. The first group was suspected of 2350 offenses during 1975 to 1977, and the second accounted for 2161 offenses during 1982 to 1984. Both groups' members averaged nearly 15.5 years of age, about 20 percent of both groups were female, 40 percent were linked to just one offense, and slightly less than half were accompanied in their crimes by confederates.

Sarnecki turned his attention to these confederates, and he isolated 18 clusters of youngsters who were suspected of committing crimes together during 1975 to 1977. Within these 18 clusters he identified three large groups that committed many more offenses than the rest: gang A, gang C, and gang X. He interviewed 29 of the 64 members of gang A and found that their best friends were also likely to be members of gang A, and more importantly, found that their best friends were also among the most delinquent members of the gang. Those who were admired and popular in the gang were also *most* criminal.

These same 29 gang members, however, could not identify fully 55 percent of their fellow gang members. Despite the rather close relationships among the core members and their affiliates, those on the periphery were not closely affiliated with one another. The core members provided most of the direction and cohesion for the gang. Moreover, *all* of the serious delinquents (juveniles who were suspected of at least 30 offenses during 1975 to 1980) were linked with one of the 18 gangs, and as a group they were responsible for nearly half (48 percent) of the delinquencies recorded in Borlänge during this period. The core members provided most of the thrust toward delinquency for the gang.

When Sarnecki looked at the 1982 to 1984 crime blotters, he found that some of the boys who had been regular offenders during 1975 to 1977 had continued into 1982 to 1984, and all three of the gangs that were most troublesome during the earlier period had continued into 1982 to 1984. The most durable gang, gang A, included a majority of the serious delinquents noted in Borlänge during the study. The members of gang A committed an average of 22.3 offenses per member, as opposed to all gang members who committed just 13.1 offenses per member.

Those who persisted in delinquency from the 1975 to 1977 period were usually much younger than their comrades during the earlier period but much older during the later period. Not only were they more delinquent (10.6 offenses per boy in 1982 to 1984), but their younger comrades were also much more delinquent (10.5 offenses per boy) than youngsters affiliated with other delinquents (5.3 per boy) in the same gangs.

These older delinquents who persisted in delinquency brought deviant attitudes, techniques, and motivations to their younger friends. They acted as bridges ushering their younger followers into delinquency. Juveniles who were not affiliated with other delinquents committed many fewer offenses (2.2 per boy), and the large majority (71 percent) were suspected of only one offense.

If some way could be found of removing these core members from the community for some time, the continuity of delinquency from one generation of adolescents to the next could be conveniently interrupted. Although many children in each age cohort would still drift into delinquency, the problem itself would not grow more sophisticated as each new generation took its place, and the carryover into adult crime would probably also weaken.

crashing through her bedroom window, intended for her neighbor, the gang member. When firemen arrived, they could not get to the flames because gangs were firing at one another in the vicinity of her apartment. Over the next several days two rival gangs fought a guerrilla war in and around her building, and several apartments on the first two floors were riddled with bullets and gutted by fire (*Wall Street Journal*, September 30, 1988: 12).

Third, gangs forge strong links with the criminal past, present, and future in their neighborhoods. Most gangs are jealous and protective of five things: their territory, their uniforms and reputations, their rackets, their close relatives, and their girlfriends. If anyone—a stranger, a rival gang member, or an unwary adult—insults any of these, it can spark an angry outburst from the gang. If the outburst is answered in kind, a gangland feud can erupt that shapes the violence and attitudes of the members for years to come. The gang escalates individual conflicts into intergroup conflagrations that assume an unending cycle of thrust and counterthrust.

Major street gangs in metropolitan areas have formed alliances with international drug kings, weapons traffickers, and even with foreign nations to carry on sabotage and other illicit activities. In 1986 El Rukn, an offshoot of the old Blackstone Rangers in Chicago, made contact with Libyan officials and offered to destroy government buildings, airplanes, and vehicles in their behalf (*Chicago Tribune*, October 31, 1986: 1, 18). Jeff Fort, the adult leader of El Rukn, was ultimately convicted and sentenced to an 80 year prison term for his part in this escapade. Many of the major gangs in large metropolitan centers have become dominant players in the drug markets of their regions. In moving into these rackets, they have shouldered aside more traditional underworld organizations such as the Italian syndicate and forged links with important political figures in their cities (see Abadinsky, 1990: 259).

In 1980, as El Rukn solidified its hold on narcotics operations on Chicago's south side, the gang's leader, Jeff Fort, was invited to discuss the situation with a syndicate kingpin in a restaurant in the Italian neighborhood. In the course of the evening Fort was subjected to verbal abuse and threats, and though he said nothing, mafia leaders felt they had made their point. That night, however, the restaurant was burned to the ground, and the syndicate quietly abandoned its operations on the south side (Abadinsky, 1985: 158–159).

In addition, El Rukn has organized voter registration drives in Chicago, worked on behalf of Jane Byrne's mayoral election, and helped Jesse Jackson in his campaigns. In 1969 its leaders—Jeff Fort and others—were invited by Senator Percy to President Nixon's inaugural party (*Chicago Tribune*, December 21, 1980: S1, 20). With organization comes power that can be flexed in a number of new directions (see also Spergel, 1990: 240–242).

Finally, gangs also are a proving ground wherein juvenile offenders learn their craft and mature into serious career criminals (Peterson and Braiker, 1981: 140–148). By associating with older, more sophisticated gang members, they become skilled at routine crimes, and they learn a wide variety of far from routine crimes. They learn how to turn criminality into a reliable source of wealth, a skill they make good use of as adult career criminals. In Los Angeles many gang members, though well into adulthood, continue their involvement with the gang and its rackets (Moore, 1988b: 11–13), and the same is true in Chicago and elsewhere.

El Rukn's leader, Jeff Fort (born in 1947), became involved in Chicago's street gangs when he helped to organize the Blackstone Rangers, a predecessor of El Rukn, in the early 1960s while still in his midteens (*Chicago Tribune*, October 18, 1981: S3, 18). Over the years, he has become a major player in Chicago's underworld through his gang affiliations. And a substantial portion of Chicago's syndicate leadership during the 1960s and 1970s (for example, Sam Giancana, Sam Battaglia, Felix Alderisio, and Marshall Caifano) found their origins in a juvenile gang, the 42 Gang, established during the 1920s in the Patch, an Italian section in Chicago (Abadinsky, 1990: 196).

THE ORIGINS OF DELINQUENT GANGS

Gangs originate in a variety of ways. Teenagers cluster during adolescence to find answers for many new and urgent questions. How do their changing appearance and stature compare with other kids'? What sense can they make of their new experiences and discoveries? Which peers can they trust with their closest secrets without being ridiculed? Adolescent cliques regularly form on the basis of a need for mutual confirmation.

But cliques are mostly ephemeral. They form and change in terms of adolescent whimsy. Attractions that are powerful one moment fade the next, and as bonds are formed and broken, cliques change. Some of these cliques may turn to delinquency, but when the social ties are not firmly established, the members usually have little interest in or respect for one another and do not stay together long (Hirschi, 1969: 145–158).[1] Only a few of these cliques ever mature into gangs.

---

[1]See Chapter 9, pages 158–159 for a thorough discussion of the extent to which juvenile gangs shape and aggravate the delinquency of their members.

Cliques evolve into gangs when they establish a power structure wherein some members are acknowledged by the rest as a nucleus around which the clique revolves. These leaders regularly have a distinct charisma, they bring color and excitement to the gang, and they focus its overall direction. Whereas cliques grant everyone more or less equal status, in a gang not everyone speaks with the same authority. As an established structure emerges, the gang muffles the incessant competition that characterizes many adolescent cliques (Spergel, 1990: 226–227). Some of the issues regarding personal competence that plague adolescents are settled by membership in the gang.

What brings these leaders to the fore? When a crisis confronts the group, some of the bolder members suggest a plan. If the plan is successful, in a new emergency these leaders are consulted again. If again they are successful, other members defer automatically to their judgment, and the group or clique has transformed itself into an organized gang.

In Los Angeles, Chicano gangs were born during World War II, when teenaged groups were confronted by servicemen who objected to their zoot suits (Moore, 1988b: 9–10). A series of confrontations between Mexican youths, the police, and sailors forced the teenagers to organize for their mutual defense. The result was that several Mexican boys' cliques were transformed into gangs that were ready and able to defend themselves against all comers. These gangs were forced by other groups to organize for violence.

Four decades later in the early 1980s much the same process produced a number of gangs in Milwaukee (Hagedorn, 1988: 57–79). During this period several teenaged groups were organized into drill team units, while others regularly engaged in breakdancing contests. As these groups took part in competitions, fighting between the different units sometimes broke out. The drill teams began to prepare for these fights, and as relations with other teams became tense, these rivalries became more important than drilling. The groups were transformed into fighting gangs. Good models of fighting gangs in Chicago just 70 miles away made the transition easier for the Milwaukee gangs.

Gang leaders are usually strongest in several important ways (see Spergel, 1990: 208). They often have colorful imaginations, they are skillful in social interaction, they are strongest physically, they are the best athletes, and they are the most delinquent (Yablonsky, 1970: chapter 13; Klein, 1971: 70–92).[2] Among other things, they provide a kind of stability and focus that organizes the gang into something more solid and permanent than a clique.

As a core of leaders settles out, a gang with a definite structure, a name, a history, a growing reputation, a distinctive uniform, hand and arm signals, and a territory evolves. This kind of group is much more difficult for a neighborhood to cope with than juvenile cliques. Efforts to control it by neighborhood leaders, well-meaning individuals, or the criminal justice system itself are rarely effective. Such efforts by adults may serve only to strengthen the gang's solidarity as well as its reputation among other juveniles.

New members are recruited in swelling numbers through its growing reputation, and as its threat intensifies, rival gangs appear to serve other teenagers in much the same way. Thus, conflicts among young teenagers that are normally one-on-one encounters become better organized and more dangerous. At the same time the gang settles the issue of who is strong and respected in their neighborhood and who is not.

---

[2]Yablonsky has also insisted that gang leaders are serious sociopaths, but Klein sees no evidence in his own research for such a claim.

Gangs are sometimes formed in juvenile correctional centers. Inmates in such centers face many of the same personal challenges that confront teenagers elsewhere but in a much more intense way. In correctional centers juveniles are subjected to intense pressures to demonstrate their manliness, and numbers often provide an advantage in such conflicts (see Bartollas, Miller, and Dinitz, 1976). When boys from the same general neighborhood find one another in a youth correctional center, their common origin and experiences provide an important bridge, and a close alliance is an easy next step. If the same youths were to continue their friendship into their neighborhood, they would form the nucleus of a delinquent clique or gang.

The Vice Lords of Chicago were born in much this way in the late 1950s. According to David Dawley (1973: 28–33), a former Vice Lord, Peppilow at 14 was a school dropout on Chicago's west side. He was part of a ring of juvenile burglars who were arrested in 1958 and sent to the Illinois State Training School for Boys at St. Charles. One day his friend, Leonard Calloway, arrived at St. Charles and was assigned to Pep's cottage. Gradually, they assembled several more members, including Toehold, Ralph Bonds, and Maurice Miller. They had not all known each other before coming to St. Charles, but they became "tight" through regular contacts in the cottage. By means of their work assignments in the kitchen and laundry, they were able to do favors for one another in the institution. Eventually, all of them returned to Lawndale, and together they established the Vice Lords. Thirty years later, direct offshoots of the Vice Lords are still very active in Chicago.

And yet gangs also solve some of the problems that adolescents face in an impersonal, competitive world. In the absence of better ways of resolving self-worth and status issues, they turn to violence and organize themselves in terms of their ability to intimidate and coerce one another. Where other more peaceful mechanisms are available—where clubs or cliques with an established reputation (school-based athletic teams, for example) have already emerged—status issues may be settled by joining one or more of these clubs. When these clubs are unavailable, as for many lower- or working-class youngsters, they are left with little choice but to form their own clubs, if they want to think of themselves as worthy individuals.

Several theorists have taken an interest in this ability of fighting gangs to settle the status questions of marginal adolescents. One of the first was Albert Cohen (1955), who did as much as anyone to spark the modern-day interest in gangs with his classic *Delinquent Boys*. Cohen suggested that working-class youngsters often encounter difficulties in school because of the conflict between their values and those of their middle-class peers and teachers.

Their teachers prefer settled, industrious children who accept instruction well. Working-class children, particularly boys, are often unwilling to sit quietly in class, to listen dutifully to their teachers, and to do their homework regularly. Instead they are unruly students who approach the learning experience reluctantly. They do poorly on their quizzes and earn their teachers' and schoolmates' scorn. They develop a poor reputation in the eyes of their classmates, and a working-class clique endorsing *their* values makes a great deal of sense to them. Moreover, since their teachers and critical classmates endorse middle-class values, these gangs often take an antagonistic stance toward middle-class values. In addition to a strong version of masculinity—motorcycles, smoking, and boozing—working-class gangs adopt an antagonistic quality in their clothing—

Nazi paraphernalia, black boots, scrubby beards, and stringy hair—all of which the middle-class abhors. Things have changed dramatically today, but in the 1950s Cohen's description of working-class gangs was right on target.

Moreover, since their delinquency expresses resentment toward middle-class dominance, it takes a peculiar turn toward nonutilitarian, malicious, and negativistic activities. They steal things they have little use for from businesses, victimize middle-class children they hardly know, and destroy things at school for no apparent reason. From the standpoint of the middle class, their behavior is irrational and obnoxious. In the 'late 1950s and 1960s, Cohen's formulation seemed to describe working-class cliques well, as they reacted against the middle class and its values.

Twenty years later Herman and Julia Schwendinger (see 1985: chapters 3, 4, and 7) studied juvenile gangs in southern California and much as Cohen predicted, they discovered two generic forms (see also Box 5.2) that were mutually antagonistic—street-corner groups and socialite groups—as well as two narrower patterns—the intellectuals and the athletes. The athletes were admired by all groups and easily joined either one of the more general cliques, but the intellectuals were despised by most of their peers and were forced to form their own small group.

According to the Schwendingers, the generic cliques—socialite groups and street-corner groups—reflect a basic conflict inherent in capitalist economies between the bourgeoisie and the proletariat, and adolescent cliques simply echo this class conflict in their relations with one another. On the one hand, they are fully aware of their parents' negative views regarding unions and the working class, and on the other, their parents' criticisms of unscrupulous and selfish business leaders; they take these prejudices with them into school.

Street-corner groups admire strength and courage, independence, loyalty to friends, and a sense of family, whereas socialites value more a sense of style—manners, social finesse, fashionable clothes and cars, parties, and dates with pretty girls. These two groups follow opposite paths, and when they coexist in the same schools, they usually become bitter enemies.

This conflict in the school yard, say the Schwendingers, imitates a broader conflict in the economy between the capitalist owners of the means of production and the proletariat. But it also reflects the roots of delinquency in the distinctive cultures of the American class system. Walter Miller suggests that the ideals (the cultural foci) of the lower class serve as springboards to delinquency for many lower-class boys. Cohen and the Schwendingers take the whole process another step further and show how conflicts between core values of the middle and the lower classes produce conflict in their adolescent offspring (see also Chapters 9 and 12).

The California cliques described by the Schwendingers—the socialites and street-corner groups—are found broadly in American high schools, as Box 5.2 focusing on Utopia High near New York City reveals. These cliques wield a heavy influence over American adolescents and condition their attitudes about fashions in clothes and music, parents, education, and adult careers.

Their influence, however, also depends upon the social focus of the school (see Chapter 9, p. 156). Where the high school is part of a working class community and working class kids predominate, *their* cliques—street-corner groups—will prevail, and middle-class children and their cliques will not be highly regarded. By the same token,

Box 5-2 **Socialites and Street-Corner Groups at Utopia High**

Ralph W. Larkin published an insightful survey in 1979 of Utopia High, near New York City. Utopia High is not its actual name, nor is it a typical American high school. For example, intellectuals and politically active students share leadership roles along with the familiar, "jock/rah-rah crowd" (Larkin, 1979: 69–73). "Greasers" are also part of the scene, and they are ranked at the bottom of the social scale along with blacks (Larkin, 1979: 76–82). Larkin's descriptions of the jock/rah-rah crowd and the greasers illustrate very nicely the Schwendingers' concept of the socialites and the street-corner groups.

The jock/rah-rah crowd operates as a social elite and its members are pointed in the direction of . . . "the collegiate subculture" consisting of fraternities, sororities, sports, parties, drinking, and campus fun. At the high school level, this excludes campus fraternities and sororities but, nevertheless, encompasses the ethic of sociality of the "collegiates" that inhabit most college campuses. At Utopia High, the jock/rah-rah crowd is referred to in these terms because the ideal type male is the athletic star and the ideal female is the cheerleader. It consists primarily of athletes and their admirers and female students involved in more traditional roles of gaining success through the achievements of their boyfriends. This crowd dates, it is the core of the "school spirit," and it provides the most willing workers for such activities as homecoming and the prom. At one time it held cultural and political dominance on the high school scene. The . . . "freakification" of youth culture in the sixties undercut their dominance as *the* leading crowd and diminished their percentage of the student population as well as their unchallenged dominance as *the* elite. . . .

The jock/rah-rah crowd is populated from the ranks of upper middle-class youth primarily of Protestant background. Their parents are middle-and upper-level executives of large corporations and successful entrepreneurs. Those who are bright enough will follow in their fathers' footsteps into the Ivy League schools. Those who are not will be attending schools where the academic requirements are not as rigorous but where thriving collegiate subculture still exists (e.g., Penn State, Southern California). . . .

The greasers, like the jock/rah-rah crowd, have their roots in the youth culture of the 1950s. . . . The greasers at Utopia High also seem to be imitating the images presented in the television show "Happy Days," which features a saccharine "greaser" as its most popular character, "The Fonz," who dresses in tight levis, white tee shirt and black leather jacket. . . . Both *American Graffiti* [the film that inspired "Happy Days"] and "Happy Days" underemphasize the negative aspects of the youth experience of the 1950s, such as gang violence, personal intimidation, invidious competition, exploitation, alienation, and loneliness that were central to fifties youth culture. . . . Though greasers like to call themselves "hard guys," the rest of the student body calls them "greasers" and, even more disparagingly, "bobos." . . .

The greasers do not seem to engage in much violence against their peers; however, they are a source of conflict within the school. It is common knowledge that most of the vandalism within the school is attributable to the greasers. . . . The

student leadership complained about [their] coming to dances and movies sponsored by student government and hanging out and milling around without really
participating in the organized activity, but rather using the event as a place to con-
gregate, get drunk, smoke marijuana and cigarettes, and make a general nuisance
of themselves. . . . In addition it is the greasers who come to school drunk. Many
of them use both marijuana and booze before they stumble onto campus
. . . . [They are also] the prime target of police activity, since they not only tend to
be drug abusers, but also participate in acts of vandalism. . . .

The greasers are predominantly from working-class backgrounds. There is no
evidence that their families have suffered more divorces than those of the upper
middle-class students; however, they do tend to live in single-parent households
more frequently than their more affluent peers. The male students tend to be primarily interested in cars or motorcycles. Those with whom I talked were planning
to work in a local automobile assembly plant. . . . The female students who hang
out with the greasers contemplate graduation from high school with no firm
plans—perhaps they will go to junior college, or take a job—but marriage is the
ultimate goal. [Larkin, 1979: 69–70, 76–78, 80–81, 82]. Exerpt from *Suburban Youth in
Cultural Crisis* by Ralph W. Larkin. Copyright © 1979 by Oxford University Press, Inc. Reprinted by permission.

when middle-class high schoolers are in the majority, their cliques—the socialites—will
be widely admired and will set the tone of student activities. Working-class cliques in this
setting will be peripheral.

In addition, the Schwendingers (1985: 183) identify several generic pressures that
foster delinquency among adolescents. First, they point to a generalized interest in adventure and minor deviancy that prompts shoplifting, vandalism, alcohol and drug
abuse, sexual acting out, reckless driving, and such status offenses as running away and
truancy. Second, they see a competitive attitude toward one's peers as sparking invidious
comparisons that lead in turn to a generalized pattern of fighting. This need to enhance
one's status, as we have seen, is the basis of juvenile cliques generally. Finally, the
Schwendingers suggest that once a delinquent clique is formed, its natural leaders tend
to intensify its delinquency through an ability to weld the group into a cohesive gang of
like-thinking comrades. With the group's support the leaders propose delinquent activi
ties that none of the members would have dared alone.

These theorists seem to be in agreement regarding the origins of delinquent gangs.
According to Kobrin (1951), Suttles (1968) and Spergel (1984), in the absence of better
alternatives, gangs help to establish juveniles in the social structure of their neighborhoods (see also Chapter 9). According to Cohen and the Schwendingers, gangs help to
answer the gnawing problems of adolescence regarding self-worth, and for the
Schwendingers, the gangs also express the fundamental contradictions of the economic
order.

Gangs, especially highly developed ones, seem to be associated with lower-class
neighborhoods and especially with inner-city ghettos. What role does the ghetto play in
fostering juvenile gangs? Most neighborhoods in America sponsor juvenile cliques, and
most of these cliques indulge in some form of nuisance behavior at one time or another.
But few become well-organized, criminal gangs prepared for systematic conflict with
other gangs and the police. Why does the ghetto tend to foster these kinds of gangs?

Once these gangs have formed in the ghetto, what role do they play there? Why do some continue as juvenile gangs with younger members regularly coming in and older members dropping out, whereas others establish a leadership cadre that remains in control for decades? Why are inner-city gangs so much more durable than other kinds of gangs?

GANGS AND THE INNER CITY

During the 1970s, America took the gang to a new level of sophistication. Gangs in the 1950s in major American cities consisted of informal cliques of young teenagers who ran around together more for companionship and excitement than predatory delinquency. They sometimes got into trouble, but for the most part they were loosely woven street-corner cliques only incidentally involved in crime. They rarely had anything to do with the underworld or adult criminals.

Today many of these gangs, though continuing the street gang traditions of the 1960s, include mainly adults who commit serious crimes with more sophisticated weapons and play a key part in the criminal rackets of their neighborhoods. Street gangs today are much better organized and led, are larger and more sophisticated, and are more widely distributed in American cities than their predecessors of the 1950s and 1960s. Many of these gangs have become significant problems in their communities, and some—supergangs—have become major law enforcement targets.

Why do America's inner cities spawn so many supergangs? For one reason the inner cities have become a convenient marketplace for illicit goods and services in the United States. Sex, drugs, and weapons are sold with near impunity in the inner cities, and all three constitute a thriving underground industry in America—but especially is this true of drugs. Immense profits with some risk can be made in drugs, from the peasant or farmer who cultivates them all the way to the street dealer who sells them.

Some street gangs have assumed a major role in distributing drugs in America (Spergel, 1990: 193–199). They are one of the few groups in the inner city that have the discipline and organization to bring drug trafficking under one roof over the protests of others already active in the area. They have the ruthlessness to control the channels of distribution. They can protect their dealers from rip-offs, and they can thwart attempts by rival groups to invade their markets.

In the late 1970s some gangs in the major cities shifted their focus away from street crime to drug cartels and gradually built up their sources of supply, their distribution networks, and their protection services. Many of these gangs were based in the inner city, where they had a natural jurisdiction. Drugs are everywhere in America, but they are most effectively administered in the inner city, where the major markets are and where local people can exercise little control over gang activities.

Still, drugs are a major factor in the deterioration of the inner city and its people. Gangs have become a prime supplier of misery to inner-city people, and constructive change will be impossible, as long as gangs dominate these areas (see Schuerman and Kobrin, 1986).

At the same time, gangs derive much of their power from their ability to control the distribution of drugs. As long as illicit drugs overrun America, the inner city will be at the mercy of the super gangs, and little of lasting benefit can be done about its problems.

The answer to problems of the inner city, therefore, is straight forward. First, interdict the flow of drugs to the inner city, and deprive the gangs of their most profitable racket. Second, suppress the gangs and divert their members to socially constructive roles in the community. Third, even if these two goals were easy, a whole generation of inner-city young people who have been concentrating on illicit activities since an early age must be reoriented to other, more wholesome paths.

Fourth, family planning and family counseling must be developed so that infants and children will have the support and guidance of responsible parents who can help them discover their talents in school and find careers in an increasingly sophisticated economy.[3] Fifth, as the gangs dwindle and inner-city families find new ways of helping their children, the schools must be strengthened, and communal groups like ethnic clubs, unions, church groups, parent-teacher associations, boy scouts, and school clubs should be encouraged.

Finally, meaningful links between communal groups and regional and national groups must be fostered so that programs at the local level will mesh smoothly with social campaigns at the regional or national level. Training programs can be organized by local leadership and geared to local needs, and they can tap state or national funding sources, bringing the resources of the broader society to bear on inner-city needs.

This prescription for solving the inner-city's gang problem is relatively simple to sketch out. But each step is very difficult to achieve, and given the political difficulties in mobilizing significant resources for such programs, the likelihood of public support is not strong. The miseries of the inner city will no doubt persist into the distant future. No simple solution is in sight.

CONCLUSIONS

Gangs have had a long history in American cities. In the 1820s when the Bowery became the theater center of New York City, its streets were lined with saloons, beer gardens, and basement dives (Asbury, 1927: chapter 2). In this neighborhood, a profusion of gangs made up of young Irishmen established themselves, not so much for criminality as for entertainment and a general good time. Gang members often belonged to volunteer fire companies and usually fell into competition with one another. From time to time this competition escalated into pitched battles. During the Civil War draft riots of 1863, gangs of young men were especially vicious in fighting the police.

These groups were more nearly cliques than gangs, though from time to time youthful leaders offered direction and structure. Their members were usually 17 or older and not self-consciously criminal. Fighting was a regular pastime, but they were not otherwise a threat to the neighborhood, and their criminality was incidental to their drinking and brawling. As time wore on, the gangs of lower Manhattan were used periodically by New York politicians for strong-arm activities. They gave some muscle to Tammany Hall

---

[3]James Short (1990: 236–238) describes the Beethoven Project, an interesting effort along these lines to provide family counseling in a Chicago housing project, the Robert Taylor Homes.

and on that basis survived in one form or another until World War II (Abadinsky, 1990: 106–114).

Other gangs have been reported in other cities. In the 1920s, Thrasher counted 1313 gangs in Chicago, and one of these, the 42 Gang, was an Italian gang that many of Chicago's gang leaders used as a springboard to the upper ranks of Chicago's Italian crime syndicate. During Prohibition, Detroit had its Purple Gang, and in Los Angeles the Zoot Suit riots fostered Mexican gangs during the 1940s. Finally, in New York City in the 1950s, Puerto Rican gangs made an appearance in response to heavy immigration from that island.

Like the early gangs in the nineteenth century as well as most in between, the Mexican gangs of the 1940s in Los Angeles and the postwar Puerto Rican gangs of New York were defensive organizations and only incidentally criminal. Their leadership was informal, their criminality unsophisticated, their immediate neighborhood was their territory, and their membership was loosely defined. Gangs in the 1940s and 1950s had not changed much from the early nineteenth century, except that now they were made up largely of juveniles. Most of the early gangs had consisted mainly of young adults.

With the growth of the drugs in the late 1960s and 1970s among young people, some juvenile gangs exploited the opportunity presented by drug trafficking. A basis presented itself for continuing as a gang even after the membership had become mostly adult. The street gangs of the early 1960s became a platform for drug-driven crime during the 1970s and 1980s. As society changes and evolves, so too do its gangs.

SUMMARY

We have shown here that gangs are a major source of delinquency in a variety of ways. They intensify the delinquency of ordinary delinquents by making them fully aware of highly sophisticated methods and techniques, and they extend delinquency by recruiting new gang members and teaching them delinquent ways. Gangs originate in different ways in different communities, but they all take a distinctive form. They unite around a specific leader who is particularly sophisticated and anti-social. They settle on a name and a territory, and before long they find themselves in conflict with other adjacent groups. They develop a reputation, and the gang becomes a brotherhood of like-minded adolescents.

Many researchers have studied gangs. Early on Cohen (1955) linked the gang to a clash in middle class and working class values. The Schwendingers (1985) took Cohen's formulation one step further and suggested that this conflict reflects a broader struggle between the bourgeousie and proletariat in capitalist society. The generic nature of this conflict in capitalist society supports the conclusion that delinquent gangs reflect broadly the economic institutions of society. The Schwendingers maintained that gangs also echo more parochial juvenile interests in risk and adventure as well as gaining a respected status among their peers.

When juvenile gangs encounter risky, illegal, but highly profitable opportunities, they are uniquely able to exploit the situation, and their affluence enables them to extend their hold on their membership into middle adulthood. Such gangs undermine legitimate economic opportunity and drive conventional families and organizations out. The viability of the community under these conditions is endangered.

REFERENCES

Abadinsky, Howard. 1985. *Organized Crime.* 2nd edition. Chicago: Nelson-Hall.

———. 1990. *Organized Crime.* 3rd edition. Chicago: Nelson-Hall.

Asbury, Herbert. 1927. *The Gangs of New York.* New York: Alfred A. Knopf.

Bartollas, Clemens, Stuart J. Miller, and Simon Dinitz. 1976. "The Exploitation Matrix in a Juvenile Institution." *International Journal of the Sociology of Law* 4:257–270.

Cernkovich, Stephen A., Peggy C. Giordano, and Meredith D. Pugh. 1985. "Chronic Offenders: The Missing Cases in Self-Report Delinquency Research." *Journal of Criminal Law and Criminology* 76, No. 3:705–732.

Cohen, Albert K. 1955. *Delinquent Boys.* Glencoe, IL: The Free Press.

Dawley, David. 1973. *A Nation of Lords.* Garden City, N.Y.: Anchor Books.

Hagedorn, John M., with Perry Macon. 1988. *People and Folks.* Chicago: Lake View Press.

Hirschi, Travis. 1969. *Causes of Delinquency.* Berkeley: University of California Press.

Klein, Malcolm. 1971. *Street Gangs and Street Workers.* Englewood Cliffs, NJ: Prentice-Hall.

Kobrin, Solomon. 1951. "The Conflict of Values in Delinquency Areas." *American Sociological Review* 16 (October):653–661.

Larkin, Ralph W. 1979. *Suburban Youth in Cultural Crisis.* New York: Oxford University Press.

Moore, Joan. 1988a. "Changes in the Youth Gang: 'Normal Deviance' and Beyond." Paper presented at the annual meeting of the American Society of Criminology in Chicago.

Moore, Joan. 1988b. "Introduction: Gangs and the Underclass, A Comparative Perspective." In *People and Folks.* Edited by John M. Hagedorn, with Perry Macon. Chicago: Lake View Press.

Peterson, Mark A., and Harriet B. Braiker, with Suzanne M. Polich. 1981. *Who Commits Crimes.* Cambridge: Oelgeschlager, Gunn & Hann.

Reiss, Albert J., Jr., and Albert Lewis Rhodes. 1961. "The Distribution of Juvenile Delinquency in the Social Class Structure." *American Sociological Review* 26, No. 5 (October):720–732.

Sarnecki, Jerzy. 1988. "Delinquent Networks in Sweden." Paper presented at the annual meeting of the American Society of Criminology in Chicago.

Schuerman, Leo, and Solomon Kobrin. 1986. "Community Careers in Crime." In *Community and Crime: Crime and Justice,* vol. 8. Edited by Albert J. Reiss and Michael Tonry. Chicago: University of Chicago Press.

Schwendinger, Herman, and Julia R. Siegel Schwendinger. 1985. *Adolescent Subcultures and Delinquency.* New York: Praeger.

Short, James F. 1990. "New Wine in Old Bottles? Change and Continuity in American Gangs." In *Gangs in America.* Edited by C. Ronald Huff. Newbury Park, Calif.: Sage Publications.

Spergel, Irving A. 1984. "Violent Gangs in Chicago: In Search of Social Policy." *Social Service Review* 58 (June):199–226.

———. 1990. "Youth Gangs: Continuity and Change." In *Crime and Justice,* vol. 12. Edited by Michael Tonry and Norval Morris. Chicago: University of Chicago Press.

Suttles, Gerald D. 1968. *The Social Order of the Slum.* Chicago: University of Chicago Press.

Vigil, Hames Diego. 1990. "Cholos and Gangs: Culture Change and Street Youth in Los Angeles." In *Gangs in America.* Edited by C. Ronald Huff. Newbury Park, Calif.: Sage Publications.

Yablonsky, Lewis. 1970. *The Violent Gang.* Revised edition. New York: Penguin.

Chapter

6

Youth, Drugs, and Alcohol

hese days, drug and alcohol use by America's youth is one of the most popular topics in the mass media. Almost every day newspapers, television and radio, and books and magazines of all sorts recount the horrors of drug and alcohol abuse and the trafficking of illicit substances. In 1989, the widely seen movie *Colors* gave a stark portrayal of the drug-related violence of two Los Angeles gangs. And the government has also played a part in stimulating national concern about drugs. The Reagan and Bush administrations put drug enforcement at the forefront of federal policing, and the cabinet-level post of "drug czar" was created with much fanfare.

Much of the national concern about drugs has focused on two problems: the spread of "crack" cocaine and the increase in street violence that many believe is associated with it. Crack may become the preeminent street drug. It is plentiful, cheap, and psychologically addicting. Because of this, crack is a prime object for abuse. As demand grows, trafficking grows, and so does the competition for a piece of the action. This contributes to an escalation in violence as drug sellers try to protect their turf and their traffic. According to some accounts, the traditional street weapons of clubs, knives, and cheap (even handmade) guns have given way to imported submachine guns with awesome firepower.

Los Angeles and Chicago have long histories of serious gang problems, but as this is being written, news reports from Washington, D.C., claim that street violence there has reached an unprecedented level, much of it connected with the drug trade and apparently involving juveniles. The number of homicides in 1989 doubled the 258 that occurred in 1988, and authorities predict that increases will continue. The police say most of the homicides are related to trafficking in crack, which first appeared on the streets of Washington, D.C., early in 1988 (*Washington Post*, October 12, 1988 p. A1, A9). During 1988, juvenile violence increased dramatically, and by October nearly 500 juveniles had been shot or stabbed. If the current level of violence continues, more than 150 children will be murdered each year in drug-related incidents. Half of these children will be 15 years old or younger.

DRUG USE AMONG YOUTHS—THE NIDA SURVEYS

The stories of juvenile drug use portrayed in the media and promulgated by high government officials show a pretty dismal picture. However, neither reporters nor politicians are constrained by the tenets of science, and their portrayal of reality generally serves other purposes. So what's the story of juvenile drug use as criminologists and other scientists see it?

First, we must acknowledge some difficulties facing the researcher. For one thing, most drug use is illegal behavior, and people are generally not anxious to tell strangers about wrongdoing. Second, the very nature of drug use means that much of the hard evidence of use disappears once the drug has been consumed. There are no telltale broken windows, missing television sets, or dead bodies. There are urine and blood tests, to be sure, but to be effective these must often be done within a matter of hours of ingestion, and in any case they cannot tell us about the number of offenses committed in any given period nor about law violations that do not involve actual consumption (such as buying or selling). Such tests also require special circumstances or voluntary compliance before the authorities can use them.

To further complicate fact finding, drug law violations are commonly referred to as "victimless" crimes. This does not mean that no one is ever hurt but, rather, that participants consider themselves willingly involved and there is rarely anyone who claims to have been victimized.

The best way to get around these difficulties is to ask youths directly about their drug involvement. The National Institute on Drug Abuse (NIDA) has conducted surveys of high school seniors since the mid-seventies. These surveys show that only a small minority of seniors admit to having used heroin, hallucinogens such as LSD, or barbiturates "during the past 12 months," and even these percentages declined steadily during the 1980s (see Table 6.1). The most widely used illegal drug is marijuana, but even here the percent admitting use during the preceding year dropped from a high of 50.8 percent in 1979 to 33.1 percent in 1988. On the other hand, rates of alcohol use have remained very high over the past decade, with around 85 percent of seniors admitting use during the 12 months preceding the surveys. The only drug to show any real increase in use is cocaine, but that, too, now shows signs of falling, as the last two columns in Table 6.1 indicate. However, the growing popularity of crack cocaine, widely available only since 1988, may send reported cocaine use up again.

Someone who admits to having used a drug during a year-long period need not be a regular user, and some students who admit use may only have tried a drug once. In fact, Table 6.1 shows that the percentage of students who admit having used a drug "during the past thirty days" is small for all illicit drugs. Hardly any students at all admit to *daily* use of a drug, and when they do, the substance is almost always alcohol or tobacco.

The NIDA surveys cannot tell us about the drug use of youths who have dropped out of school, and to that extent they clearly underreport actual use. Nevertheless, the national picture of drug use by juveniles in school should be somewhat comforting to parents who believe that there is an epidemic of illicit drug use among the nation's children and that it grows bigger every day. On the other hand, the continued popularity of alcohol and the likelihood of more growth in the use of crack, especially in urban areas, are cause for concern. This is underscored by the NIDA finding that student knowledge of where to get illicit drugs correlates strongly with rates of use. In 1975 only a handful of interviewed subjects thought it was easy to get cocaine; by 1986 more than half of those interviewed thought it would be easy to get it.

Other Surveys of Drug Use Among Youths

National surveys are useful for assessing gross trends, and they can tell us how patterns of drug use vary throughout the country and among different population groups. For example, the NIDA surveys show that recreational use of marijuana and cocaine is much more prevalent among male students than among female students, in larger cities than in rural areas, in the west than in the south, and among students with no plans to graduate from university (Johnston, O'Malley, and Bachman, 1987).

On the other hand, researchers interested in examining the causes and consequences of drug use generally study samples of youths drawn from single communities. Not only is this less costly and time consuming, but also the research can be designed to answer specific questions not appropriate for nationwide surveys, and the data can be related to other information not available at the national or even regional level. Of course, the major limitation of such studies is that their findings may not generalize to other communities.

A couple of examples will shed additional light on drug use among adolescents. In one study, 1101 youths were surveyed at a South Bronx, New York, junior high school (Dembo et al., 1986). The youths were asked about their use of various drugs, from tobacco and alcohol to solvents, LSD, narcotics, and marijuana. Alcohol was by far the most widely used drug—at least once by 47 percent of the students, and during the preceding 6 months by 37 percent. Marijuana was used by 19 and 16 percent, respec-

Table 6.1   REPORTED DRUG USE*

Type of drug	1978 (a)	(b)	1981 (a)	(b)	1984 (a)	(b)	1986 (a)	(b)	1988 (a)	(b)
Marijuana	50.2	37.1	46.1	31.6	40.0	25.2	38.8	23.4	33.1	18.0
Hallucinogens	9.6	3.9	9.0	3.7	6.5	2.6	6.0	2.5	5.5	2.2
Cocaine	9.0	3.9	12.4	5.8	11.6	5.8	12.7	6.2	7.9	3.4
Heroin	0.8	0.3	0.5	0.2	0.5	0.3	0.5	0.2	0.5	0.2
Sedatives	9.9	4.2	10.5	4.6	6.6	2.3	5.2	2.2	3.7	1.4
Alcohol	87.7	72.1	87.0	70.7	86.0	67.2	84.5	65.3	85.3	63.9
Cigarettes	na	36.7	na	29.4	na	29.3	na	29.6	na	28.7

*(a) used within the past year; (b) used within the past 30 days.

Source: Lloyd D. Johnston, Patrick M. O'Malley, and Jerald G. Bachman. 1989. "Illicit Drug Use, Smoking, and Drinking by American High School Students, 1975–1987." In *Sourcebook of Criminal Justice Statistics, 1988*. Edited by Katherine M. Jamieson and Timothy J. Flanagan. Washington D.C.: U.S. Department of Justice, 1989:356–359.

tively. In contrast, fewer than 6 percent indicated they had *ever* used any of the other drugs (excluding tobacco).

A study from Ontario, Canada, looked at drug use among students aged 12 to 19 (Smart and Adlaf, 1986). Three different samples were interviewed, the first in 1968, the second in 1977, and the most recent in 1985. Alcohol and tobacco were not included because the study focused only on illicit drugs (marijuana, LSD, opiates, cocaine, heroin) and "psychotherapeutics" (stimulants, sedatives, and tranquilizers). The study is interesting because it looked at changing patterns of drug use rather than whether or not students used drugs.

The findings show that from 1968 to 1977 the proportion of drug-using students reporting exclusive use of stimulants and tranquilizers dropped off sharply but was offset by a corresponding increase in the proportion reporting use of illicit drugs or exclusive use of marijuana. After 1977, a different picture emerged: The proportion reporting exclusive use of marijuana declined slightly, but the proportion of students reporting *multiple* (or "poly") drug use increased significantly. By 1985 just over half of the drug-using students admitted having used two or more illicit drugs during the preceding 12 months. Confirming earlier research, the authors conclude that "virtually all users of illicit drugs, other than cannabis [marijuana], are polydrug users" (Smart and Adlaf, 1986: 718).

EXPLAINING JUVENILE DRUG USE

Various theories have been advanced to explain why individuals become involved with drugs and alcohol. Because the drug- and alcohol-related behavior of juveniles is very often illegal, most of the explanations are similar to those offered for other kinds of delinquency and crime. However, Gottfredson and Hirschi (1990) go further than this. They argue that drug use is *inherently* analogous to crime in that it brings short-term pleasure, is easy and simple to do, involves little skill or planning, and tends to be risky or thrilling. Hence no special theory is needed to explain it.

Nevertheless, Gottfredson and Hirschi (1990: 42–43) distinguish between drug *offenses,* drug *use,* and drug *abuse,* indicating that the drug "problem" can be conceptualized in different ways. One typical drug offense is drunk driving; another is illustrated by the adult who sells liquor to a minor. A typical example of drug use is the youth who smokes cigarettes or marijuana on a daily basis; a typical example of drug abuse is someone who is addicted to "hard" drugs and must commit crime or sell drugs to others in order to support the addiction. These distinctions suggest that while the same "cause" may underlie drug use, drug abuse, and drug offenses (the pursuit of pleasure is one possibility), the context and consequences of drug use vary. A good general explanation of drug-related behavior will be sensitive to such variations.

People tend to become involved with drugs or alcohol at an early age, and both the prevalence and incidence of use peak in the late teens and early twenties (Temple and LaDouceur, 1986; Snyder et al., 1987). In this respect, drug use mirrors other risky behaviors, among them burglary, robbery, murder, rape, and embezzlement (see Gottfredson and Hirschi, 1990). This is further evidence that a special theory may not be needed to explain the drug problem.

Another thing that we need to bear in mind in considering theories of drug involvement is the distinction between *initial* use, *continuation* of use, and *cessation* of use. The reasons people start using drugs may not be entirely the same as the reasons they continue using them, or eventually quit doing so. Once again, a satisfactory general theory must accommodate these distinctions.

The vast majority of people who say they have used drugs or alcohol also report that their use has been limited and sporadic. Heavy use of drugs and alcohol is confined to a small percentage of users (Douglas and Waksler, 1982), and most of these eventually reduce their consumption, with many quitting altogether by the time they are 30. Drug using "careers" have been described among regular users, some lasting longer than others, some involving polydrug use, some centered around a single drug, and some associated with trafficking and other crime.

The 1972 National Commission on Marijuana and Drug Abuse (in Thio, 1988: 340) identified five types of drug-using behavior: (1) *experimental use,* where a passing curiosity results in short-term trial of one or perhaps a number of different drugs; (2) *recreational use,* where occasional drug use is part of having a good time, often in the company of friends; (3) *situational use,* where a particular drug is used as a means of coping with a specific situation—for example, the need to stay awake or to improve performance; (4) *intensified use,* where recreational or situational use escalates into a daily habit, but the user still goes about everyday business normally; and (5) *compulsive use,* where drugs become a dominant feature of the users life and where psychological and sometimes physiological dependence occur.

The drug problem is clearly complex. The following theories attempt to make sense of the picture, but no single theory appears adequate to explain all the facts about drug-related behavior among youths.

Physiological Explanations

Directed primarily at continuation of drug or alcohol use rather than initial use, physiological theories stress the involuntary nature of drug use (Abadinsky, 1989: 113). The most prominent versions argue that drugs are consumed in response to a bodily need, or craving, over which the individual has no control. This need may exist prior to and independently of the drug use itself, or it may develop as a result of use. In either case, the pharmacology of drugs—their chemical effect on a person's nervous system—is thought to correct some sort of neural deficiency. The correction then becomes the stimulus for further use.

And so it is with addiction. Regular use of such drugs as alcohol and opiates results in a chemical equilibrium that must then be maintained or else the addict suffers withdrawal. Withdrawal can be extremely distressing, even fatal. As many addicts have pointed out, each "fix" is necessary to prevent withdrawal, and in doing so it makes them feel normal again (Brecher, 1972). The chemical balance is temporarily restored.

Recent research suggests that habitual (but not first) use of cocaine may be the result of a deficiency in dopamine (DA), a drug that bodies produce in order to activate the sympathetic nervous system, which prepares them for action. Apparently, cocaine stimulates dopamine production, but as its effects wear off, the body "reads" the decline in DA level as a deficiency that must be corrected. In chronic or compulsive users "this

DA depletion could be experienced . . . as craving for cocaine, which would explain the need for successive cocaine doses throughout the day" (Gold, Washton, and Dackis, 1985; cited in Abadinsky, 1989: 114).

Some authors have suggested that the compulsivity and pain associated with addictive withdrawal may have been overstated. In many cases, the doses taken by addicts are too low to produce severe withdrawal symptoms, and "heroin addicts commonly detox themselves—that is, they take their doses down in stages to avoid withdrawal symptoms as a way of reducing their tolerance and making it possible to achieve a high state with less heroin, hence less money" (Douglas and Waksler, 1982: 221). These addicts exercise some degree of control over their drug use, and in itself this challenges the notion that heavy use of addictive drugs is involuntary and explained by physical compulsion. We shall return to matters of control and choice in a later section.

None of this negates the importance of the physiological aspects of drug use. Drugs clearly do have direct physiological effects, and in most cases these effects are clearly part of the reason people keep on using them. Some drugs are distinctly pleasurable. The best example is probably cocaine. Cocaine is a stimulant that works directly on the "pleasure" or "reward" centers of the brain. It is so powerful that it undermines the brain's ability to regulate such functional necessities as sleeping, eating, and handling stress. The high has been described as elation, vigor, sexual arousal, and warmth (Grabowski, 1984). Because its effects are so pleasurable, cocaine is a prime target for abuse, though there is considerable disagreement about whether it is physiologically addicting.

Many social scientists accept the view that the physiological effects of drugs are important in explaining continued use but believe there is much more to the story. In particular, physiological theories have little to say about the onset of drug use, and they are not very helpful in explaining why an individual gets involved in polydrug use, especially when this involves drugs with opposite pharmacological effects. Physiological theories are also not very useful for predicting sporadic drug use.

Psychological Explanations

As with other "problem" behaviors, drug use has been a prime area for psychological theory and research. There must be something different about the person who uses drugs, especially if that drug use is excessive. Psychological testing seems to confirm this conclusion (Craig, 1986); Heroin addicts, for example, have been found to be hostile, demanding, aggressive, rebellious, impulsive, and irresponsible. But as Abadinsky (1989: 114) points out, so have many outstanding athletes (see also Gottfredson and Hirschi, 1990).

Various personality theories of drug use can be found in the psychological literature. Appropriately, many of these focus on the adolescent period, when personality development is reaching maturation and individual differences can be more easily detected. This is also the period when drug use commonly starts and during which it may escalate. The personality factors "explaining" drug involvement constitute a mixed bag—among them are poor self-conception, low self-esteem, inadequate ego development, neurosis of one sort or another, narcissism, and immaturity (see Jurich and Polson, 1984; Khantzian, 1985; Abadinsky, 1989).

Some psychologists argue that particular personality problems explain why an adolescent will stay with one kind of drug rather than another. Thus, restless and aggressive individuals look for "ego-constricting" drugs such as heroin. Heroin produces feelings of euphoria, relaxation, and calmness. On the other hand, adolescents who are typically shy, bored, or depressed will tend to use amphetamines and cocaine, stimulants that are "ego-expanding" (Khantzian, 1985).

Despite the large volume of psychological research on drugs, it is virtually impossible to draw any confident conclusions about the links between personality and drug use. And to complicate matters, there is considerable evidence that even addicted drug users are behaviorally and psychologically normal (or only marginally different) when compared to nonusers (see Nathan, 1988). Indeed, except for their use of illegal drugs, many drug users are quite conventional—they abide by social rules, they limit their pleasures, they engage in legitimate activities most of the time, and they seek to reduce the dangers surrounding their drug use.

This sort of finding suggests that people use drugs not because of abnormalities or pathology but rather as a consequence of normal social conditions and processes to which they are exposed and in which they are involved.

Learning Theory

This observation by no means rules out psychology as a fruitful perspective in the explanation of some aspects of drug and alcohol use. On the contrary, learning theory has made a significant contribution to our understanding of both the onset and continuation of drug use.

Rooted in the behaviorism of the late B. F. Skinner, learning theory proposes that when behaviors are rewarded, they are positively reinforced and will occur again; behaviors that have unpleasant consequences are negatively reinforced and will be avoided. In terms of drug use, the reinforcement may come from the psychoactive effects of the drug itself and/or from the situation or environment in which it occurs. Thus, the negative reinforcement of withdrawal prompts the addict to "shoot up" again (Lindesmith, 1968). Alternatively, the pleasurable and thus positively reinforcing effects of cocaine prompt the user to snort, smoke, or inject it again. Abadinsky (1989: 124) identifies other positively reinforcing aspects of heroin and cocaine use:

> . . . the power of these substances to provide physiological and psychological rewards explains why some will continue to use them in the face of considerable hardship—*drugs overcome competing reinforcers*. Being known as a "junkie" or a "cokie," while it may have negative consequences in the wider society often provides a positive reward insofar as it allows entry and acceptance into the drug subculture. Daily activities can be concentrated on a clearly identifiable goal—drugs. The illegal aspects of drug use provide a level of excitement that some persons find quite rewarding.

Since learning is a social experience, many learning theories of drug use are more aptly described as *social* learning theories. They consider the behavior of individuals to be a product of interrelated psychological and sociological processes.

A case in point is the differential association-reinforcement theory of Burgess and Akers (1966). These authors modified Edwin Sutherland's original theory of differential association and combined it with a behaviorist theory of learning. Applied to the opiate user, the modified theory explains both the acquisition and maintenance of drug use: Individuals *become* drug users because the reinforcing effects of a drug combine with social reinforcers such as peer group approval. They *continue* using for the same reasons. If addiction results, continued use is further reinforced through the addict's avoidance of withdrawal. However, even when addicts succeed in breaking their physiological dependence, they may still *relapse* into use because of reinforcers in the social environment (Akers, Burgess, and Johson, 1968).

Sociological Explanations

Sutherland's theory of differential association postulates that learning takes place when people associate with each other in intimate groups. Sutherland was primarily interested in the content of the learning. If a child spends a lot of time with peers whose attitudes and behavior favor marijuana use, that child is more likely to use marijuana than is a child who spends a lot of time with friends who frown on its use and are nonusers themselves. Through association with other users the child will also learn the techniques of marijuana use and the values and attitudes that support it.

Associational theory is persuasive, especially when we hear time after time that people who have used alcohol and drugs recall being introduced to them by friends or other intimates. Furthermore, those who are already familiar with one type of drug often recall that they were introduced to new drugs in the company of drug-using friends.

Drug Subcultures Because drug use tends to be a repetitive social behavior, norms and values develop over time that distinguish it from other forms of activity and provide it with rituals. Examples of drug-related norms and rituals include the "proper" methods of consumption, the sharing of drugs and drug paraphernalia, the use of a special drug language and conventions for buying and selling, and the adoption of rationalizations and justifications for the behavior. Since juvenile drug use carries a certain amount of risk—if not from the authorities, then from the drugs themselves or the circumstances surrounding their use and distribution—these norms and rituals help protect participants from danger, while at the same time they promote and protect the supply and distribution of drugs. Over time, a *subculture* of drug use emerges. Participation in a drug subculture encourages continued drug use, despite societal disapproval and police repression. Eventually, the participant may "learn to define himself as an addict, learn new justifications for his drug use, and new and negative attitudes toward the laws which try to prevent drug use" (O'Donnell, 1969: 84).

Alcohol use by juveniles also tends to be initiated and maintained within peer group associations, but because alcohol use is widely condoned by the larger society and is legal for adults, there is less need to be secretive and protective and less need to rely on alcohol-using peers for definitions favorable to use. Indeed, the same has been said of prescription drugs. These are not "bad" drugs that need to be redefined as okay and whose pleasurable use must be learned from others (Douglas and Waksler, 1982: 225–226).

Decisions About Drug Use   Drug use does not just happen; people make conscious decisions to try drugs. Even when a drug is available and others are encouraging use, a novice may still refuse to try it. Goode (1972) suggests that in these cases the newcomer does not like, trust, or feel close to those encouraging use. But apart from this, a novice may still refrain because of a perception that the drug is dangerous or that other risks are too high.

These indications of choice and rationality are confirmed in recent studies of heroin addiction. Although these studies focused on young adults rather than juveniles, the subjects' drug using behavior began in childhood and progressed to heroin addiction. Judging from physiological theories, one would expect self-control and rational decision making to decline as addiction takes hold. The new studies challenge this view.

For example, in their study of 124 black inner-city heroin addicts in Chicago, New York, Washington, D.C., and Philadelphia, Hanson and colleagues (1985) found that life with heroin was far from a mindless, driven existence. To be sure, the addicts spent much of their day concentrating on getting the money for a fix, but they did so in a variety of rational ways, determined largely by their knowledge, skills, and connections. Many worked at legitimate jobs, but nearly all found they had to supplement their income by borrowing and hustling. The most unskilled, opportunistic addicts sought money in the quickest, least violent, and least risky ways, whereas more skilled and connected addicts committed planned crimes with partners or raised money through systematic drug trafficking.

An English study by Trevor Bennett (1986) of six groups of addicts explored heroin addiction as a career involving three stages: initiation, continuation, and cessation. He predicated his study on the assumption that people are self-determining, deliberate, and responsible and that their behavior is goal directed, episodic, and self-limiting. Ninety percent of the addicts were initiated into heroin use by friends, and many had made a conscious decision to try heroin some time before they actually did so.

After initiation, most of Bennett's subjects progressed slowly toward addiction, many taking over a year to reach the point where they used heroin daily. Evidence of purposive decision making appeared in the accounts of continuation given by many addicts: Some gave up use for long periods of time, one "gave up opioids during the summer months so that he could pursue his favourite sports" (25), and many varied the amount of heroin consumed from day to day.

All Bennett's subjects were current users, and half indicated no interest in quitting. The others were confident they could quit but expected to do so only if certain other things happened, for example, if they moved away from their friends or if their lives changed dramatically in some other way. A new job, family responsibilities, and involvement in other "straight" activities have been identified as reasons why addicts quit (see also Winick, 1962). Unfortunately, a good job, a stable family life, and other benchmarks of conventionality are out of reach for many inner-city addicts (Hanson et al., 1985). Submerged in a street subculture of hustling and crime, the ghetto addict's horizons rarely extend beyond the immediate neighborhood and a small group of drug-using friends. Rational decision making therefore occurs within a narrow physical and social space. But it still occurs.

The fact that drug addicts can and do engage in rational decision making in no sense lessens the impact on behavior of social forces. Inevitably, behavioral decisions are influenced by the nature and availability of incentives and disincentives, and these vary widely. More to the point, the individual rarely has any real control over them. Rational decision making is limited and constrained by the social setting in which it occurs. A person who decides to try or to continue using a drug makes that choice in the face of reinforcement and opportunities to which he or she is exposed. In sum, the rewards *for* drug or alcohol use and the constraints *against* use are rooted in social relationships and social conditions.

Peers and Parents   We have noted that initiation and continuation of drug-using behavior often appears to be influenced by a child's association with others who use drugs. Most of the anecdotal evidence and much systematic research point to the conclusion that drug-using peers, parents, and siblings figure prominently in the biographies of juveniles who use drugs or alcohol regularly (for references to the extensive literature see Elliott, Huizinga, and Ageton, 1985).

In some contexts—gangs or partying, for example—drug use may even be expected. By not doing it, youths risk negative sanctions that can range from mere disapproval to ridicule, ostracism, and even violence. Noncompliance is grounds for suspecting a person's commitment to the group, and when the behavior is both illegal and risky, nonuse may be taken as evidence that a person could be a snitch.

There seems to be little question that people who turn on to drugs are likely to have grown up in an environment where drug use was common. What is more, no matter whether it is cocaine, heroin, marijuana, or psychedelics, many studies have shown generational continuity in drug use and in progression from legal to illegal drugs (see Brecher, 1972; Goode, 1972). What parents and older siblings do, children often end up doing. Of course, many parents who themselves use drugs or alcohol do not approve of their children using them. Yet, example is a powerful teacher, and when this is bolstered by expressions of approval, the combination sends strong messages to children. It should come as no surprise that parental drug use and drinking correlate highly with drug and alcohol use by offspring (see Barnes and Welte, 1986).

Some studies suggest that peer group influence on alcohol and drug use is more important than parental influence (see White, Pandino, and LaGrange, 1987). The "near universal recognition" (Selnow and Crano, 1986: 48) that peer affiliations are important probably surprises no one, since we can all remember that much of our own childhood was spent in the company of friends with whom we took risks, tried new adventures, and on occasion did "bad" things. Our peer associations both defined and facilitated much of our acting out. The more loose time we had, the more likely we would fend off boredom by trying something new. All the better if we knew it was frowned on by authorities and therefore entailed some risk and symbolized our growing independence.

The periodic combination of opportunity, loose time, absence of surveillance by authorities, appropriate peer influence, and a facilitating context (for example, partying, a celebration, a rite of passage, an opportunity to impress someone) draws many youths into occasional drug use. On the other hand, some peer affiliations actually reduce the risks of adolescent drinking and drug use. Studies show that youths who participate in more or less formal, goal-directed peer associations, such as organized sports, 4-H clubs, or the Boy Scouts, are less likely to use alcohol or drugs than youths who participate in more ad hoc associations, such as gatherings at the local video arcade or fast-food parking lot (Selnow and Crano, 1986). Participation in formal peer associations reduces the likelihood of drug involvement because it (1) lessens opportunities for acquiring drugs and the amount of unsupervised free time to consume them, (2) raises the costs and risks of nonconformity, and (3) encourages internalization of conventional values and rules.

The relationship between juvenile drug use and peers, parents, and opportunities is by no means fully understood, and debate continues as to whether drug use reflects weak bonding to conventional society, or social learning, or opportunities and situational pressures, or some combination of all three. Some recent studies that have attempted to integrate various different perspectives have shown promise (e.g., Elliott, Huizinga, and Ageton, 1985) but have also garnered severe criticism (e.g., Hirschi, 1987). The position taken by an increasing number of researchers appears to be that some sort of theoretical integration is superior to reliance on a single perspective.

One recent integrative study concludes yet again that association with drug-using peers is the best predictor of adolescent drug and alcohol use, but it also suggests that the connection between peers and drug use might be more simple than had previously been thought: "It is not so much that adolescents use drugs because the drug use of their friends makes drugs seem right or safe, they apparently use drugs *simply because their friends do*" (Johnson, Marcos, and Bahr, 1987: 336).

This suggests that youths who participate in both drug-using and non–drug-using peer groups will move between them, chameleon-like, exchanging one behavior for another according to the particular friends they are with at the time. This explains why many youths move in and out of drug-related behaviors, acquiring neither a regular pattern of use nor an identity as a user.

A caveat is in order. Some of the studies we have cited, including the last one, were conducted with relatively small samples of mainly white youths from mainly middle-class backgrounds in a single community. Clearly, their findings may not generalize to other categories of youths or to other communities. Nevertheless, regardless of class, race, or community, the preponderance of research does confirm that drug use is strongly influenced by the behavior of peers.

CRACK AND THE INNER CITY

Nationwide surveys in America have shown that self-reported drug use varies little by social class or race (see Elliott, Huizinga, and Morse, 1985; Johnston, O'Malley, and Bachman, 1987). However, media reports indicate that cocaine use, in the form of crack, is apparently becoming more and more extensive in the nation's inner-city areas, especially among Hispanic and black youths.

Attempts to explain this apparent link between the spread of crack and the inner city have focused on the life-styles of lower-class youth, on the prevalence of street gangs, and on the socioeconomic conditions under which they live. There is an obvious economic side to the issue: Cocaine is getting cheaper, and crack is inexpensive and plentiful. In 1982, for example, cocaine cost roughly $500 a gram on the street; by 1988 it cost less than $100 (Flanagan and Jamieson, 1988: 289). And judging from Drug Enforcement Administration (DEA) and U.S. Customs seizures, cocaine trafficking is continuing to grow. In 1977, less than 1300 pounds of cocaine was seized by both services combined; in 1987, the DEA confiscated 82,042 pounds alone, and the Customs service another 52,000 pounds (Flanagan and Jamieson, 1988: 402–403).

This means that a pleasant but pernicious drug is within easy reach of American youths, especially those who associate with gangs or who live in neighborhoods where drug trafficking flourishes. In many large cities, random drug testing of youths arrested on charges of crime or delinquency indicates that a majority test positive for cocaine (National Institute of Justice, 1990). While this tells us nothing about the drug use of youths who are not arrested, nor of the extent of use by arrested youth, it is evidence of cocaine's widespread availability, and there is no reason to believe that its use is confined to youths in trouble with the law.

The increasing involvement of youth gangs in drug trafficking is also well documented, in both popular and scientific literature. Illicit drugs have been a feature of street-corner society for decades (see, e.g., Schwendinger and Schwendinger, 1985; Merry, 1981), but the lure and profitability of crack has elevated trafficking to a major gang activity, and competition among rival gangs in Chicago, Los Angeles, and Washington, D.C., has led to turf wars that have left many youths dead and injured and the authorities at a loss to know what to do about it (*NCTAP NEWS*, April, 1988).

The fact that crack- and drug-related gang wars are flourishing in the inner city is partly explained by the existence in those areas of traditions of street drug use. The economic and social underpinnings of black market enterprise are already in place—for example, meager incomes, hustling traditions, anonymity, vice, and organized crime. Furthermore, high rates of truancy and school failure combined with high rates of unemployment put large numbers of youths on the streets, where the trafficking typically takes place. Whether as observers, customers, sellers, lookouts, "steerers" (who direct customers to a drug supplier), "coppers" (who pass money and drugs from buyers to sellers), or "touters" (who promote a particular dealer's drugs), many of these youths become involved in the drug scene at some level.

The ease and profitability of trafficking in crack has brought a whole new dimension to the street drug scene. "Crack houses" (where the cocaine is processed into crack) are springing up in inner-city residential neighborhoods—there are reputed to be 50 crack houses in Denver, Colorado (*NCTAP NEWS*, April, 1988, pg. 7)—and gang members carry beepers around so they can be called the moment the next batch of crack is ready for distribution. There are indications that crack trafficking now involves youths of 10 and 11 years old (and even younger) who act as lookouts and even run the crack from place to place. The $5 or $10 they make for each job is a lot of money among their neighborhood peers, and the experience and connections provide opportunities for them to move up the trafficking ladder as they grow older.

The use of crack is not confined to the inner city. There is mounting evidence that suburban youths and young adults are turning on to the drug in growing numbers (*NCTAP NEWS*, October, 1988). Notwithstanding the growing awareness among youths nationwide that crack is dangerous (see Johnston, O'Malley, and Bachman, 1987), the availability, price, and hedonistic appeal of crack cocaine are apparently a strong lure.

At present, little is known about crack use in the suburbs, and it may be that much of the use is experimental and irregular. On the other hand, once trafficking is established in a neighborhood, the potential profits promote growth in enterprise networks, and growing numbers of potential users find themselves coming in contact with growing numbers of pushers. Besides all this, crack's strong potential for abuse makes it likely that growing numbers of users will move beyond experimental use, thus feeding further black market growth. When it was expensive and scarce, cocaine was widely regarded as the drug of choice for the rich; now that it is cheap, its pleasures—and dangers—can be experienced by all.

DRUG USE AND DELINQUENCY

Many of the drugs used by adolescents are illicit substances, which means that they are illegal to use even if used by adults. Marijuana, LSD, cocaine, and heroin are examples. In contrast, alcohol and tobacco are not illicit substances, although in most jurisdictions they may not be sold to minors and use by minors is restricted. It is therefore virtually impossible for juveniles to avoid breaking the law when they get involved in recreational drug and alcohol use. In this sense, drug and alcohol use are part of the broad spectrum of juvenile offenses.

Yet many people also believe that drug and alcohol use *cause* other crimes and delinquencies. Not long ago it was common to read that marijuana caused fiendish behavior or that heroin turned normal law-abiding people into crazed robbers and rapists, and alcohol has long been blamed for criminal behavior ranging from shoplifting to rape, assault, and murder.

The consensus among scientists now appears to be that there is nothing inherent in *any* substance that directly causes a person to rob, rape, or murder. However, there is also no question that some drugs do produce psychoactive effects that may alter a person's capacity to make decisions, to control physical movements, or to react to external stimuli. Where some drugs (e.g., cocaine, amphetamines) stimulate the central nervous system, others (e.g., opiates) produce opposite effects.

These psychoactive effects do not in themselves cause delinquent or criminal behavior. But their combination with other cultural, social, personality, and situational factors—for example, having an argument, driving a car, being at a party, taking a risk—may help turn conventional behavior into crime. Or they may turn behavior that is already illegal into more serious crime.

Among readily available drugs, alcohol is the substance most often associated with criminal outcomes. Alcohol lowers reaction times as well as inhibitions and reduces motor coordination, but at the same time it stimulates feelings of power. This dangerous combination helps explain much of the carnage on the nation's highways, but it is neither a sufficient nor a necessary ingredient in crime.

Despite the lack of a direct causal connection between psychoactive substances and crime, many people still cling to the idea that drugs cause people to do bad things. There are various reasons for this. One is that the imputation of cause helps us account for a person's criminal behavior while denying that the person really meant to behave that way. Alcohol and drugs are thus convenient rationalizations or excuses for bad behavior. It should come as no surprise that many offenders claim to have been "under the influence" during their crimes (see Flanagan and Jamieson, 1988: 497). Another reason pertains to enforcement: The belief that drugs cause us to do terrible things provides public support for the severe penalties and intrusive enforcement strategies often used against drug offenders.

If there is no established direct causal connection between drugs and alcohol per se and antisocial behavior, this does not mean that use of these substances bears no relationship to crime and delinquency. There is substantial evidence that regular use of drugs is strongly related to crime, the more so the heavier the use.

Studies of heroin addicts in Baltimore and Harlem show that daily users participate in crime at a much higher rate than less frequent users. In Harlem, daily users generated an average of $11,000 in cash per year from crimes of all sorts, including an average of 316 drug sales (Johnson et al., 1985). In Baltimore, a sample of 354 known users arrested by the police between 1952 and 1976 committed four to six times the number of crimes when they were frequently using drugs compared with when they were not using drugs or using them only occasionally (Ball, Shaffer, and Nurco, 1983). These findings have been confirmed in a study by Anglin and Speckart (1988). Not only did daily use predict stepped up criminal involvement, but as the level of use increased, there was a corresponding shift toward more profitable types of crime.

Most studies of chronic criminal offenders show that heavy drug use and drug sales are prominent in their backgrounds, often beginning in their early teens (e.g., Peterson and Braiker, 1981; Dunford and Elliott, 1984). What is not clear is how much of the crime committed by these serious offenders is explained by their drug use. The costs of sustained drug use create a financial pinch that forces most users—especially the young and those from poverty areas—to commit crimes to supplement their legitimate sources of income. This *instrumental* crime may be carried on individually or in groups, but the eventual conversion of spoils to cash or drugs usually takes place within peer networks. Clearly, it is difficult to disentangle the offenses that are drug-use related from those that are not.

There is mounting evidence that just as drug use may lead to instrumental crime, so crime may lead to drug use. The notion that criminal activity generates drug use makes intuitive sense for various reasons: (1) People who "earn" money like to spend some of it on pleasurable things, (2) a risky but successful venture should be celebrated, (3) a risky venture may need some special courage or other mental preparation, (4) the peer networks that facilitate delinquency and crime also facilitate drug use, and (5) drugs may substitute for cash or other profits from crime.

In causal terms, the argument is that income-producing crime often precedes drug use, especially drug use that is expensive. Various studies have found that while a majority of chronic delinquents and adult offenders are also serious drug users, this does not hold the other way around (e.g., Elliott, Huizinga, and Morse, 1985; White, Pandino, and LaGrange, 1987). Serious drug use is more likely to be an aspect of the life-styles of serious delinquents than chronic criminality is of the life-styles of serious drug users. In part this is because chronic drug users are more likely to come from relatively affluent circumstances than are chronic delinquents. On the other hand, as illegal income increases so does discretionary buying power, which means that more money is available for purchasing drugs. A recent study of 3575 drug-treatment clients offers support for this view (Collins, Hubbard, and Rachel, 1985).

SOCIETAL REACTIONS TO DRUG AND ALCOHOL ABUSE

There is nothing inherent in any activity that makes it a crime. Things and people become criminal or delinquent because persons in authority label them as such. Sometimes similar activities are labeled differently—some are called crimes; others are not. This is especially true of the world of drugs. Most of us are consumers of drugs, but some of us do nothing illegal, whereas others do. In order to fully appreciate the criminological aspects of drug use we have to consider its legal side as well.

Psychoactive substances have been a part of American life since the country's founding, but only in this century have drugs been universally linked with crime and delinquency. Indeed, the nineteenth century has been called a "dope-fiend's paradise" (Brecher, 1972). Opiates and marijuana were widely available, and both were used extensively as medicines. However, by the early twentieth century a mixture of politics, business interests, ethnic prejudice, and moral entrepreneurship had resulted in passage of various laws and ordinances, culminating in the Harrison Narcotics Act of 1914, which outlawed opiates and cocaine, and the Marijuana Tax Act of 1937, which effectively outlawed marijuana.

There were two major unintended consequences of the Harrison Act. First, many previous opiate users now became heavy users of barbiturates. Middle-class, middle-aged white women had been the largest group of opiate users before Harrison, largely due to the dispensing of opium for so-called female problems. After Harrison, these same people became the largest group of sedative users (Goode, 1972: 193).

Second, a new class of opiate users began to emerge—inner-city blacks and Hispanics. Ravaged by the Depression and concentrated in anonymous, decaying slums, inner-city populations offered profitable black market opportunities that were soon seized upon by unscrupulous entrepreneurs and organized criminals. From 1920 to 1933, the 13 years of Prohibition increased demand for illicit drugs and encouraged development of underground networks of supply and distribution.

Prohibition was repealed for various reasons: (1) because many Americans wanted to enjoy an alcoholic drink free from criminal stigmatization, (2) because the liquor industry was losing billions of dollars, (3) because enforcement was manifestly inefficient and corruption was widespread, (4) because of an alarming growth in organized crime and associated gangland killings, and (5) because many state officials resented federal control of local affairs.

Interestingly, the major accomplishments of Prohibition appear to have been the boost it gave to illicit drug trafficking, and through its repeal, the reinforcement it lent to the notion that alcohol is not really a drug and should not be criminalized. As if to stress the difference between alcohol and narcotics, no one clamored for repeal of the Harrison Act.

This double standard is reflected time and again in the societal response to alcohol and drugs. Drunks who kill with their cars are somehow exempt from the harsh reactions that are stirred when we learn that someone is involved with illicit drugs. Few people have qualms about the recreational use of alcohol, but many speak out against the recreational use of marijuana or cocaine.

An entirely different class of drugs also belongs in this story of double standards and special interests. These are the legal drugs that are sold over the counter, sometimes as medicines (e.g., aspirin), sometimes as ingredients in food and drink (e.g., caffeine). In America, drugs have become a way of life. They are big business, and even children cannot escape the marketing ploys of the legal drug pushers: Aspirins are named after saints, vitamins look like Flintstones, and beer that isn't beer is sold as if it were beer.

Small wonder, then, that there is much confusion about drugs and that no constructive policy has ever been developed. Although alcohol shows the strongest links with the crimes Americans fear most—assault, rape, murder—and with accidental death and injury, people are given every encouragement to believe that alcohol is not as bad as heroin, cocaine, LSD, or even marijuana. Even recent efforts to curb drunk driving—contributing to around 25,000 deaths and countless injuries each year—pale in comparison with the millions of dollars and hours spent annually on drug enforcement.

And what of the huge drug enforcement effort? By many accounts it has been unsuccessful at every level. Even the General Accounting Office of the U.S. government agrees (see *NCTAP News,* January, 1989). The interdiction effort at the nation's borders has been a disaster, cooperative law-enforcement efforts with cocaine-producing countries have produced no significant declines in production or smuggling, and the cost to taxpayers continues to soar.

At the street level, according to FBI figures, arrests of juveniles on non–alcohol-related drug offenses increased from a mere 1458 in 1960 to 65,864 in 1975 and 79,601 in 1981; the number remained at around 80,000 arrests per year throughout the 1980s. If the use of crack continues to spread, however, we may well see a surge in juvenile arrests.

There is little evidence that a heavy hand accomplishes positive results in the war on drugs. Surely a major reason is that the messages sent to children are contradictory. They are told not to take drugs, yet drugs of all sorts are legally advertised and sold all around them. They are warned (sometimes incorrectly) that illicit drugs are addictive, yet some drugs known to be addicting (e.g., nicotine, alcohol) are legal. They are chastised for drug use by parents and teachers who themselves smoke or drink. They are warned of the death and destruction caused by cocaine or heroin abuse, yet they can see that the death and disease from abuse of alcohol and tobacco are far greater. But some officials never seem to learn: The 1989 Omnibus Drug Initiative Act speaks of drug education but plans to deny federal loans to students with drug convictions and to require capital punishment for drug (not alcohol!) related murders. Against this background, it is small wonder that a child's friends should be so influential.

SUMMARY

It should come as no surprise that occasional drug use is widespread among adolescents. After all, drug use is widespread throughout the population, and there are many environmental reinforcements for it. The fact that nonmedicinal drug use is largely illegal for adolescents makes it all the more attractive at a time when experimentation, risk-taking, and challenges to authority are important components of identity-building. Add the periodic combination of opportunity, loose time, absence of adult surveillance, and presence of drug-using peers, and the situational inducements are in place.

There is little evidence that adolescent drug use requires a special theory to explain it, although the addictive nature of alcohol and some other drugs adds an element not present in the etiology of other behaviors. Addiction is clearly part of the reason some youths keep on using such drugs, although even here its role may have been overstated. To persistent users, alternative behaviors may be seen as less attractive or realistic in the face of social, cultural, and economic circumstances and recurring situational inducements.

The notorious problem these days is growing use of crack cocaine among inner-city youth and the well-publicised rise of crack-peddling and related violence among city gangs. Combine the fact that crack is readily available, inexpensive, and pleasurable with concentrated user populations, traditions of hustling and illegal markets, and enterprising street gangs with easy access to weapons and portable communications, and a burgeoning traffick in the drug is predictable, as is an increase in instrumental crime. Unfortunately, public officials are no closer to constructing effective drug-related policies than they were in the days of the Harrison Act. In our view, a heavy hand and mixed messages to youth about drugs have not helped.

REFERENCES

Abadinsky, Howard. 1989. *Drug Abuse: An Introduction.* Chicago: Nelson-Hall.

Akers, Ronald L., Robert L. Burgess, and Weldon I. Johnson. 1968. "Opiate Use, Addiction, and Relapse." *Social Problems* 15:457–469.

Anglin, Douglas M., and George Speckart. 1988. "Narcotics Use and Crime: A Multisample, Multimethod Analysis." *Criminology* 26:197–233.

Ball, J. C., J. W. Shaffer, D. N. Nurco. 1983. "Day-to-Day Criminality of Heroin Addicts in Baltimore—A Study of Continuity of Offense Rates." *Drug and Alcohol Dependence* 12:119–142.

Barnes, Grace M., and Jack W. Welte. 1986. "Patterns and Predictors of Alcohol Use Among 7–12th Grade Students in New York State." *Journal of Studies in Alcohol* 47:53–62.

Bennett, Trevor. 1986. "A Decision-Making Approach to Opioid Addiction." In *The Reasoning Criminal.* Edited by Derek B. Cornish and Ronald V. Clarke. New York: Springer-Verlag.

Brecher, Edwin. 1972. *Licit and Illicit Drugs.* Boston: Little, Brown.

Burgess, Robert L., and Ronald L. Akers. 1966. "A Differential Association-Reinforcement Theory of Criminal Behavior." *Social Problems* 14:128–147.

Collins, James T., Robert L. Hubbard, and J. Valley Rachel. 1985. "Expensive Drug Use and Illegal Income: A Test of Explanatory Hypotheses." *Criminology* 23:743–763.

Craig, Robert T. 1986. "The Personality Structure of Heroin Addicts." In *Neurobiology of Behavioral Control in Drug Abuse.* Edited by Stephen J. Szara. Rockville, Md.: National Institute on Drug Abuse.

Dembo, Richard, Gary Grandon, Lawrence La Voie, James Schmeidler, and William Burgos. 1986. "Parents and Drugs Revisited: Some Further Evidence in Support of Social Learning Theory." *Criminology* 24:85–104.

Douglas, Jack D., and Frances C. Waksler. 1982. *The Sociology of Deviance.* Boston: Little, Brown.

Dunford, Franklyn W., and Delbert S. Elliott. 1984. "Identifying Career Offenders Using Self-Report Data." *Journal of Research in Crime and Delinquency* 21:57–85.

Elliott, Delbert S., David Huizinga, and Barbara J. Morse. 1985. "The Dynamics of Deviant Behavior: A National Survey." *Progress Report*. Boulder, Colo.: Behavioral Research Institute.

Elliott, Delbert S., David Huizinga, and Suzanne S. Ageton. 1985. *Explaining Delinquency and Drug Use*. Beverly Hills: Sage Publications.

Flanagan, Timothy J., and Katherine M. Jamieson. 1988. *Sourcebook of Criminal Justice Statistics*. Washington, D.C.: U.S. Department of Justice.

Gold, Mark S., Arnold M. Washton, and Charles A. Dackis. 1985. "Cocaine Abuse, Neurochemistry, Phenomenology, and Treatment." In *Cocaine Use in America: Epidemiologic and Clinical Perspectives*. Edited by Nicholas J. Kozel and Edgar H. Adams. Rockville, Md.: National Institute on Drug Abuse.

Goode, Erich. 1972, *Drugs in American Society*. New York: Knopf.

Gottfredson, Michael R., and Travis Hirschi. 1990. *A General Theory of Crime*. Stanford: Stanford University Press.

Grabowski, John. 1984. *Cocaine: Pharmacology, Effects, and Treatment of Abuse*. Rockville, Md.: National Institute on Drug Abuse.

Hanson, Bill, George Brescher, James M. Walters, and Elliott Bovelle. 1985. *Life with Heroin*. Lexington, Mass.: Lexington Books.

Hirschi, Travis. 1987. "Review." *Criminology* 25:193–201.

Johnson, Richard E., Anastasios C. Marcos, and Stephen J. Bahr. 1987. "The Role of Peers in the Complex Etiology of Adolescent Drug Use." *Criminology* 25:323–339.

Johnson, B., P. Goldstein, E. Preble, J. Schmeidler, D. Lipton, B. Spunt, and T. Miller. 1985. *Taking Care of Business*. Lexington, Mass.: Lexington Books.

Johnston, Lloyd D., Patrick O'Malley, and Jerald D. Bachman. 1987. *National Trends in Drug Use and Related Factors Among American High School Students and Young Adults, 1975–1986*. Washington, D.C.: National Institute on Drug Abuse.

Jurich, Anthony P., and Cheryl J. Polson. 1984. "Reasons for Drug Use: Comparisons of Drug Users and Abusers." *Psychological Reports* 55:371–378.

Khantzian, Edward T. 1985. "The Self-Medication Hypothesis of Addictive Disorders: Focus on Heroin and Cocaine Dependence." *American Journal of Psychiatry* 142:1259–1264.

Lindesmith, Alfred C. 1968. *Addiction and Opiates*. Chicago: Aldine Publishing Co.

Merry, Sally Engle. 1981. *Urban Danger: Life in a Neighborhood of Strangers*. Philadelphia: Temple University Press.

Nathan, Peter E. 1988. "The Personality Is the Behavior of the Addict." *Journal of Consulting and Clinical Psychology* 56:183–188.

National Institute of Justice. 1990. *DUF: 1988 Drug Use Forecasting Annual Report*. Washington, D.C.: U.S. Department of Justice.

O'Donnell, John A. 1969. *Narcotics Addiction in Kentucky*. Washington, D.C.: U.S. Government Printing Office.

Peterson, Mark A., and Harriett B. Braiker. 1981. *Who Commits Crime: A Survey of Prison Inmates*. Santa Monica: Rand.

Schwendinger, Herman, and Julia Siegel Schwendinger. 1985. *Adolescent Subcultures and Delinquency*. New York: Praeger.

Selnow, Gary W., and William D. Crano. 1986. "Formal v. Informal Group Affiliations: Implications for Alcohol and Drug Use Among Adolescents." *Journal of Studies in Alcohol* 47:48–52.

Smart, Reginald G., and Edward M. Adlaf. 1986. "Patterns of Drug Use Among Adolescents: The Past Decade." *Social Science and Medicine* 23:717–719.

Snyder, Howard N., Terrence A. Finnegan, Ellen H. Minick, Melissa H. Sickmund, Dennis P. Sullivan, and Nancy J. Tierney. 1987. *Juvenile Court Statistics.* Washington, D.C.: U.S. Department of Justice.

Temple, Mark, and Patricia Ladouceur. 1986. "The Alcohol-Crime Relationship as an Age-Specific Phenomenon: A Longitudinal Study." *Contemporary Drug Problems* 15:89–115.

Thio, Alex. 1988. *Deviant Behavior.* 3rd edition. New York: Harper and Row.

White, Helene Raskin, Robert J. Pandino, and Randy LaGrange. 1987. "Longitudinal Predictors of Serious Substance Abuse and Delinquency." *Criminology* 25:715–740.

Winick, Charles V. 1962. "Maturing out of Narcotics Addiction." *Bulletin on Narcotics* 14:1–7.

Chapter

7

Status Offending

Status offenders are the foundation upon which juvenile justice was built in the first place. True, the early houses of refuge were also intended to protect juvenile felons from the ravages of prison, but young felons were few and far between in the early decades of the nineteenth century. The bulk of the youthful offenders who found their way into houses of refuge were status offenders—children who refused to attend school or obey their parents and roamed the city streets in search of adventure or crime. Many had parents too poor to raise them, but many also had parents who could not control them. By default they became street nomads.

The mayor of Boston, John Bigelow, complained in 1848 that ". . . hundreds of children are kept from the schools by their parents, and brought up to support them in idleness and drunkenness by pilfering our wharves, and are regularly educated for the brothel and the dram-shop, the poor house and the jail" (*Boston Evening Transcript*, January 3, 1848: 2). And one year later the Chief of Police of New York City, George W. Matsell, acknowledged that upwards of 3000 children roamed the city's streets at night. He warned that "each year makes fearful additions to their ranks . . . and from this corrupt and festering fountain flows a ceaseless stream to our lowest brothels—to the Penitentiary and to the State Prison!" (quoted in Hawes, 1971: 91).

These juveniles could not fit themselves into newly established school routines or urban family patterns, and to cope with their mushrooming emergence in the 1820s and 1830s the cities were forced to build custodial havens, houses of refuge, where children could receive an education, religious instruction, and tolerant, humane supervision— what they were missing to that point. Since these institutions were designed to protect children from their vulnerability, the courts took wayward children into custody using the doctrine of parens patriae and sent them to the houses of refuge. This same doctrine was also used to remove children from "inadequate," negligent parents and to compel juveniles to attend the public schools.

The first two forms of custody—custody over wayward, dependent, or neglected children—were challenged in nineteenth-century courts (see *Ex parte Crouse*, 4 Whart. 9, 1838; and *People v. Turner*, 5 Ill. 2800, 1879), and in both cases parens patriae was upheld.[1] Thus, in terms of parens patriae the state had an obligation to step in where key social institutions—the family or school—were faltering and to supplement their care.

These state court decisions acknowledged the family's concurrent obligations toward the child (see Garlock, 1979: 365–366). They assumed that the courts only shared the governance of children with families and that a sound family had *priority* as long as it exercised responsible control over the child. Parens patriae recognized the primacy and sanctity of the family and expected the court to intervene in family matters only when the family failed to act responsibly toward its children. Further, the legislatures were forced by challenges to the parens patriae doctrine to spell out precisely what constituted irresponsibility by a child's parents. The family was an essential factor in not only the child's welfare but also the community's, and the courts under parens patriae were required to act with delicacy in family matters.[2]

During the next 170 years the definition of a status offender was expanded as the social obligations of juveniles were specified more fully. In addition to incorrigibility, school misbehavior, and truancy, status offending came to include the frequenting of brothels, gambling dens, taverns, rail yards, pool halls, or other unwholesome places; associating with undesirable companions whether adult or juvenile; underage drinking or smoking; and curfew violations. As late as the 1940s at least one-third of the children who came before the juvenile courts were status offenders (Tappan, 1949: 29).

Shortly after World War II, Paul Tappan (1946) published his path-breaking paper, "Treatment Without Trial," and detailed how juveniles were regularly denied basic due process rights in the juvenile court.[3] Since status offenders were especially vulnerable to invasions of their due process rights (see Chapter 13), in 1962 New York state created a family court that had jurisdiction over all juvenile cases, whether delinquent, status offending, dependent, or neglected. Later the New York Court of Appeals ruled (*In re Ellery C.*, 1972) that separate dispositions for delinquents and status offenders (i.e., PINS or Person in Need of Supervision) were required. Most of the remaining states undertook to provide similar methods for treating status offenders. Some removed status offenders from the juvenile court entirely. Others prohibited the commingling of status offenders and delinquents but continued confining status offenders. A few simply con-

---

[1]The new doctrine was not upheld immediately because the Illinois Supreme Court ruled in *People v. Turner* that even though the court had every right to take custody of neglected children under parens patriae, it could not do so under a law that defined a neglected child as one who is "a vagrant, or is destitute of proper parental care, or is growing up in mendicancy, ignorance, idleness, or vice." The law was simply too vague. Later, after the law was repaired, a second challenge, *In re Ferrier* (103 Ill. 367, 1882), was rejected by the Illinois Supreme Court (see Garlock, 1979: 398–399).

[2]Parens patriae is based on the assumption that the family—beyond the individuality of its members—enjoys a certain privacy in relations with the state. Parens patriae lays down guidelines wherein the state may take action against parents and their childrearing responsibilities, but in specifying these ground rules, parens patriae acknowledges the family's primary rights. The "privacy" of the family in family matters is rooted firmly in this area of civil law, and in the Constitution's Fourth Amendment as well.

[3]Tappan ignored the fact that most delinquents were brought into the juvenile court under parens patriae, which did not invoke constitutional due process protections in the same way that criminal charges would. Nevertheless, Tappan's paper stirred much soul-searching among thoughtful juvenile justice professionals and pointed the way to far-reaching Supreme Court decisions in juvenile due process in the 1960s and 1970s.

tinued the traditional practice of mixing status offenders and delinquents in all phases of juvenile justice.

Through these reforms, better treatment was envisioned for status offenders than under previous delinquency laws. But that apparently did not happen (see Andrews and Cohn, 1977: 45–113; and *In the Matter of Ellery C.,* 32 NY 2d 588, 1973).[4]

Underlying much of this controversy was the assumption that delinquents and status offenders were two different species. Whereas delinquents had violated the criminal law and could be dealt with via custodial dispositions if need be, status offenders had not done so and did not deserve confinement. If they could not be handled effectively as voluntary clients, according to this argument, they ought not to be dealt with at all. Under no circumstances were they to be exposed to the same punitive, custodial programs as those confronting incarcerated delinquents.

Had punitive, custodial programs been unqualified successes in reclaiming juvenile offenders, it might have been different. But the evidence was not encouraging on this score, and the juvenile courts had no authority to assign status offenders to those kinds of programs.

THE NORMALIST'S APPROACH

Normalists[5] see status offenders as different from delinquents mainly because the Constitution and the Fifth Amendment protect the former but not the latter from custody in penal institutions. They point out that by granting judges very broad powers over juveniles, parens patriae has been on balance a destructive doctrine in the juvenile court. Status offenders, most of whom do not need court intervention let alone penal confinement, often have been confined with delinquents in detention centers and training schools and stigmatized unnecessarily. Since juvenile judges have used their discretionary powers unfairly, their authority over status offenders should be removed.[6]

---

[4]Andrews and Cohn's argument consisted of comparisons of the courts' handling of PINS cases with the handling of delinquents under the new law. As might be expected, PINS were dealt with basically in terms of their relationships within the family, whereas delinquents were dealt with in terms of their offense. When relationships were strained, or when the family itself was weakened, PINS were more likely than delinquents to be referred to court, to be detained, adjudicated, and given "regulating" dispositions. In terms of the standards of fairness usually upheld in the criminal courts, the juvenile court was not providing equal justice for status offenders.

Remarkably, Andrews and Cohn concluded from all this that juvenile courts could not predict which juveniles might benefit from court intervention and that even if they could, they could not provide them services effectively. They recommended that family court jurisdiction over PINS be abolished.

Their research would have been more to the point had it tested whether the family court was having beneficial effects on PINS (i.e., that PINS were more likely to mature into responsible, constructive adulthood under the family court's jurisdiction than when left to themselves).

[5]Smith et al. (1980: 121–122) were among the first to describe several different approaches to status offenders, and subsequently Malcolm Klein used the term *normalist* informally in his evaluation of the deinstitutionalization of status offenders.

[6]American legal reformers prefer to deal with defects in criminal justice agencies not by correcting their flaws as reformers elsewhere do but by restricting the discretion of criminal justice practitioners. Problems in law

Normalists believe that immature behavior in the home and school is simply part of growing up. Since most children go through it and grow out of it with few lasting problems, the juvenile court need not intervene in most such cases. Brief supportive counseling is often all that is needed.[7] The overreach of the juvenile court is nowhere displayed more clearly than in its hovering control of status offenders.

From the normalists' standpoint the key factor preventing misbehavior among juveniles is not the juvenile court and its programs but the close, informal relationships that grow up naturally between juveniles and parents, teachers, and peers. These relationships form a social web that envelops most juveniles and is the basis of constructive behavior at home and school. Such juveniles run very little risk of misbehavior.

From their standpoint the task of juvenile justice when confronting status offenders is (1) to evaluate the quality of their informal relationships and (2) to repair them where weakened. *Repair* in this case means involving constructive parents, siblings, teachers, neighbors, and peers in solving the problem.

Naturally, much depends on the goodwill of these people toward the juvenile, and one of the first steps in beginning crisis management is to relay the adolescent's point of view to his "web" (i.e., his parents, siblings, teachers, neighbors, and peers) and explain their feelings toward him. This process should help to patch up any breaches so that the juvenile can reestablish his niche in the web of relationships. Occasionally, this process of reconciliation breaks down and the only alternative is an out-of-home placement—a foster home, short-term shelter care, or a medium-term group home.

Sometimes juveniles themselves need a period of persuasion and reorientation before they can begin an effective negotiating process with their social webs, and involvement in multiple service centers, such as the YMCA, Youth Service Bureaus, or neighborhood centers, that combine organized recreation, group counseling, employment referrals, or academic tutoring may also be necessary. When the child is ready, overtures can begin and the process of reintegration can get underway.

Normalists believe that social service agencies are at best stopgap measures and are not replacements for the natural relationships that make up children's lives. They hope through intervention to restore the child to its usual social relationships and heal old wounds. Once this has been achieved, natural social processes can again exert their influences.

If used obtrusively, professional agencies or programs can have many unwanted side effects. Despite their best efforts, such programs disrupt a child's first line of defense against further misbehavior by removing it from its natural social web in favor of a residential program. Further, they introduce deviant children to other offenders and inadvertently help them forge antisocial alliances. Third, they may foster antiadult attitudes in children through institutionalized staff-inmate conflicts in older, routinized organizations. Finally, they breed a kind of manipulative dependency in which kids learn to display superficially cooperative attitudes in exchange for a variety of program benefits.

---

enforcement and adult corrections have been attacked in much this way. Such policies seem to stem from a pervasive fatalism regarding criminal justice shortcomings in America.

[7]California cut substantially the use of detention for status offenders by offering brief crisis-intervention counseling services to its 601 (status) offenders (Feeney, 1977). When it proved effective, several other states followed with similar services.

For these reasons normalists strongly urge a complete deinstitutionalization of status offenders (DSO). Status offenders should be diverted from secure detention and kept out of long-term custodial care at all costs.

The ability of Japan to hold down its delinquency rates relative to Western countries probably reflects the success of the Japanese in weaving a close web of informal relationships among children and their parents, teachers, neighbors, and police. Japan has few of the formal programs mentioned above because it has placed heavy emphasis upon strengthening the informal relationships in the child's social web. Even though it expects much from its teenagers at home and school, Japan's delinquency rate is minimal (see Chapter 10).

THE DEINSTITUTIONALIZATION OF STATUS OFFENDERS

The attempt to deinstitutionalize status offenders got underway, as we have seen, when New York drew a sharp distinction between status offenders and delinquents. It received an additional boost in 1974 when the federal Office of Juvenile Justice and Delinquency Prevention initiated a nationwide effort to take status offenders out of institutions by generously funding individual states to deinstitutionalize status offenders. As part of that effort Solomon Kobrin and Malcolm Klein were commissioned to evaluate these programs.

After carefully assessing eight community-based programs, scattered from coast to coast, for status offenders, they report (Kobrin and Klein, 1983: chapter 7) that the best predictor of a status offender's continued offending is his personal characteristics. Female and younger status offenders with many prior offenses were most likely to continue offending, but older male offenders whose father's occupational status was high and whose referral offense was possession of alcohol were less likely to recidivate. Least important in predicting further offending was the type of service furnished. Neither the kind of service offered nor the quality of the service staff made any systematic difference in the clients' subsequent offending.

With regard to drug offenders and runaways, however, there was evidence that long-term residential care (foster home or group home placement) was helpful (Kobrin and Klein, 1083: 267). Predatory offenders derived little benefit from any program.

Kobrin and Klein (1983: chapters 5 and 6) discovered in addition that the manner whereby the deinstitutionalizing effort was blended with the established judicial system powerfully affected the effectiveness of the program. Several of the projects made use of diagnostic screening centers to determine which kind of program was best suited to each child, and most developed crisis intervention counseling services and residential centers, as well as a variety of multiple service centers. In addition, a number made use of aggressive advocacy programs in which the youth's point of view was conveyed to key people in the web of relations.

In several cases the new structures and new methods of working with status offenders sparked bitter conflicts with more conservative juvenile justice groups in the community. For example, the evaluation centers and their assignments of children to programs drew the whole deinstitutionalization effort into power struggles with local judges and probation officers as to what kinds of program were best for the children and who was most qualified to provide them. Moreover, some centers adopted a confrontational posture toward the local juvenile justice system, and in the process further alienated the very groups whose cooperation they were seeking (Kobrin and Klein, 1983: 141–143). Finally, the new programs these DSO projects developed provoked bitter quarrels with social service agencies that were working with the same status offenders but using different methods (154). On the other hand, when key local juvenile justice groups agreed with the DSO effort and were in close sympathy with innovative approaches to that end, new programs thrived (Kobrin and Klein, 1983: chapter 5).[8]

ARE STATUS OFFENDERS REALLY DIFFERENT FROM DELINQUENTS?

Since status offenders have not violated the criminal code, they are not subject to the penal law. But they have violated the norms and rules governing juvenile conduct, and under parens patriae the courts have a mandate to assume guardianship over status offenders for their own welfare. The matter becomes largely a question of the court's ability to help status offenders.

How might its effectiveness be measured? Two distinct approaches are possible. Are the juvenile courts effective in correcting the conditions that brought the child to the attention of the court in the first place? Or, do they improve the child's chances of advancing into a constructive, fulfilling adulthood beyond what they would have been had the courts done nothing. Of course, both approaches need further specification, but they present two different ways of evaluating the juvenile court's effectiveness.

In the first case, the standard of comparison is the child's pathology upon admission to the program, and on this basis most therapeutic efforts, including even those of hospitals and medical doctors, would not be regarded as highly successful. Many patients improve without any intervention. But even where the patient is helped, often the symptoms are only relieved; the illness itself is not cured. In the second case, however, the standard of comparison is the child's likely course of behavior had nothing been attempted. On this basis most therapies would be seen as successful because the symptoms, though not entirely removed, are often diminished.

Should the juvenile court impose "treatment" upon status offenders when its effectiveness in the first sense is in doubt? Consider for a moment a child whose mental illness is incurable but whose behavior is self-destructive. Such a child deserves help under parens patriae when no one else can care for him, even though he is no threat to the community and there is no hope of restoring him to full mental clarity. Any court refusing help for such a child would certainly be blameworthy. The question is not whether the court's handling of the case can clear up the malady, but whether the child's overall situation is incrementally relieved by the court's intervention. Is the child with

---

[8]Henry McKay and Clifford Shaw were especially adroit in working with community groups and their informal authority structures in setting up their Chicago Area Projects in the 1930s. One of the factors that distinguished *their* Chicago Area Projects from postwar versions in the same areas was community support (see Schlossman et al., 1984: section III).

mental illness better off under the court's care than he would have been had he been left alone?

Consider a 14-year-old female status offender who strenuously resists the efforts of social service agencies to establish a foster family placement in favor of her self-indulgent desire to enjoy the city's nightlife. Her situation is perfectly analogous to the first example. If such a child steadfastly refused the advice of social service professionals, as seems likely, she risks drug addiction, prostitution, AIDS, and possibly early death. Does the juvenile court have a responsibility in such cases to intervene under parens patriae, even though the court's efforts accomplish little more than keeping the girl alive until she reaches young adulthood?

No one can be certain her fascination with the danger and excitement of the streets will ultimately wane, nor that placing her in a secure setting will not bring its own kind of antisocial attitudes and experiences. No one can say with confidence that a secure setting would be better for her than the streets.

But it is likely that in the majority of cases a secure placement, even though not a perfect placement, would be preferable to a life on the mean streets. The burden of proof should be on those who argue that the streets would be better.

The argument usually turns on whether the pathology itself was cured, or just moderated, whether the girl was cured of all interest in the streets by court intervention, or just some of her antisocial behavior was improved but not removed. The inability of the court to remove or cure status offenders' problems is viewed as its inability to help them. Andrews and Cohn (1977), for example, argued for abolition of the court on the basis that it could not foresee who would need what services and that its services were inadequate. But it would be better to compare the effects of court intervention with status offenders to their lives without court intervention. Although more may be harmed by court intervention than not, the question is, are they better off as a group than status offenders who are left to their own devices? This crucial question has not yet been answered definitively.

But a related question has been answered clearly. Do status offenders have a right to treatment? Yes they do! If juveniles are confined for treatment purposes, the court is obligated by the Eighth and Fourteenth Amendments (see *Martarella v. Kelley*, 349 F. Supp. 575, [S.D.N.Y., 1972]; *Morales v. Truman*, 364 F.Suppl 166 [Tex., 1973]) to make a good faith effort to provide appropriate treatment. Since status offenders are most likely to be confined for treatment purposes, the right to treatment applies most directly to them. Moreover, the treatment itself must be appropriate to the problem; that is, the treatment must be professionally recognized as appropriate. It need not guarantee success, but it must be recognized as sound by professionals in the field.

Although status offenders and delinquents are legally different, the juvenile court may still take custody of status offenders when conditions are threatening to the welfare of the child, and when the court can offer a program that holds some promise of helping. Fortunately, very few status offenders or their families reject the best efforts of social service professionals, and in most cases they are very willing to accept well-intentioned, sound advice. Thus, most status offenders and their families do not need coercive intervention, because they are willing to follow the advice of social service professionals. The legal difference between status offenders and delinquents does not mean that the juvenile court must leave status offenders alone. It means only that the court must be aware of its limits as well as its responsibilities toward status offenders.

The evidence is also clear regarding the behavior of status offenders in comparison with delinquents. Status offenders are much less likely to become chronic offenders (more than four offenses) than are delinquents (see Clarke, 1975; Kobrin, Hellum, and Peterson, 1980; but also Thomas, 1976). Indeed, a majority of them are never convicted of a second offense of any kind (see Clarke, 1975; Kobrin, Hellum, and Peterson, 1980: 226; but also Erickson, 1979). These children, in other words, seem to confirm the expectations of the normalists: Young people usually outgrow the problems of adolescence, and often a little patience is all they need.

A panel study of nearly 1200 junior high pupils in San Diego, for example, found that of 221 children who had been involved in status offenses in junior high school, 42 (19 percent) reported medium or high status offending in high school and only 2 (0.9 percent) reported medium or high delinquency in high school. A substantial number of these junior high school students were involved in both status offending and delinquency (39.7 percent) in high school, but a majority (56.7 percent) had either no further offenses or only status offenses to report in high school (see Weis, 1980: 68).

Although most status offenders show less likelihood of further offending than delinquents, they also include a small minority who commit mainly truancy, curfew, and liquor law violations and go on to repetitive delinquency and status offending. Such children are often male, older, and more advanced not only in terms of their delinquency but also in terms of their problems. They are more similar to delinquents than most status offenders and constitute a distinctive group within this broad category (Shelden, Horvath and Tracy, 1989). They may need humane, custodial care in much the same way a serious delinquent does. Such children have progressed further toward delinquency than most status offenders, and their attitudes about offending are more sophisticated. From their standpoint, the law and the juvenile justice system have lost legitimacy (see Matza, 1964). They believe most parents, courts, and police are as dishonest as most teenagers and do not deserve the respect or obedience of teenagers. Many of their friends reinforce these attitudes and include them in thefts, burglaries, fights, drinking bouts, and drug parties. Experience with positive, admirable adults and a vacation from their street peers may be needed before rehabilitation can get underway. Thus, the court may need to confine some advanced status offenders in custodial programs that can provide valuable experiences with adults while limiting contact with disturbing family members and delinquent friends.

Without authority to place such children in custodial programs, the court can do little until they have progressed to serious delinquency. Most status offenders do not develop in this direction, but some do, and juvenile judges must be alert to indicators of imminent chronic offending, estrangement from parents and teachers, and close relationships with other delinquents.

Normalists assume that such status offenders are rare and beyond the scope of the juvenile court anyway. From their standpoint, they should be handled informally by social agencies insofar as they receive any attention at all. Normalists would only take custody after they had become delinquent.

Others who favor a deterrent approach—the *Traditionalists*—believe that early intervention is the key to rechanneling advanced status offenders along positive paths.

They seek to break their links with delinquent friends, encourage constructive relationships with adult guardians and teachers, and counsel them on the advantages of stable careers, good family relationships, and constructive friends. According to the traditionalists, the parens patriae notion that the juvenile court should take custody of status offenders just as it does delinquents is still valid.

The treatment approach to these advanced status offenders, as outlined by the *Rehabilitationists,* also favors early intervention with advanced status offenders, but not so much to interrupt destructive relationships with adults and peers as to establish more wholesome activities, new routines, and new relationships with prosocial adults so that a broad foundation for constructive social attitudes, skills, and relationships can be set. Custody for its own sake as a method of deterring antisocial behavior may have some limited utility, but it should not be allowed to displace more positive, beneficial programs.

To facilitate the development of these programs and to give the juvenile court a greater range of dispositions, some have proposed the establishment of locally based Youth Service Bureaus (see Sherwood, 1972). As envisioned, Youth Service Bureaus assess the treatment needs of status offenders and minor delinquents, they invite local social service agencies to initiate community based programs for youths, and they assign children to these programs according to their needs. They serve as a clearinghouse for status offenders and minor delinquents in which each child is classified according to its needs and provided an appropriate treatment program in the community. The juvenile court has few resources to support treatment initiatives in the community, and a new agency such as the Youth Service Bureau is badly needed to assume such responsibilities (see Chapter 13).

But in practice, Youth Service Bureaus have run into serious difficulties. Often their local managers are not sympathetic with the views of older, more experienced professionals in the juvenile court and social agencies. Instead of facilitating their efforts, Youth Service Bureaus regularly find themselves in conflict with local professionals. Juvenile judges and the police resent their efforts to assign children to local treatment programs without considering the threats such children may present, and probation officers and treatment professionals resent their willingness to consider innovative or even antagonistic methods—youth advocacy, for example—in defiance of more traditional approaches utilized in the community. Without cooperation from local juvenile justice professionals, however, Youth Service Bureaus can serve no useful purpose, and a great many have just disappeared.

NEEDED: A VERSATILE COURT

All three of these approaches—the normalist, the traditionalist, and the rehabilitationist approaches—are commendable—but at different times with different kinds of youngsters. The normalists are correct when they observe that most status offenders will do well if left largely alone. The child's status offending has alerted him, his family, and his teachers to a problem, and the best course for the juvenile court is to encourage all three in devising and carrying out an effective plan. The court should make social service professionals available as need requires, but with these children and their parents it need not become coercive. They are already motivated to put their troubles behind them.

In following this perspective, California has made effective use of family crisis intervention with status offenders (Feeney, 1977). Counseling and brief family mediation can serve the needs of most status offenders and their families very well, while avoiding secure detention for most children.

The traditionalist's stance toward the advanced status offender also has something to recommend it. It is often true that advanced offenders must be made aware of their errors by some straight talk from the judge and, if necessary, confinement before gentler rehabilitative programs and counseling can be brought into play.[9] Once a child has softened his resistance to positive change, rehabilitationists can do their jobs more effectively. Traditionalists and rehabilitationists must work cooperatively, because delinquents and advanced status offenders may require custodial intervention coupled with skillful counseling and innovative treatment programs such as wilderness challenge programs.

The prevalent approach to status offending in the juvenile court today is the normalist perspective. The Institute of Judicial Administration and the American Bar Association have urged the states to adopt what amounts to a normalist policy toward status offenders.

As we have seen, the normalist approach works well for mild status offenders, but it often runs into difficulty particularly with female advanced status offenders who, though estranged from parents and school, have not yet become clearly involved in delinquency. Programming for such girls must be based upon voluntary cooperation. And since advanced status offenders are usually uncooperative with parents, teachers, or social service professionals, the court's inability to order cooperation may force her parents to leave the girl to her fate.

Cooperation under custodial conditions is not ideal, but at least the child's participation in a rehabilitative plan for a reasonable period can be assured.[10] Advanced male status offenders are more likely to commit delinquencies and do not usually pose a problem for normalist courts.

The traditional approach places heavy emphasis on custodial programs that are useful in focusing a youth's attention upon difficult problems, but such efforts amount to overkill with children whose parents and teachers are already willing (or at least can be persuaded) to help in coping with the child's difficulties. When informal groups such as the family and the school can be involved in the child's behalf, they are usually more effective than anything the juvenile justice system can provide. In such cases the judge's formal authority is usually unnecessary.

---

[9] The fact, for example, that members of the treatment group in Marguerite Warren and Ted Palmer's community treatment program received many more short term detentions than members of the control group can probably be explained by their parole officer's sensitivity to their need for "softening up." (See Lerman, 1975: chapter 3, for an alternative explanation.)

[10] Some will argue that self-improvement can only be effective when clients enter such programs voluntarily. That may be true, but millions of children are *compelled* everyday to attend school in the hope that despite their reluctance, they will get something out their education. We are not prepared to base their education upon their willingness to cooperate.

Custodial dispositions without a genuine commitment to the child's personal growth, however, can only make matters worse. Since custodial programs are useful primarily in providing a framework for rehabilitative programs, the rehabilitationist is a necessary partner in any venture down this path.

The juvenile court brings a unique blend of abilities to the juvenile justice system, and status offenders offer a complex challenge to the juvenile court. Unlike all other forums, the juvenile court can evaluate the problems of juveniles on the basis of keen insights into (1) adolescent psychology, (2) the Constitutional rights of juveniles, (3) the community's responsibilities toward its children, (4) the proper role of parents and relatives vis-a-vis growing teenagers, (5) the contributions of schools and peers to teenager's problems, (6) the subtle strengths and weaknesses among a wide variety of social welfare agencies, and (7) an appreciation of the community's fears and sensitivities. On this basis it estimates the best path for each child, whether delinquent or status offender. Since each child usually presents his own mosaic of problems, it is important that the court be allowed enough discretion to accomplish its purposes, whether punitive, facilitative, or rehabilitative. It is foolhardy to limit the court to just one approach.

No other forum that deals with children has the same breadth of expertise. Most other agencies represent only one or two strengths in dealing with children, whether legal or social welfare groups, and as a result some segments in the juvenile offender spectrum suffer in their hands. The breadth of the juvenile court's perspective is fundamental to its success as an institution.

But the court cannot be all things to all people. It is neither a punitive nor a treatment agency in its own right. It can only allocate children to other agencies. Its primary function is to weigh all aspects of a child's condition, and define an intelligent way of meeting its problems. If the juvenile court is taken out of the business of assessing status offenders, a similar agency will still be needed. This agency will face the same problems the court faces but with fewer skills and fewer alternatives. It will suffer the same complex problems but without the same breadth of remedies. Some such forum for assessing the issues of juvenile misbehavior is needed, and it is hard to imagine a more narrowly focused agency that could do it better. The court needs a variety of approaches to match the variety of its youngsters, and instead of limiting its perspective to one or another of the popular ones, it should maintain its broader jurisdiction so that all facets of the status offending problem can be handled effectively.

CONCLUSIONS

All this points to the need for competent, experienced, fair-minded judges and probation officers who can guide juvenile justice in serving the needs of status offenders and delinquents. In all honesty, however, disturbing evidence exists that juvenile justice is moving in the opposite direction.

During the pre–World War II period it was not uncommon in the juvenile court for court personnel to assign children to custodial institutions without considering whether other, better assignments might be advisable. Many young status offenders were assigned along with serious delinquents to custodial centers where their family or school problems received virtually no attention, while many serious delinquents without family or school problems were left in the community. Gradually, as a result of their inability to initiate treatment programs in the community (see Chapter 13) the juvenile courts began to depend heavily on custodial institutions with the result that ultimately their dispositions were suspected of being arbitrary and their procedures were drastically narrowed. The court's competence to deal with the full range of juvenile offenders was called seriously into question. Injustice in procedures and unfairness in dispositions, for example, were major factors in the *In re Gault* (387 U.S. 15 [1967]) decision.

To correct unjust routines that had crept into juvenile justice, changes in the juvenile law were imposed and adjustments in its jurisdiction were made. If the court could not maintain a commitment to justice and fairness within the framework of parens patriae, the doctrine itself must be limited. Eliminating status offenders from its jurisdiction was one answer. But nothing is an unalloyed good, and removing status offenders from the court's jurisdiction raises its own problems.

Families and schools need the support of the juvenile court to bolster their own efforts with their juveniles. Not only does the court give parents and teachers more confidence in their methods and goals, but it also conveys to the community that these institutions are essential to the well-being of juveniles.

We participate in a society that recognizes, even hallows, freedom for individuals, including juveniles. But freedom is only of benefit to those with plans for using freedom intelligently. Few juveniles have had time or experience enough to develop a sound direction in their own lives. But with no plan, freedom becomes an incoherent maze of unconnected decisions—some of which inevitably go wrong. Most juveniles need wise help in putting their lives together. Superficial impulse-ridden decisions abound, and their lives proceed all too often toward dead ends.

Parents and teachers have retreated from their traditional roles as socialization agents, and the moral development of juveniles has been left largely to peers. Now is *not* the time for the court to add to this flimsiness by limiting its own influence upon those who need it most—the status offenders. Now is the time for the juvenile court to find how best to apply its strengths to the problems of children. Surely the flaws of the juvenile court are not so profound that its jurisdiction over status offenders must be abandoned. Surely these flaws can be repaired so that status offenders can be served justly and effectively.

SUMMARY

Children and the family were early victims of industrialization, and status offenders were prominent in nineteenth century custodial institutions for wayward and delinquent children. Parens patriae was the doctrine under which cities and states took custody of wayward children, and in a series of appeals state supreme courts in Illinois and Pennsylvania affirmed its authority. But status offenders were held along with delinquents in most states, and by the 1950s it was not unusual to find status offenders and particularly female status offenders being held in custody longer than most delinquents.

When it became clear in the 1950s that juvenile custodial institutions were primarily punitive and not rehabilitative, parens patriae was no longer relevant to their situation, and status offenders were deinstitutionalized and decriminalized. They were for the most part normal teenagers encountering problems normal during adolescence. They required, therefore, minimal intervention.

The normalist approach to status offenders held that status offenders and their families could overcome most of their problems if provided, at most, crisis intervention. Intrusive social programs imposed by the juvenile court might even make matters worse. Custody was rarely if ever needed in dealing with status offenders, according to the normalists.

In behalf of this approach, deinstitutionalization was pressed forward in several states by establishing community-based programs for status offenders. The most important factor affecting the success of these programs was the depth of the child's problem. Where the problem was deep rooted, success was unlikely in community-based programs. Another factor was the skill with which these programs were blended with existing community-based programs. Where they were merged carefully with existing agencies and their philosophies, success was likely. But where the programs conflicted with existing community programs or with judicial philosophies, they were likely to fail.

Status offenders are clearly different from delinquents and deserve a different form of treatment. Most offend only once. Only a small minority go on to repetitive delinquency or advanced status offending, but such children may well need custodial intervention. The normalist philosophy does not recognize such children and their problems, but both the traditionalist approach and the rehabilitative approach do. Both would apply custodial measures as soon as the advanced nature of the child's problems became apparent. Traditionalists would stress the deterrent affect of institutionalization to encourage children to accept the family or school without serious resistance. Rehabilitationists, on the other hand, would apply such therapy as the case may require to reconcile the child, the family, or the school. All three approaches—the normalists, the traditionalists, and the rehabilitationists—probably have an insight into the problems of at least some portion of the status offender population. The challenge lies in finding the right approach for the right child. A versatile court is needed that can draw accurate distinctions among the several different kinds of status offenders and apply the relevant solution. Status offenders need a juvenile court that can adjust easily to the wide variety of juveniles that make up its caseload. Fastening on a single perspective in serving either status offenders or delinquents can severely undermine the versatility of the court.

REFERENCES

Andrews, R. Hale, Jr., and Andrew H. Cohn. 1977. "PINS Processing in New York: An Evaluation." In *Beyond Control.* Edited by Lee E. Teitelbaum and Aidan R. Gough. Cambridge: Ballinger Publishing Company.

Clarke, Steven H. 1975. "Some Implications for North Carolina of Recent Research in Juvenile Delinquency." *Journal of Research in Crime and Delinquency* 12, 1:51–60.

Erickson, Maynard L. 1979. "Some Empirical Questions Concerning the Current Revolution in Juvenile Justice." In *The Future of Childhood and Juvenile Justice.* Edited by LaMar T. Empey. Charlottesville: University of Virginia Press.

Feeney, Floyd. 1977. "The PINS Problem—A 'No Fault' Approach." In *Beyond Control: Status*

Offenders in the Juvenile Court. Edited by Lee F. Teitelbaum and Aidan R. Gough. Cambridge: Ballinger Publishing Company.

Garlock, Peter D. 1979. " 'Wayward' Children and the Law, 1820–1900: The Genesis of the Status Offense Jurisdiction of the Juvenile Court." *Georgia Law Review* 13, No. 2:342–447.

Hawes, Joseph. 1971. *Children in Urban Society.* New York: Oxford University Press.

Kobrin, Solomon, Frank R. Hellum, and John W. Peterson. 1980. "Offense Patterns of Status Offenders." In *Critical Issues in Juvenile Delinquency.* Edited by David Shichor and Delos H. Kelly. Lexington, Mass: Lexington Books.

Kobrin, Solomon and Malcolm Klein. 1983. *Community Treatment of Juvenile Offenders.* Beverly Hills: Sage Publications.

Lerman, Paul. 1975. *Community Treatment and Social Control.* Chicago: University of Chicago Press.

Matza, David. 1964. *Delinquency and Drift.* New York: John Wiley & Sons.

Schlossman, Steven, Gail Zellman, and Richard Shavelson, with Michael Sedlack and Jane Cobb. 1984. *Delinquency Prevention in South Chicago* Santa Monica, Calif.: Rand.

Shelden, Randall G., John A. Horwath, and Sharon Tracy. 1989. "Do Status Offenders Get Worse?" *Crime & Delinquency* 35, 2:202–216.

Sherwood, Norman. 1972. *The Youth Service Bureau.* Washington, D.C.: National Council on Crime and Delinquency.

Smith, Charles P., et al. 1980. *Reports of the National Juvenile Justice Assessment Centers: A Preliminary Assessment of the Status Offender and the Juvenile Justice System: Role Conflicts, Constraints, and Information Gaps.* Washington, D.C.: U.S. Department of Justice, Office of Juvenile Justice and Delinquency Prevention.

Tappan, Paul. 1946. "Treatment Without Trial." *Social Forces* 24:306–311.

——— . 1949. *Juvenile Delinquency.* New York: McGraw-Hill.

Thomas, Charles W. 1976. "Are Status Offenders Really So Different?" *Crime and Delinquency* 22:438–455.

Weis, Joseph G. 1980. *Reports of the National Juvenile Justice Assessment Centers: Jurisdiction and the Elusive Status Offender.* U.S. Department of Justice, Law Enforcement Assistance Administration, Office of Juvenile Justice and Delinquency Prevention, Washington, D.C.: U.S. Government Printing Office.

Chapter
8

Delinquency and Gender

This chapter is about delinquency and gender, but the emphasis will be on female delinquents. "It is not uncommon," Allison Morris (1987: 1) writes, "for criminology textbooks, even critical reviews, to contain nothing at all on women. . . . Criminology, like most academic disciplines, has been concerned with the activities and interests of men." Since women make up over fifty percent of the population, one might well ask: Why the neglect?

The answer is obvious, according to Morris. The field was founded by men and has been dominated by males ever since (see also Leonard, 1982). If nothing else, this would tend to focus theory and research away from women and their concerns in favor of the experiences and activities of males. Such an emphasis is easily justified: Females are less of a "problem" since they commit fewer and primarily petty crimes when compared with males (see Datesman and Scarpitti, 1980: 4–7).

Some authors believe this neglect has been detrimental to the study of crime and delinquency. Morris (1987: 2) suggests that prominent theories about crime are really theories about men's crime and therefore may not be valid when applied to women. She continues,

> A theory is weak if it does not apply to half of the potential criminal population; women, after all, experience the same deprivations, family structures and so on that men do. To study only men or boys to assess whether or not delinquency springs from, for example,

poverty, makes little sense. Similarly, to refer to the "subcultural style" of working-class boys as a solution to the problems of redevelopment, housing, depopulation and community solidarity begs an important question: how do working-class *girls* solve these problems? Theories of crime should be able to take account of both men's and women's behavior and to highlight those factors which operate differently on men and women.

In this chapter we will investigate female delinquency with three goals in mind: first, to describe what is currently known about the relationship of gender to the frequency and severity of offending; second, to highlight the areas of significant difference between girls and boys; and third, to identify promising theories that might account for the facts.

THE GENDER FACTOR IN DELINQUENCY

Published data on delinquency and gender are largely confined to statistics on arrests, court referrals, and dispositions. Each data source uncovers a different slice of reality, as we saw in Chapter 2. Nevertheless, none can tell us about true rates of delinquency (for either sex), for they cover only those juveniles who happened to get caught and officially processed. There are at least four other limitations as well: (1) Children of all ages are often lumped together; (2) historical analysis is hampered because information on gender was not routinely disseminated in the past; (3) the national picture is obscured by jurisdictional variations in legal definitions and in collection and reporting procedures; and (4) sampling is rarely representative because of the voluntary and costly nature of reporting juvenile court data.

Some of these problems are currently being addressed by state and federal agencies, and things should improve for future students of crime and delinquency. In the meantime, it is safe to say that the official picture has not changed much over the past few decades: *Girls are less delinquent than boys.* This is true in terms of prevalence (fewer girls are arrested than boys), incidence (delinquent girls commit fewer offenses than delinquent boys), and gravity of offense (girls are less likely to commit serious offenses, especially crimes of violence). Much the same situation exists in other countries (Morris, 1987: 20–21). Summarizing the research on gender and crime, Gottfredson and Hirschi (1990: 145) conclude that gender differences are invariant; that is, "men [and boys] are always and everywhere more likely than women [and girls] to commit criminal acts."

Differences between boys and girls are illustrated by nationwide arrest data compiled by the FBI for the years 1965 to 1986 (FBI, 1988). Arrest rates for boys are uniformly greater than those for girls, although the differences vary by age and by offense. The gap between male and female rates increases with age, largely because girls' delinquency involvement tapers off sooner than that of boys. As for the nature of offending, the gap between boys and girls is greatest for crimes of violence (robbery and weapons offenses in particular) and least for theft, drug abuse violations, and sex offenses (excluding rape).

Based on some of this FBI data, Table 8.1 shows the average of the age-specific ratios of male to female arrest rates for children 17 and under. The larger the number, the greater the difference in favor of males. Thus, the first number in the table (7.5) means that the 1966 Crime Index arrest rates for boys were on the average 7.5 times greater than those for girls across the various age categories.

Table 8.1 FACTORS BY WHICH MALE ARREST RATES EXCEED
FEMALE ARREST RATES, CHILDREN 17 AND
UNDER, SELECTED YEARS

Offense	1966	1971	1977	1983	1986
Crime Index*	7.5	5.0	4.3	4.2	4.0
Violent crimes**	12.5	11.4	10.5	10.1	9.8
Robbery	22.3	12.7	12.1	13.7	12.9
Weapon offenses	30.3	19.3	13.7	14.8	14.0
Burglary	29.0	20.0	15.3	13.6	11.5
Stolen property	14.6	12.1	10.3	9.2	10.0
Larceny-theft	3.2	2.8	2.5	2.7	2.7
Sex offenses***	2.8	4.0	8.9	13.9	11.1
Drug abuse	6.6	3.2	4.6	4.4	5.1

*Crime Index offenses are homicide and nonnegligent manslaughter, forcible rape, robbery, aggravated assault, burglary, larceny-theft, motor vehicle theft, and arson.

**Violent crime is homicide and nonnegligent manslaughter, forcible rape, robbery, and aggravated assault.

***Sex offenses exclude forcible rape.

Source: Compiled from Federal Bureau of Investigation, 1988. *Age-Specific Arrest Rates and Race-Specific Arrest Rates for Selected Offenses, 1965–1986.* Washington, DC.: Department of Justice.

The table confirms the greater frequency and seriousness of boys' delinquency involvement (as measured by arrests). However, the gender gap varies from one offense to another, and in some cases it narrowed over the period while in others it increased. On the whole, the gap between boys and girls narrowed substantially during the 1960s, then remained largely stable over the next 15 years. The most notable changes have occurred for burglary and for sex offenses. In the case of burglary, arrest rates for girls increased over the period while those of boys decreased. In the case of sex offenses, the reverse happened; girls' rates decreased while boys' rates increased (FBI, 1988). We will consider what these changes mean later in the chapter.

The FBI routinely collects information on arrests for the status offense of "runaway" but did not include such data in the recent publication from which Table 8.1 is compiled. Had it done so, the figures would certainly have stood out. This is because girls are arrested as runaways far more often than boys. In fact, runaway is the second most common offense for which girls are arrested after larceny-theft, which is primarily shoplifting. Indeed, arrests on runaway charges did not decline during the 1980s despite calls for more lenient treatment of status offenders (Chesney-Lind, 1987a). Equally important, the ratio of male to female arrests on runaway charges has remained largely unchanged since 1980, averaging 0.75 (FBI, 1981–1988).

Another official source of information on gender and delinquency is provided by the juvenile court. A recent national study shows that boys make up the bulk of court referrals: 1983 estimates put boys at over 80 percent of referrals for offenses against the person, against property, and involving drugs; over 70 percent of referrals for curfew and liquor law violations; and almost 60 percent of truancy referrals. Based on what we have already seen, it should come as no surprise that the only offense for which girls were referred to court more often than boys was for being a runaway.

Self-Report Studies

The official picture of gender and delinquency shows that girls are less delinquent than boys. This is largely confirmed by studies that tap self-reported delinquency. However, the differences between boys and girls are less marked for all but the most serious crimes.

Self-report studies confirm that the bulk of female offenses are petty crimes and status violations, but this is also true of boys. On the other hand, girls admit to aggressive delinquency, especially fighting, more often than one might suppose from official statistics. In a survey of 588 youths in Boston, Morash (1986) found that 37 percent of the girls admitted acts of aggression, albeit usually in the lower range of severity when compared with the violence of aggressive boys. Some gang studies have also found that girls do many of the same things boys do, including fighting (e.g., Campbell, 1984, 1986).

Gender comparisons of chronic delinquents show that at the high end of criminal involvement, girls sometimes surpass boys in self-reported incidence rates. Among the 128 chronic offenders interviewed by Cernkovich, Giordano, and Pugh (1985), larger proportions of girls than boys admitted that they frequently (i.e., two to three times a week) committed theft, robbery, hard drug sales, breaking and entering, and aggravated assault. One should not make too much of this, however, for the proportions involved were small, and chronic delinquents represent a small proportion of all delinquents. Girls, like boys, are most often sporadic delinquents who mostly commit petty offenses.

GENDER AND OFFICIAL REACTIONS TO DELINQUENCY

Are boys and girls treated similarly when their delinquency comes to the attention of authorities? For example, is the delinquency of girls more (or less) likely to be officially recorded than that of boys? And are girls treated more harshly than boys once they are arrested?

One way to answer the question about official recording is to consider how well self-report rates of delinquency correlate with official rates for each sex. Other things being equal, if more boys than girls admit committing offenses (a question of prevalence), more boys than girls should have official records. And, if individual boys admit committing more offenses than do individual girls (a matter of incidence), those boys should be more likely to accumulate an official record for the offenses in question. In short, the closer the correspondence between self-report and official records, the less the likelihood of bias or discrimination at the initial stage of official reaction.

Robert Sampson (1985) examined this issue using a sample of 1214 males and 398 females living in Seattle, Washington. As we would expect, he found crime was less prevalent among girls than boys, and serious crime was much less common. On the question of correspondence between self-report and official records, he found no evidence of gender discrimination or bias in either prevalence or incidence. He warns, however, that the results might not generalize to other jurisdictions. (We face this problem whenever findings are based on only one jurisdiction or population.)

Official processing of juvenile offenders consists of various steps: referral to court, prosecution, judicial hearing, and court disposition. The number of offenders passing through each step successively declines as cases are dismissed or removed from juvenile court jurisdiction. Of the estimated 1,247,000 cases entering the nation's juvenile courts in 1983, less than half made it to a court disposition (Snyder and Finnegan, 1987: 11). Gender differences, of course, could emerge at any stage.

Using contents of the National Juvenile Court Data Archive, Snyder and Finnegan (1987) found some important differences in the processing of girls and boys. First, girls were three times more likely than boys to be referred to court for *status* offenses: Only 12 percent of boys were referred for status offenses, compared with 34 percent of girls. Second, girls were nearly twice as likely as boys to be referred to the court by nonpolice sources, usually parents and schools. Third, girls charged with status offenses were more likely than boys charged with such offenses to be incarcerated while being processed through the system. This resulted from two things: (1) runaways had the highest rates of detention among status offenders, and they comprised a much larger proportion of the female than male status offenders; and (2) liquor law violations had low rates of detention yet comprised a much larger proportion of the male status offense cases (Snyder and Finnegan, 1987: 25). When offense categories were looked at individually, boys were usually more likely than girls to be detained during processing, although differences were small for most offenses.

Arrest, jail, and prison data show that females who enter the sanctioning system are more likely than males to have been involved in status, property, or drug offenses (Bureau of Justice Statistics, 1988: 46). However, since these offenses also make up the bulk of male crimes (see also Canter, 1982), one could argue that women are being treated more harshly than men. "The difference is not in the behaviour of the sexes, but in society's response to that behaviour" (Morris, 1987: 95).

This sort of argument deserves serious attention and is often incorporated in the charge that criminal justice authorities actively discriminate against women and girls (e.g., Heidensohn, 1985; see also Morris, 1987: 94–100). McCarthy and Smith (1986) have reviewed much of the available literature on the judicial processing of juveniles and conclude that the findings are mixed. Their own study of family court records on 649 delinquency referrals found no gender differences in dispositions at various stages of the process. Unfortunately, this study did not include referrals on status charges and therefore cannot address the argument that it is precisely in the realm of status offenses that girls are singled out for sanctions. A careful study that included status offenders is by Datesman and Scarpitti (1980). Girls who committed status offenses did receive harsher dispositions than boys. This was especially true for repeat offenders and those accused of "ungovernability" and running away.

The "girls receive harsher treatment for lesser crime" argument is taken up by Meda Chesney-Lind (1987a, 1987b, 1988), who believes the condition has existed for decades, if not centuries. During the period 1929 to 1930 in Hawaii, she notes, over 80 percent of the girls referred to court were charged with "immorality" or "waywardness." In the early days of America's first juvenile court in Chicago, half the delinquent girls but only one-fifth of the delinquent boys were sent to reformatories (Chesney-Lind, 1987b: 2). During the eighteenth and nineteenth centuries women, not just girls, suffered much for petty crimes. Citing work by Heidensohn (1968), Chesney-Lind (1986: 83) describes the transportation to Australia of maids, servants, and laundresses convicted of petty (and often first) offenses:

> The numbers of women transported for these offenses are sobering. Between 1787 and 1852, no less than 24,960 women, fully a third of whom were first offenders, were sent to relieve the "shortage" of women in the colonies. They were shipped in rat-infested holds where the death rate in the early years was as high as one in three and where women were systematically raped and sexually abused at the hands of the ships officers and sailors. Their arrival in Australia was also a nightmare: no provision was made for the women, and they were forced to turn to prostitution to survive.

Some studies from abroad also indicate that females at the low end of delinquency fare worse than males when it comes to official reactions (for reviews see Chesney-Lind, 1987a; Morris, 1987: 97–100). Of particular interest is the finding that females are more likely to lose their freedom. This has been recently confirmed in England in a study sponsored by the Home Office (similar to the U.S. Department of Justice). In 1985, convicted men were twice as likely as convicted women to get a noncustodial community service sentence, and women who reached the higher levels of prison sentences did so by virtue of an accumulation of minor crimes rather than by committing serious crime (Jackson and Smith, 1987).

Deinstitutionalization

Some people might object that the picture we have drawn is overly pessimistic and ignores recent significant decreases in the proportion of youth who are processed through the juvenile courts for status offenses. Indeed, between 1975 and 1983 the number of status offense cases handled by the nation's juvenile courts declined by 39 percent; in addition, the proportion of status cases involving detention prior to final disposition declined from 40 percent to 11 percent (Snyder and Finnegan, 1987). These declines are directly attributable to the 1974 Juvenile Justice and Delinquency Prevention Act, which called for greater leniency in dealing with status offenders and less use of secure detention. States that did not adopt these goals risked losing federal funds, and this threat helped make *deinstitutionalization* of status offenders a national strategy.

Some experts believe deinstitutionalization was doomed from the start. For example, Charles Logan and Sharla Rausch (1985) point out that it makes little sense to have deinstitutionalization without a corresponding *decriminalization* of status offenses. So long as the offenses remain on the books, judges are being asked to enforce laws that have no teeth. On the other hand, the goals of deinstitutionalization are undermined so long as status offenders are processed by the criminal justice system, which is coercive and repressive almost by definition. Hence there can be no effective deinstitutionalization without a corresponding *divestiture*, where responsibility for handling "problem" (but noncriminal) children is placed outside the criminal justice system.

Even with decriminalization and divestiture it is unlikely that deinstitutionalization will work if authorities (and parents) believe problems such as incorrigibility, running away, and ungovernability cannot be solved in normal environments such as family and school. Another place will be found to house these problem children. Paul Lerman (1982) and others (Schwartz, Jackson-Beeck, and Anderson, 1984) have argued that decreases in the numbers of status offenders housed in criminal justice facilities during the seventies and eighties were offset by increases in the numbers of juveniles held in facilities under control of the child welfare, mental health, and chemical dependency systems.

A growing privatization of juvenile justice has also been taking place, with insurance companies, parents, and even the state contracting with private agencies and groups to house problem children. The result is not a relaxing of control but an extension of control with less public oversight (Lemert, 1981; Cohen, 1985; Whitehead and Lab, 1990: 320–321). Alcohol and drug treatment, all sorts of therapy organizations, and other forms of medicalized "community control" are taking in more and more problem children, many of whom would have been processed as status offenders a decade ago, if at all (see Polk, 1987). Far from meeting the goals of deinstitutionalization, there is evidence that these programs actually involve more intensive supervision and control than traditional detention (Lerman, 1982).

A counterargument is perhaps that most commitments to private facilities are not court ordered but voluntary. However, whether a commitment is considered voluntary or not depends on who you ask. The children being committed may feel they have little choice in the matter even though police and courts were not involved. The fact that it is a child's parents who define her as ungovernable or "difficult" and turn to outside help does not make a commitment voluntary. The following case illustrates:

> Sarah is a 16 year old girl who lives with her parents in a small community. She is bright, and, when she applies herself, is a good student. Sarah has no history of serious delinquency or chronic status offense behavior. Sarah does not get along with her parents. They argue and fight constantly. Her father, who is a prominent university administrator, is angry and embarrassed over the fact that Sarah dresses "punk." She wears "weird" clothes, heavy bright makeup and colors her hair orange. Her father is upset over the fact that when Sarah is out with her friends, who also dress "punk," everyone knows who she is and more particularly, who her family is.
>
> Sarah's parents placed her in a psychiatric unit of a large private hospital. She was admitted for being unmanageable and emotionally disturbed. She stayed in the hospital for a month and a half and was released. When she returned home, she continued to dress "punk" and associated with her old friends.
>
> Some time later, Sarah's parents talked her into going to Minnesota with them for three days of "educational testing." They flew to Minnesota, rented a car, and, before even checking into a hotel, drove to the facility where the testing was to take place. As soon as they drove into the driveway, Sarah knew that this was not a school. She refused to get out of the car while her parents spent several hours inside talking to administrative staff. Finally, several men surrounded the car and Sarah realized that she had no alternative but to go inside. Sarah was kept for more than 9 months in this psychiatric facility which, to this day, she still refers to as the "looney bin." [Schwartz, Jackson-Beeck, and Anderson, 1984: 382–383]

Although appropriate national and state data are virtually nonexistent, estimates suggest that "wayward," "runaway," and "ungovernable" girls will be found disproportionately among those under privatized control (Costello and Worthington, 1981–1982, in Chesney-Lind, 1987a). This is not surprising when we consider that most people take the behaviors in question to mean there has been a breakdown in familial control. It also fits the idea that girls "need" different treatment than boys, especially "protection" and supervision (see Figueira-McDonough, 1987). A study of detention practices at one secure facility in England illustrates the emphasis on protection (Morris and Wilkinson, 1983). Over the course of a year, 8 of 32 girls admitted to the facility were detained for delinquency, the rest for running away and a variety of stereotypical problem behaviors. When social workers were asked to explain why they had recommended secure placement, the reasons "in most cases" were protective (cited in Morris, 1987: 95).

- "She was so vulnerable. . . . We didn't know where she was, who she was with."
- "It was for her own safety."
- "She was going to kill herself; it was real, not attention-seeking."

The strategy of deinstitutionalization has been undermined by yet another recent trend: the increasingly hard line taken by the Reagan and Bush administrations and by many state and local authorities in their dealings with juvenile offenders. Behavior previously termed "incorrigible" or "wayward" is being redefined as criminal at a time when courts are taking a tougher line (Curran, 1984). Offenses previously ignored or trivialized are now being treated as "real" crimes. In one suburban community, for example, runaways who break into their parent's home and steal so they can stay away longer are now charged with burglary (Mahoney and Fenster, 1982). Such practices inevitably raise the felony offense rates of girls, because it is girls who are singled out as runaways.

THREE IMPORTANT QUESTIONS

Our review of the data on gender and delinquency leaves us with three important questions:

1. Why are girls less delinquent than boys?
2. Why are girls treated more harshly than boys for lesser offenses?
3. Do we need a special theory to explain the delinquency of girls?

The remainder of the chapter will address these issues.

Why Are Girls Less Delinquent Than Boys?

One of the persistent themes in the social and behavioral sciences is that gender differences in behavior are influenced by biological differences between the sexes. But no one seems sure about the amount and direction of that influence. Even Cesare Lombroso, who spoke of "born criminals" and believed that females were less advanced evolutionarily than males, was willing to concede that biological impulses could be actuated or constrained by the environment, and females were not exceptional in this regard (Lombroso and Ferrero, 1895). Nevertheless, the idea that gender differences in behavior are biologically based remains an influential theory.

The study of children is important for the biological perspective, since biological influences should appear early in life and pinpointing them is harder once socialization is underway. That very difficulty probably explains why early sociological theories often left room for the influence of innate factors in the explanation of delinquency. Thus, W. I. Thomas (1925: 168–172) proposes a social role theory of delinquency, and then suggests that males are "inherently" aggressive and females "inherently" acquiescent.

The most comprehensive review of research on the biological force in crime and delinquency is by Wilson and Herrnstein (1985: 104–125). Their perspective is sociobiological, meaning that biology and society interact to influence behavior. Recognizing that the largest and most persistent gender differences are found in rates of violent crime, their conclusion is basically that girls are constitutionally less inclined to aggression, and this condition is reinforced by socialization.

The direct evidence for a constitutional difference in aggressive temperament consists mainly of findings on sex hormones. At best it is equivocal, as Wilson and Herrnstein (119) admit. Higher levels of male hormones (androgens) such as testosterone have been found among some aggressive prisoners, and some clinical studies have shown that injections of female hormones (estrogens) eliminated aggressive behavior in violent rapists. However, research is still in its infancy, and results will remain questionable until more controlled experiments are done with males and females whose hormonal levels are measured prior to, during, and after commission of aggressive acts. Needless to say, this sort of experimentation is beset with practical and ethical difficulties.

No less controversial are the studies purporting to show a connection between menstruation and crime. The argument is this: during the menstrual cycle, especially its early phase, many women experience an emotional "down," and feelings may turn hostile. Some studies (reviewed by Wilson and Herrnstein, 1985: 120–121) suggest that at these times women are more susceptible to crime. Indeed, one author (Marsh, 1981) goes as far as to suggest that 80 percent of all female crime is committed during the menstrual cycle.

Of course, menstruation theories of crime are hardly applicable to prepubescent girls, and in any case they don't address gender differences. But considering that menstruation continues for many years, one fact about gender differences hardly fits the menstruation argument: The gap between male and female rates of serious crime *increase* during adolescence, and female rates drop off earlier than male rates do—decades before menopause. Morris (1987: 50–51) suggests another thought: It is not menstruation *per se* that affects women's behavior, but its social construction. People come to believe that menstruation *causes* behavioral problems and apply that explanation even to murder. Morris cites cases where magistrates let murderers off on the grounds that they were menstruating at the time of the crime.

Socialization and Gender   When we start talking about how other people react to behavior we enter the domain of socialization, the process by which individuals learn the ropes of living among others. No matter whether sex differences have biological roots (and certainly some do), if children of different sexes are treated differently by parents, peers, teachers, and other authority figures, they will come to see themselves differently. Through this process they come to adopt a *female* identity or a *male* identity, as the case may be, and their behavior reflects it.

Use of the word *gender* as opposed to *sex* acknowledges the importance of socialization in distinguishing between the sexes. Theories using socialization to explain why girls are less delinquent than boys come in various forms but boil down to assertions that rule-violating behavior is an expected result of growing up male, but it is an indication of failed socialization in females.

In many societies, for many centuries, the conventional imagery of the "proper" female describes a person who is passive, demure, nurturing, acquiescent (to males), and dependent (on males). Males, on the other hand, are active, aggressive, authoritative, and independent. Males take risks, females shouldn't; males don't need (and wouldn't accept) much supervision, females do (and will); males look for excitement and adventure, females look for love and lasting relationships; males are competitive and confrontational, females cooperative and empathetic; males are preoccupied with sexual conquest, girls with having a family.

These are stereotypical images, of course. But as indicators of criminal propensity they certainly favor boys over girls, and to that extent they match the high end of delinquency involvement. They also match a lot of what we know about gender differences in attitudes and in parental control. Girls *are* less likely to take risks (e.g., Hagan and Palloni, 1988); girls *are* less concerned with physical prowess (e.g., Morash, 1988); girls *are* more empathetic and caring than boys (e.g., Morash, 1983, 1988); girls *are* more interested in maintaining relationships (e.g., Morris, 1964; Cernkovich and Giordano, 1987); girls *are* more likely to feel shame and guilt when they offend others (e.g., Morris, 1964); girls *are* more closely supervised and controlled (e.g., Thrasher, 1927, and numerous studies since).

Consistent with these gender differences, studies show that females overestimate and males underestimate the legal risks of delinquency and crime (see Richards and Tittle, 1981; Lanza-Kaduce, 1988). Other studies have shown that females are less willing to steal than males are when the amount involved increases (Farrington and Knight, 1979). This may reflect a sense of increased risk or danger, but might just as well reflect concern for the victim. In any event, these gender-differentiated attitudes imply that the gap between male and female crime rates increases along with the seriousness of offenses. As we have seen, this is exactly what available data show.

Opportunities and Gender   The greater supervision and control of girls (and women generally) restricts their routine participation in activities that are open to males, and therefore the experiences and opportunities that may lead to crime. Furthermore, as long as girls remain "housebound" and schooled for mothering, they will not learn how to "make it" in what is essentially a man's world, except in the limiting contexts of marriage and "women's work." In essence, women become auxilliaries in a man's world, and it should come as no surprise that this is true regardless of the legality of their activities. For example, students of delinquent gangs have documented an auxilliary role for girls—as helpers, girlfriends, and lookouts (Thrasher, 1927; Klein, 1971; Campbell, 1984). Females are excluded from full participation not only because they are more closely supervised but also because their socialization (unlike that of males) does not emphasize competition and exploitation (Schwendinger and Schwendinger, 1985; Messerschmidt, 1986). They are also excluded because of simple sexism, as a recent study showed. Darrell Steffensmeier and Robert Terry (1986) questioned 49 experienced male thieves about the kinds of attributes they considered valuable in crime. The most important ones were trustworthiness, physical strength, being calm and cool, emotional stability, reliability, and having endurance. In comparison to men, women were perceived as more likely to lack these qualities.

Some authors believe that important social changes are improving opportunities for women, including the opportunity to commit crime. The expansion of Western economies has drawn many women into the labor force and out of the home, and the women's liberation movement has been an important force in the quest for equality between the sexes. The result, Adler (1975) and Simon (1975) believe, has been a convergence of gender roles as many of the experiences and opportunities previously reserved for males (and a few "lucky" or "deviant" females) open to more and more females. According to Adler, a "virilization" of women is taking place, and the new masculine female will become less distinguishable from her male counterpart in all areas of life, including crime. The changes, because they affect home life and socialization, presumably filter down to young girls as well. This "liberation/opportunity" thesis predicts that the crime rates of women and girls will both increase and broaden to include new offenses.

The theory has not stood up well under empirical scrutiny. Specific tests of the virilization (or "masculinity") hypothesis have found no support in studies of girls' delinquency (e.g., Cullen, Golden, and Cullen, 1979; Thornton and James, 1979). And Giordano and Cernkovich (1979) found that girls who expressed more liberated attitudes tended to be *less* delinquent than those who conformed to traditional gender roles. A similar finding was reported by James and Thornton (1980) in their study of Nashville youth. Figueira-McDonough (1986), on the other hand, suggests that the impact of liberated attitudes may differ with the kind of school environment girls are exposed to: The more traditional and restrictive the environment, the greater the pressures for liberated girls to deviate.

The lack of support for gender equality theories of crime and delinquency lends credence to the idea that the underlying causes of criminality may be the same for both males and females (Steffensmeier, Allan, and Streifel, 1989). Those females who enjoy a wider range of social roles and who escape the chains of poor education and unemployment experience the same kinds of benefits as their male counterparts: greater self-esteem, reduced stress, a steady income, and more to lose from nonconformity.

As for the new opportunities around which the theory revolves, most scholars have followed Smart (1979) and Leonard (1982) in arguing that there has been little real change. Females are still more likely to hold low-paying jobs that are often auxilliary to the "more important" and better paid jobs of men. Morris (1987: 72) suggests that many women actually have less freedom today than 40 years ago. They are expected to contribute to family income, and yet childcare facilities are woefully inadequate. This is particularly burdensome on young single mothers, many of whom are still teenagers.

Messerschmidt (1986: 72–76) reveals another way that contemporary females who work outside the home actually have less freedom, especially if they also have children. Such women inevitably work longer hours since they are now subject to the double burden of wage labor *plus* housework and childcare. Messerschmidt finds no evidence that boyfriends, brothers, or husbands are taking up the slack in household chores and childcare. In many families where mothers work, it is the daughters, not the sons, who take on added responsibilities.

With more mothers working outside the home, children are less subject to parental supervision, and some observers believe this will increase delinquency, especially among girls. Studies indicate that girls are subject to more supervision than boys and that they are more strongly influenced by *maternal* supervision (Hill and Atkinson, 1988). Girls who report less maternal supervision (or difficulties in their relationships with their mothers) also report more delinquency (see also Riley, 1986).

Power-Control Theory of Gender and Delinquency   John Hagan and his colleagues (1985, 1987) have developed a "power-control" theory of delinquency that links parental control to the exercise of power in explaining gender differences. In traditional, *patriarchal* families, males hold the power and control the destinies of family members, especially wives and daughters. Mothers stay at home and are responsible for the routine supervision and discipline of their children. However, because fathers hold power within the family and control mothers economically through their labor outside the home, sons (in emulation of their fathers and in preparation for the adult male role outside the home) are left freer to deviate and to take risks, while daughters are subject to more supervision and control. Thus, in patriarchal families, sons have more power and are subject to less control, while daughters have less power and are subject to more control.

The greater power and freedom granted sons results in more male than female delinquency. But while *all* males are freer to deviate than females, some males are freer than others. Those with the greatest freedom to deviate are males with the greatest power, which means they are subject to the least control by other males. Needless to say, the power to control others is distributed unevenly in the class structure, with more at the top than at the bottom. In other words, delinquency rates should be greater among higher-class males. In this way, Hagan brings gender and class together, predicting that persons who are both male *and* members of the highest ("employer") class will exhibit the highest rates of delinquency; those who are female and in the lowest ("surplus population") class should exhibit the lowest rates.

Hagan's survey of 458 adolescents in Toronto generally confirmed the theory: Those reporting the greatest delinquency involvement were higher-class males. However, the data also showed that the effects of gender declined with each step down the class hierarchy. In other words, the gender differences in delinquency were greatest in the employer class and least in the surplus population class. In fact, there were no significant differences in the self-reporting of delinquency among boys and girls from the lowest class. A child's membership in a family with unemployed or underemployed parents overwhelmed the effects of sex.

Freedom from parental control proved to have a significant impact on gender differences both within and between social classes. The greater the freedom enjoyed by girls, the less the difference between boys and girls in their rates of delinquency. The deterrent impact of maternal control was greater than that of paternal control, especially for girls, and the authors suggest this is due to its effect on "taste for risk" and on the perceived risk of being punished. Males, more so than females, are taught to value risk taking, and this encourages a lower perceived risk of being punished. The authors conclude that "males are apparently more delinquent than females in the employer class because they are less controlled by their mothers and less likely to perceive the risks of getting punished as threatening (Hagan, Gillis, and Simpson, 1985: 1173).

In a subsequent paper (Hagan, Gillis, and Simpson, 1987), the concept of class was refined to include the relative power of mothers and daughters outside the home. The authors recognize that many mothers work outside the home and believe that authority derived from work bears upon dominance and control at home. Households in which both mothers and fathers have authority at work are called "balanced," and the authors expect to find more egalitarian relationships in such households than in "unbalanced" families. Unbalanced families are ones in which the father has authority at work, but the working mother does not, and ones in which the mother does not work outside the home at all. Delinquency predictions are then as follows: Girls who live in balanced households will be treated more like boys than girls in unbalanced households, hence be subjected to less control and encouraged to develop a taste for risk.

Published applications of power-control theory have so far been restricted to common forms of delinquency, for example, petty theft, simple assault, and property damage. The theory is not offered as an explanation of gender differences in status offending or in serious, violent delinquency (but see Hagan, Gillis, and Simpson, 1990: 1035, for references to as yet unpublished work that extends power-control theory to a wider range of crimes and delinquencies). The authors believe that class, gender, and perceptions of risk may relate quite differently to these forms of delinquency. In addition, they cite methodological problems in the case of serious delinquency. For example, the prevalence of offending is relatively low and concentrated among males at the lower end of the social-class scale. To generate enough variation in rates of offending it would be necessary to interview a huge sample.

Chesney-Lind (1987a: 20) has a more fundamental objection to power-control theory. In the first place, she calls it a "not-so-subtle-variation on the earlier 'liberation' hypothesis: Now a mother's liberation causes daughter's crime." Second, she notes that recent increases in labor force participation have not been accompanied by increases in girls' delinquency rates. During the past decade, when both female labor force participation and the number of female-headed households grew, rates of female delinquency remained the same or declined.

Notwithstanding these various objections, power-control theory constitutes an important attempt to identify sources of variation in the gender ratio in juvenile delinquency. As with all promising theories, more tests will probably lead to further refinements, and in this manner we shall move closer to understanding gender differences in delinquency and crime.

Why Are Girls Treated More Harshly Than Boys?

We saw earlier that girl delinquents are treated more harshly than boy delinquents. For example, a higher proportion of girls are sent to training schools, girls are more likely than boys to be referred to juvenile court for status offenses, and girls are incarcerated more often than boys when they have a record of minor offenses.

Even in states widely believed to have enlightened criminal justice policies, girls fare worse than boys. Consider Minnesota. In 1986, 3941 juveniles were detained in *adult* jails and lockups. Females under age 18 comprised nearly a quarter of the incarcerated juveniles. Although most of the children detained had committed relatively minor crimes, girls were twice as likely as boys to have been charged with status offenses (Schwartz, Harris, and Levi, 1988).

One prominent explanation of gender disparities in reactions to delinquency has come out of feminist literature. The harsher treatment of girls is believed to result from two processes—the sexualization and medicalization of delinquency (see Chesney-Lind, 1973; Hancock, 1981). The argument is as follows: The acts for which girls are often referred to authorities (incorrigibility, running away, waywardness, immorality) are "sexualized" because they are considered evidence of sexual misconduct even though no sexual behavior may actually have been involved; in turn, the sexual deviance is seen as evidence of a problem in need of "treatment." In contrast, sexual activity is expected of boys (hence is not really misconduct at all), and it even defines a "healthy" boy.

Traditional patriarchal rules dictate that girls who misbehave sexually must be punished (with or without "treatment"). Parents, teachers, and other authority figures are thus encouraged to treat the problem seriously. And the laws are cleverly written (almost always by men) so that all areas of sexual behavior may be classified as delinquent or criminal when engaged in by girls or women. In this way any female behavior remotely connected with sex becomes something that legal officials are authorized to detect and punish.

The medicalization of problem behavior further ensures that girls will lose freedoms more often than boys who engage in similar behavior. Many states have moved to decriminalize status offenses such as promiscuity and incorrigibility, but the behaviors in question are still classified as problem behaviors requiring social control. More and more, that control takes the form of medical treatment of one sort or another under either state or private sponsorship. The fact that proportionately more girls are found in such treatment programs indicates that traditional patriarchal values are still strong. Considering that such treatment is rarely, if ever, the choice of the "patient," girls, not boys, suffer more because of it.

Chesney-Lind (1988) calls this kind of justice *paternalistic* in that girls are considered in need of care, protection, supervision, and control. The state assumes the role of parent. For their part, parents contribute to a double standard of justice by initiating complaints about daughters more often than about sons. And there is evidence from at least one study (Johnson, 1986) that complaints about girls from female-headed families are much more likely to receive official attention than complaints about other children. Undoubtedly, the authorities feel that girls raised in female-headed families couldn't possibly be getting sufficient parental control.

Chesney-Lind (1988) reviews studies that describe another side to the double standards of juvenile justice: Females who are incarcerated are often housed under tighter security, are permitted fewer privileges (e.g., phone calls, exercise, work release), and are more isolated than their male counterparts. To be sure, this often reflects the more limited facilities available for incarcerating females. But it also increases the harshness of the detention experience and may increase a girl's vulnerability to sexual assault by guards or other male adults with access to them.

Underlying the harsher treatment of girls is a tradition of sexism in criminal justice—itself a reflection of sexist traditions in the larger society—and throughout the history of Western civilization (Rafter and Natalizia, 1982). Simply put, girls (and females generally) are not accorded the same treatment as boys (and males generally) because they are not considered their equal. Considering that girls commit far less crime than boys, and usually less serious crime at that, their harsher treatment at the hands of authorities must be especially galling to women. In protecting sexuality as a male preserve, furthermore, parents and judicial authorities play into the hands of traditional patriarchal values and thus delay any significant moves toward dismantling the double standard of justice.

In criminology, more theoretical and research work needs to be done that will further our knowledge of what is happening to young women in the arms of the law and that will link our explanations of the phenomenon to broader theories of gender inequality. There seems to be a general agreement among feminist authors that while many of the ills of the system have been amply documented, solutions rest on destroying the roots of sexism in systems of domination and control.

Do We Need a Special Theory to Explain the Delinquency of Females?

We have seen in this chapter that there are significant gender differences in crime and delinquency. Not only are females less likely than males to commit serious offenses, but when they do commit offenses, they tend to do so less often than males and to end their careers in crime earlier. In addition, the female delinquency that most often comes to light through the intervention of authorities (including parents and school officials) is more likely to represent violations of patriarchal authority relations (running away, incorrigibility, promiscuity) than is the official delinquency of boys.

Despite these differences, Allison Morris (1987: 65) believes that similar delinquent motivations probably exist for both sexes—for example, anger, poverty, excitement, addiction, and all sorts of personal problems. Where some writers (e.g., Carlen, 1985) argue that the crime and delinquency of females represent purposive strategies of survival in the face of powerlessness and sex discrimination, Morris points out that most females still do not turn to crime. And Leonard (1982: 191) observes that a theory of female criminality linked to relative powerlessness must still account for the apparently contradictory fact that females are labeled criminal relatively rarely.

When criminologists focus on the gender gap in crime and delinquency, they inevitably look for ways that males and females differ, hoping that some of these differences will explain differences in criminality. Such explorations typically try to establish first whether the factors known to be associated with male delinquency and crime are also associated with female delinquency and crime. Usually they are: Girls with delinquency records, like boys with delinquency records, are more likely to have delinquent friends, are more likely to come from backgrounds of poverty and stress, and are more likely to have experienced discipline problems at home and in school.

This does not suggest that female delinquency requires a special theory; quite the opposite. Girls respond to criminal opportunities and influences in ways similar to boys—their rates of delinquency and crime increase. The gender gap in crime can then be explained by the following proposition: Exposure to criminal opportunities and influences is less extensive among females. We already know why this is likely to be true. For example, females are more closely supervised than males; females are taught to nurture and to avoid physical confrontation and displays of aggression; the associations of girls (like those of boys) are likely to be in same sex groups—and delinquency is less extensive among girls.

Many feminist writers would reject this line of argument because it hardly goes beyond traditional role and opportunity theories. But so far no gender-sensitive feminist theory of crime and delinquency has been forthcoming. Leonard, Morris, Chesney-Lind, and Daly have made significant contributions to the development of a feminist literature on crime and delinquency, but all stop short of providing a theory. If a special theory is needed to explain female delinquency, it has not yet been written by feminists or by anyone else.

In a recent article by Kathleen Daly and Meda Chesney-Lind (1988), the authors point out that while theory building in the area of gender and crime is still in its infancy, there is evidence that female criminologists take a different tack from their male counterparts. Female criminologists are more tentative, they believe, and their claims less global than those of male criminologists. By the same token, in their empirical work female criminologists "are more interested in providing texture, social context, and case histories; in short, in presenting accurate portraits of how adolescent and adult women become involved in crime" (Daly and Chesney-Lind, 1988: 122). They do this by extensive use of observations and interviews. This is how Christine Alder (1986) found out that while unemployed young women in Melbourne, Australia, desperately wanted to find work, their lack of a job rarely resulted in criminal behavior. Alder documents widespread feelings of alienation, powerlessness, and hopelessness among unemployed females, but little crime. Such work opens the door to nontraditional ideas about delinquency and crime. But it also suggests that theories that purport to explain male criminality may not generalize to the crimes of girls and women.

So we come back to the question posed at the beginning of this section. The experiences of girls growing up are clearly different from those of boys, even when the growing up occurs in the same family or neighborhood. Yet, as we have seen, the delinquency and crime committed by both boys and girls is most often petty and sporadic. The one thing that stands out about female delinquency (especially that which is officially reported) is that it most often represents real or imagined violation of patriarchal authority (usually sexual misconduct). It is in this connection that the search for a special theory appears to make the most sense.

SUMMARY

Girls are less delinquent than boys in almost all respects. Not only are they less likely to commit offenses, when they do the offenses are usually less serious and they rarely involve violence. On the other hand, the reactions to girls' delinquency tend to be more severe than the reactions to boys who commit similar offenses. In particular, girls are far more likely than boys to be incarcerated for status offenses and the growing privatization of juvenile justice appears to have made matters worse. Girls' problem behavior tends to be sexualized and medicalized, and this process brings it into the catchment of a wider control net.

Explanations of the gender gap in crime and delinquency range from biological theory—males are inherently more aggressive than females—to opportunity theory—males have greater exposure to situations conducive to crime—to theories centering on gender–based differences in power and freedom—males have more of both than do females. Although much theoretical work on gender differences still needs to be done there is widespread agreement on one factor in the gap: girls are subject to greater adult supervision and control than are males. Beyond this, however, the waters remain murky.

Doubts as to the need for a special theory explaining female crime and delinquency are reinforced by findings that many of the factors linked to the delinquency of boys turn up also as factors in female delinquency. Foremost among these are early signs of discipline problems at home and school, and having friends who are also delinquent. Furthermore, the fact that the most seriously delinquent girls, like the most seriously delinquent boys, come from backgrounds of stress, dysfunction, and discrimination also suggests common structural sources.

REFERENCES

Adler, Freda. 1975. *Sisters in Crime: The Rise of the New Female Criminal.* New York: McGraw-Hill.

Alder, Christine. 1986. " 'Unemployed Women Have Got It Heaps Worse': Exploring the Implications of Female Youth Unemployment." *Australian and New Zealand Journal of Criminology* 19:210–225.

Bureau of Justice Statistics. 1988. *Report to the Nation on Crime and Justice.* 2nd edition. Washington, D.C.: U.S. Department of Justice.

Campbell, Anne. 1984. *The Girls in the Gang: A Report from New York City.* Oxford: Basil Blackwell.

———. 1986. "Self-Report of Fighting by Females." *British Journal of Criminology* 26:28–40.

Canter, Rochelle J. 1982. "Sex Differences in Self-Report Delinquency." *Criminology* 20:373–393.

Carlen, P. 1985. *Criminal Women.* Cambridge: Polity Press.

Cernkovich, Stephen A., Peggy C. Giordano, and Meredith D. Pugh. 1985. "Chronic Offenders: The Missing Cases in Self-Report Delinquency Research." *Journal of Criminal Law and Criminology* 76:705–732.

Cernkovich, Stephen A., and Peggy C. Giordano. 1987. "Family Relationships and Delinquency." *Criminology* 25:295–319.

Chesney-Lind, Meda. 1973. "Judicial Enforcement of the Female Sex Role: The Family Court and the Female Delinquent." *Issues in Criminology* 8:51–69.

———. 1986. "Women and Crime: The Female Offender." *Signs: Journal of Women in Culture and Society* 12:78–96.

———. 1987a. "Girl's Crime and Woman's Place: Toward a Feminist Model of Female Delinquency." Working Paper No. 334. University of Hawaii, Youth Development and Research Center.

———. 1987b. "Female Status Offenders and the Double Standard of Juvenile Justice: An International Problem." Paper presented at the annual meeting of the American Society of Criminology, Montreal.

———. 1988. "Girls in Jail." *Crime and Delinquency* 34:150–168.

Cohen, Stanley. 1985. *Visions of Social Control: Crime, Punishment and Classification.* New York: Polity Press.

Costello, Jan C., and Nancy L. Worthington. 1981–1982. "Incarcerating Status Offenders: Attempts to Circumvent the Juvenile Justice and Delinquency Prevention Act." *Harvard Civil Rights–Civil Liberties Law Review* 16:41–81.

Cullen, Francis T., Kathryn M. Golden, and John B. Cullen. 1979. "Sex and Delinquency: A Partial Test of the Masculinity Hypothesis." *Criminology* 17:301–310.

Curran, Daniel J. 1984. "The Myth of the New Female Delinquent." *Crime and Delinquency* 30:386–399.

Daly, Kathleen, and Meda Chesney-Lind. 1988. "Feminism and Criminology." *Justice Quarterly* 5:101–143.

Datesman, Susan, and Frank Scarpitti. 1980. "Unequal Protection for Males and Females in the Juvenile Court." In *Women, Crime and Justice.* Edited by Susan Datesman and Frank Scarpitti. Oxford: University Press.

Farrington, David P., and Barry Knight. 1979. "Stealing from a 'Lost Letter': Effects of Victim Characteristics." *Criminal Justice and Behavior* 7:423–435.

Federal Bureau of Investigation. 1981–1988. *Crime in the United States.* Washington, D.C.: U.S. Department of Justice.

———. 1988. *Age-Specific Arrest Rates and Race-Specific Arrest Rates for Selected Offenses, 1965–1986.* Washington, D.C.: U.S. Department of Justice.

Figueira-McDonough, Joscfina. 1986. "School Context, Gender, and Delinquency." *Journal of Youth and Adolescence* 15:79–97.

———. 1987. "Discrimination or Sex Differences? Criteria for Evaluating the Juvenile Justice System's Handling of Minor Offenses." *Crime and Delinquency* 33:403–424.

Giordano, Peggy C., and Stephen A. Cernkovich. 1979. "On Complicating the Relationship Between Liberation and Delinquency." *Social Problems* 26:467–481.

Gottfredson, Michael R., and Travis Hirschi. 1990. *A General Theory of Crime.* Stanford: Stanford University Press.

Hagan, John, A. R. Gillis, and John Simpson. 1985. "The Class Structure of Gender and Delinquency: Toward a Power-Control Theory of Common Delinquent Behavior." *American Journal of Sociology* 90:1151–1175.

———. 1990. "Clarifying and Extending Power–Control Theory." *American Journal of Sociology* 95:1024–1037.

Hagan, John, John Simpson, and A. R. Gillis. 1987. "Class in the Household: A Power-Control Theory of Gender and Delinquency." *American Journal of Sociology* 92:788–816.

Hagan, John, and Alberto Palloni. 1988. "Crimes as Social Events in the Life Course: Reconceiving a Criminological Controversy." *Criminology* 26:87–100.

Hancock, Linda. 1981. "The Myth that Females Are Treated More Leniently Than Males in the Juvenile Justice System." *Australian and New Zealand Journal of Sociology* 16:4–14.

Heidensohn, Frances M. 1968. "The Deviance of Women: A Critique and an Inquiry." *British Journal of Sociology* 19:160–176.

———. 1985. *Women and Crime: The Life of the Female Offender.* New York: New York University Press.

Hill, Gary D., and Maxine Atkinson. 1988. "Gender, Family Control, and Delinquency." *Criminology* 26:127–145.

Jackson, Hilary, and Lorna Smith. 1987. "Female Offenders: An Analysis of Social Inquiry Reports." Home Office Research and Planning Unit, Research Bulletin No. 23. London: HMSO.

James, Jennifer, and William Thornton. 1980."Women's Liberation and the Female Delinquent." *Journal of Research in Crime and Delinquency* 17:230–244.

Johnson, Richard E. 1986. "Family Structure and Delinquency: General Patterns and Gender Differences." *Criminology* 24:65–84.

Klein, Malcolm W. 1971. *Street Gangs and Street Workers.* Englewood Cliffs, N.J.: Prentice-Hall.

Lanza-Kaduce, Lonn. 1988. "Perceptual Deterrence and Drinking and Driving Among College Students." *Criminology* 26:321–341.

Lemert, Edwin M. 1981. "Diversion in Juvenile Justice: What Hath Been Wrought?" *Journal of Research in Crime and Delinquency* 18:34–46.

Leonard, Eileen B. 1982. *Women, Crime, and Society.* New York: Longman.

Lerman, Paul. 1982. *Deinstitutionalization and the Welfare State.* Newark, N.J.: Rutgers University Press.

Logan, Charles H., and Sharla P. Rausch. 1985. "Why Deinstitutionalizing Status Offenders Is Pointless." *Crime and Delinquency* 31:501–517.

Lombroso, Cesare, and Guglielmo Ferrero. 1895. *The Female Offender.* New York: Appleton.

Mahoney, Anne R., and Carol Fenster. 1982. "Female Delinquents in a Suburban Court." In *Judge, Lawyer, Victim, Thief.* Edited by Nicole Rafter and Elizabeth Stanko. Boston: Northwestern University Press.

Marsh, T. 1981. *Roots of Crime: A Biophysical Approach to Crime Prevention and Rehabilitation.* N.J.: Nellen.

McCarthy, Belinda R., and Brent L. Smith. 1986. "The Conceptualization of Discrimination in the Juvenile Justice Process: The Impact of Administrative Factors and Screening Decisions on Juvenile Court Dispositions." *Criminology* 24:41–64.

Messerschmidt, James W. 1986. *Capitalism, Patriarchy, and Crime. Towards a Socialist Feminist Criminology.* Totowa N.J.: Rowman and Littlefield.

Morash, Merry. 1983. "An Explanation of Juvenile Delinquency: The Integration of Moral Reasoning Theory and Sociological Knowledge." In *Personality Theory, Moral Development, and Criminal Behavior.* Edited by W. S. Laufer and J. M. Day. Lexington, Mass.: Lexington Books.

———. 1986. "Gender, Peer Group Experiences, and Seriousness of Delinquency." *Journal of Research in Crime and Delinquency* 23:43–67.

———. 1988. "The Sex/Gender System and the Etiology of Boys' Delinquency." Revised version of a paper presented at the annual meeting of the American Society of Criminology, Montreal, 1987.

Morris, Allison. 1987. *Women, Crime and Criminal Justice.* Oxford: Basil Blackwell.

Morris, Allison, and C. Wilkinson. 1983. "Secure Care: Just an Easy Answer?" *Community Care* 8:22–26.

Morris, Ruth R. 1964. "Female Delinquency and Relational Problems." *Social Forces* 43:82–89.

Polk, Kenneth. 1987. "When Less Means More: An Analysis of Destructuring in Criminal Justice." *Crime and Delinquency* 33:358–378.

Rafter, Nicole Hahn, and Elena M. Natalizia. 1982. "Marxist Feminism: Implications for Criminal

Justice." In *The Criminal Justice System and Women*. Edited by Barbara Raffel Price and Natalie J. Sokoloff. New York: Clark Boardman.

Richards, Pamela, and Charles R. Tittle. 1981. "Gender and Perceived Chances of Arrest." *Social Forces* 51:1182–1199.

Riley, David. 1986. "Sex Differences in Teenage Crime: The Role of Lifestyle." Home Office Research and Planning Unit, Research Bulletin No. 20. London: HMSO.

Sampson, Robert J. 1985. "Sex Differences in Self-Reported Delinquency and Official Records: A Multiple-Group Structural Modeling Approach." *Journal of Quantitative Criminology* 1:345–367.

Schwartz, Ira M., Marilyn Jackson-Beeck, and Roger Anderson. 1984. "The 'Hidden' System of Juvenile Justice." *Crime and Delinquency* 30:371–385.

Schwartz, Ira M., Linda Harris, and Laurie Levi. 1988. "The Jailing of Juveniles in Minnesota." *Crime and Delinquency* 34:133–149.

Schwendinger, Herman, and Julia Siegal Schwendinger. 1985. *Adolescent Subcultures and Delinquency*. New York: Praeger.

Simon, Rita J. 1975. *Women and Crime*. Lexington, Mass.: Lexington Books.

Smart, Carol. 1979. "The New Female Criminal: Reality or Myth?" *British Journal of Criminology* 19:50–59.

Snyder, Howard N., and Terrence A. Finnegan. 1987. *Delinquency in the United States, 1983*. Washington D.C.: U.S. Department of Justice.

Steffensmeier, Darrell J. 1980. "Sex Differences in Patterns of Adult Crime, 1965–1977." *Social Forces* 58:1080–1109.

Steffensmeier, Darrell J., Emilie Allan, and Cathy Streifel. 1989. "Development and Female Crime: A Cross-National Test of Alternative Explanations." *Social Forces*, 68:262–283.

Steffensmeier, Darrell J., and Robert M. Terry. 1986. "Institutional Sexism in the Underworld: A View from the Inside." *Sociological Inquiry* 56:305–323.

Thomas, William I. 1925. *The Unadjusted Girl*. Boston: Little, Brown.

Thornton, William E., and Jennifer James. 1979. "Masculinity and Delinquency Revisited." *British Journal of Criminology* 19:225–241.

Thrasher, Frederic M. 1927. *The Gang*. Chicago: University of Chicago Press.

Van Voorhis, Patricia, Francis T. Cullen, Richard A. Mathers, and Connie Chenoweth Garner. 1988. "The Impact of Family Structure and Quality on Delinquency: A Comparative Assessment of Structural and Functional Factors." *Criminology* 26:235–261.

Whitehead, John T., and Steven P. Lab. 1990. *Juvenile Justice: An Introduction*. Cincinnati: Anderson Publishing Co.

Widom, Cathy S. 1978. "An Empirical Classification of Female Offenders." *Criminal Justice and Behavior* 5:35–52.

Wilson, James Q., and Richard J. Herrnstein. 1985. *Crime and Human Nature*. New York: Simon and Schuster.

Chapter
9

Community: Neighborhoods, Family, Peers, Schools

Ohe of the most important groups as far as delinquency is concerned is the community. The community establishes the structure within which its members found their families, form their friendship groups, and develop their careers. The community includes *neighborhoods* where people with similar traditions, life-styles, and goals settle; *formal associations* like the Boy Scouts, the Rotary Club, the PTA, or the local church or temple that help to bring families and neighborhoods together to form a community; *formal work organizations* like Ace Hardware or the local factory; and agencies of *government* such as city hall, the courts, the police, and fire departments.

The community also embraces a number of groups that involve mainly teenagers— *informal peer groups* and *formal organizations* centering on youths: the high school and its athletic teams and school clubs, teen centers, as well as the local McDonalds where teenagers gather after school. In addition, it usually contains representatives of juvenile justice: a juvenile court, substance abuse programs, a group home for troubled youths, and possibly a shelter home or detention center.

The community takes all these groups and people and organizes them so that all can live more or less secure, fulfilling lives without hindering others from doing the same. Some communities place special emphasis upon the economic well-being of their members; others give importance to the social and moral focus of their members. Still others focus on order and security, ignoring to a certain extent their needs for individuality.

Some communities do a better job than others in providing for their members, and some are inviting to only specific levels in society—the working class, the middle class, or social elites, for example.

An almost endless variety of communities is possible. But as far as juveniles are concerned, the family, neighborhood, schools and especially their peer groups are the stages upon which most play out their adolescence. These groups shape the destinies of nearly all the community's teenagers, and the community is the dominant group in the lives of most teenagers.

We will examine in this chapter what makes a community effective in shepherding its teenagers toward adulthood by looking at the social forces that restrain as well as some that encourage misbehavior. We will also look at the neighborhood, family, schools, and teenage peer groups as they mold and shape this process.

TYPES OF COMMUNITIES

Communities come in two distinct forms: simple and complex. *Simple communities* are especially effective in fostering upbeat, positive social attitudes, though they usually are a bit too tame for some teenagers. *Complex communities*, on the other hand, though they provide a good variety of interesting activities, are less able to restrain and channel their young people into constructive social paths. Simple communities shape youngsters by surrounding them with adults and children who are in basic agreement regarding ideals, acceptable behavior, and appropriate outlooks. A consensus exists on most aspects of life in the community, and most juveniles are well aware that the community as a whole will criticize them if they stray from the accepted path. The unanimity and cohesiveness of the community are intimidating, and only the most determined rebels—adolescent or adult—will continue in open defiance of community feeling.

Sociologists describe this kind of solidarity—a consensus in values, a common cultural heritage, and social stability—with exotic names: *gemeinschaft* (Ferdinand Toennies), mechanical solidarity (Emile Durkheim), or the folk community (Robert Redfield). They are all describing the same community—one in which the members settle into a status based on race, gender, and occupation that envelops them throughout their lives in dealing with other members. In these communities, agreement prevails regarding the social values, routine behaviors, and social worth of individual members. Deviation in any respect draws attention and often community-wide reaction. And yet community members at different levels are expected to follow different behavioral paths. Juveniles play a different role than adults, wealthy members act differently than poor people, and boys behave differently than girls. Deviance for one is not always deviance for others.

The members of simple communities are familiar with one another, and their reputations are important. Gossip is a powerful force. Few who go astray escape notice, and only a few are willing to risk their reputations by attempting any kind of deviant behavior. Such communities are stable, and little serious crime or delinquency is encountered among them (Maccoby, Johnson, and Church, 1958). Small towns and villages particularly in the American midwest and south regularly approach this degree of solidarity.

Complex communities exhibit a different kind of unity. These communities are much more heterogeneous: Roman Catholics, Jews, and Protestants; Asians, Hispanics, blacks, and whites; stockbrokers and college professors, plumbers, carpenters, and factory workers. These groups share some values (the economic advantages and cultural diversity of urban life), but they also endorse very different ideas on many subjects. Such communities have a much smaller fund of shared values, and they are much more diverse in almost every way. And yet they, too, exhibit a characteristic form of solidarity that sociologists have called *gesellschaft* (Toennies) or organic solidarity (Durkheim).

First, they usually recognize each group in the community and insist, publicly at least, on its social value. Simple communities often discriminate relentlessly against a stigmatized minority in their midst, but complex communities usually frown upon open discrimination because each group separately is a minority in the larger community. If prejudice gathered strength, it could devastate any one of them. Complex communities usually endorse, formally at least, an egalitarian ideal both in policy and action. Economic, ethnic, religious, or racial prejudices lurking beneath the surface must be dampened, and the long-term benefits of communal cooperation must be emphasized. Different groups in the community depend upon one another for their well-being, and this fact tends to blunt some of the friction that often arises among the many different groups.

But even more important, the several groups of the community are obliged from time to time to review policy on such matters as the public schools, the police, taxes, residential zoning, or welfare. Framing policies that all can endorse becomes increasingly difficult if factions contend vigorously with one another and regularly veto each other's proposals. A policy that can guide the community as a whole is essential, and to this end the various groups must find a middle ground so that cooperation and compromise are possible on issues of key importance.

To this end these communities develop a number of mediating groups that blend the diverse interests of factories, schools, and businesses together with such groups as families, ethnic or religious communities, and diverse economic neighborhoods (see Kornhauser, 1959; chapter 2). Political parties dramatize the benefits of cooperation by uniting racial and economic groups in behalf of common interests, and public education provides a common foundation of belief and understanding. Religious groups (e.g., Roman Catholics) unite several social classes, and secular groups such as professional and social associations—the Rotary Club, Kiwanis, American Legion, Knights of Columbus, Masonic Order, or Boy Scouts—do the same. Complex communities are united by a variety of social and economic forces that help to counteract their natural centrifugal tendencies. As a united, effective community their complexity allows them to pursue a much broader range of goals, and politically and economically they are much stronger than simple communities.

Their strength, however, is the basis of a most difficult problem: dealing with large numbers of migrants that are attracted to the promise of complex communities. The abundance of everything, its sophisticated political and cultural life, its international dimension, its fine educational centers, and its generosity toward newcomers all attract migrants from less-developed areas. The groups that come in are usually not prepared for life in a complex, advanced community and show several weaknesses. They often

Table 9.1   CRIME RATES (PER 100,000) IN THE UNITED STATES, 1989

City size	Violent crimes	Property crimes	Crime index
250,000 and over	1614.1	8425.0	10066.1
100,000–249,999	950.8	7603.7	8554.5
50,000–99,999	671.7	6099.9	6771.6
25,000–49,999	500.4	5435.2	5935.5
10,000–24,999	366.6	4459.9	4826.5
9,999 and under	317.2	4121.6	4438.8
Rural counties	198.2	1923.3	2121.5

Source: FBI. The Uniform Crime Reports 1989, 154–155. Table 14.

have difficulty in finding a common ground with people unlike themselves. Nor are they as well prepared for advanced educational programs or demanding, sophisticated careers. They are not ready for full participation in the community, though they are eager to do so, and the community expects that ultimately they will. Migrants are seen as backward, superstitious, and unruly and are often shunned by well-established members.[1]

Many migrants become discouraged and follow a path that skirts the mainstream of community life. Some get involved in an underground economy. Others become absorbed into peripheral religious or ideological groups, and still others occupy themselves with informal groups of similarly dislocated people. As their numbers grow, however, such migrants pose a difficult problem of assimilation and require careful planning and organization. Otherwise they will fall into a perpetual underclass and become a dispossessed, unassimilated, shunned group that is defeated and without hope.

Complex communities, therefore, despite their best efforts to embrace diversity and to bridge factions, often find themselves with a sizable number of newcomers who are imperfectly assimilated and distinctive ethnic, religious, and racial groups that are imperfectly united in values and goals. As a consequence, these communities are less effective than simple communities in mobilizing informal social restraints, and they display much more crime and delinquency.

As Table 9.1 shows, in 1989 the distribution of crime and delinquency in the United States came very close to the pattern anticipated by this comparison of simple and complex communities. Complex communities are naturally much larger than simple communities. Note that the largest cities in the United States (those with a population of 250,000 or more) suffer 8.3 times as much violent crime as rural counties but only 4.4 times as much property crime. Complex communities foster a disproportionate number of violent robberies and rapes relative to simple villages.

In Japan metropolitan centers encourage the development of villages in their midst and thereby combine the social unity and support of simple communities with the diversity and versatility of complex communities. Each is strengthened by the other. See Box 9.1 on the following page for details.

---

[1]Young people, though not migrants, qualify in all other respects as newcomers.

Box 9-1   **Japanese Communities**

Many Japanese cities—Tokyo, for example, or Osaka—in spreading over broad regions have engulfed many simple villages so that today these small communities have in effect become large neighborhoods in a vast metropolitan area. Many of them have retained their traditional character and are stronger for it. As neighborhoods they include many families who have lived together for long periods and accept without reservation their common heritage and beliefs. They feel a deep respect for elders and authority and a commitment to diligence, self-discipline, and responsibility. Above all they accept the primacy of group opinion and feeling. A close consensus exists in many such communities regarding basic ideals and values, and those who deviate, including juveniles, are made to feel the shame of their misdeeds by their family, neighbors, and acquaintances. As simple neighborhoods their solidarity is formidable.

These small communities within major metropolitan centers are further reinforced via town associations that unite families and neighborhoods with such secondary groups as small work organizations, schools, and the police. These mediating groups strengthen the neighborhoods in the struggle against deviance and serve to guide and coordinate their response.

Schools take an active role in encouraging parental interest in the accomplishments of their children. Each school organizes a parent-teacher association that insures contacts between parents and teachers through periodic school visits by the parents and home visits by the teachers. These visits help forge a cooperative spirit among the key adults who socialize children and enlist the parents, particularly the mother, in supervising the child's progress. Teachers and parents work together in fostering the proper moral attitudes as well as in encouraging the children in their studies.

In addition, teenagers in both middle school and high school are urged to join student clubs that pursue such activities as sports, crafts, the arts, and specialized topics during and after school. About 60 percent of all high school students become members (Rohlen, 1983: 274). These clubs serve to bind the children to school and wholesome activities, while also fostering good social skills. In addition, a sizable portion of male high school students attend cram schools, *yobiko*, at night and on weekends to prepare for college entrance exams (see U.S. Department of Education, 1987: 32–36, 44–46).

The local police work closely with neighborhoods and schools in anticipating and preventing delinquency. Each community usually forms a town block association, *chokai*, that serves to coordinate local efforts in a variety of areas, including crime and delinquency prevention. Subcommittees, *bohan kyokai*, are formed with the police to spearhead anticrime programs, including informal neighborhood patrols and poster campaigns to foster preventive attitudes and efforts (Wagatsuma and Devos, 1984: 29–33).

Police officers regularly visit school officials to learn more about difficult or troubled children and to cement good working relations. When finding these children in the community, they have a better perspective in helping them. The police are brought in quickly with school problems, and work in a constructive way to counsel predelinquents and their parents. The emphasis is upon finding and working with children who seem headed for serious difficulty.

Children who persist in misbehavior or who waste too much time in entertainment centers and video parlors are offered counseling in psychological guidance centers, and those who are taken to court for a minor offense are often assigned a volunteer probation officer who lives in the neighborhood and works closely with the child in dealing with his or her problem.

As in most industrial societies, Japanese adolescents have developed a youth culture with distinctive dress styles, popular music, and youthful ideas and beliefs, but peer groups have had little opportunity to crystallize in Japan as in Western societies (Rohlen, 1983: 272–281). Japanese teenagers are virtually surrounded with adults who encourage the proper ideals and attitudes and who support them in their academic duties. The key groups in the community as far as juveniles are concerned—their parents, neighbors, teachers, counselors, volunteer probation officers, and the local police—all work closely with one another to discover and deal with troubled children. The community as a whole applauds these efforts, and only a few deviant children stray very far down the wrong path.

The result in Japan is that in 1987 only 15.2 juveniles per 1000 young people under 20 were "given guidance" by the police for serious offenses like felonies, violent crimes, larcenies, and grand theft (Japanese National Police Agency, 1988: 52). In the United States in 1984 we had an offending rate involving index offenses and the same age group (10 to 19 years) of 29.8 per 1000 (Federal Bureau of Investigation, 1985: table 35; U.S. Bureau of the Census, 1986: table 6). For a closely comparable estimate of the relative levels of delinquency in the two countries, see Rohlen (1983: 294–301).

SOCIAL CONTROLS IN THE NEIGHBORHOOD

The school, peer group, and family combine to establish another field of controls in the neighborhood in addition to that created by the larger community—one that is very important to modern adolescents.

Family

The family plays a major role in shaping a child's attitudes toward school and peers. Several studies have shown (Hirschi, 1969: 131, 142–144; Wiatrowski, Griswold, and Roberts, 1981: 536–537) that high school students who have good rapport with their fathers and mothers are more likely to have a good attitude toward school and to care what their teachers think in comparison with students who are not on good terms with their parents. Similarly, those youngsters who are closest to their parents have prosocial friends as well.

The family is the first line of defense against juvenile misbehavior, but in America this bulwark is crumbling rapidly. Young men and women cohabitate routinely today (U.S. Bureau of the Census, 1989: table 1). In 1970 married couples made up fully 70.5 percent of all households, but by 1989 such couples had dwindled to 56.1 percent. Households of nonrelatives including mainly unmarried couples, on the other hand, grew by 126 percent between 1980 and 1989. Many unmarried couples stay together, but many ultimately separate, and the children usually stay with the mother. If they do marry, they are nearly as likely to divorce as to stay together. About 45 percent of first marriages today are dissolved through divorce. But even if they stay together, nearly one-third develop serious instability—chronic discord, incompatibility, infidelity, and unhappiness.

Years ago the family provided shelter, protection from unwanted intrusion, and material well-being for its members. The family also served as the individual's port of entry to many other institutions in the community—to religious fellowship, marriage partners, and extended kinship groups. It was responsible for its members and a single person, whether a man or a woman, was more vulnerable by far than those firmly established in families.

As the family's monopoly in satisfying these needs has dwindled, its stability has come to rest squarely on the personal compatibility of the spouses. Stable employment is readily available to both women and men, and even teenagers enjoy a measure of autonomy as a result of their incomes from part-time jobs. If the family is no longer the broad sustaining force it once was, it still provides both parents and children supportive companionship.

But companionship alone is a frail basis for family stability. It waxes and wanes, but more important, the family is no longer the sole source of companionship for either parents or teenagers. When companionship wanes in the family, or is available with someone else outside the family, the family itself has lost its purpose.

Instability, however, has its costs, and those who pay most heavily in the long run are the children. Parental discord often involves bitter quarrels over the children. Childrearing practices are a frequent point of contention, and disagreements often confront children with conflicting demands from their parents. Parents are models for their children, and parental quarreling encourages children to use hostility and abuse in their own relationships. Further, quarrels focusing on the children often invite them to choose one parent over the other. Finally, as family turmoil takes its toll, the parents lose any desire to give their children the kind of guidance and supervision they need, so that often the children are left to follow their own whims and inclinations.

Parental discord is at the root of much poor parenting, and research suggests that weak parental involvement, low levels of supervision, ineffective discipline, and parental rejection are all closely related to delinquency. Mild forms of deviance particularly seem to result from family malfunctioning—status offending, drug abuse, property offenses, and auto theft, for example (see Johnstone, 1978)—especially among boys (see Gove and Crutchfield, 1982).

Parental interest and involvement with children has been the focus of many studies (see Loeber and Stouthamer-Loeber, 1986: 41–43) in which delinquent boys were compared with nondelinquents. The results show clearly that weak parental involvement, and particularly weak fatherly involvement, are strongly related to delinquency and aggressiveness by sons. Supervision has also been studied (Loeber and Stouthamer-Loeber, 1986: 43–51) and found to be strongly related to official delinquency but only mildly related to self-report delinquency. The weaker the supervision, the more chronic and the more versatile the child's delinquency. Parental supervision is particularly important in neighborhoods where delinquency is prevalent. In such neighborhoods strict supervision is probably more important even than a supportive, stable home life (Wilson and Herbert, 1978).

Parental rejection of children, especially by the father, severs communication and nullifies parental influence. It is a strong correlate of aggressiveness and delinquency. Parental rejection, moreover, is a strong predictor of *future* delinquency and not just a parental reaction to the child's delinquency (Loeber and Stouthamer-Loeber, 1986: 54–55).

Parental disciplinary style also influences the child's delinquency. Nagging and scolding as well as extreme strictness, leniency, and inconsistency or unfairness have all been associated with delinquency or aggressiveness (Loeber and Stouthamer-Loeber, 1986: 52–55). Even though child abuse is often found in the background of violent delinquents, less extreme forms of physical punishment do not seem to be a factor in delinquency, and the same is true of love withdrawal and a lack of parental reasoning in administering discipline (see Loeber and Stouthamer-Loeber, 1986: 52–53).

All these factors—parental involvement, supervision, and discipline—are themselves undermined by parental discord, and if Gottfredson and Hirschi (1990: 97–105) are correct, poor parenting is at the root of weak self-control among adolescents and ultimately delinquency. Where sharp discord is chronic in the family, parental skills are weak, and delinquency gains a foothold.

Still, family discord is not the only basis in the family for delinquency. Other factors such as parental deviance, family disruption, or the child's own impact on the family also make a difference. Deviance, violence, or criminality in the parents seem even to carry over from one generation to the next. If the father or the mother has a history in any of these, their sons are likely to follow suit (Loeber and Stouthamer-Loeber, 1986: 71–72).

Many studies have examined family disruption, particularly broken homes as a cause of delinquency. Disruption through divorce is common, but since it usually is accompanied by discord and all that that entails for the children, divorce is not a good measure of disruption. Disruption arises in a variety of ways: through death, debilitating illness, or illegitimacy. Disruption, however caused, results in one parent—usually the mother—carrying the burden of childrearing alone. And single mothers (see Stouthamer-Loeber et al., 1984) whether happy or not, are less effective with their children than happily married mothers, and accordingly, boys with police contacts are more likely to come from low-supervision households where the father is absent than from intact families (Goldstein, 1984). Nevertheless, family disruption and discord together are much more powerful in causing delinquency than simple disruption, as in the death of the father (Loeber and Stouthamer-Loeber, 1986: 77–78; van Voorhis et al., 1988). Discord followed by disruption seems to compound the influence of each.

Another very strong criminogenic factor is sibling delinquency. If one boy is delinquent, his brothers are very likely to be delinquent, too. In a study of families in London, 4.3 percent of the families produced 46.9 percent of the delinquents (see Farrington, Gundry, and West, 1975), and the Gluecks (1950) report that 65.2 percent of their delinquents had delinquent brothers, whereas only 25.8 percent of their nondelinquent controls did.

Older siblings portray delinquency for their younger brothers as well as guiding them directly into misconduct. Moreover, since sibling relationships are virtually inescapable, delinquent brothers present a persistent criminogenic pressure for their younger siblings. If one child is especially aggressive, the siblings are also usually aggressive and are much more likely to assault others when they reach adolescence (see Loeber, Weismann, and Reid, 1983). Curiously, boys with two sisters, one older and the other younger, seem to be most delinquent, followed by boys with up to three male siblings (Wilkinson, Stitt, and Erickson, 1982). The mechanisms whereby sisters affect their middle brother, however, remains to be clarified.

Family factors combine with neighborhood circumstances to provide a system of forces that protect the family from delinquency or conversely render it vulnerable. Race, for example, in interaction with the qualities of different neighborhoods seems to make a big difference (see Rosen, 1985). Black sons with strong paternal relationships in working- or middle-class families withstand delinquency much better than their counterparts in families where the paternal relationship is weak. But black sons from lower-class families who frequently talk with their fathers, even though their relationship is otherwise weak or antagonistic, are much *more delinquent* than those who rarely if ever talk with their fathers. Interestingly, Robins and Hill (1966) found much the same, and Austin (1978) found similar results for black girls. Austin explains this pattern by suggesting that relationships between mothers and children in lower-class black families become especially close and conventional when the father is absent. In lower-class black families the father exerts a criminogenic influence on both boys and girls, though in lower-class white families he has a more positive influence.

A misbehaving child himself can shape the family in ways that render his own delinquency easier. For example, he may resist parental attempts to impose controls so strongly that eventually they give up and for the sake of peace abandon any attempt to impose reasonable controls. Shouting and threats can force parents into permissive rules, but it can also spur parental rejection of the child. As we have seen, both permissiveness and rejection often produce delinquency.

The structure of the family also organizes the way controls play on its teenagers. Where the family is patriarchal, girls tend to be controlled more closely by their mothers, they (the girls) tend to be less adventuresome and less risk-oriented outside the home, and their delinquency level is markedly less than their brothers'. Where the family is egalitarian—where the mother and father wield power more equally—girls enjoy greater freedom and their delinquency tends to rise (Hagan, Simpson, and Gillis, 1987: 799–815; Hagan, 1989: chapter 7), while their brothers receive more balanced attention from their parents and their delinquency declines.

Hagan et al. indicate that as more mothers find employment and their power in the family increases, more girls will become delinquent. Thus, one of the factors in the sharp rise in delinquency among girls since 1960 could well be a shift in family structure toward a more balanced, egalitarian pattern. Hagan et al. do not show why greater freedom for girls should lead to delinquency, but if it means that girls will move more readily into dating and the youth culture, it is easy to see how more girls would be drawn into mild delinquency.

Delinquents in Hirschi's study (1969: 131, 142–144, 149–152) were much more likely to have poor relationships with both their mother and father, negative attitudes toward school and their teachers, and to disapprove of their delinquent peers. On this basis Hirschi concluded that peers only become important for an adolescent's delinquency, when the family has already lost control. As long as the parents and children enjoyed close relations, the children avoided delinquent companions.

The family seems to be a foundation for sound development through adolescence. When parent-child relations are solid, the child avoids destructive, malicious peers, adjusts well to the rigors of school, and in general makes a good adjustment during adolescence. When parent-child relations are flawed, the child selects malicious, delinquent peers, and cannot tolerate school.

Peers

Peers seem to make a difference. Hirschi's study showed that the family is the basis of teenagers' sound adjustment, but an impressive series of studies point to a different conclusion that peer groups, schools, and community all interact to define a child's development in adolescence.

During the early part of this century wave after wave of immigrants from eastern and southern Europe settled in cities along the eastern seaboard. In the midst of world war and social upheaval crime rates worsened, and criminologists speculated that the delinquency wave of the post-World War I period was a result of immigrants who flooded into America's eastern cities. A whole series of studies looked into this question, and in a nutshell they found that first generation juveniles—those born abroad and brought to this country as children by their parents—showed a lower rate of delinquency than native born juveniles. But as they looked further, it turned out that second generation juveniles—those born in this country to foreign born parents—had much higher delinquency rates than their American peers. Finally, in succeeding generations the delinquency rate of ethnic children fell to the same rate as that of their American peers (see Shulman, 1961: 76–77).

Those children who were closest to their parents but had little in common with native born youngsters (i.e., those who were born abroad and brought with them a foreign accent and old world values) were relatively immune to delinquency. Those who were closer to their American peers but distant from their parents (i.e., American-born children of foreign parents) were *more* delinquent than their American peers. Those ethnic children who were readily absorbed into the peer groups of their neighborhoods were vulnerable to delinquent pressures, but those children who were less attractive to their peers were exposed less to anti-social pressure.

A later study begun during the early 1950s by Reiss and Rhodes (1961) of 9238 white high schoolers in Tennessee came up with strong supportive evidence. They examined delinquency in relation to neighborhood and school structure. In some schools middle class children were prevalent in the area and were the most numerous group in the high school. Their peer groups no doubt set the tone among students, and working class kids were peripheral to student social life. In such schools middle class students were more delinquent than their working class peers and indeed, more delinquent than other middle class kids in other kinds of schools. In schools where working class kids and peer groups dominated, they were most delinquent. Thus, when the youngsters for structural reasons are peripheral to the dominant teenage groups in the school, they are less vulnerable to peer group pressures including delinquency pressures.

Finally, a recent study in Hawaii further corroborated these results (Ferdinand, 1990). Upwards of 19,000 delinquents processed by the Hawaiian juvenile courts between 1982 and 1985 were examined in relation to their socio-cultural backgrounds, and when their ethnicity in relation to that of their neighbors was taken into account, their delinquency rates were dramatically affected. Caucasian, Japanese, and Filipino juveniles living in areas dominated by *their* ethnic group showed much higher levels of delinquency than their counterparts in a distinctly minority status group in their neighborhood. In these several studies a foreign background, socio-economic status, and ethnicity all seemed to affect how teenagers relate to their peers and as well their likelihood of getting involved in delinquency. Peers do make a difference.

Although Hirschi found that the quality of a juvenile's peers was governed by his relations with parents, these studies point to an independent peer influence. Children in the mainstream of youth culture are more prone to delinquency than those who are not.[2]

Hirschi also found that early dating (i.e., cross-gender relationships) is closely related to delinquency, and Wiatrowski et al., (1981: 535) using a nationwide sample of tenth graders found much the same—that youngsters who dated heavily were also more likely to be delinquent. Why should dating be related to delinquency, when neither Hirschi nor Wiatrowski et al. could find any impact of peer relationships on delinquency?

Hirschi (1969: 163–170) suggests that his delinquents often pressed hard toward adult behavior—particularly adult behavior that was ordinarily denied young teenagers. For example, Hirschi's delinquents were likely to date, smoke, and drink much earlier than non-delinquents. Thus, some adolescents were drawn early to the freedoms and pleasures of adulthood, and since most of these pleasures were forbidden to young people, these same youngsters were especially vulnerable to delinquency.

In a related study, Greenberg, Carey, and Popper (1987) discovered that the death rates of white youths ages 15–24 from violent causes (homicide, suicide, auto accidents, or non-auto accidents) in the western states of Arizona, Idaho, Montana, Nevada, New Mexico, and Wyoming have for decades been about twice as high as violent deaths among white youth in the four northeastern states—Connecticut, Rhode Island, Massachusetts, and New Jersey. Death rates in the six western states were highest in the most rural counties and *exceeded* even those for inner city black youth in the six highest crime centers in the United States—Atlanta, Baltimore, Dayton, Forth Worth, St. Louis, and Washington, D.C.

The most risky western counties offered adolescents little stability and few guidelines to a promising adult life. Rewarding employment was scarce, organized religion (Mormonism) had little influence, and the youth culture promoted a macho hedonism—fighting, heavy drinking, and dating. These counties offered young people little help in preparing for adulthood and little hope that it would prove interesting or fulfilling, but they did offer an exciting youth culture. They had much in common with Hirschi's young delinquents in Richmond, California. Adulthood promised them little more than a chance to indulge one's appetites in several directions.

Datesman, Scarpitti, and Stephenson (1975) found an analogous pattern among

---

[2]The assumption here is that some peer groups exert significant criminogenic pressures on their members. The next question is, what kinds of *mainstream* cliques exert these kinds of pressures.

some white female status offenders. Status offending by some teenage girls was closely linked with their concept of femininity. Though their parents placed tight restrictions on their behavior, they repeatedly defied parental rules in order to run around with boys. Since the girls' self-esteem was geared to their ability to attract boys, when they were successful in getting a boy's attention, even though against their parents' wishes, the girls felt good about themselves—better in fact than other girls, whether delinquent or non-delinquent.

Teenagers who have few prospects in adulthood but can participate in the fun and games of a male-dominated adolescent culture tend to fall into a peculiar kind of juvenile impulsivity in which the males focus on reckless, macho activities, and the females try to attract the males. It all starts out innocently enough, but in effect this version of youth culture lures both males and females into a very costly hedonism that is also mildly delinquent. Some die early, some get pregnant prematurely, some are drawn into substance abuse, and some get charged with status offending or delinquency.

Another question raised by Hirschi's research is the impact of delinquent peers upon one another. As noted above, Hirschi's delinquents had little regard for each other, especially for those they actually knew. He concluded on that basis that delinquent gangs and cliques play little role in aggravating the delinquency problem. Only youngsters who have already become delinquent are receptive toward other delinquents or gang members, and Wiatrowski, Griswold, and Roberts (1981) found similar results in their study.

The issue turns basically on whether Hirschi and Wiatrowski et al. included in their research significant numbers of gang delinquents. It now appears they did not. Since both their samples were based on surveys of junior and senior high school students, their results reflected mainly the attitudes of relatively minor delinquents. The most serious juvenile offenders (i.e., gang delinquents) cannot be studied by means of a self-report survey of high school students (Cernkovich et al., 1985: 705–732) because they either are in juvenile institutions or have dropped out of school. These are also the juveniles who are most likely to have close relationships with other delinquents.

In contrast to Hirschi's findings, serious delinquents actually report a strong sense of kinship and camaraderie with their delinquent friends. Giordano, Cernkovich, and Pugh (1986) compared nondelinquents with serious delinquents and found on the whole that serious delinquents were much more closely bound to their gangs than nondelinquents were to their friends. They concluded that highly conforming youths were

> least attached to friends . . . , [had] the lowest levels of caring and trust, the lowest rates of self-disclosure, . . . [and were] least likely to admit to the group's influence on their own behavior. . . . In contrast, the more delinquent groups [were] more likely to believe that they may be influenced by friends and that they exert considerable influence on the group. [Giordano, Cernkovich, and Pugh, 1986: 1192–1193]

An important study by LaGrange and White (1985) throws further light on this problem. They looked at criminogenic factors in delinquency according to age and found that 15-year-old juveniles were influenced by parental attitudes, ties to school, and delinquent associates—all the variables that stood out in Hirschi's research. Although delinquent associates had some influence on the delinquency of 15-year-olds, parents and school were most important.

Eighteen-year-old delinquents, however, were affected by delinquent associates only. School and parents had no effect, probably because they were no longer part of the delinquent's life, and a low socioeconomic status had a moderate effect (see also Agnew, 1991). Since Hirschi's research sample consisted of high school students and his findings coincided with the results reported by LaGrange and White for 15-year-olds, the conclusion is inescapable that he had few if any of the older gang delinquents who do maintain close relationships with other delinquents. Hirschi's failure to analyze his research sample in terms of age suggests caution in interpreting his findings regarding the relationships between delinquents and their delinquent peers.

Delinquent gangs have also been known to intensify seriously the delinquency problem in a neighborhood (see Campbell, 1984: 49–50; Spergel, 1984: 201–203; and Horowitz, 1982). Klein (1971: 135–166), for example, found in a study of gangs in Los Angeles that delinquency among new gang members rose sharply *after* they entered their gang.

On balance, the evidence seems to suggest that gangs exercise considerable influence over their members and thereby aggravate any delinquent tendencies they may already have had. This is not to suggest that social controls in the family are unimportant, only that they operate apart from gangs with regard to delinquency.

Schools

Along with families and peer groups, the schools also play a crucial role in delinquency. Much delinquency occurs in or around schools, and their general organization plays a big part in determining how much and what kind of delinquency they must cope with.

During the school year teenagers spend less than one-fifth of their waking hours in school, but a much larger percentage of their crimes are committed in or around schools, particularly in the junior high schools. Children between 12 and 15 years old commit 68 percent of their robberies and 50 percent of their assaults at school, and juvenile vandalism hits the schools hard, too. Although schools in all areas suffer from delinquency, it is especially common in large cities where 15 percent of the schools have reported serious problems (U.S. Department of Health, Education, and Welfare, 1978: chapter 1). In one fashion or another the schools experience a sizable amount of juvenile misconduct, and the question is, how can they control it?

Schools after all are not primary groups and cannot exercise the same informal restraints on behavior that closely knit families or peer groups often do. Research suggests, nonetheless, that schools can manage the experience of their students so as to balance any negative impact that classroom failures may have with more positive accomplishments, and they can provide the kind of structure that will contain the impulsivity of immature students.

One of the most damaging experiences a child can suffer is repeated failure at school. It tarnishes his reputation among his peers, it undermines his relationships at home, and it weakens his teachers' confidence in him. Youngsters who regularly face defeat in the classroom confront fundamental challenges to their self-esteem and sense of effectiveness that are very difficult to overcome.

Polk and Richmond suggest that such children often react to failure by rejecting their rejectors. They see school as dull and boring, they abandon any notion of continuing on to college, they are likely to spend several evenings a week with peers who have already dropped out, and they reject extracurricular activities connected with school (Polk and Richmond, 1972: 63–69). These attitudes and behavior, moreover, bear little relationship to the students' social class. Rejecting the rejectors is as prominent among middle-class adolescents who have difficulty in school as among working-class kids in the same predicament.

Indeed, these reactions may be *more* typical of middle-class kids than working-class kids. In an insightful study of 1600 high school students in California, Stinchcombe (1964: chapter 6) found that alienation and rebellion in school were most intense among *lower-middle-class boys* who despite heavy parental pressure to succeed were still failing. Their strain was sharp and their alienation pervasive. Hirschi (1969: 132) also found in his study of Richmond, California, high school students that "academic incompetence [leads] to poor school performance to disliking of school to rejection of the school's authority to . . . delinquent acts."

But Hirschi rejected any idea that strain encourages delinquency. In fact, he even disdained any direct assessment of strain and delinquency. Still, the reality of strain in school as a factor in delinquency is obvious even in his own research.

If strain from school failure is such an important source of delinquency, the schools should certainly take steps to soften its impact. To determine how extracurricular activities could counter the stress of school failure, Schafer (1972: 98–100) surveyed a broad system of school-sponsored, extracurricular athletic activities and found that they did inhibit student misconduct. Such activities involve students in adult-guided activities after school, while occupying large blocks of their leisure time. Clubs involve students with one another and provide a good basis for strong bonds based upon common interests and goals. Where such clubs are available, students have a chance to show their accomplishments in nonscholastic areas, allowing those that cannot excel academically to demonstrate real ability in other areas (Agnew, 1984).

Not only do students relate closely with peers and school activities, they also feel some reluctance when opportunities for mischief present themselves. Extracurricular activities that are effectively organized strengthen student bonds with conventional adults as well as peers and, thereby, reinforce the field of controls in the school. This seems to be one of the secrets of Japanese schools in curbing delinquency.

Some urban school systems, taking this idea one step further, have organized work-study programs for students who are primarily vocationally oriented. Instead of going to school full time and working part time at unrelated tasks after school, such students can elect to alternate full-time work with full-time study. Both their work experience and their studies focus on vocational goals and derive, thereby, added meaning. In addition, the workplace provides a pervasive system of relationships that guide the student-worker along constructive social paths, much as extracurricular clubs do in schools. Such programs have proven effective antidotes to delinquency in New York City and elsewhere.

Further, school administrators have discovered that the skillful exercise of authority is a major contributor to student conformity (Department of Health, Education, and Welfare, 1978: 132–135). Schools in which the principal defines rules and punishments clearly and administers them fairly, together with a corps of teachers who understand the uses and limits of authority and who work closely with one another in upholding the rules—such a cadre of administrators and teachers in many inner-city parochial schools provides a good working environment for themselves and their students.

Schools, however, must also coordinate their efforts with families and neighborhood peer groups, and where the links between parents, peer groups, and teachers are weak or their goals conflicting, the child has an opportunity to choose a delinquent path. Under these conditions the school may be forced to compensate by taking extraordinary measures—either because delinquent gangs threaten the children or because local families provide little support for their children's efforts in school. But where the schools work in close harmony with the families and children, the child is more likely to succeed in his or her academic responsibilities.

Unfortunately, too little attention has been given to fitting the school to the social community (compare Burzik, 1988; Schwartz, 1987). As Jackson Toby (1983: 30–38) has pointed out, since 1950 American urban high schools have become socially isolated from local neighborhood and family groups, and the urban high school no longer routinely enlists family and neighborhood support for its educational goals. In the aftermath of the post-Sputnik movement to consolidate small, secondary schools into large high schools of 1000 and more with professional administrators and highly specialized faculty and curricula, the local school has been lifted out of the neighborhood and made into a foreboding institution particularly to working-class parents, who themselves are often poorly educated.

Primary schools still fit comfortably in their neighborhoods and still mainly serve local families. Since the 1950s, however, consolidated junior and senior high schools have served communities (i.e., a combination of neighborhoods), and the teachers are less likely to know the parents or children outside of school. As a result, faculties in the junior and senior high schools have encountered renewed difficulty in enlisting the parents and children in their academic enterprise, and their overall effectiveness has suffered even further.[3]

These changes in the schools, together with a heightened concern for children's rights and tighter school attendance laws that force unsuccessful students to remain in school until the age of 16, have meant that since 1950 the ability of urban high schools to enlist students, families, and neighborhoods in support of academic goals has been drastically reduced. Informal controls in and around secondary schools have been weakened, and the authority of its teachers and administrators has been seriously eroded. One result has been a sharp increase in school-based delinquency.

TWO TYPES OF SOCIAL FIELDS

Two kinds of social fields, one with roots in fragmented neighborhoods and the other in an integrated, cohesive community, have important implications for the development of juveniles. The *fragmented neighborhood* typically includes a variety of ethnic or religious groups more or less competitive with one another, along with various social groups—the Kiwanis, American Legion, and labor unions—that have little in common with one another and usually go their separate ways. It also provides few contacts between adults

---

[3]The senior high schools, through their athletic teams, stand as a source of pride in many communities and contribute substantially to their sense of solidarity. At the same time many schools suffer in badly divided communities as feuding juvenile factions vent their anger toward each other in and around the schools, adding further to the schools' isolation. The public schools in America have assumed symbolic meanings in many of the communities they serve, and an intelligent management of the schools as a cultural resource to elevate the community would seem to be both a convenient and necessary course.

and children, or between parents, youth workers, and teachers. In a fragmented neighborhood the children have few informal contacts outside the family with adults, and they receive little guidance or even supervision as they move through adolescence. Weekend soccer leagues, summer swimming teams, Boy Scouts, or religious clubs for young people are rare, and for better or worse they are left much to themselves to devise their own social life. Their path into adulthood is largely a matter of chance.

The *integrated, cohesive community* presents the other side of the coin. All the community often belongs to the same ethnic or religious group, and ethnic or religious ceremonies are often a central part of community life. Social groups share in this life, and their membership is usually overlapping. They share the same goals and cooperate extensively in community-wide projects. Young people are expected to participate in these groups, and mens' groups often establish wives', sons', and daughters' auxiliaries. Churches organize Cub and Boy Scout or Brownie and Girl Scout chapters, and summer and fall are taken up with a variety of sport leagues for young people.

Adults are interested in helping young people make sound decisions, and juveniles come to know a wide circle of both adults and juveniles in the community. In the process they develop a clear picture of the paths readily open to juveniles in the community. They also come to know which juvenile peer groups are highly regarded and which ones are not. In many subtle ways the adult community charts their path, and although juveniles are largely unaware of the fact, their development is closely monitored and supervised by the adults in the community.

In a classic article Solomon Kobrin (1951) examined delinquency in these two distinct communities. He identified two types of delinquent gangs, a fighting gang and a criminal gang, and explained them in terms of the structure of the community and neighborhood.

According to Kobrin (1951: 658–660), fighting gangs tend to appear in neighborhoods that are complex and fragmented. When the community contains many distinct ethnic, religious, and racial groups; when different factions in the community—the middle class, the working class, labor unions, professional groups, and religious groups, for example—pursue their goals with little coordination or concern for one another; and when the neighborhoods provide little meaningful contact between parents and teachers, or between business groups and school, the young people rarely receive adult help or even supervision during adolescence. They band together in cliques to fill their social vacuum, and as they contend among themselves for status, the more durable ones evolve into fighting gangs.

When the community is relatively simple and the neighborhood, including even its criminal groups, is closely integrated, a different kind of gang—the criminal gang—tends to appear, according to Kobrin. When the community includes a dominant ethnic group and the several subgroups are woven together via a common political party, local schools, or religious congregation into a cohesive whole, the families, schools, and teenagers all endorse similar values and goals. When these conditions are present, teenagers confront a highly structured social field in which their path to adulthood is clearly defined, career lines are understood, and adolescents face few dilemmas as they move into adulthood.

Ordinarily, such communities would suffer little delinquency, but if they harbor well-established crime families who participate in their social life, a criminal career is also available to adolescents—particularly those who have shown some aptitude for deviant activities. Thus, a few juvenile cliques will follow the scams of their adult idols in organized crime and pursue such crimes as drug dealing, gambling operations, auto theft for profit, and gun trafficking (Cressey, 1970: 129–138). The sophistication of the adult gangs filters down to the juveniles, and their criminality begins to resemble that of their older mentors. These sophisticated juvenile gangs are not common, but they are found in many major urban centers in the United States (see Cloward and Ohlin, 1960; Spergel, 1964).

Not all simple communities tolerate criminal families. When they do not, deviant juveniles are much less sophisticated, less well organized, and much less common (Cohen and Short, 1958: 24). Although they still tend to form cliques and informal groups, their delinquency is routine—theft, vandalism, victimization of other juveniles—and not much else.

Following Kobrin's line of reasoning Irving Spergel and his students (Spergel, 1984: 200–203; Curry and Spergel, 1988: 381–406) surveyed Chicago's violent street gangs and were able to show that neighborhood structure does affect the ways in which juvenile gangs develop. The violent gang itself is large, age stratified, and organized by an inner core of leaders who direct the activities of the rest. Its membership is drawn from minority youths with limited economic prospects who are willing to compete violently with one another for position and reputation. It usually has a name, an insignia or colors, a tradition, and a turf over which it claims sovereignty. The leaders are frequently young adults who have proven their mettle in gang exploits and developed special skills in combat and in criminal activities. These are gangs in the fullest sense of the term.

According to Spergel such gangs evolve in one of two ways. Violent gangs may form in highly fluid communities with many minorities—Hispanics, Vietnamese, and others. The families may be relatively stable and close, but the neighborhood is weakly integrated and offers juveniles little prospect for a conventional adult life. Street gangs provide an immediate answer to problems of social worth and position as well as protection from rival gangs in the area. They can also promise significant adult careers in organized crime. The gangs that evolve under these conditions tend to be well organized and especially violent.

Gangs also form in stable, lower-class, heavily black neighborhoods with high rates of family breakdown, mental illness, poverty, delinquency, and vice. Despite these obvious handicaps, such communities are surprisingly well integrated. Secondary organizations—particularly social agencies such as employment services, veterans organizations, children and family services, and elderly welfare groups—have close links with families and other local groups like the churches, schools, probation and parole offices, and courts. These organizations bring a new kind of social structure to lower-class neighborhoods that otherwise would have very little. They offer both a leadership corps and a unifying focus for individuals and families who have already lost much of their commitment and pride in their neighborhood. The gangs that appear in such communities place less value on violence and focus more on opportunities for profit in the underground economy—the rackets.

The relevance of Spergel's typology of gangs to Kobrin's paradigm is clear and seems to bear out the essentials of the latter's analysis. When a community is well integrated, if delinquency appears, it is focused and well structured. When the community is loosely integrated, a more violent, volatile pattern of delinquency appears.

Spergel (1984: 209–219) discovered that gang-related homicides from 1978 to 1981 in Chicago were concentrated mainly in recently settled, Puerto Rican communities with little poverty and only moderate levels of delinquency. At the same time Spergel discovered that of the ten poorest black neighborhoods in Chicago with very high levels of delinquency, only one also had an extremely high rate of gang violence.

Taking his ideas even further, Kobrin looked at high crime rate neighborhoods in Los Angeles and discovered (see Schuerman and Kobrin, 1986) that a cohesive, homogeneous neighborhood with little delinquency follows a characteristic pattern as it changes into a high crime area. As single family homes give way to multifamily dwellings and as married couples with children are replaced by broken families and unrelated individuals; as the neighborhood shows increasing residential turnover, a growing portion of females in the labor force, a rising minority population, and a growing ratio of children to adults, the neighborhood also shows increasing levels of crime and delinquency.

During the early phase social deterioration *precedes* the growth of crime and delinquency. But near the end of the cycle crime and delinquency grow faster than social problems in the neighborhood. As adult crime and gang delinquency take root in the neighborhood, they undermine even further whatever resources remain and thereby accelerate the rise in deviant behavior. As with the family, by weakening the neighborhood even further, crime and delinquency undermine its unity and make deviant behavior even less controllable.

CULTURAL EMPHASES IN THE NEIGHBORHOOD

Several criminologists have pointed out that since different neighborhood groups attach importance to different ideals and qualities, they tend to orient their members along different patterns of behavior. Miller (1958) sees lower-class members focusing on trouble, toughness, smartness, excitement, fate, and autonomy and predisposed to commit offenses reflecting these qualities. Cohen (1955: 24–32) found working-class gangs subscribing to versatility, short-run hedonism, and group autonomy along with nonutilitarian, malicious, and negativistic behavior. Schwendinger and Schwendinger (1985) found a generic type of working-class juvenile clique—the street-corner group—that exhibited an aggressive, iconoclastic delinquency as well as a middle-class clique—the socialites—that pursued a pattern of drinking, dating, sports, and parties. They traced the origins of these cliques to class conflict that arises normally within a capitalist economic system. Finally, as noted, some poor communities suffer an extremely barren social structure so that little is promised to adolescents beyond the basic pleasures and freedoms of adulthood. These impoverished communities in turn foster a violent, reckless, and hedonistic youth culture that gives more significance to autonomy and pleasure than preparation for the future.

The American youth culture, therefore, reflects a variety of cultural themes, depending on the broader class structure and the social opportunities and limitations of the community. Different communities present different youth cultures according to the importance their groups give to the cultural themes described above. Whatever shape it takes, youth culture is a major force in the life of American young people, whether they live in the upper-middle class of Boston's suburban north shore or in the poverty of rural

Nevada. It colors their misbehavior as well as their ideals and aspirations for adulthood. It is also, no doubt, one of the main factors in the current low intellectual level of American high schools. Although it is a key factor in the delinquency of many young people, it reflects forces that do not permit easy manipulation. No doubt, the prevention of delinquency is not a simple undertaking.

CONCLUSIONS

The community, as it bears upon juveniles, includes neighborhoods, families, schools, and adolescent peer groups as well as a great variety of formal organizations and informal associations. These social groups, as they relate to one another, confer upon the neighborhood a distinctive structure. In some, these groups link closely with one another, and their activities blend nicely. They establish the appropriate pathways for their juveniles, who in turn move smoothly into an honorable adulthood. Such communities are well organized.

Other neighborhoods have yet to establish good working relations among their several groups, and as a result different segments of the community have little confidence in the rest and pay them little heed. Such communities are only very loosely organized. Their juveniles are left to themselves in finding their proper role both as adolescents and as young adults.

Still other communities are divided into factions, so that some groups and neighborhoods compete and conflict with the rest. The best efforts by some are undone by others, and the community seems to be at war with itself. Such communities are disorganized, and their disorganization prompts deep divisions often along socioeconomic, ethnic, or racial lines. But this is something more than a regulated competition among equals. Some segments are condemned as immoral and disreputable. They are shunned by the rest and forced into peripheral neighborhoods and economic pursuits. In this chapter we have not dealt at length with this type of community, but it is described in greater detail in Chapter 12 in the section on conflict theory.

All three communities set the stage for their adolescents, and juvenile delinquency varies predictably from one type of community to another. Well-organized communities, if they include elements of organized crime, give rise to juvenile criminal gangs that pursue a form of predatory delinquency oriented to an underground economy. Otherwise, they produce juveniles who fall short in realizing the ideals of the community and through stress are shunted into delinquency. Loosely organized communities and disorganized communities produce fighting gangs that dominate the social life of juveniles in the community. In addition, disorganized communities inflict substantial levels of stress on segments of their neighborhoods, and some few adolescents also find their way into delinquency via strain and labeling.

Delinquency, as it takes root in a community, increases the risk to individuals and organizations, so that the economic base is weakened and the ability of the community to provide for its juveniles is even further undermined. The organization of the community affects its delinquency, and delinquency in turn affects its organization.

By the same token the structure of the family, school, and peer groups also shape the character of delinquency in the community. When the family is troubled, the older siblings delinquent, or the parents themselves pursue illicit activities, the children are likely to turn to delinquency. When the family is structured along traditional patriarchal lines, the girls are less but the boys are more delinquent than when the family is egalitarian. And when the faculty and administration of a high school agree on their academic mission and standards of behavior, students tend to be less delinquent than when faculty and school administrators are not in accord.

Juvenile social groups come in all shapes and sizes and pursue a variety of values depending on the values of their parents, their class position, and the structure of their neighborhood. Some juvenile cliques may insulate their members against anomie and serious delinquency, but they probably also encourage them in some mild forms of delinquency. As urban high schools have consolidated and absorbed a variety of neighborhoods into their catchment areas, the youth culture has successively embraced girls, rural families, as well as working-class and lower-class youths. Friction among these several juvenile groups is still sharp but based more upon differences in style and viewpoint than upon claims of superiority.

Cliques of delinquents are less cohesive and less influential than their more conventional counterparts. Established gangs, however, are older and much more cohesive. Although cliques of delinquents may not aggravate delinquency much, the gangs intensify the problem significantly.

The organization of the community affects its families, schools, and peer groups, and these groups in turn directly affect their members. Strangely enough, in integrated, cohesive communities, rigorous competition in school spurs the students to fulfill their potential, but those who are least capable suffer extreme stress and lose interest. Children who are only weakly committed to the ideals of the community are less inclined to compete and less uncomfortable under these circumstances. Social forces at several different levels affect conformity in the neighborhood and its delinquency as well. Different social forces, however, spur strain so that some unfortunate individuals are relegated to a peripheral status and denied many of the rewards and privileges of the community.

SUMMARY

Communities are either simple or complex. Simple communities include a tightly woven web of families and neighborhoods united behind a single perspective and code of values. Complex communities are much more heterogeneous with different kinds of religions, races, social classes, and nationalities that are nevertheless brought together by such mediating groups as the Boy Scouts, the American Legion, the Roman Catholic Church, or the Masonic Order. Though their solidarity is often much thinner and narrower than with simple communities, complex communities are usually much more powerful and resourceful. Most communities with serious delinquency problems are complex communities.

The family comes under severe pressure in the complex community. Most members of the modern family including the older children and the mother as well as the father depend primarily on the family for personal support and comfort. Personal survival is no longer an issue, and many, including the older children and mother, may leave the family when it ceases to serve their purposes. Even when they remain, family discord often arises and affects the family in a myriad of ways—mainly to reduce the rapport and affection between one or both of the parents and the children.

Peer relations also play an important part in the lives of most adolescents. Juveniles who are in the mainstream of teenage social life with many friends are at greater risk of delinquency than those who are isolated from most peers (first-generation Americans, or those who are a small minority). At the same time young juveniles (under 16 years of age) whose friends are mainly delinquent, even though they have little sense of rapport or friendship with them, are also likely to be delinquent, as well as older juveniles (17 years of age, for example) with close friends who are delinquent. Finally, those who foresee minimal promise in adult life and adopt a philosophy of short-run hedonism (inner city juveniles; rural, lower-class, western juveniles; or juveniles in Appalachia) are also likely to become delinquent.

Since schools are a major factor in sifting successful from unsuccessful adolescents, they too play a major role in shaping delinquents. Failure in school is a regular precursor of delinquency. Unfortunately, schools in America have grown larger and more remote to local residents, making the job of those (the PTA, for example) who would like to involve parents more fully in the education of their children much more difficult. In the absence of close parental monitoring many high schoolers' motivation to learn has proven too weak and many fail.

Neighborhoods also affect delinquency. Fragmented neighborhoods are often divided along racial, ethnic, religious, gender, age, social class, or professional lines. Poor relationships among these several factions provide little opportunity for adults as a group to guide juveniles into productive, honorable careers. Integrated, cohesive neighborhoods, on the other hand, weave these several factions into a single cultural whole in which each pursues the values and goals of the rest. They are united in presenting juveniles a cultural focus and purpose for adulthood.

Both kinds of neighborhoods foster delinquency but with different emphases. Fragmented neighborhoods tend to encourage violent, fighting gangs that seek to gain a reputation via their violence, whereas integrated, cohesive neighborhoods support criminal gangs that eagerly pursue illegal but profitable scams. The structure of the neighborhood molds the expression of their delinquency by focusing the concerns of adolescents alternatively upon status or profits.

REFERENCES

Agnew, Robert S. 1984. "The Work Ethic and Delinquency." *Sociological Focus* 17:337–346.

———. 1991. "The Interactive Effect of Peer Variables on Delinquency." *Criminology* 29, No. 1:47–72.

Austin, Roy L. 1978. "Race, Father-Absence, and Female Delinquency." *Criminology* 15, No. 4 (February):487–503.

Bursik, Robert J., Jr., 1988. "Social Disorganization and Theories of Crime and Delinquency: Problems and Prospects" *Criminology* 26, No. 4:519–551.

Campbell, Anne. 1984. *The Girls in the Gang*. Oxford: Basil Blackwell.

Cernkovich, Stephen A., Peggy C. Giordano, and Meredith D. Pugh. 1985. "Chronic Offenders: The Missing Cases in Self-Report Delinquency Research." *The Journal of Criminal Law & Criminology* vol. 76, No. 3:705–732.

Cloward, Richard A., and Lloyd E. Ohlin. 1960. *Delinquency and Opportunity: A Theory of Delinquent Gangs.* New York: The Free Press.

Cohen, Albert K. 1955. *Delinquent Boys: The Culture of the Gang.* New York: The Free Press.

Cohen, Albert K., and James F. Short, Jr. 1958. "Research in Delinquent Subcultures" *The Journal of Social Issues* 14:20–37.

Cressey, Donald R. 1970. "Organized Crime and Inner-City Youth." *Crime & Delinquency* 16 (April):129–138.

Curry, G. David, and Irving A. Spergel. 1988. "Gang Homicide, Delinquency, and Community." *Criminology* 26, No. 3:381–406.

Datesman, Susan K., Frank R. Scarpitti, and Richard M. Stephenson. 1975. "Female Delinquency: An Application of Self and Opportunity Theories." *Journal of Research in Crime and Delinquency* 12 (July):107–123.

Dawley, David. 1973. *A Nation of Lords.* Garden City, N.Y.: Anchor Press/Doubleday.

Farrington, David P., G. Gundry, and D. J. West. 1975. "The Family Transmission of Criminality." *Medicine, Science and the Law* 15:177–186.

Federal Bureau of Investigation. 1986. *Uniform Crime Reports.* Washington, D.C.: U.S. Government Printing Office.

Ferdinand, Theodore N. 1990. "Ethnicity, Neighborhood, Gender, and Delinquency in Hawaii." Paper presented at The American Society of Criminology meetings in Baltimore.

Fyvel, T. R. 1964. *Troublemakers.* New York: Schocken Books.

Giordano, Peggy C., Stephen A. Cernkovich, and M. D. Pugh. 1986. "Friendships and Delinquency." *American Journal of Sociology* 91, No. 5 (March):1170–1202.

Glueck, Sheldon, and Eleanor Glueck. 1950. *Unraveling Delinquency.* Cambridge: Harvard University Press.

Goldstein, H. S. 1984. "Parental Composition, Supervision, and Conduct: Problems in Youths 12 to 17 Years Old." *Journal of the American Academy of Child Psychiatry* 23:679–684.

Gottfredson, Michael, and Travis Hirschi. 1990. *A General Theory of Crime.* Stanford, CA: Stanford University Press.

Gove, Walter R., and Robert D. Crutchfield. 1982. "The Family and Juvenile Delinquency." *The Sociological Quarterly* 23 (Summer):301–319.

Greenberg, Michael R., George W. Carey, and Frank J. Popper. 1987. "Violent Death, Violent States, and American Youth." *Public Interest* No. 87 (Spring):38–48.

Hagan, John. 1989. *Structural Criminology.* New Brunswick, N.J.: Rutgers University Press.

Hagan, John, John Simpson, and A. R. Gillis. 1987. "Class in the Household: A Power-Control Theory of Gender and Delinquency." *American Journal of Sociology* 92, No. 4:788–816.

Hirschi, Travis. 1969. *Causes of Delinquency.* Berkeley: University of California Press.

Horowitz, Ruth. 1982. "Adult Delinquent Gangs in a Chicano Community." *Urban Life* 11, No. 2 (April):3–26.

Japanese National Police Agency. 1988. *White Paper on Police 1988.* Tokyo: Police Association.

Jensen, Gary F. 1972. "Parents, Peers and Delinquent Action: A Test of Differential Association Theory." *American Journal of Sociology* 78:562–575.

Johnstone, John W. C. 1978. "Juvenile Delinquency and the Family: A Contextual Interpretation." *Youth and Society* 9 (March):299–313.

Klein, Malcolm. 1971. *Street Gangs and Street Workers.* Englewood Cliffs, N.J.: Prentice-Hall.

Kobrin, Solomon. 1951. "The Conflict of Values in Delinquency Areas." *American Sociological Review* 16:653–661.

Kornhauser, Ruth Rosner. 1978. *Social Sources of Delinquency.* Chicago: University of Chicago Press.

Kornhauser, William. 1959. *The Politics of Mass Society.* New York: The Free Press.

LaGrange, Randy L., and Helene Raskin White. 1985. "Age Differences in Delinquency: A Test of Theory." *Criminology* 23, No. 1:19–46.

Loeber, Rolf, and Magda Stouthamer-Loeber. 1986. "Family Factors as Correlates and Predictors of Juvenile Conduct Problems and Delinquency." In *Crime and Justice,* vol. 7. Edited by Michael Tonry and Norval Morris. Chicago: University of Chicago Press.

Loeber, Rolf, W. Weismann, and J. B. Reid. 1983. "Family Interaction of Assaultive Adolescents, Stealers, and Nondelinquents." *Journal of Abnormal Child Psychology* 11:1–14.

Maccoby, Eleanor E., Joseph P. Johnson, and Russell M. Church. 1958. "Community Integration and the Social Control of Juvenile Delinquency." *Journal of Social Issues* 14, No. 3:38–51.

McCord, Joan, and William McCord. 1975. "The Effects of Parental Role Model on Criminality." In *Readings in Juvenile Delinquency,* 3rd edition. Edited by Ruth Shonle Cavan. Philadelphia: J.B. Lippincott.

Miller, Walter B. 1958. "Lower Class Culture as a Generating Milieu of Gang Delinquency." *The Journal of Social Issues* 14, No. 3:5–19.

Polk, Kenneth, and F. Lynn Richmond. 1972. *Schools and Delinquency.* Englewood Cliffs, N.J.: Prentice-Hall.

Reiss, Albert J., Jr., and A. Lewis Rhodes. 1961. "Delinquency and Social Class Structure." *American Sociological Review* 26, No. 5:720–732.

Robins, L., and S. Hill. 1966. "Assessing the Contributions of Family Structure and Peer Groups to Juvenile Delinquency." *Journal of Criminal Law, Criminology, and Police Science* 57:325–334.

Rohlen, Thomas P. 1983. *Japan's High Schools.* Berkeley: University of California Press.

Rosen, Lawrence. 1985. "Family and Delinquency: Structure of Function." *Criminology* 23, No. 3 (August):553–574.

Schafer, Walter E. 1972. "Participation in Interscholastic Athletics and Delinquency." In *Schools and Delinquency.* Edited by Kenneth Polk and Walter E. Schafer. Englewood Cliffs, N.J.: Prentice-Hall.

Schuerman, Leo, and Solomon Kobrin. 1986. "Community Careers in Crime." In *Crime and Justice,* vol. 8. Edited by Michael Tonry and Norval Morris. Chicago: University of Chicago Press.

Schwartz, Gary. 1987. *Beyond Conformity or Rebellion.* Chicago: University of Chicago Press.

Schwendinger, Herman, and Julia R. Siegel Schwendinger. 1985. *Adolescent Subcultures and Delinquency.* New York: Praeger.

Shulman, Harry Manuel. 1961. *Juvenile Delinquency in American Society.* New York: Harper & Brothers.

Spergel, Irving. 1964. *Racketville Slumtown Haulburg.* Chicago: University of Chicago Press.

———. 1984. "Violent Gangs in Chicago: In Search of Social Policy." *Social Service Review* 58 (June):199–226.

Stinchcombe, Arthur L. 1964. *Rebellion in a High School.* Chicago: Quadrangle Books.

Stouthamer-Loeber, M., K. B. Schmaling, and R. Loeber. 1984. "The Relationship of Single Parent Family Status and Marital Discord to Antisocial Child Behavior." Unpublished paper. Pittsburgh: University of Pittsburgh.

Sykes, Gresham M., and David Matza. 1957. "Techniques of Neutralization: A Theory of Delinquency." *The American Journal of Sociology* 22 (December):664–670.

Toby, Jackson. 1983. "Violence in School." In *Crime and Justice*, vol. 4. Edited by Michael Tonry and Norval Morris. Chicago: University of Chicago Press.

U.S. Bureau of the Census. 1986. *Current Population Reports.* "School Enrollment—Social and Economic Characteristics of Students." P 20, No. 409, September: table 6.

U.S. Bureau of the Census. 1989. "Households, Families, Marital Status, and Living Arrangements." *Current Population Reports.* Series P 20, No. 441, March: table 1.

U.S. Department of Health, Education, and Welfare. 1978. *Violent Schools—Safe Schools*, vol. 1. Washington, D.C.: U.S. Government Priting Office.

U.S. Department of Education. 1987. *Japanese Education Today.* Washington, D.C.: U.S. Government Printing Office.

Van Voorhis, Patricia, Francis T. Cullen, Richard A. Mathers, and Connie Chenoweth Garner. 1988. "The Impact of Family Structure and Quality on Delinquency: A Comparative Assessment of Structural and Functional Factors." *Criminology* 26, No. 2:235–261.

Wagatsuma, Hiroshi, and George DeVos. 1984. *Heritage of Endurance.* Berkeley: University of California Press.

Wells, L. Edward, and Joseph H. Rankin. 1988. "Direct Parental Controls and Delinquency." *Criminology* 26, No. 2:263–285.

Wiatrowski, Michael D., David B. Griswold, and Mary K. Roberts. 1981. "Social Control Theory and Delinquency." *American Sociological Review* 46 (October):525–541.

Wilkinson, K., B. G. Stitt, and M. L. Erickson. 1982. "Siblings and Delinquent Behavior." *Criminology* 20:223–240.

Wilson, H., and G. W. Herbert. 1978. *Parents and Children in the Inner City.* London: Routledge & Kegan Paul.

Chapter
10

Comparative Delinquency: Europe and Asia

Delinquency is like any other cultural system: It changes and adapts as society evolves. Developing societies such as Uganda and Mexico create a rising demand for workers and invite a vast migration of rural folk into major urban centers. Since the uprooted poor often lack basic social or economic resources to care for their children, many urban children are left on their own. Because they have no public facilities to care for such children, developing nations often encounter herds of vagrant children—street urchins—in their commercial centers eking out a living from begging, scavanging, and petty crime. These children are a nuisance because they annoy established classes with their begging and petty crime and because all too often they become adult criminals who prey upon society in more dangerous ways.

Before long, however, these developing countries build custodial institutions for vagrant children in which some of their social and physical needs can be provided. These benign institutions in crowding mildly deviant children together enable them to establish informal groups in which the methods and values of delinquency are glorified. On this basis informal cliques form, drawn from all sections of the city. Upon release they reassemble to exploit opportunities in crime and to acquaint other children with the glories of deviance. Within two or three generations delinquency has been institutionalized in such cities, and the problem has become an integral part of the urban landscape.

Cities that are just beginning to industrialize often sport a timid, unsophisticated kind of delinquent who expresses both the adjustment problems of poor youth and the social deficiencies of the urban environment. Cities that have already begun to cope with the problems of youth, paradoxically, often face a more serious type of delinquency, more broadly based and more predatory (see Ferdinand, 1986).

At first, delinquency reflects the weaknesses and limited means of rapidly developing societies. But as development proceeds and cities adjust their administrative bureaucracies to the needs of an urban population, delinquency advances to a more sophisticated level. Today, in fully developed societies, well-established delinquent groups socialize juveniles into a deviant culture that sets them apart from the rest and prepares them for adult criminality.

For this reason it would be unwise in comparing delinquency in developing and developed societies to expect the same theories and perspectives to account for both. By the same token, we must be careful in adopting the methods of other societies to prevent or control delinquency. Since different societies face different problems, it would be naive to expect the prevention techniques of Japan, for example, to work as well in the United States as in Japan. We must be aware of the relative levels of development in societies to understand clearly their differences in delinquency and its control. Any comparisons in this area must be done carefully. Not only are the traditions of other countries vastly different, but their juvenile laws also are different.

Nevertheless, cross-cultural comparisons of delinquency can be very revealing, just as tracing historical trends in delinquency in single societies can be. Both techniques, if used intelligently, can provide a sound scientific basis for explaining why delinquency of one era or society differs so sharply from that of another.

Why are delinquent gangs in Mexico City or San Juan, Puerto Rico, little more than adolescent cliques roaming through the streets, while Hispanic and black gangs in Chicago or Los Angeles engage periodically in deadly shoot-outs with rival gangs? Why are delinquency rates so low in Tokyo and Zurich, while in Amsterdam, Stockholm, and Los Angeles they are much higher? Sound answers must be based on sound analyses of the patterns of each society.

By cataloging the sociohistorical forces that affect delinquency in different kinds of societies, we can begin to identify the basic factors that are responsible for delinquency in the first place. But all this must be done with a keen eye toward social and cultural differences that can disguise the underlying nature of delinquency.

JAPANESE DELINQUENCY

The Japanese juvenile justice system is as thorough as any in following the trends of delinquency in society. Since both the legal system and the penal system are organized nationally—not locally or regionally as in the United States—throughout Japan the courts and institutions follow uniform policies in dealing with juveniles. Since each center carefully reports its annual experience to its national headquarters in Tokyo, it is convenient for the Japanese government to aggregate the experiences of the nation's juvenile courts and institutions. By doing so over the years it gradually assembles a long term picture of delinquency in Japan. Figure 10.1 shows the rate of penal code juvenile offenders in Japan from 1936 to 1988.

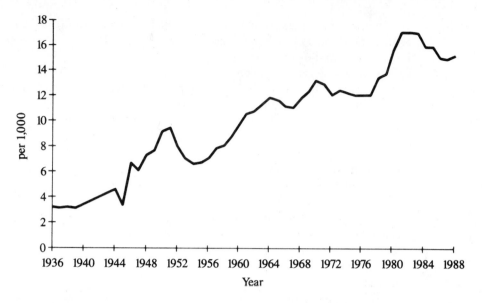

Figure 10.1 Delinquency rates per 1,000 in Japan. *Source:* Ministry of Justice. 1989. *Summary of the White Paper on Crime.* Research and Training Institute: Tokyo, Table 15, p. 41.

From 1922 to 1948 juvenile tribunals dealt with youngsters 17 years and under. Young people 18 and over were regarded as adults and were handled under the criminal code. After 1948 the juvenile code included teenagers 14 to 19 years old, and the number of arrested juveniles rose 26 percent between 1947 and 1949 (see Figure 10.1).[1] Beginning in the 1970s the police stepped up their monitoring of minor offenders, and arrests for bicycle "borrowing" and simple theft rose by 253 percent. Heightened police supervision continued into the 1980s and helped to produce a major peak in the rate of delinquency in 1981 (Yokoyama, 1986a: 110). Although serious crimes showed a steady decline after 1965, minor offenses such as larceny and bicycle theft rose by 21 percent and 809 percent respectively (Yokoyama, 1986a: 109, table 3) and contributed to an overall increase in the delinquency rate of 48 percent (11.7 to 17.2 per 1000) between 1965 and 1981 (Figure 10.1).

Since 1980 these trends have continued. By 1988 female delinquency had increased 37.3 percent and male delinquency 16.3 percent. The police continued to focus on younger, minor delinquents, and as a result middle school students increased their share of male delinquency from 36 percent in 1980 to 43 percent in 1988. Among female delinquents the portion of middle school students rose from 27 percent in 1980 to 39 percent in 1988. Most of these increases focussed on minor thefts with girls showing a 30.1 percent increase, and boys an increase of 11.5 percent.[2]

---

[1]Traffic offenders were separated from penal code offenders after 1962, and many crime statistic series reflect this change, although Figure 10.1 does not. Prior to 1955 juvenile traffic offenders were relatively rare.
[2]Dr. Ayako Uchiyama kindly provided the statistics describing 1980 through 1988.

By way of comparison, the *adult crime rate* in Japan steadily decreased during this same period. In 1948 a postwar peak—20 arrests per 1000—was recorded by the police for violations of the penal code, excluding road-traffic violations. By 1987 the crime rate for the same offenses had fallen to 13.4, for a decline of 33 percent over 39 years (Japanese Ministry of Justice, 1989: 21–22, table 9). Although delinquency increased substantially in the postwar period, adult crime declined.

Several developments contributed to this pattern of delinquency in Japan. After World War II the Japanese nation was shattered. Its economy was battered and prostrate. Its sociopolitical system was discredited and disorganized. Its people were demoralized by the fierce bombardment of their homeland during the war and, then, by their government's surrender. The rapid demobilization of Japan's military forces brought large numbers of men back into civilian life and a foundering economy. Many adolescents were homeless or with only one parent, and many families had barely enough to sustain themselves. Starvation was a threat, and minor crime by both adults and juveniles provided needed support for desperate families.

The result was a sharp increase in both crime and delinquency in the immediate postwar period. During this period theft and violent crime were common, and adult offenders were mostly older, urban males. Delinquency was also the work of older, socially marginal males who offended repeatedly (Mugishima and Matsumoto, 1973).

But as the economy shifted to peacetime production and gradually reabsorbed young adults as well as demobilized soldiers, social stability and moral confidence returned. Crime and delinquency both declined. The spreading prosperity dispelled pessimism among young people and eased their reintegration into urban neighborhoods. It also enabled Japan to give more attention to the education of the young.

Compulsory education required young people to attend school to the age of 16, and great care was taken to insure that they not only received formal instruction but also were guided in constructive attitudes and cooperative relationships. Moreover, it was broadly understood that the child's success in school affected not simply his or her future, but the honor of the parents and siblings as well.

Nevertheless, school was arduous, and those whose abilities were meager or whose commitment to parents and their honor was limited often found it difficult to excel. Thus, some Japanese children experienced only humiliation and stress in school, and a sense of helplessness and fatalism began to dominate *their* attitudes.

Although each child was encouraged to join a variety of school-sponsored clubs and activities, informal peer groups began to form in the junior and senior high schools and helped to rechannel the values of young students. Just as teenagers elsewhere think about social status, peers, excitement, and fashionable clothes, Japanese youngsters also began to value the emblems of wealth and status. Status claims also forced many boys to compete aggressively with one another, and those who were slightly unusual either in appearance or in background occasionally became the butt of severe hazing or bullying (U.S. Department of Education, 1987: 37).

Around 1956 delinquency began to climb, and between 1956 and 1970 it rose fully 87 percent. During this fifteen year period the ratio of boy to girl delinquency remained high—11 to 1—and only about 55 percent of all delinquents were in school. The rest were high school dropouts or beyond school age (Uchiyama, 1990, tables 4, 5, 8, and 9).

The resurgence of Japanese industrial power in the 1960s lifted the standard of living of nearly everyone and created a vast market among the young for goods that could establish them as attractive persons with social sophistication and taste. It also dulled their sense that the "good things" in life come only to those who work hard and maintain a stern discipline over themselves and their needs. In fact, the good things in life came easily to attractive young people. Delinquency began to change.

It began to reflect less the broader society and more the condition of teenagers in Japan. Delinquents were getting younger and embracing a broader segment of the adolescent population (Mugishima and Matsumoto, 1973). But they were less likely to mature into chronic delinquents than in the postwar period. School failure and weak family structure were still prominent in the background of delinquents (DeVos, 1980), but peer groups were also beginning to shape the thinking and behavior of Japanese teenagers, though still not so pervasively as in the United States (Yokoyama, 1986a; U.S. Department of Education, 1987, 46).

In 1977 delinquency began a substantial rise to a level in 1981 fully 54 percent higher. As noted earlier this increase reflected an emphasis among Japanese police upon reducing minor juvenile offending. There is evidence, however, that delinquency itself also began to change. Beginning in 1971 the ratio of female delinquents began to increase from its pre-1970 level of about one female delinquent for every eleven male delinquents to about 1:5 in 1977, where it has remained throughout the 1980s. Moreover, the proportion of students among delinquents increased from the 1970 level of 53 percent to about 74 percent in 1985, while the proportion of non-students among delinquents sank from 47 percent in 1970 to only about 22 percent in 1985 (Uchiyama, 1990: tables 4, 5, 8, 9). These subtle changes began before the police became especially active in supervising pre-delinquents in the mid-1970s, and they continued after police initiatives were well underway. The changes in police policy toward minor delinquents in the mid-1970s could well have been a response to changes in the nature of delinquency. It was becoming more juvenile and less criminal.[3]

Delinquency slowly spread from the poor and socially deprived to the middle classes. As greater wealth came within their grasp, young people became more relaxed, more spontaneous, more impulsive, more dependent upon their peers, and less inhibited by adult disapproval. They began to buy fashionable goods, motorbikes, and occasionally, thrilling, attention-getting motorcycles.[3]

To entertain young adults pachinko parlors opened in nearly every neighborhood, where players sometimes spent hours before simple games of skill, and whole sections of major cities—Shinjuku in Tokyo, for example—were devoted to nighttime amusements of all types. Girls with difficulties at home or in school found their way to these entertainment centers and fell easily into a variety of questionable relationships with other young people.

Japan's thriving economy and rising standard of living in the 1960s relieved serious poverty and brought a comfortable life-style to nearly everyone. It reduced the number of deeply demoralized people, and serious crime and delinquency fell steadily during the postwar period. But this same economic advance increased demands on juveniles both

---

[3]Recently, small but growing numbers of Japanese teenagers have also been dropping-out of school (*Wall Street Journal*, February 8, 1991: p. A10).

formally in terms of school achievement and informally in terms of youthful values and goals. Although serious delinquency declined throughout Japan, minor delinquency in the form of minor theft, hot-rodding, and glue sniffing were becoming troublesome (Yokoyama, 1986a: table 3; Yokoyama, 1986b; and Morita, 1985).

Additionally, shortly after the war, demobilization of the armed forces spawned sharply increasing birth rates—much as in the United States—with the result that just as the economy was hitting its stride in the late 1950s and early 1960s, a rising tide of teenagers began to gather. As their numbers grew, they sensed their growing social importance, and the impact of their materialistic values and ideas seemed to complement the growing industrial capacity of the nation. The baby boom in postwar Japan amplified the impact of young people in the late 1960s and early 1970s.

Preventing Delinquency in Japan

In response to the growing problem, the Japanese undertook a carefully conceived strategy to combat delinquency. We described in Chapter 9 the close cooperation between town associations, parents, schools, police, Big Brothers or Big Sisters, and volunteer probation officers in dealing with predelinquent children. Juveniles who show signs of failing in school or falling into delinquency receive close attention from all these groups. In addition, after 1975 the Japanese police stepped up their efforts to curb predelinquents through close supervision and counseling. Juvenile Guidance Centers were established in many urban neighborhoods to help parents deal with difficult teenagers and to help children who were unhappy with their lives (Yokoyama, 1989:45), and the Japanese Correction Bureau set up in the 1950s a network of Juvenile Classification Homes where problem children could receive careful diagnostic testing and treatment recommendations.

But curiously, the Japanese did not emphasize community-based, professional treatment programs for delinquents. Their strategy was to prevent delinquency by first identifying youngsters who were drifting away from socially acceptable paths and then strengthening their ties with family and school, nudging them back onto their proper paths. Rifts in family and neighborhood relations were mended by bringing Big Brothers or Big Sisters, police, Juvenile Guidance Centers, and volunteer probation officers together with parents, child, and school so that troubled juveniles would have even less opportunity to misbehave.

Very few were sent to community-based treatment programs. In 1985 just 0.2 percent (374 youngsters) were referred to treatment programs out of the 190,852 offenders sent to family courts. Altogether 96 percent of the children appearing before these courts either were placed on probation or had their cases dismissed (Yokoyama, 1989: 49, table 2). The emphasis in Japan was upon preventing delinquency before it could occur.

If all this attention, formal and informal, went for naught and the child persisted in delinquency, he or she stood a good chance of being sent to a juvenile custodial institution. Few Japanese communities offer systematic treatment programs for persistent delinquents. Although a variety of community-based treatment programs are available for such delinquents in most medium to large cities in the United States and in western

Europe, Japanese community leaders have less confidence in such programs, and persistent delinquents, sooner rather than later, are placed in custodial centers.

Juvenile Justice in Japan

Juvenile training schools in Japan, 54 in all, are scattered throughout the country. They are graded in terms of the length of their programs (short term or long term), the age and gender of the inmates, and their criminal tendency (advanced or not). Short-term programs last three to six months and focus on juveniles who need intensive discipline but otherwise have only a weak inclination toward delinquency. Long-term programs, lasting up to two years, are for more sophisticated delinquent youths. These programs focus upon improving social skills and work habits and provide living guidance and vocational, and educational programs. Above all, they encourage a cooperative and compliant demeanor among juveniles.

Japanese juvenile institutions are small by American standards. In 1988, male institutions with short-term programs averaged about 40 boys, male institutions with long-term programs held about 91 inmates on any given day, and female institutions averaged about 52 girls on a daily basis (Japanese Ministry of Justice, 1990: 55, table III-3). These institutions all emphasize reeducating the child, and they provide psychiatric treatment only for those who show clear clinical symptoms. The assumption is that delinquency is a willful act and the juvenile can decide to follow a more constructive path if he or she so wishes. Through their programs, the institutions attempt to guide the juvenile to such a decision.

Overall, the effort to control delinquency in Japan is intelligently designed to take full advantage of the closely knit Japanese community. As can be seen in Chapter 9, the rate of delinquency is slight by Western standards, and the policy of depending heavily on informal relations to redirect errant juveniles utilizes the formidable pressures of the Japanese family and neighborhood in ways that almost ensure the juvenile's reorientation. Should these informal pressures be insufficient, the juvenile is given a taste of coercive institutional life, and he or she learns firsthand the condition of the criminal in Japan. Unsophisticated children are kept separate from those with advanced criminal tendencies, but both receive a candid demonstration of what the future may hold if they fail to change their direction. Most juveniles change.

No careful measures of recidivism are reported publicly for juvenile residential programs, but anecdotal reports suggest that it is very low for some institutions. The strategy of concentrating on delinquency prevention seems to be effective. Moreover, the policy of institutionalizing children who give clear evidence of incorrigibility may also be effective, though the evidence here is less solid.

DELINQUENCY IN THE WEST

The place of the individual in Western communities differs sharply from that in the Orient. In Asian countries the individual is measured by group standards, but in the West the individual's duty to the community is much weaker than the responsibility to his or her own conscience. In the West individuals are more fundamental than their groups.

The Enlightenment and French Revolution in the eighteenth century, the Marxist revolution in the late nineteenth and early twentieth centuries, and *perestroika* in recent years were all prompted by an awareness that traditional leaders and politics were unable to guide society in ways that would advance the welfare of its citizens. Whenever the regime in power proved inadequate to the task of governing, its legitimacy was challenged by a different corps of leaders with an alternative style and set of values who felt justified in seizing the helm by revolution, if necessary. The individual has claims on the polity and the community that *must* be fulfilled. Moreover, the individual's self-interest often outweighs the obligations to community, and individual freedoms as well as educational programs designed to foster individuality have been considerably broader. This means basically that individualism has flourished in the West, affecting not only the levels of crime and delinquency but also the administration of criminal justice.

Sweden

Sweden and the Netherlands strongly resemble one another. Both are prosperous capitalist societies and have a tradition of highly centralized governmental bureaucracies as well as a tolerance toward minorities and stigmatized groups. Both have a juvenile justice system founded on the social welfare model, and both have an active drug culture that is readily accessible to teenagers, though the Netherlands through its decriminalization of soft drugs has favored an extraordinary development in this area. Both nations have experienced sharp rises in delinquency in the postwar years.

Since World War II, for example, delinquency has been the fastest growing segment of the Swedish crime problem. In 1950 about 11 males per 1000 between the ages of 15 and 17 were charged with offenses in Swedish courts, but by 1987 this rate had more than tripled, to 37 per 1000. As recently as 1975, however, delinquency had been much higher. Between 1975 and 1987, for example, the delinquency rate dropped by about half (Sarnecki, 1989: 8, diagram 3).

Lower-working-class boys seem to be the main problem. Lower-working-class arrestees outnumber their upper-middle-class counterparts about 3 to 1, and boys outnumber girls by about 24 to 1 (Wikstrom, 1990: 13).

As in much of the West, a large portion of male teenagers drifts into minor delinquency. In 1953 the prevalence of arrests among males under 26 years was 31 percent, and among females in the same age group, 6 percent were recorded in the police files. These figures would undoubtedly have been higher if measured today via self-report questionnaires (Wikstrom, 1990: 12). Serious delinquents in Sweden tend to have hostile relations with their parents; they are academically poor and are frequently school dropouts; they are involved with other youngsters in drugs and crime and often join established cliques (Sarnecki, 1989). These cliques foster delinquency, and their core members account for much if not most of the delinquency in Sweden (see Box 5.1, Chapter 5).

Sarnecki (1988), for example, reported that (1) a core of teenaged gang members— 5.6 percent of all suspected delinquents—offended at a much higher rate than all the rest (see also Wikstrom, 1990: 12); (2) they doubled the delinquency rate of noncore aquaintances; and (3) they formed new delinquent groups as they grew older. All in all, they accounted personally for about 48 percent of the delinquency committed while they were active in their town. If these core members had been identified and incapacitated, Sarnecki (1988:27) speculated, that fact alone would have resulted in a significant reduction in Swedish delinquency.

For Swedish chronic offenders, delinquency seems to represent an inability to get involved in the constructive routines of family, peers, neighborhood, and school. These rootless, anomic juveniles invent delinquency as an expression of their discomfort, but their delinquency only serves to confirm and intensify their alienation as they move into adulthood.

Although numerically only a tiny part of the Swedish delinquency problem, these core delinquents are surprisingly active and account for a very substantial portion of the criminality in Sweden both as juveniles and as adults. Delinquent cliques are found in many of the medium-sized and large cities of Sweden, and rootless delinquents circulate freely from one town to another, greeting other delinquents whom they met earlier during stays in juvenile justice centers (Sarnecki, 1984b: 10).

It is safe to say that Sweden has spawned a loosely integrated network of chronic delinquents who are hedonistic, predatory, and alienated. They pose a significant problem in adulthood not only because they continue to pursue crime but also because they suffer a whole host of other problems—downward social mobility, unemployment, divorce, drug and alcohol abuse, poor physical and mental health, and early death, among others (Sarnecki, 1984a: 3–9).

Juvenile Justice in Sweden   The Swedish juvenile justice system is often regarded as one of the most progressive in the world. It presumes children under 15 years are incapable of crime, and no matter what the offense, such cases are reviewed not by a juvenile court but by a local Social Welfare Committee composed of social workers, clergymen, school teachers, medical doctors, lawyers, and other community leaders.[4] The Social Welfare Committee is responsible for several facets of the treatment function in Sweden. It funds and implements treatment programs at both the local and national levels; it develops plans for resolving the children's problems, if possible; it coordinates local services ranging from medical to social to psychiatric treatment in behalf of the child.

The committee may also elect to do nothing aside from a stern warning, and in most cases that is the decision. Since misbehavior is often a part of growing up, the police and the Social Welfare Committee are particularly tolerant of youthful behavior that has the earmarks of adolescent impulsiveness or poor judgment.

The Social Welfare Committee can also provide guidance and support in the form of a social caseworker who regularly contacts the child and family. Children may be placed in a foster home or group home for children, and if necessary, the Committee may appeal to the local court for permission to assign a child to a reformatory for children. But this alternative is rarely used. Custodial care programs must be reviewed every six months by the court until the involuntary placement is terminated.

---

[4]This section was guided by two reports on the Swedish juvenile justice system (Sarnecki, 1989; Janson and Torstensson, 1984).

Juveniles 15 to 17 years old may be charged with criminal offenses and, if convicted, punished according to penal law. But here the court also enjoys wide latitude. After consultation with the Social Welfare Committee, the prosecutor may elect to waive prosecution if the teenager promises to cooperate with the Social Welfare Committee. About 45 percent of juveniles 15 to 17 years old receive such a waiver, and these are most common in minor theft cases but rare with violent crimes or vandalism.

Based on a juvenile's confession of guilt, the prosecutor may administer a sanction—a day-fine or restitution, for example—but again, only if the offender willingly accepts it (about 38 percent receive such punishments). The juvenile may be tried under the criminal law (in about 13 percent of the cases) and receive a fine, a suspended sentence or probation, or be sent to a custodial institution (0.2 percent).

Young adult offenders 18 to 20 years old face much the same range of outcomes, but here the vast majority are punished by the prosecutor or the court following conviction. Only 9 percent receive a prosecution waiver, and only about 1 percent are transferred to the Social Welfare Committee. The rest—90 percent—are treated as adults and punished according to Swedish penal law.

In sum, misbehavior among young juveniles under 15 is regarded as socially or psychologically determined and noncriminal. Between 15 and 17, the juvenile is presumed innocent, with the burden of proof placed on the prosecutor to establish that the offender deserves to be handled as an adult. A small proportion of Swedish juveniles are handled in this fashion, and only a tiny portion are assigned to custodial settings. Young adults 18 to 20 years old may also be handled as juveniles, but only a very small number actually are.

The Netherlands

In Holland, delinquency is much the same as in Sweden. Since 1961, arrests of children 12 to 17 years old have risen from about 7.3 per 1000 to 14.2 per 1000 in 1981 (Junger-Tas and Block, 1988: 14), for a 94 percent increase over 20 years. Much of this increase involves home burglaries, breaking into and stealing from autos, bicycle theft, car theft, and vandalism, primarily by males 14 years old and older. Girls constitute only a small portion of the total—7.9 percent in 1975 and 9.8 percent in 1981—and younger teenagers 12 to 13 years old are negligible as far as delinquency is concerned (Junger-Tas and Block, 1988: 15–18). Since 1981 delinquency has drifted downward as in Sweden.

Although drug use is common among alienated Dutch teenagers, such behavior is not closely monitored by the police, and drug abuse is not a common charge in court. Illegal drug dealers are pursued vigorously, but few juveniles are arrested for drug use. If drug users commit other offenses for their drug habits, they are duly charged, but they are not dealt with in criminal justice as drug offenders.

When viewed via self-report studies, the scope of Dutch delinquency is seen to be much wider. A representative sample of 1,980 Dutch teenagers gathered by Junger-Tas and Block (1988: 22–65) revealed that 54 percent of the boys and 24 percent of the girls admitted to at least one incident of shoplifting, theft at school, bicycle theft, joyriding, violent offenses, vandalism, or soccer hooliganism. Further, although the socioeconomic status of the parents bore little relationship to their child's delinquency, attending vocational schools as opposed to public preparatory schools made a big difference. Thirty-four percent of those attending lower vocational schools admitted delinquent offenses, but only 20 percent of the students preparing for university did.

Not only was the type of school important, but also the quality of the child's performance in school was a key factor in his or her delinquency. *Bonding with school* as measured by the child's feeling for teachers and school, and *school functioning* as assessed by both the child's academic success and his or her misbehavior in school were both related to delinquency.

Bonding and school functioning served as measures of the child's integration in school, and school integration defined in this sense was much more important in the child's delinquency than even family integration. More specifically, the child's success in learning and complying with school rules played a very large role in his or her delinquency. Similar results have been reported in virtually every country studied, but the curious fact is that these results in the Netherlands were taken by the authors to mean that *social controls theory* was most effective in explaining delinquency (Junger-Tas and Block, 1988: 73).

If the quality of the child's adjustment in school is governed by his or her academic success and compliance with the rules, strain theory (see Chapter 12, pp. 212–214) is probably more relevant. Those who do poorly or cannot conform to basic regulations receive much criticism from parents and teachers, and their self-esteem suffers. They fail in their quest for school success not only in the eyes of those closest to them but worst of all in their own eyes. Is not strain theory most appropriate to this particular pattern of events?

Juvenile Justice in Holland[5]   As in Sweden, the Dutch juvenile justice system is based on the social welfare model. The juvenile justice system pursues rehabilitation as its overall goal in handling juvenile offenders and works mainly with juveniles between 12 and 17 years old. It consists of a juvenile court that deals directly with youth in violation of the law and a Child Protection Council that works hand in hand with the court in developing treatment plans for children who come before the court. The court and council follow a social welfare philosophy and seek the least obtrusive solutions for children in need. In some serious cases, however, juveniles of 16 or 17 years can be transferred to the criminal courts and tried as adults.

The juvenile court has a wide range of alternatives. The court may sentence the teenager to (1) supervision within the family, under the guidance of social caseworkers and involving outpatient services; (2) supervision away from the family, in some form of residential care (foster homes or group homes); or (3) penal measures (fines or imprisonment).

The plain fact, however, is that the rehabilitative arm of the Dutch juvenile justice system has been shrinking recently, while its punitive arm has been increasing. Fewer juveniles have been placed under supervision either within or outside the family, pretrial detention of juveniles has grown more punitive, and custodial confinement has increased over the past few years. A distinct hardening of the Dutch juvenile justice system has occurred since the 1970s.

---

[5]This section is based largely on an essay by Junger-Tas (1984).

The answer may lie in the fact that since the 1970s a sizable and growing number of Dutch youth have assumed a loosely structured, iconoclastic life-style. They move into unoccupied quarters, they engage in begging and minor criminality, they are truant from school or unemployed, and drug dependency is common. They lead a carefree but aimless existence and seemed headed for a short adult life.

Still, these young people have proved especially unresponsive to the traditional array of social welfare programs, and as a result, several major cities—Amsterdam and Rotterdam, for example—have established Youth Advisory Centers in which the guiding philosophy stresses not helping young people adapt to the social order but helping them deal with the discrepancies between their hopes for the social order and its lapses or failures. If a young person doesn't like the system, how can he or she help change it? In addition, these centers focus upon some of the urgent health, shelter, social, and legal problems young people bring to the city.

The efforts of these centers in reaching out to rootless young people certainly fill a niche in the Dutch juvenile justice system that is otherwise unserved. But they may also perpetuate a dependency based upon anomie that leads to further deterioration for those involved.

Switzerland

In some ways, Switzerland has more in common with Japan than with Sweden or the Netherlands. As with the Japanese, the Swiss are a closely knit, conservative, affluent nation. Young people have good rapport with their elders, communities embrace their members, and juveniles develop a commitment to basic Swiss values and goals. Most people live in urban communities of at least 10,000 and feel a deep pride in Swiss accomplishments—their vaunted standard of living, their efficiency as a banking and industrial nation, and their very low crime rate. Indeed, much of the country's serious crime is the work of foreign visitors (Clinard, 1978: 49–51).

At the same time Switzerland has a decentralized government, as in the United States, in which much of the governing is done at the canton level. The Swiss are also a remarkably diverse people, with four major languages and ethnic traditions. Whether measured by crime victim surveys, insurance claims for property losses, public attitudes about crime, or prosecution rates, the overall Swiss crime rate is far below that of much of Europe (see Clinard, 1978).

In the 1960s when crime rates in Sweden and the Netherlands were soaring, Swiss crime was falling (Clinard, 1978: appendix C). Between 1960 and 1971, conviction rates for violent crimes and for crimes against morality actually fell, and rates for crimes against property showed a minuscule 1.1 percent increase. Petty larceny had a sizable jump, from 1.1 convictions per 100,000 in 1961 to 6.8 in 1971, but it was the only crime to show a sharp increase.

Still, drugs, both hard and soft, are a growing problem in Switzerland, particularly in the major urban centers. The AIDS epidemic further complicates the problem, and in response some communities provide free sterile hypodermic needles to drug users. Although there is little detailed evidence to clarify this problem, we do know that drug abuse in Switzerland is largely a young people's problem.

As in Japan, it seems as though well-structured, supportive communities with well-defined career lines for young people only intensify the plight of those few who for whatever reason cannot follow conventional pathways into adulthood. Substance abuse is appealing because it dulls the sense of depression and failure that often engulfs those who fall off the conventional path.

In most other respects Swiss youth are highly conventional. Swiss compulsory secondary education is particularly formal, emphasizing scholarship and strict discipline in the classroom. Academic standards are high and demand a major investment in time and commitment by the students (Vaz and Casparis, 1971). As in Japan, a youth culture is making its presence felt, but it is still weak in comparison with those in the United States, the Netherlands, or Sweden (Casparis and Vaz, 1978). Youth gangs are rare and loosely organized. Delinquents form themselves into cliques, but these cliques are based more on convenience than a sense of close kinship.

Overall, the ease with which Swiss youth find satisfying employment in their expanding economy almost guarantees them a rewarding place in most communities and a full life. This together with the firm ties they have to family and school keep delinquency at a minimum.

WHAT HAVE WE LEARNED?

In Japan and Switzerland juveniles are presented with a well-structured, full experience during adolescence. In school they are expected to study hard and avoid trouble not only for their teacher's or parent's sake but also for their own futures. Police and juvenile authorities provide both supportive counsel and strict limits for those few who deviate from the usual path. Juveniles whose deviance persists in the face of official counsel are exposed to harsh, custodial pressures, and one way or another most juveniles reach adulthood prepared to accept adult responsibilities. Few delinquents become adult criminals.

In Sweden and the Netherlands, however, other factors have conspired to strengthen delinquency. The confidence that Dutch and Swedish authorities have placed in community-based programs to reorient misbehaving youth has among other things fostered relations among delinquents that carry over to their lives in the community. Both countries have fostered a loosely structured web of alienated juveniles and young adults in which drug abuse and minor crime are common. Both countries have placed strong emphasis upon humane, professional treatment of predelinquents and delinquents, but today themes of disillusionment toward treatment and rehabilitation are heard increasingly in both countries.

Could it be that many marginal young people in the West are no longer receptive to the notion that with society's help—in the form of social and psychiatric treatment—they can be fitted comfortably into a conventional adult life? A malaise seems to have gripped some young people, such that full, productive membership in adult society is not seen as necessary or even desirable, though a lifetime of temporary relationships, idleness, illness, poverty, and social dependency is viewed with deep ambivalence, too. Could it be that the United States could learn much from the social experiments of the

Dutch and the Swedes, as well as from the firmness and stability of Swiss and Japanese society?

SUMMARY

The emergence of juvenile justice in developing countries clearly has a significant impact on the forms their delinquency assumes. It affects delinquency in several ways, but in the process makes comparisons among different countries difficult. Any comparisons among nations must take into account not simply their distinctive cultural and social patterns but their distinctive juvenile justice practices as well.

In this chapter we looked at delinquency in Japan, Sweden, the Netherlands, and Switzerland and noted the peculiarities of each nation's juvenile justice system. Drugs and stable delinquent cliques are common in Sweden and the Netherlands with the result that a nihilistic hedonism seems to dominate the outlook of many of their delinquents. Rehabilitative efforts have not been effective in either country, and delinquency rose to unprecedented heights during the 1970s. More recently, however, delinquency has receded slightly from elevated levels. Both countries have retreated somewhat from a narrow focus on rehabilitative, permissive policies vis-a-vis juveniles, but neither has invented an acceptable substitute.

In Japan and Switzerland adolescents are provided a rigorous educational system providing little room for self-determination. Gangs and drugs are largely contained, and in Japan the juvenile justice system bends every effort to curb minor delinquency before it can gather headway by mobilizing support teams of neighbors, parents, teachers, and local police who in concert focus extra attention on deviant youth. They offer professional counseling and diagnoses to unhappy children and families, and these measures have been effective in preventing most minor delinquents in Japan from becoming repetitive, serious offenders. Minor delinquency has risen substantially in Japan since the 1960s, but serious delinquency has not.

In Switzerland sound measures to curb minor delinquency have not been so widely implemented, and pockets of deviant young people have begun to make themselves felt in major Swiss cities. Nevertheless, there is little evidence that delinquency in Switzerland has risen since 1960, while it was skyrocketing elsewhere in western Europe and the United States.

Delinquency has not been squarely confronted in either Sweden or the Netherlands, and efforts to control serious delinquency have depended heavily on the maturation of offenders in relatively permissive programs. Both countries, however, offer a broad range of cultural and educational opportunities to their adolescents and most youth have eagerly accepted them. A small remnant of serious delinquents persists in these countries despite all efforts to reform them, and in Japan and Switzerland as well.

The rigor and stability of adolescent life in these countries relative to that in the United States prevents most delinquency, but this same rigor and stability probably also spell difficulty for those few who simply cannot fit themselves to the narrow demands of school and parents. They are forced by their own idiosyncracies into persistent deviance. A deviant subculture in northwestern Europe serves these more serious delinquents, and the juvenile justice system makes it easy for them to form themselves into cliques and even gangs. The absence of gangs and hard drugs in Japan forces persistent young delinquents into an alternative path as recruits to organized crime—the Yakuza. In Europe and Japan as in the United States serious delinquents form the foundation of serious crime in adulthood.

REFERENCES

Casparis, John, and Edmund W. Vaz. 1978. *Swiss Society and Youth.* Leiden: E.J. Brill.

Clinard, Marshall B. 1978. *Cities with Little Crime.* London: Cambridge University Press.

De Vos, George. 1980. "Delinquency and Minority Status: A Psychocultural Perspective" in *Crime and Deviance: A Comparative Perspective.* Edited by Groeme Newman. Beverly Hills: Sage Publications.

Ferdinand, Theodore. 1986. "A Brief History of Juvenile Delinquency in Boston and a Comparative Interpretation." *International Annals of Criminology* 24, nos. 1 & 2: 59–81.

Janson, Carl-Gunnar, and Marie Torstensson. 1984. "Sweden." In *Western Systems of Juvenile Justice.* Edited by Malcolm W. Klein. Beverly Hills: Sage Publications: 191–211.

Japanese Ministry of Justice. 1989. *Summary of the White Paper on Crime.* Tokyo: Research and Training Institute.

———. 1990. *Correctional Institutions in Japan 1990.* Tokyo: Correction Bureau.

Junger-Tas, Josine. 1984. "Holland." In *Western Systems of Juvenile Justice.* Edited by Malcolm W. Klein. Beverly Hills: Sage Publications: 121–146.

Junger-Tas, Josine, and Richard L. Block. 1988. *Juvenile Delinquents in the Netherlands.* Amstelveen, Netherlands: Kugler Publications.

Morita, Yohji. 1985. "Personality Traits and Underachievement of Deviant Adolescent Hot Rodders." *Japanese Sociological Review* 36, no. 1 (June): 48–65.

Mugishima, F. and Y. Matsumoto. 1973. "An Analysis of Delinquent Differentiation Related to Boy's Social Origin and Educational Attainment—A Comparison of Two Cohorts." Reports of the National Research Institute of Police Science. 14: 55–63.

Rohlen, Thomas P. 1983. *Japan's High Schools.* Berkeley: University of California Press.

Sarnecki, Jerzy. 1984a. *Stockholm Boys Born 1943–1951—A Follow Up Study.* Stockholm: National Council for Crime Prevention.

———. 1984b. *Juvenile Delinquency and Societal Change in Sweden.* Stockholm: National Council for Crime Prevention.

———. 1988. "Delinquent Networks in Sweden." Paper presented at the American Society of Criminology meetings, Chicago.

———. 1989. *Juvenile Delinquency in Sweden.* Stockholm: National Council for Crime Prevention.

U.S. Department of Education. 1987. *Japanese Education Today.* Washington, D.C.: U.S. Government Printing Office.

Uchiyama, Ayoko. 1990. Personal Communication.

Vaz, Edmund W., and John Casparis. 1971. "A Comparative Study of Youth Culture and Delinquency: Upper-Middle Class Canadian and Swiss Boys." *International Journal of Comparative Sociology* 12, no. 1: 1–17.

Wikstrom, Per-Olof H. 1990. "Delinquency and Urban Structure." In *Crime and Measures Against Crime in the City*. Edited by Per-Olof H. Wikstrom. Stockholm: National Council for Crime Prevention.

Yokoyama, Minoru. 1984. "Why Doesn't Japan have Diversion Programs for Juvenile Delinquents?" Paper presented at the 27th World Congress of International Institute of Sociology, Seattle, Washington.

———. 1986a. "The Juvenile Justice System in Japan." In *Youth Crime, Social Control and Prevention: Theoretical Perspectives and Policy Implications*. Edited by M. Brusten, J. Graham, N. Herriger, and P. Malinowski. Pfaffenweiler, Germany: Centaurus-Verlagsgesellschaft: 102–113.

———. 1986b. "Social Control of Juvenile Traffic Offenders in Japan." *Kangweon Law Review* (Republic of Korea) 2 (1986): 142–60.

———. 1989. "Net Widening of the Juvenile Justice System in Japan." *Criminal Justice Review* 14, no. 1: 43–53.

11

Thinking About Theory

What is theory, and how does it differ from other forms of knowledge, for example, from philosophy? How can two different theories be compared? What makes some theories better than others? How can different kinds of theories be integrated with one another? What part should theory play in our study of delinquency? These are the kinds of questions we are going to explore in this chapter.

WHAT IS THEORY?

A theory is basically a series of interlocking statements regarding the nature of our world. We all make reasonable assumptions (to us anyway) about the social, moral, or natural world, and insofar as we attempt to organize our beliefs into a logical system, we have a theory, according to Abraham Kaplan (1964: 61–71), a widely acclaimed philosopher of science. Theories differ from philosophies of the social, moral, or natural world in that theories dwell less on what ought to be (i.e., on ethics) or on how we can know what is (i.e., on epistemology) than on what is. Philosophical analysis focuses more on questions of the nature of knowledge or of virtue in social life or politics, whereas theories provide estimates of what exists and why.

Theories consist of three broad classes of logically linked statements: (1) untested *assumptions* about their empirical domains; (2) inductive and deductive *statements* that coordinate and amplify the implications of the assumptions; and (3) flowing from these assumptions and statements some testable *conclusions* regarding specific events or processes in nature. The untested assumptions and their implications make up the body of the theory, and its value depends upon the validity of the assumptions—how accurately do they capture the basic nature of the phenomenon they attempt to explain?—and the relevance of the conclusions to the issues of the age. The assumptions establish the boundaries of the theory (i.e., the kinds of problems the theory attempts to address), and the implications of the theory in the form of deductive statements and conclusions describe the specific meaning of the theory for its domain.

Strain theory, for example, assumes that juveniles seek basically to conform to conventional ideals and values. Delinquency arises as a result of moral dilemmas that social structure poses for juveniles. A dilemma facing many juveniles is how to follow the ideals and values of their peers as well as those of their parents and teachers. Ideally, they would like to honor both, but in some cases this is not possible. Doing well in school is only possible by devoting evenings and weekends to study, when their peers also make demands on their time. Their grades plummet; their parents and teachers lose confidence in them; and they find their friends mainly among peers in a similar condition. A likely result is delinquency.

The assumption of strain theory is that initially teenagers would like very much both to do well in school and to please their peers. Where this assumption does not apply, some other theory is needed to explain delinquency. But where this conflict is sharp, only one set of values can be honored, and juveniles are forced to choose. Those who align themselves with their peers against the values of their parents and teachers run the risk of estrangement and delinquency. Strain theory cannot tell us the form their deviance will take, but it predicts that estrangement from parents and teachers is very likely to be followed by some kind of deviance.

Some juveniles avoid this dilemma by concealing the full extent of their deviant behavior from their parents and teachers or by pursuing values their peers and parents both can endorse, for example, by excelling in team sports. Still, the conflicts of teenagers are not easily solved, and even though they would like to conform to their parents' wishes, if these entail sharp conflicts, some form of deviance becomes likely. Strain theory sees delinquency as one outcome to moral dilemmas. Naturally, different theories make different assumptions and predictions regarding delinquent behavior.

Using this view of theory, humans have probably theorized about a wide variety of issues since the dawn of self-consciousness, but it has only been since the sixteenth century that we have begun to check our theories systematically against the facts of nature. Copernicus theorized in 1543 that the Sun and not the Earth was the center of the solar system. The Church strenuously rejected his idea, and Copernicus's theory was not widely accepted until the 1630s, when Kepler and then Galileo showed that Venus and Mars orbited the Sun, not the Earth, and that the moons of Jupiter orbited that planet. Only then was Copernicus's heliocentric theory of the solar system taken seriously.

Clearly, the assumptions of broadly accepted theories are often closely attuned to prevalent ideologies (compare Laub and Sampson, 1991). Copernicus's theory encountered serious opposition, because of its contradictions with the Church's teachings at the time. Thomas Kuhn, a modern philosopher of science, has gone so far as to suggest (1962: chapter 10; see also Fuchs, 1986) that a basic shift in scientific theories depends not simply upon a swing in the evidence against a given theory, but also upon a popular ideological shift away from the theory's underlying assumptions.

In the 1970s and 1980s, political opinion took a sharp swing to the right, and since 1968 the only Democrat elected to the presidency has been Jimmy Carter. During this period more severe punishments for both juvenile and adult offenders have been instituted by many states, and Travis Hirschi's social control theory—a conservative theory—has become a popular explanation of delinquency. More liberal theories, which see delinquency as stemming from strain or social conflict, have fallen out of favor. The national mood is sympathetic with the notion that strengthening the family, school, and community as well as the penal code and the police is the best way to curb crime and delinquency. This is not to say that evidence is unimportant to theory, but only that a theory's fit with popular political or moral viewpoints also plays a part in its general acceptance.

WHAT MAKES SOME THEORIES BETTER THAN OTHERS?

How can we evaluate theories honestly without bias and determine their relative merits? Although theories are judged popularly in terms of widely accepted ideologies and beliefs, these criteria are among the weakest reasons for supporting any theory. A better measure of a theory's value is its agreement with carefully gathered empirical evidence.

What kind of evidence can be used in evaluating a scientific theory? Scientific theories attempt to explain natural processes by specifying their basic nature in a set of initial assumptions and by predicting from these to natural events.

The existence of the planet Pluto was suggested in 1930 by fluctuations in the orbit of Neptune that could not be explained in terms of prevailing pictures of the solar system. Theories of planetary motion suggested a nineth planet beyond the orbit of Neptune, and when astronomers looked where it was supposed to be, they found exactly what the theory had predicted. Today, incidentally, similar aberrations in Pluto's orbit uncovered by the Voyager satellite suggest still another planet beyond Pluto.

Similarly, in the late nineteenth century, Mendeleyev's periodic table of elements predicted the existence of several additional elements, and when scientists searched for them, they found the noble gases neon, krypton, xenon, and radon. Theories are very useful in pointing to obscure events that otherwise would hardly have been noticed. Such predictions, when proven, are powerful evidence for the validity of a theory. But they are by no means the most common way by which theories are verified.

Most evidence bearing upon theories is not so dramatic. In fact sometimes it is not even relevant. For example, in summarizing several studies of social control theory, Shoemaker (1984: 175) concluded that it accounted for between 25 and 50 percent of the variance in delinquency. But such a claim is hardly warranted, because as Hirschi (1969: 34) has pointed out, "The question 'Why do they [delinquents] do it?' is simply not the question the theory is designed to answer. The question is 'Why don't we do it?'" Hirschi is saying that weak controls cannot predict directly to delinquency. They can only predict to the likelihood of some kind of unconventional behavior.

Weak controls may open the door to *some form* of personal idiosyncrasy—for example, advanced computer programming or drug experimentation—but the kind of deviance that finally emerges depends upon other, more immediate forces. Since delinquency, strictly speaking, is not part of the target domain of control theory, control theory cannot explain delinquency, and evidence that controls are related to delinquency is not directly relevant to its validity. Shoemaker's claim that social control theory explains up to 50 percent of the variance in delinquency is at best premature.

Consider as well the following example. Control theory suggests that children's conforming behavior should be related *positively* to their feelings (inner controls) about the teacher's opinions, but strain theory suggests that conformity should be related *negatively* to feelings (strain) of being picked on unfairly by their teachers. Two different theories and two contradictory conclusions. Or are they contradictory?

Carefully gathered evidence reported by Travis Hirschi (1969: 126, table 35) appears to support control theory in that self-reported delinquent acts are clearly linked with a concern for teacher's opinions. The greater the student's concern, the fewer the delinquent acts. But Hirschi (1969: 127) also concluded based on the same data, this time incorrectly, that strain theory is invalid, because even when strain is carefully controlled, the opinions of the juveniles' teachers still have a powerful effect on their behavior. Controlling for strain eliminated it as a factor in nonconforming behavior, and the data cited by Hirschi were irrelevant to strain theory. They could neither prove nor disprove it.[1] The fact that his data still supported control theory indicated to Hirschi that it was more powerful than strain theory.

A Theory's Domain

Scientific theories are differentiated from each other by their target domains or ranges (see Dubin, 1982: 134–135; Gibbs 1972: 67–68), that is, by the segment of the natural world they seek to explain. Psychological theories of delinquency attempt to explain the personalities of delinquents, and sociological theories focus on the social and cultural aspects of delinquents.

The target domain determines also the evidence to be used in testing the theory (see Lieberson, 1985: 102). Since psychological theories attempt to identify the personality patterns of delinquents, their domains include delinquency that arises from emotional, motivational, and attitudinal factors. Sociological theories address the social settings of delinquency and their relationships to broader social processes, and their domains embrace socially based delinquency. It is obvious that psychological theories of delinquency should be evaluated in terms of psychological evidence and not sociological evidence.

Gangs, for example, have a profound effect upon teenagers that become gang members and often aggravate their delinquency (Sarnecki, 1988). But to interpret the gang members' advanced delinquency as a result of psychological factors could well amount to explaining their socially based actions in terms of emotionally or motivationally based pressures (Yablonsky, 1962: chapter 12). Such a conclusion may be warranted with some

---

[1]The same data, incidentally, when rearranged show clearly that strain is also related to nonconforming behavior when controls are held constant.

gang members; that is, they would have become serious delinquents even without the gang. Nevertheless, we must recognize that group-based values impinge on all members and shape their actions accordingly. Using data drawn from gangs to explain a psychopathic theory of delinquency is a serious but common mistake and can result ultimately in unnecessarily discrediting the theory.

A Theory's Scope

When we do have sound data that bear directly on a theory's domain, it is possible to determine how much of its domain is explained by the theory, that is, what percentage of the variance of delinquency in the theory's domain is explained by the theory (see Box 11.1) for an explanation of the variance of delinquency).

Box 11.1 ## Variance and Delinquency

Most variables including delinquency display a wide range of intensity. Some juveniles attempt only a few minor offenses, some commit a few minor offenses, many commit some minor offenses and a few serious ones, and still others commit several serious offenses. Any measure of delinquency inevitably finds different levels of intensity or seriousness among juveniles, and this variability is a direct measure of the variance of delinquency.

To some extent this variance arises because the basic causes of delinquency (temperament, personality, family structure, or peer group pressure, for example) also show variability. If personality is a cause of delinquency, and it varies widely, it will induce a similar variability in delinquency. It is possible, therefore, to measure exactly how much personality and delinquency vary together, and thus determine precisely the degree of their covariance.

The extent to which a causal variable—personality—covaries with delinquency depends ultimately upon the strength of its relationship with delinquency. Since we can determine both the level of this covariance and the total amount of variance of delinquency, we can measure the percentage of the variance in delinquency that is attributable to personality. This percentage can also be measured for other causal variables (e.g., for temperament, family structure, and peer group pressures), and accordingly, we can compare the contributions of each of these factors to delinquency. Thus, the portion of variance of delinquency attributable to each causal factor can be determined precisely. This variance, as we have seen, is a good measure of a theory's scope.

A perfectly controlled experiment of a perfect theory would explain 100 percent of its domain, but all theories are imperfect, and most experiments fail to control some relevant factors. Hence, most experiments show most theories of delinquency as imperfect in explaining delinquency.[2] For example, strain theory and cultural deviance theory both attempt to explain nonconformity. Since nonconforming behavior is part of each theory's domain, both are often regarded as competitive in explaining nonconformity.[3] And the percentage of nonconforming behavior that each accounts for provides us with a convenient estimate of which theory has the most predictive power.

Similarly, if we were interested in testing whether parental bonds or peer pressures were more effective in shaping teenage behavior, assuming we controlled for all other relevant factors, it would be a simple task to identify which factor was most powerful in changing juveniles. It is possible to compare the power of two distinct theories by comparing their explanatory power.

When we compare two theories in this fashion, we are assessing their relative scopes (see Gibbs, 1972: 67). Theories that can account for most of the phenomena in their target domain have a greater scope than theories that account for only a small portion of the same domain (see Elliott, 1985: 125–126). As theories mature, new insights and assumptions are added, new implications are recognized, and new conclusions are drawn. As a theory's implications are developed, its ability to account for the problems and issues of its domain expands. Its scope improves (see Box 11.2).

It would be possible, of course, to compare the generality of two distinct theories with very different domains by comparing their scopes (i.e., by comparing the amount of variance that each explains). But the comparison would not have much meaning. Classic Freudian theory ignored the broad issue of the self and as a result had a narrower scope vis-a-vis its own domain. Labeling theory, on the other hand, deals narrowly with the effects of official stigmatization on inexperienced delinquent children. Their two domains are distinct, and to show that the scope of classic Freudian theory is low in comparison with that of labeling theory (even though the latter deals with a much narrower problem) is of little value. Comparing broadly different theories in terms of their relative scopes does not advance our knowledge or understanding very much. The scope of a theory is most useful in comparing it with "competitive" theories.

Theoretical Parsimony

In addition to scope, theories are also evaluated in terms of their ability to explain their domains parsimoniously. To many of us theory seems a complex way of dealing with relatively simple phenomena. Delinquency theory seems much more complicated than delinquency itself, for example.

But delinquency theory attempts to summarize and explain all facets of delinquent

---

[2]But two perfect theories of delinquency describing the same domain (e.g., delinquency) might still exhibit scopes of less than 100 percent, because the forces they describe would exert distinctive influences on nonconforming behavior. The independent variables of a *perfect* theory would display an imperfect correlation with its dependent variables so long as other influential factors were active. Weak correlations need not mean a poor theory; they may mean only that other factors were poorly controlled.

[3]Naturally, each theory must be evaluated in terms of data related to its specific domain. Strain theory must be tested with data that examines the relationship between strain and nonconformity, and cultural deviance theory must be validated with data that deals with the relationship between cultural deviance and nonconformity. This warning is so obvious it seems unnecessary, but this is exactly the mistake made by Hirschi mentioned above.

Box 11-2 **A Theory Is Like a Map**

A theory is much like the map that many students use when they head south during spring break. The key points on the map—the cities and villages; the lakes, forests, and mountains; the state parks, Civil War battlefields, universities, and prisons—are linked together by a web of interstate highways, local roads, railroads, bridges, and rivers. But even the most precise maps must leave out certain features. Road maps ignore most skyscrapers, water towers, radio or TV broadcast towers, small airports, and airline routes. Aeronautical charts, however, ignore many roads and bridges and concentrate instead on airports, airplanes, and tall structures. The map's purpose dictates its focus.

A theory, like a map, is a conceptual model of a part of the natural world. It gathers, organizes, and interprets what we know about a part of the world, and like the map it abstracts only the relevant features, that is, the features that are important to the theory. Any given theory will ignore some features, even though they may be crucial for answering other kinds of problems. In essence, a theory provides a perspective—a way of looking at a limited facet of the natural world. If it is valid, it can lead to marvelous insights.

Just as maps are good only for their designated territories, theories are useful only in their own domains. Theories describe relationships between fundamental ideas and are relevant only to their peculiar part of the world. Psychology can explain why and how some delinquents feel little remorse for their victims, but it is probably of little value in explaining why most delinquents hate and fear the police. The one deals with a psychologically based emotion; the other describes attitudes derived from social interaction. Two different theories may describe the same general phenomenon but from very different vantage points. When they do, each theory abstracts different features from the common domain according to its particular interest.

Two distinct maps need not be mutually contradictory just because they abstract different features from the same area, and two distinct theories addressing the same problem (e.g., the causes of remorse, fear, and hatred) need not be mutually contradictory, even though they are explained from very different points of view. They are described by two different maps using different viewpoints of the same reality.

behavior, and when we consider that its domain is very broad and there is much to explain, delinquency theory is actually a very succinct statement of the nature of delinquency. Nevertheless, theories are evaluated in terms of the principle of Occam's razor, that is, by their ability to account for their domains in the simplest possible terms. The most coherent, straightforward, and succinct theory is the best theory, all else constant.

Theorists, however, have a tendency to elaborate their work beyond all reason, and the more vague the problem or subtle the evidence, the more complex the theory (see Cohen, 1985: 190–191). Countless examples abound, particularly in criminology.

To balance this tendency scientists have adopted the principle of Occam's razor to prune overly elaborate theories until only the bare essentials remain. Of two theories that explain the same domain with equal effectiveness, the theory that does so simply is much preferred.

To sum up, it is important when testing a theory to compare it with phenomena that are relevant to its domain, just as a map of Georgia cannot be judged by driving through Florida. A theory's domain is determined by its basic assumptions and by the problems it explores. Theories can also be distinguished by their success in explaining their domains, that is, by their scopes. Some well-developed theories, by accounting for most of their domains, enjoy a broad scope. But others, newer and less well developed, explain only a small portion of the problems of their domains and exhibit only a limited scope. Normally, the more mature a theory, the more complete its structure, and the broader its scope. All in all, theories are defined by their assumptions, logical structure, domain, and scope.

Theories that deal with different domains cannot contradict one another. They deal with different parts of the world and are not easily comparable. As Lieberson suggests, "it is impossible to use empirical data in nonexperimental social research to evaluate the relative importance of one theory versus another . . ." (Lieberson, 1985: 106).

Theories are best evaluated by comparing their predictions and conclusions with the state of their own domains and by checking the logic of their propositions. Failures in either respect challenge the validity of a theory and signal a need for revision.

As theories are revised and improved, their ability to explain their domain improves. In particular, their ability to explain both the fine-grained features and the broad issues of their domains increases, which is another way of saying their scope improves. Pointing the way to meaningful inquiry and significant research, theory is an important tool of science, including the systematic study of delinquency.

THEORY AND SCIENCE

Theory is the beacon that lights the avenues of science. Theorizing has been part of our repertoire since the beginning of time, but it was not until theories were linked with empirical studies by Kepler and Galileo that theory began to depend upon objective evidence for its authority. When theory and research were routinely combined, we began to see systematic critiques of existing theories and their regular refinement. With the union of theory and experimentation, science was born.

Many students and even some scholars believe that the essence of science is experiment, that there is no knowledge without verified facts. But a too heavy dependence on experimentation (i.e., an exaggerated positivism) results not in science but in the unorganized accumulation of facts. Some historians gather facts about the past guided mainly by their curiosity, and they pile fact upon fact with little rhyme or reason. Other historians (see Richard Hofstadter's *The Age of Reform,* for example) provide a plausible structure for the facts. Historical events rarely reveal clear patterns, but the best historians discover threads of meaning in history; that is, they develop something akin to a theory of history and show how isolated facts actually build to an intelligible, historical climax.

Science, as with history, follows a thread of meaning. The gathering of evidence is guided by theoretical intelligence such that each investigation contributes to the structure of science. As the structure is completed, it points to ever more obscure but crucial experiments. The planet Pluto was discovered not by chance nor by idle curiosity, but through theoretically guided investigations.

Theory guides science to important discoveries. Nature presents an unlimited number of questions to study, and without theory science wanders aimlessly in its quest for understanding. Theory is the mind of science.

THEORY AND DELINQUENT BEHAVIOR

Since theory is based upon objective facts, delinquency theory must be assessed ultimately in the behavior of juveniles. This means that our conclusions regarding delinquency, whether drawn from social, psychological, or legal theories, must all describe the behavior of juveniles. Even though these theories all deal with abstract, disembodied processes, our theories must somehow be fashioned to correspond to the forms of delinquent behavior.

Delinquents not only violate the juvenile code, but they also are biological beings with all the needs, abilities, and maladies that that implies; they are human beings with feelings, emotions, and neuroses, and social beings in overlapping social networks and cultural heritages. All these very distinct forces converge on juveniles just as they do on all of us to shape our behavior. The challenge to the theorist is to mold theoretical conclusions as nearly as possible to the juvenile's behavior in life. The theorist must, in other words, identify holistic syndromes—biological, psychological, social, as well as legal—that correspond to the delinquent's multifaceted nature (Diesing, 1971: chapters 14, 23).

The formulation of theoretical types simplifies the validation of theories. First, it provides realistic tests that identify *clusters* of characteristics that should relate to delinquency and not just single factors. The meaning of any given factor—IQ, socioeconomic status, family structure, labeling, or impulsivity—derives ultimately not simply from its own inherent nature but also from its context.

Families without fathers, for example, seem to affect different juveniles differently (Datesman and Scarpitti, 1975: 51; Austin, 1978: 492–493). Although most children in single-parent families are more delinquent than children in intact families, black boys and girls in mother-only families commit *less* delinquency than black children in intact families. The relationship between family and delinquency depends upon an interaction between race and sex. Holistic clusters of factors (family structure, race, and sex) provide a much sounder basis for evaluating the causes of delinquency than studies using single factors as independent variables, and they yield more clear-cut answers.

Second, holistic clusters also suggest useful methods for assessing delinquency. They identify the qualities that should be related to delinquency and point to the types of delinquents that should be tested. Since they are constructed to correspond closely to delinquent patterns of behavior, the questions of measurement and research design are relatively straightforward.

Finally, this method of structuring theoretical conclusions also provides a useful way of assembling multidimensional models of delinquency. If we have a typology of personality types that relates to delinquency, it is relatively easy to combine these personality types with characteristic social situations or physiological patterns that also relate to delinquency to determine how the several typologies combine interactively to shape delinquency. In principle, more typologies could be melded to the original cluster until all relevant factors have been included. Such a model, no doubt, would be cumbersome, with several hundred distinctive patterns, but it would also provide an authentic modeling of the patterns of delinquency as well as an effective tool in delinquency research.

These synthetic typologies (i.e., typologies that blend together several different models of delinquency) would enable us to coordinate simultaneously the implications of several different models of delinquent behavior (see Ferdinand, 1966; see also Gibbons, 1985). But they do not constitute a new, integrated theory of delinquency. The theories themselves—for example, personality theory, sociological theory, or physiological theory—would not be unified, only their implications for delinquency.

Some researchers (Elliott, 1985; but see also Hirschi, 1979) have sought to develop a comprehensive theory of delinquency by compacting several different kinds of explanatory factors into a single model of delinquency. However useful in guiding research, such efforts do not constitute a logical integration of the theories, and they cannot yield a comprehensive theory of delinquency.

CONCLUSIONS

We have seen that theory is essential to science, and that without it, science becomes little more than aimless empiricism. But we must maintain some balance; careful testing of theory is also crucial. Theory and experimentation are at the heart of science, and without both, science flounders. Much of human history has been spent in idle speculation about the universe, unaided by validating empirical study, and though much of it was fundamentally false, it was defended as true by churchmen, philosophers, statesmen, and citizens alike. It would be folly to elevate either theory or experimentation as the *most* important part of science. Both are necessary if science is to be directed to the solutions of our problems.

Science must be used wisely, however, for its powers can also be turned to malicious purposes. Our leaders and statesmen must be skilled not only in administration and persuasion, but also in understanding science and how it can serve the long-range interests of all human beings. There is no magic formula, of course, but despite some terrible mistakes, history contains many instances in which science has deftly relieved vast human suffering.

A theory's domain sets the agenda for the theory. It determines the issues, and it locates the evidence to be used in testing the theory. A theory's domain is one of its most basic features, because it plays an important role not only in defining the theory but also in comparing it with other theories. Theories with similar domains can be readily compared in terms of their scopes, that is, their relative power in explaining common problems. But theories are rarely seen as entirely valid or invalid, only as partially valid. A theory's scope is a measure of its validity.

Theories are also evaluated in terms of their relevance to popular ideologies. Social control theory emphasizes the importance of personal character, family, community, church, and school (not to mention the juvenile justice system) in preventing delinquency. It has a distinctly conservative ring, and as conservatism has become dominant in American political life, social control theory has achieved a kind of vogue. Conflict theory, on the other hand, tends to see the root of delinquency in societal flaws and has, therefore, a more liberal bent.

Theory, as with most of our enterprises, grows both by quantum leaps and by incremental nudges. Thus, Darwin fashioned the idea of natural selection and transformed our understanding of the ways in which species evolve. Freud discovered the unconscious and revolutionized psychology, and Einstein's special theory of relativity did the same in physics. Each of these was a startling departure from accepted theorizing in its domain.

Most often, however, a theory grows via the contributions of hundreds of scientists working carefully and imaginatively in their laboratories testing its conclusions. Few succeed in developing a general theory that transforms their discipline as Darwin's, Freud's, or Einstein's did. Most devote themselves to patient, skeptical testing of current theories in the hope that inspiration will reveal a better way of organizing the knowledge within their particular area. Occasionally, a new idea does suggest itself, and for a few weeks or months the theorist/researcher becomes an ardent explorer in a fascinating quest for evidence and explanation.

The popular image of the scientist suggests a disheveled eccentric pursuing esoteric problems. From the inside, however, science and theory building are perhaps the freest adventures that human beings can undertake. Most of what we do in life is limited by social, moral, and reality considerations. Theory building, however, is only limited by our imaginations. It is one of the few endeavors that permits the individual full mastery.

SUMMARY

Theory is a conceptual model describing the real world and is evaluated both in terms of its ability to predict the nature of reality and its compatibility with the dominant ideologies of the age. A theory is described in terms of its domain (the sector of reality that by virtue of its conceptual model it attempts to describe) and its scope (the portion of its domain that it actually does describe). Both the domain and scope of a theory are determined ultimately by the focus of its conceptual model and can only be tested by means of data directly relevant to this focus. Most theories are limited both in domain and scope, and it is difficult to compare distinct theories in terms of their effectiveness. Theories with distinctive conceptual models and foci cannot be evaluated with the same data, because their domains are too dissimilar.

But theories that yield conclusions regarding reality can be checked both by means of their conceptual models (are they logically flawless and parsimonious?) and by their relevance to empirical data. Theory is the intellect of science and guides studies along fruitful, productive lines. It often leads to surprising conclusions and startling discoveries about nature.

REFERENCES

Austin, Roy L. 1978. "Race, Father-Absence, and Female Delinquency." *Criminology* 15, No. 4 (February):487–503.

Cohen, Morris Raphael. 1953. *Reason and Nature.* New York: The Free Press.

Cohen, Stanley. 1985. *Visions of Social Control.* New York: Polity Press.

Cortes, Juan B., with Florence M. Gatti. 1972. *Delinquency and Crime: A Biopsychological Approach.* New York: Seminar Press.

Datesman, Susan, and Frank Scarpitti. 1975. "Female Delinquency and Broken Homes: A Reassessment." *Criminology* 13:33–55.

Diesing, Paul. 1971. *Patterns of Discovery in the Social Sciences.* Chicago: Aldine Press.

Dubin, Robert. 1982. *Theory Building.* 2nd edition. New York: The Free Press.

Elliott, Delbert. 1985. "The Assumption that Theories Can Be Combined with Increased Explanatory Power." In *Theoretical Methods in Criminology.* Edited by Robert F. Meier. Beverly Hills: Sage Publications.

Ferdinand, Theodore N. 1966. *Typologies of Delinquency.* New York: Random House.

Fuchs, Stephen. 1986. "The Social Organization of Scientific Knowledge." *Sociological Theory* 4, No. 2 (Fall):143–150.

Gibbons, Don C. 1985. "The Assumption of Efficacy of Middle-Range Explanation: Typologies." In *Theoretical Methods in Criminology.* Edited by Robert F. Meier. Beverly Hills: Sage Publications.

Gibbs, Jack. 1972. *Sociological Theory Construction.* Hinsdale, Ill.: The Dryden Press, Inc.

Glueck, Sheldon, and Eleanor Glueck. 1956. *Physique and Delinquency.* New York: Harper & Brothers.

Hirschi, Travis. 1969. *Causes of Delinquency.* Berkeley: University of California Press.

———. 1979. "Separate and Equal is Better." *Journal of Research in Crime and Delinquency* 16:34–38.

Hofstadter, Richard. 1955. *The Age of Reform.* New York: Alfred A. Knopf.

Kaplan, Abraham. 1964. *The Conduct of Inquiry: The Methodology of Behavioral Science.* New York: Chandler Publishing.

Kornhauser, Ruth Rosner. 1978. *Social Sources of Delinquency.* Chicago: University of Chicago Press.

Kuhn, Thomas S. 1962. *The Structure of Scientific Revolutions.* Chicago: University of Chicago Press.

Laub, John H., and Robert J. Sampson. 1991. "The Sutherland-Glueck Debate: On the Sociology of Criminological Knowledge." *American Journal of Sociology* 96, No. 6:1402–1440.

Lieberson, Stanley. 1985. *Making it Count.* Berkeley: University of California Press.

Sarnecki, Jerzy. 1988. "Delinquent Networks in Sweden." Paper presented at the American Society of Criminology meetings in Chicago.

Shoemaker, Donald J. 1984. *Theories of Delinquency.* New York: Oxford University Press.

Yablonsky, Lewis. 1962. *The Violent Gang.* New York: Macmillan.

Chapter
12

Social Theories of Delinquency

W e saw in Chapter 11 that a theory consists of some basic, untested assumptions, a series of interpretive statements that spell out meanings inherent in these assumptions, and a set of conclusions that relate the theory to the empirical world. These assumptions, statements, and empirically oriented conclusions make up the *conceptual model* of the theory and set the domain of the theory—the natural field to which the theory applies. Theories are generally evaluated by their scope—their ability to explain their domains—and by their agreement with popular ideologies.

   In this chapter we will identify two broad categories of social theories, theories of conformity and theories of anomie, in terms of their assumptions regarding the sources of delinquency and the domains they seek to explain. Social control theory and cultural deviance theory explore the reasons why individuals adhere to the standards of their groups, and we treat them here as social theories of conformity. Strain theory, including labeling theory, and conflict theory explain how conforming individuals and groups gradually become alienated from conventional values and turn to deviant behavior. We describe them here as social theories of anomie. Each theory will be explained in terms of its basic conceptual model and its ideological implications.

SOCIAL CONTROL THEORY

In light of Chapter 9 we can begin to see how social controls in the community are relevant to delinquency. The two most important factors in the community affecting the behavior of its members are its cohesiveness and its structure. Simple communities are small and cohesive, their controls are pervasive and powerful, and they show little deviancy of any kind.

When the community is complex, it embraces many different kinds of groups, it is much larger, its consensus is narrow, and its social intimacy and cohesiveness are limited. Still, webs of interdependency restrict communal groups and their members, mediating groups blend together their diverse purposes, and those involved in these criss-crossing urban nets often show surprisingly little deviance.

But those who are peripheral to these coordinated, interdependent networks of activity in complex communities—the black underclass, the rural poor of Appalachia and the western states, and the young—are weakly constrained by social structure or cohesiveness in any form and are especially prone to deviant behavior.[1] Evidence abounds in Chapter 9 that structure and cohesiveness affect delinquency.

When the family is troubled, juveniles are less readily governed by the parents. When it is patriarchal, the mother is more restrictive toward her daughters, and they show much less delinquency than in more egalitarian families. Boys are affected in the opposite direction. Similarly, community schools that are well governed and closely integrated with families in their neighborhoods spread a web of controls over school children that sharply curtails their delinquency, as in Japan. Structure distributes delinquency in communities by channeling supervision and social controls along distinctive lines.

Social controls relate to delinquency primarily in their absence. When social controls are weak, delinquency is high, and when they are strong, delinquency is slight. Control theory can easily explain the absence of delinquency, but explaining its presence requires additional statements as to the forces that trigger delinquency, which control theory cannot provide. Delinquency is beyond the domain of control theory, as are other types of idiosyncratic behavior such as neurotic, psychotic, and, for that matter, creative behavior.

Since control theory is obviously at its best in explaining conformity, the proper domain of control theory is conforming behavior. To extend social control theory to delinquency Kornhauser (1978: 38–39) suggested that it assumes an obstreperous human nature. According to Kornhauser, humans are naturally unruly and defiant of social convention. When social controls are weak and unable to contain adolescent rebelliousness, delinquency results.

But delinquency still must be *explained*. If adolescent rebellion or impulsiveness are responsible, we still need to explain them. Simply assuming what we seek to explain cannot suffice. We need a theory of delinquency that shows how human personality

---

[1]The young show much more deviant behavior, including delinquency, in complex urban communities than in closely knit simple villages. Following World War II, many homeless young people left the rural areas of Japan (where crime levels were very low) for its major urban centers (where crime levels were higher), and in their rootless condition were probably responsible for a major share of the crime wave that swept Japan during the postwar period.

takes the meanings of culture and the opportunities of social structure and focuses them into deviant behavior. Without such a theory, delinquency, neurosis, and human genius are nothing more than different forms of unexplained human variability.

Social control theory, which seeks to explain conforming behavior, makes no assumption about the rebellious, antisocial character of humans. On the contrary, social controls theory assumes that humankind is naturally receptive to the demands and requirements of social structure and wants nothing more than to conform. If it assumed humans' unruliness, and explained delinquency on that basis, it would be assuming what it wants to explain—a silly mistake, indeed.

Despite its simplicity, social control theory accounts for a substantial portion of delinquency, and its scope is quite high. The relationship between strong controls in the community, family, and school and low levels of delinquency is strong. About 20 to 25 percent of male juveniles in the United States have official histories of delinquency, and the absence of social controls is often a prerequisite for (i.e., a necessary but not a sufficient "cause" of) delinquency.[2] Weak social controls are associated with most forms of delinquency, even though they cannot explain its occurence nor why it takes the forms it does.

Finally, since control theory focuses on social forces that assert themselves over the individual, it is a "conservative" theory. Those who feel that we are well served by our heritage and that our first task as citizens is to live up to the nation's ideals should feel comfortable with the social and political ideas implicit in social control theory. If Americans are well served by their institutions and traditions, American society should strengthen these institutions and their influence to help us live according to our social and moral responsibilities as citizens.

Progressives, on the other hand, believe that the institutions and traditions of society contain flaws and that the well-being of Americans is best served if these flaws are constantly examined and corrected. They tend to see social controls as a necessary evil. Social controls are needed to contain the frailties and excesses of humans, but the creativity of human nature and the freedom to express it are probably more essential to the good life than order and stability.

CULTURAL DEVIANCE THEORY

Cultural deviance theory closely parallels social control theory. Both are based on an assumption that human beings want to conform to the ideals and norms of their groups. Human beings are by nature responsive to the social rewards and punishments of groups and, if left to themselves, usually obey group commandments without reflection or reservation. People by nature are conformists. To explain conforming behavior we must understand group processes and their dynamics. Cultural deviance theory assumes that deviant groups develop norms and goals in much the same way that conforming groups do and that they apply many of the same pressures to achieve conformity (compare Kornhauser, 1978: 29).

---

[2]A *necessary* cause must be present but is not in itself enough to trigger the result. A *sufficient* cause is enough by itself to trigger the result.

The primary difference between conventional groups and deviant groups is the relationship between *their* values and those of the broader community. Deviant groups must face the fact that they are *deviant* in the eyes of the larger community, whereas conventional groups need not. The question of their *own* legitimacy is central with deviant groups (see Matza, 1964: chapter 2).[3]

Although most scholars would probably acknowledge this last point, Kornhauser (1978: 37–38) clearly disagrees. From her vantage point, cultural deviance theory implies that when delinquent groups contend with legitimate groups, police power and not legitimacy determines the outcome. Thus, from her perspective, gang members believe that morally the community is no better than themselves and that gang members are hunted by the police (and not the reverse) only because the community and the police are more powerful.

We must remember, however, that it is not just political groups and the police that condemn delinquent gangs. Parents, teachers, neighbors, community leaders, and the mass media all decry the bloodshed and destruction of gangs. Such broad denunciations—many from groups in their own immediate neighborhood—speak to the moral illegitimacy of delinquent gangs and not simply to their political defensiveness. The moral legitimacy of gangs is a *major* problem for their members, and this is one reason why defense mechanisms are so important (compare Sykes and Matza, 1957)—they help to justify the gang's deviancy.

If their moral legitimacy is suspect, the issue—How are delinquent gangs such as La Cosa Nostra, or the Yakusa of Japan established in the first place?—becomes an even more difficult question. Where do their deviant goals come from, and how can they flourish in the face of strenuous counter measures? These are some questions that cultural deviance theory must address.

The Origins of Delinquent Values and Gangs

Since cultural deviance theory cannot explain the origins of deviance, its beginnings must be understood in terms of other models. Strain theory and community structure have been two common explanations.

Albert Cohen   In a trailblazing work more than 35 years ago, Cohen (1955: 129–137) postulated that working-class youths faced with status frustration in middle-class schools react by rejecting middle-class values and endorsing their opposite. If the middle-class endorses moderation, balance, and decorum, frustrated and rejected working-class kids will endorse spontaneity and vulgarity. If the middle-class admires self-discipline and diligence in pursuit of long-range goals, working-class kids will subscribe to impulsiveness and self-indulgence. For Cohen, class conflict is the key to working-class gangs. It produces reaction formations against middle-class values, schools, and teachers in which

---

[3]This is a basic problem of groups in conflict with their community and is a fundamental assumption underlying conflict theory. Hence, conflict theory is also relevant to delinquent gangs in that it helps to explain how they adapt to their illegitimacy in the eyes of the community.

working-class kids redeem themselves by inverting their critics' value schemes.[4] The basic question of working-class legitimacy is thereby resolved. It is "nice" middle-class kids who accept the values of their teachers and seek their approval who are held up for scorn by their working-class schoolmates.

Reiss and Rhodes (1963: 135–149) undertook to test Cohen's thesis that working-class delinquents were especially alert to status differences with their peers and found, as expected, "a positive relationship between delinquent behavior and the perception that peers have better clothes and housing" (1963: 141). When the social class of delinquents was considered, lower-class delinquents were most likely to admit that others in their school had better clothes and housing than they. A majority of the adolescents including the delinquents, however, rejected any idea that their peers had better material possessions. While a sense of status deprivation seems to be a factor in the delinquency of some teenagers, it is by no means a universal or even a common factor. Status deprivation is at best a partial explanation of working-class delinquency.

But Cohen never proposed status deprivation as a universal explanation of working-class gang delinquency. He proposed simply that it was a factor in the *origins* of working-class gangs. Once a working-class gang had evolved, other social processes—gang contagion, for example—could become a more powerful factor in its members' delinquency, and status deprivation might play little, if any, role. Since Reiss and Rhodes did not distinguish between individual delinquents and gang members, nor between new and experienced delinquents, it is difficult to separate those who were in the process of "inventing" working-class delinquency from those who were merely following the expectations of their fellow gang members. The fact that only a minority of the delinquents felt status deprivation is not a critical finding as far as Cohen's theory of working-class gangs is concerned.

Richard Cloward and Lloyd Ohlin   These two scholars (1960) offer a different explanation for gang delinquency. They identify three patterns: conflict, criminal, and retreatist gangs, two of which—the conflict gang and the criminal gang—tend to form on the basis of community structure. Following Kobrin (see Chapter 9, pp. 163–165), they postulate that tightly structured, ethnic neighborhoods with pockets of organized crime in their midst produce criminal gangs, whereas loosely structured neighborhoods in which juveniles are offered little guidance or supervision produce conflict gangs (see also Suttles, 1968: part 4).

Retreatist gangs that focus on "kicks," indulgence in drugs, alcohol, and sex, embrace juveniles who are unacceptable both to conventional groups and to well-established delinquent gangs. Those who can make it in established peer groups—whether prosocial or antisocial—follow those paths; those who cannot, invent a third, hedonistic, pattern all their own.

---

[4]Cohen failed to expand his thesis of class conflict, especially insofar as Marxism is concerned. In the 1950s, McCarthyism and a deep fear of Marxist thinking were rooted in American culture. By the 1980s, this fear had evaporated, and the Schwendingers were more free to explore the roots of working-class delinquency in class conflict à la Marx.

Social structure seems to stimulate delinquent gangs either by providing cultural models in the form of adult cells of organized crime (which, of course, must also be explained) or by creating structural lacunae wherein juveniles are left free to shape their own social destinies. Under conditions of intense status competition, teenagers move toward combative peer groups that carry on fierce rivalries with one another. When some teenagers are ineffective in both conventional and delinquent groups, they form a third pattern of delinquency, which expresses their defiant illegitimacy in exaggerated forms of self-indulgence.

Walter Miller   Miller (1958) holds that gang delinquency reflects a recombination and redefinition of sociocultural values already in lower-class neighborhoods. Miller speculated that several focal concerns (i.e., attitudes and ideals admired in the lower class) led directly to lower-class gang delinquency. The lower class generally, according to Miller, subscribes to six focal concerns: trouble, toughness, smartness, excitement, fate, and autonomy. *Trouble* refers to the complications and criticism that follow law-violating behavior. The lower class does not especially condemn law-violating behavior so much as it fears the trouble that comes with it. Sexual adventures may be fun, but the trouble they sometimes entail in the form of social diseases, complications with parents or spouses, and illegitimate children seriously cloud an otherwise interesting idea.

Toughness describes the individual's courage in facing and overcoming extreme odds. It suggests a willingness to go head to head in combat under conditions that most would flee from. Toughness is a type of mental determination that permits a person to defeat an otherwise stronger opponent. *Smartness* is a different kind of mental strength. It describes someone who uses wits and cunning to gain the better of his opponents. Here the victory comes through mental quickness, even trickery, and not through mental toughness or courage. Toughness and smartness are often contrasted, and of the two, toughness is probably more highly prized in the lower class. But smartness is also valued because it uses the easy way.

Excitement brings an element of spice, novelty, and adventure to everyday routines. It can bring trouble in its wake if it involves immoral or illegal behavior, but even when it does, the adventure is still appreciated. *Fate* is seen as kindly or unkindly but beyond the ability of humans to alter. Some are lucky, and things break their way. Others are unlucky. Events are not indifferent to humankind, but human beings are powerless to shape them in any direction. A sense of fatalism pervades the lower class.

Autonomy describes an impatience or even resentment that lower-class members often feel particularly against bureaucratic controls. Work organizations, welfare, the military, school, and labor unions—all present a comprehensive system of controls that prescribe closely what they can and cannot do. The lower-class person feels little kinship with these organizations and superficially at least, resents their controls. And yet as Miller suggests, lower-class people more or less unconsciously welcome the comprehensive care and support that such organizations also provide. Their controls are noxious, but their benefits are welcomed.

It is easy to see how these values might lead a group of lower-class teenagers into delinquency, particularly if they are vying for status and evaluating one another in terms of these six focal concerns. Toughness, smartness, excitement, and autonomy, if expressed too vigorously or toward the wrong persons, could easily put a youngster on the path to delinquency. Similarly, the idea of fate as being beyond human influence, when linked with a focus on excitement, could well encourage an overly reckless attitude in a variety of situations. Lower-class boys, therefore, in just being themselves are led into difficulty by their own values.

Still, Miller's thesis has been vigorously criticised on a number of points. Kornhauser, for one, sees little value in it (1978: 206–229). First, she rejects Miller's assertion that lower-class focal concerns actually include these six, pointing out that few studies of the lower class have found anything close to what Miller reports. She contends that many, if not all, of Miller's focal concerns are situationally induced and not culturally prescribed. For example, the conviction that fate (and not human will) shapes the outcome of events may be more a reflection of lower-class experience than a value, and the same can be said of trouble and autonomy. Since few lower-class individuals have much control over their fate, such convictions are probably just a resignation to reality. Miller's focal concerns are more individual adjustments to a lower-class situation than cultural values implicit in its heritage.

Although Kornhauser is probably right that many of Miller's lower-class values are adaptations to situations commonly faced by lower-class individuals, her critique is little more than a quibble, because these adaptations, when passed down from parents to children, also become part of the cultural heritage of the class. Furthermore, it is not true that researchers have not found such focal concerns among lower-class children. Parker (1974) reports attitudes and values very similar to those described by Miller among working-class lads in Dublin, though like Kornhauser he also regards them as situational adaptations.

In her evaluation of Miller's thesis, Kornhauser ignores his central idea that the focal concerns of delinquent gangs are assembled from elementary ideas and beliefs of the larger community. But in evaluating Miller's idea we must be careful. Miller is not contending that delinquent gangs and their values are little more than extensions of lower-class cultural life. Rather, he is suggesting that these beliefs are the *raw material* from which deviant groups fashion a new value schema to serve their own situations. This idea has been utilized by a number of other theorists (see Cohen and Short, 1958: 24; or Ferdinand, 1966: 94–141), including the Schwendingers.

The Schwendingers   Herman and Julia Schwendinger have taken Miller's basic insight and broadened it considerably. They have utilized it to understand not simply delinquent gangs but conforming groups as well, and not just the specific beliefs and values of these groups but also the social dynamics of juvenile status groups as these affect juvenile behavior.

The Schwendingers (1985: chapters 3, 4, and 7) identify two main types of juvenile groups: street-corner groups and socialite groups. Each is shaped by the historical experience of its social stratum; the life-style of its members' parents and neighbors; the dynamics of its own group process; and by the racial, ethnic, age, and gender balance of its membership. Any given group is an amalgam of factors that colors its specific values and behavior. Each group displays its own "personality"—its own unique patterns. The Schwendingers regard these patterns as "stradoms," or "stratified domains," that are ranked in terms of criteria peculiar to the groups and not simply in terms of the socioeconomic status of their members.

Male street-corner juvenile groups mark the appearance in capitalist industrial economies of large numbers of marginal individuals who have difficulty in finding stable employment. The capitalist economy uses wages as incentives and needs a large pool of willing laborers. Those whose skills are not in strong demand receive small wages and are marginally employed. Their marginality in the work force, in turn, damages their social esteem. They are not in strong demand as spouses or as friends; they often have no place to go where they are appreciated, except the street corner. Their marginality is a controlling or master attribute; it lowers their social esteem no matter what other qualities they may possess.

Marginality reproduces itself via the family and socialization. Marginal parents beget children whose limited motivation and sophistication in school reduces their success, which in turn limits their promise as workers in adulthood. A pool of surplus labor gathers, and male street-corner groups make an appearance and expose their members to other deviant pressures in the community.

Adolescent socialite groups also represent a long history in capitalist societies. As early as the seventeenth century in England, when expanding commerce gave rise to an urban-based bourgeoisie, it was possible to identify a class of young people who paid close attention to life-style as an indicator of social worth. *Bon vivants* who evaluated one another in terms of their opulent dress style, eating habits, lavish entertainments, and contempt for routine conventions were not rare in London. A similar pattern evolved in nineteenth-century America among the offspring of rich industrialists, and provided a prototype of the socialites that are found today among teenagers all over the United States.

These two groups—teenage street-corner and socialite groups—are characteristic of capitalist societies in that they express a basic conflict rooted in capitalist economies between the bourgeoisie and the proletariat.[5] They should appear, and do appear (see Fyvel, 1964), in Europe and Japan in addition to the United States. Societies with other kinds of political economies presumably would display adolescent groups with different value schemes.

In addition, several more specific pressures push juvenile groups toward delinquency, according to the Schwendingers (1985: 183). A general fascination among the young for mild forms of deviance sometimes takes them into shoplifting, vandalism, alcohol or drug abuse, sexual acting out, traffic violations, or routine status offenses. It is perhaps the most common source of delinquency among juveniles. The forms of delinquency that actually occur depend largely on the specific values and interests of the groups in question, but most juvenile groups find a ready response to suggestions of deviant behavior on the part of at least a portion of their members.

---

[5]This conflict between the bourgeoisie and the proletariat has not produced a proletarian revolution in the United States, partly because the U.S. Constitution has not backed unequivocally the claims of the bougeoisie against the proletariat. Had the Constitution supported the capitalists across the board, the proletariat would have had no alternative but to pursue a revolutionary course. Without a basic conflict between the legitimate claims of the proletariat and the Constitution, most of the claims of labor against the capitalists could be won via means other than revolution. Thus, conflict theory, technically speaking (see pp. 215–217), is not applicable here.

A more distinct kind of pressure begins to appear among most adolescents around the age of 14—the question of their status with respect to one other. This question forces many into self-aggrandizing attitudes, and since these attitudes are belittling to others, they often spark skirmishes among individual youngsters. This yearning for personal status is the basis for much socializing that also begins around this age, providing an additional inducement for invidious comparisons and more fights. When mixed with ethnic or racial divisions within the neighborhood, these rivalries can approach deadly proportions. Thus, when the quest for status gathers momentum in adolescence, it may prompt distinctly violent forms of delinquency as teenagers attempt to clarify their relative worth.

Finally, as juveniles become proficient in various forms of delinquency, opportunities for profit in an underground economy may appear. Heavy drug use among peers encourages drug dealing, heavy sports betting stimulates illegal betting syndicates, strong demand for sports cars provides incentives for auto thievery, and a ready market for sexual favors makes prostitution attractive to teenaged boys and girls. The market for illegal services and products prompts a third form of criminal activity among juveniles who have access to the rackets in their neighborhoods.

These three pressures are all fitted to the character of the juveniles' groups. All three can exist together in a given group or singly in different groups. But they provide a nudge toward delinquency for *most* juvenile groups and provide a basis for understanding why most juvenile groups, whether male or female, middle class or working class, show similar levels of minor delinquency.

The Schwendingers raise several important issues that deserve serious consideration. First, they suggest that adolescents take their cues from the values of their parents and neighbors. Second, they hold that the social classes themselves reflect the values and conflicts inherent in the basic organization of society. Little wonder that teenage socialites like to be seen as managers of school politics and fashion trendsetters, or that street-corner groups see themselves as strong and courageous. These are the values of major economic classes under capitalism. The seeds of cultural deviance lie in the organization of society and the specific adjustment problems that this organization imposes upon juveniles.

The Dimensions of Cultural Deviance Theory

The domain of cultural deviance theory is deviance that occurs in groups. Although its very name, cultural deviance theory, implies that it is solely concerned with values and cultural processes, three of the four perspectives reviewed here (those of Cohen, Cloward and Ohlin, and the Schwendingers) see structural factors also as of basic importance to delinquent gangs. Thus, the domain of cultural deviance theory includes the gang and all its aspects and not just its culturally based values and beliefs.

Kornhauser (1978: 237) suggests that apart from cultural values, gangs influence their members by means of primary group and collective behavior processes. In addition to cultural factors, delinquents experience threatening situational pressures that force gang membership. Primary bonds with fellow gang members may also lure them into gang activities, and group contagion often induces extreme delinquent acts during the heat of battle. These kinds of forces affecting juvenile groups would also be relevant to the domain of cultural deviance theory.

It is important also to draw a distinction between well-established delinquent gangs and adolescent cliques that may also pursue delinquent activity from time to time. Gangs and cliques behave differently, and complaints raised by both Hirschi and Kornhauser regarding cultural deviance theory seem to be based upon a confusion in these terms (see also Chapter 9, pp. 159–161). Gangs have an established structure with an older, stable leadership, and their membership has a sense of the reality of the gang—its reputation, its history, and its territory. They respond to its pressures. Cliques rarely display any of these. They are temporary, loosely structured, less deviant, and less able to mobilize their members in any direction.

Within this domain we are also interested in the kinds of deviance that gangs pursue, and the Schwendingers identify three distinct possibilities: minor types of mischief that appear spontaneously among most adolescents, physical violence that stems from attempts to establish reputation and status among peers, and crimes stimulated by demand for illegal services and goods from an underground economy. Both individual delinquents and gangs may follow any or all of these patterns, but when gang members are involved, group contagion and primary bonds tend to strengthen the basic deviant tendency.

A related issue that cultural deviance theory examines is the source of deviant values. Kornhauser indicates that such values are often situationally based attitudes that reflect the common experiences of group or class members. Few theorists reject this idea, but several take the idea further by suggesting that situations giving rise to these attitudes are usually themselves determined by broader social forces.

Cohen, for example, saw a conflict between working-class kids and their middle-class teachers as a source of antisocial attitudes; Cloward and Ohlin saw the structure of the community as determining whether a gang followed a conflict or criminal pattern; and Schwendinger and Schwendinger saw the fundamental values of both street-corner and socialite teenaged groups as dependent ultimately upon the class position of their parental models in capitalist society. The sources of deviant values lie in the dilemmas and conflicts inherent in the structure of an adolescent's community. Structural anomolies underlie cultural conflicts. We will explore this issue in detail in the next section.

The domain of cultural deviance theory is not as broad as that of social control theory, because cultural deviance theory applies only to gang or clique members who commit delinquency—not to all conformists as does social control theory. Although no more than one-fifth of all delinquents are members of gangs, between 60 and 80 percent of the rest are members of delinquent cliques. The domain of cultural deviance theory embraces certainly a *majority* of all delinquents.

Cultural deviance theory also encounters several competitors within its domain. Personality theory suggests that impulsivity and psychopathy underlie delinquent behavior, including gang delinquency, and conflict theory helps to understand the impact of the gang's illegitimacy on its delinquency (see the next section). Thus, within its proper domain cultural deviance theory must contend with psychological as well as social theories of anomie. These competitors, however, are not hostile invaders or combatants; they are allies and should be utilized along with cultural deviance theory to sharpen even further our ability to explain group delinquency.

As for its ideological relevance, cultural deviance theory seems to be neutral. Along with other forms of crime and vice, conservatives regard gang delinquency as a serious threat to community development and security and periodically call for its suppression. Thus, cultural deviance theory is useful to conservatives because it highlights sources of chronic delinquency in the structural and cultural weaknesses of the community and points to a convenient way of suppressing it by curtailing the underground economy in drugs and other contraband.

Progressives, on the other hand, see gang delinquency as a symptom of social weakness in America's inner cities that requires serious attention and urgent reform. They turn to cultural deviance theory as a way of specifying these broader social problems and resolving them. Cultural deviance theory is relevant to both political agendas, though the prevention of gang delinquency through social reform seems more intricate and more difficult, given the pervasive forces at work, than gang suppression.

THEORIES OF CONFORMITY

These two perspectives—social controls theory and cultural deviance theory—combine to explain *all* forms of conforming behavior. The same arguments apply to both forms, and the two perspectives are analogous in most respects. They assume a passive human being who is eager to accept the limits and requirements of the immediate groups, and differential association and its most recent version social learning theory are sufficient to explain why and how individuals become socialized to the group. Those who associate early, often, and intensively over the long term with delinquents or nondelinquents to the exclusion of the other will tend to adopt the perspective and techniques of their associates.[6]

Neither social controls theory nor cultural deviance theory can explain eccentricity, though several scholars have tried. Cloward and Ohlin made provision for those who are rejected both by conventional and established delinquent groups in their retreatist gangs. These scholars were forced to appeal to other theories to explain the origins of the gang. Cloward and Ohlin implicitly assumed a ganging tendency to explain their retreatist gang. Other theorists have proposed that antisocial behavior at bottom stems from human frailties (i.e., a generalized tendency to deviance and status striving), according to the Schwendingers, and a generalized unruliness, according to Gottfredson and Hirschi as well as Kornhauser. None of these theorists, however, has proposed a

---

[6]To be sure, social controls theorists have not looked sympathetically to differential association theory for an explanation of why some people conform and others do not (compare Hirschi, 1969: 13–15; Jensen, 1972; and Kornhauser, 1978). In answer to their doubts, Matsueda (1982) compared the predictions of differential association theory with those of social control theory and concluded that "differential association theory is supported over control theory" (Matsueda, 1982: 500). Using differential association theory, Matsueda was able to specify more accurately the outcome of different control situations.

But the two theories are not in basic contradiction. Social control theory à la Hirschi and Jensen provides broad estimates of the level of delinquent behavior, whereas differential association theory in the hands of Matsueda specifies closely the conditions under which delinquency arises in social groups.

careful explanation of human eccentricity, and our understanding of these basic forces is still limited.

Finally, several theorists and especially the Schwendingers have pointed out that ultimately the problem of delinquency is linked to the political economy of the nation as a whole. They suggest that we cannot explain delinquency by focusing simply on the community and the neighborhood. Social groups are defined in the crucible of political and economic conflict, and these conflicts in turn give meaning to adolescent competitions.

More than one level of analysis is relevant to delinquency, and we must trace the theoretical connections among these several levels: from community to region to nation and even to world system. These several levels of analysis must be looked at separately, but they are causally linked, and we also must grasp these broader linkages to understand fully the social origins of delinquency.

THEORIES OF ANOMIE

Theories of anomie—that is, strain theory, labeling theory, and conflict theory—have much in common with theories of conformity. They assume, first of all, that children are fully committed to conventional behavior and that under normal circumstances, they mature into adulthood with little difficulty. Social order and strong social controls stand at the heart of both types of theory.

With theories of anomie, however, the fundamental issue is How are conventional children, who are initially committed to prevailing values, transformed into deviant children? Theories of anomie may have much in common with theories of conformity, but they take theories of conformity a step further by attempting to explain the sources of deviant behavior in nominally conformist children.

Their answer focuses on flaws and contradictions in the social structure itself, or on the child's articulation with social structure. Sometimes the community is structured so that some juveniles are *denied* any opportunity to fulfill the ideals of the community. No matter what they do, these children cannot win the approval of the community and are consigned to lowly positions. Sometimes, however, the community is attentive to a child's best efforts, but only the talented and skilled may receive its full approval. The rest receive less recognition or even ridicule and are shunted to lower levels of responsibility and reward.

Whether the child's failures result from basic flaws in social structure or his or her inability to adjust to conditions in the community, the result is much the same. The child is gradually isolated from those who thrive with the community's blessing. Those who fail, suffer alienation from conventional values and fall into anomie. Their anomie in turn opens the door for many varieties of unconventional behavior that may well include delinquency.

They may also take a more constructive avenue, however. Anomic juveniles are sometimes spurred to a wide variety of innovative activities (compare Holden Caulfield in J.D. Salinger's *Catcher in the Rye*). But here we give primary attention to the deviant paths that anomic juveniles often follow.

When the social structure is primarily at fault in denying social approval and rewards to members of the community, a spirit of conflict between the denied group and the favored group is nourished, which may result in overt political confrontations. Theories that deal with these conflicts and their resolutions are called *conflict theory*. On the other hand, when some members are rejected by the community after a vigorous competition in which they have failed, their failure and subsequent deviant activity is explained by strain theory.

Strain theory and conflict theory have much in common. Both assume that the child is committed at first to conventional values and conforming behavior, and both assume that the commitment is eroded by a persistent inability to win the community's approval. Both also assume that anomie is the spur that prompts an alternative path.

But strain theory and conflict theory differ in their account of the juvenile's anomie and subsequent behavior.[7] From the standpoint of strain theory, the juvenile's failure is largely a moral failure. He has failed to live up to the community's standards and his esteem has suffered a bitter blow. He sees *himself* as morally at fault and personally responsible. His subsequent deviance powerfully reflects both a sense of moral degradation and a diffuse anger at his group-based humiliation.

In conflict theory the juvenile sees his class or group as the victim of unjust discrimination and not morally deficient at all. His plight results from the unfairness of the community in applying its values unjustly so that some juveniles have little if any chance to win social esteem in the usual manner. In strain theory the juvenile's reactions are basically diffuse, personal and individualistic, but in conflict theory his reactions are directed by the ideologies of his groups against particular enemies. In strain theory the individual feels discouragement, resentment, and frustration (i.e., stress), but in conflict theory he feels anger and seeks revenge. In strain theory the discriminating standards are treated as legitimate; in conflict theory their legitimacy is directly challenged.

Strain and its deviant personal reactions can be readily transformed into retreatism or rebellion through group membership, and the relief such groups can provide deviant individuals offers powerful incentives for anomic individuals to find and join such groups. They confer a sense of personal legitimacy upon individuals who have failed, and thereby encourage them in their deviant path.[8] Since the same individual may progress from seeing social failure as personal incompetence to seeing it as class or racial discrimination, strain theory and conflict theory may be relevant to any given individual during different phases of social adjustment. Strain theory and conflict theory are not contradictory, but their domains (though obviously distinct at any given time) may show substantial overlap over time. Let us turn to these two conceptual models and their differences.

---

[7]Merton (1957: 153–157) recognizes this fundamental difference between strain theory and conflict theory in his distinction between rebellion and retreatism. In retreatism the anomic individual feels resentment and rejects cultural goals as well as institutional means to these goals in favor of more idiosyncratic ones, but in rebellion the individual seeks to establish new cultural goals and institutional means of society on the basis of group-based ideologies and effort.

[8]Moral relativism implies that one group's endorsement is as good as any other's, but as we have already seen, deviant groups within a larger community still must justify themselves to their members.

Strain Theory

Strain theory describes the stress and anguish that arises from a juvenile's repeated failure to win a key social group's approval. This group could be the immediate family, relatives, peers, teachers, or neighbors. It could be just one group, or it could involve a set of groups. The more central the group to the individual's self-esteem, or the larger the number of groups stigmatizing the individual, the greater the alienation and anomie. As the juvenile's reputation is tarnished, his commitment to the group's values is weakened and his vulnerability to alternative values grows. In the beginning, however, he must feel some obligation to and identify with the group in question. His membership in the group is meaningful and his reputation is important. Where there is little commitment, theoretically speaking there can be little strain.[9]

Furthermore, as strain develops, it progresses through several different phases (Scheler, 1961: chapter 1). At first embarrassment and shame at having failed spark renewed efforts to win approval. If these efforts result in even more failure, withdrawal and anomie result, and the group's values no longer matter as much as they once did. Finally, as failure continues and biting criticism is heaped upon the youth, frustration and resentment and even defiance and revenge emerge as the dominant emotions. A conforming group member is transformed gradually through strain into an alienated member and ultimately into a resentful, defiant member. Since strain erupts into delinquency only in its later stages, efforts to link strain to delinquency must focus on these later stages. Delinquency only becomes an alternative when strain has matured into resentment and the juvenile has become marginal in his groups.

Labeling theory is highly relevant here, because it describes how a juvenile's strain can be institutionalized—how strain can usher him along a path that results in his being identified socially as a delinquent. When a resentful juvenile confronts an authoritative adult who condemns the juvenile's behavior and labels him as immoral, the label flags him as a failure generally. If the youngster gives vent to his frustration and resentment in counterattacks (secondary deviance) against his accuser, his label and deviant status are confirmed.

The merits and weaknesses of labeling theory have been widely debated (see Wellford, 1975; Gove, 1975), but Kobrin (1976) has argued that labeling, by offering strategic rewards to exemplary members, plays an important role in impressing the values and ideals of the community on the consciences of its members. It helps community members identify with the community and its basic values. But labeling also assigns the alienated, defiant juvenile to a marginal status.

There is ample evidence supporting the notion of strain and its role in producing marginality among youths. We have already noted in Chapter 9 (see p. 161) the impact of school failure upon teenagers, and many criminologists have described the key role of family conflict in producing both adolescent strain and juvenile delinquency. Alienation from conventional peers may also play a role in delinquency, according to Hirschi (1969,

---

[9]Thus, control theory and strain theory see opposite outcomes stemming from close ties with conventional groups. From a control theoretical viewpoint, close ties with conventional groups produce *low* levels of delinquency, but from a strain theoretical viewpoint close ties with these same groups coupled with stress yield *high* levels of delinquency.

145–152), though there is also good reason to believe that alienation from peers can also inhibit delinquency.

As noted in Chapter 9, children who are a sociocultural minority in their high school show much less delinquency than those who are part of the school majority. The social majority establishes the dominant peer groups in the school, and these in turn follow a less inhibited path that is likely to include minor delinquency. Thus, being deeply involved in the dominant groups in school can lead to higher levels of delinquency, and strain in peer relationships would in this case contribute to lower levels of delinquency.

The *domain* of strain theory, therefore, includes juveniles (1) who have identified closely with key groups in their neighborhood, but (2) who have failed miserably in the eyes of these groups and experienced considerable strain, and (3) as a result have become estranged and resentful. Some will find greater freedom in their alienation, but those who are labeled as deviant through bitter confrontations with authorities will move toward delinquency. Strain in the family and school creates a pool of embittered, iconoclastic juveniles with little confidence in adults. Many will invent delinquency in their isolation and estrangement.

Strain theory's domain is not broad, for it describes only teenagers who have had a troubled time in school or in the family. And even among these, juveniles who discover constructive ways of dealing with their alienation and avoiding delinquency will also fall outside its domain. Strain theory will not apply to most delinquents, because other more pervasive factors (weak social controls or cultural deviance) will account more directly for their delinquency. But strain theory is useful in understanding how well-socialized, conventional young people can nonetheless turn against their groups and reject their values and ideals, opening the way for criminogenic pressures to make themselves felt.

Much of the research to evaluate strain theory has been carried on incidentally within studies of social controls, with the result that many evaluations have proved to be negative (compare Hirschi, 1969). A second problem grows out of the fact that strain theory has not yet been carefully defined, with the result that some researchers are uncertain as to the meaning of strain or how to measure it (compare Polk, 1969: 214–224). Thus, few definitive studies of strain and its impact have been done.

Surely its domain is much narrower than all but conflict theory, but much needs to be done both in terms of developing the theory and in determining its scope. How well it covers its domain cannot at this point be estimated.

The ideological implications of strain theory and labeling theory are far reaching. Since strain theory assumes that the juvenile is rejected for good reasons by the group, the implication is that somehow the juvenile did not measure up to the group's standard. Those who thrive in the competition are morally stronger than those who do not, and those who fail are weeded out for good cause. Under conditions of free and open competition, a certain, sizable portion is bound to fall short. Failure and strain are inherent in the nature of free institutions.

Since strain is inevitable in free society, manipulation of strain in society is possible only with regard to the levels of skill that different competitors bring with them. Since much of the fault for strain in society lies with the individual's values and skills, the remedy lies in reinforcing the individual through training and education—a conservative policy. In the late nineteenth century much the same message was carried by social Darwinism and was warmly received by conservatives.

The other side of strain, however, is that among young people it helps to decrease their commitment to social institutions. Estrangement among young people, especially among those groups who have faced systematic discrimination, is growing to dangerous proportions. Methods of reducing *their* strain are needed if a steady stream of committed, capable young people is to mature into adulthood. Something is wrong with our educational and social institutions, especially as they deal with underprivileged groups, that badly needs to be fixed. For progressives, the root of the problem lies with the institutions, not the individuals.

American society has created a variety of underprivileged groups—inner-city blacks and the rural poor of Appalachia, the South, and mountain states of the west—that need substantial help if they are ever to enjoy the advantages of full citizenship. The basic fault lies not with their moral strengths or skills. The fault lies in the uneven development of American society. Those who live in economically favored areas find socially rewarding lives. Those who live in economically depressed areas, live desperate, demeaning lives. Free competition assumes that all have a chance to prepare themselves equally for the competition. No society can make competition perfectly equal, but society has a responsibility to lift up those who have thus far been denied through deliberate discrimination or uneven economic development an equal chance. To fail in this effort is to encourage an even greater polarization of the United States into the very rich and the very poor—a politically dangerous and inhumane course.

For the progressives, strain theory identifies the institutional failures that are responsible for the uneven competition. The remedy should focus not only on individual help but also on institutional adjustments (progressive income taxes, regional economic help, regional educational incentives) that can redress some of the unevenness of society up to now. Competition in society is valuable, but we must take special pains that even those who have been badly treated may still have a chance to lift themselves up through grit and ability. That has always been the promise of America, and the progressives want to extend that promise as widely as possible.

Labeling theory, to progressives, seems to suggest that juvenile justice is a dangerous, clumsy giant as it tramples around and among juveniles, arresting many, throwing some into institutions, committing others to detention centers, and placing many on probation. If juvenile justice were more selective, bringing only those who truly deserve its attention into official proceedings, less damage would be done. Labeling theory implies that the narrower the net, the fewer good kids will be damaged and the more socially effective the system. The progressives believe that if we were successful at improving social and economic institutions, delinquency and crime would shrink to much smaller proportions. Labeling via formal proceedings is at best a stopgap measure. Placing more emphasis upon the justice system at the expense of social programs is a mistake.

Conservatives, however, see the justice system as essential and labeling as inevitable. It places those who persist in antisocial behavior on notice that their course carries heavy personal costs. Without an aggressive justice system the whole of society would suffer, and the few who get caught up in its proceedings pay a small price, which they richly deserve, for the credibility of the justice system as a whole. Labeling may have negative consequences for a few—especially the innocent and young—but there is no way to avoid labeling if the broad benefits of a just and deterring system are to be realized.

Conflict Theory

Another group of juveniles who go through similar dilemmas but for very different reasons are those involved in social conflict. Juveniles who are strained in their communities are led to believe they lack a key quality that is crucial for full membership in their groups. As a result, their reputation is tarnished and a comfortable place in these groups is unattainable for them.

But other juveniles are denied membership in groups for (from their standpoint, at least) immoral or illegitimate reasons. Although few high school cliques today are organized strictly along religious or racial lines, such groups do at times reject some potential members on such grounds. It is not common, but it happens.

When it does happen, the cliques involved are applying criteria that have been thoroughly discredited in society and that most other groups have rejected on moral grounds. Any juvenile clique openly displaying such prejudiced attitudes would be vulnerable to severe criticism and would seriously damage its reputation in many neighborhoods. Youngsters rejected on racial or religious grounds would have solid grounds for believing that such a group is morally unworthy of them as members. Their rejection would provide a good basis for antagonism not only between the rejecting clique and the individual but also between the clique and all members of the rejected group as well. Thus, an exclusion of individuals on religious or racial grounds could spark a conflict between the offending clique and the excluded religious or racial group.

Instead of strain, those who were rejected would feel indignation and anger, and they would challenge the moral legitimacy of groups acting in this fashion. Conflict might even ensue, but we would still have only a quarrel among two local groups. It would not threaten the individual's or the group's allegiance to the community as a whole. Anomie would be minimal in both groups, and *conflict theory* would not apply to confrontations between antagonistic political, racial, or religious groups because these conflicts are more political than they are moral.

But suppose the conflict were between an individual, his religious or racial group, and his social community. The individual and all members of his group would feel indignation and anger, but now they would see moral unworthiness in the community and its values, and not simply in a competitive group. Now, the legitimacy of the whole community and its values would be questioned, and the individual would be alienated from the norms of the community—just as the strained individual is. The principle difference between the strained individual and the conflicted individual is their understanding of their social rejection.

If the individual blames himself, he accepts the group's evaluation and experiences degradation and alienation. But if he views the moral fault as in the community, he sees it as morally deficient, and he challenges its legitimacy. Some who have faced social prejudice and discrimination often accept the prejudiced views of their rejectors and regard their membership in an excluded group as a mark of shame and humiliation. Others in the same situation feel moral indignation toward a community that shows prejudice and reject the community and its values. The former should be understood in terms of strain theory, the latter in terms of conflict theory.

Communal discrimination alienates targeted groups from the moral community and forces them to seek an alternative morality. Defiance, including delinquency and rebellion, are distinct possibilities.

Conflict creates moral dilemmas much like those facing the strained individual and leads to alienation and anomie. The conflicted individual feels the same moral isolation and anger. But with his immediate group's moral support he can reject the antagonistic group and its prejudiced values and follow a different path. Like the strained person, he cannot live comfortably in such a community.

During the 1960s many juveniles and young adults almost over night were caught up in protests focusing on the Vietnam War, civil rights, and university governance, while celebrating drugs, casual sex, and dissonant rock music. It was basically a youthful cry for freedom from responsibility, career, war, and racial discrimination, and it drew many into a life of drugs, casual living, and youthful defiance toward adult convention. In a few short years many were drawn into a wide variety of petty crimes, and delinquency rates skyrocketed.

Unfortunately, little solid research has been done on the youth of this period, but they seem to illustrate clearly the impact of conflict (not strain) on youth. The young people of that period subscribed wholeheartedly to more permissive standards in several areas—drugs, sex, and music—but to a more rigorous moral code in others—the Vietnam War, South Africa, and racial discrimination—than their parents. The conflict in values between the young and the old was sharp, and traditional morality was scorned. The Vietnam War was seen as an attack not only on the Vietnamese people but on young America as well, and in their alienation and anomie, young people, including many teenagers, felt free to follow their own intuitions. Many were angry and alienated, many rejected traditional values, and many became delinquent or criminal.

Under normal circumstances not many juveniles are caught up in community politics in their own right, and political turmoil and conflict usher few juveniles into delinquency. Perceptive teenagers are drawn to politics or law to improve the community, but few would be driven to direct attacks on those who display intolerable values in the community.

Juveniles may participate in the political conflicts of their elders by harassing groups their parents are prejudiced toward, and they may even feel some of the hostility of their parents toward these same groups. Juvenile conflict is usually a result of their supporting the values of their parents and elders and *not* their spontaneous alienation from, anger against, and defiance toward their moral community.

During the 1960s, however, many young people fell into a moral conflict with their community, and it led them to a new moral stance and distinctly different political views. The permissiveness, but little of the anger and moral indignation of the 1960s, continues among young people today.

Conflict theory is especially useful in pinpointing structural deficiencies in the community that force specific groups into a rebellious stance in the community. Marx and his dialectical analysis of capitalism, of course, stand out, but conflict theorists have also shown much interest in the effects of slavery and racial discrimination on African Americans, and more lately gender politics has also inspired their imagination. Conflict theory's strongest contribution has been its explanation of the social and economic contradictions that kindle conflict among competitive groups within the larger society.

Complex communities and some simple communities display many forms of moral corruption and prejudice. And political conflict at the adult level among opposing racial, religious, economic, and political factions is not uncommon. Moreover, these quarrels alienate many adults, raise their anger to explosive levels, and pit them against one another and sometimes even their societies as well. These adult struggles are often echoed in neighborhood conflicts among juvenile cliques. Adult conflicts give meaning and direction to juvenile delinquency and should be understood in terms of conflict theory. If the delinquents themselves would have fallen into some form of deviance anyway, conflict theory is at best only a partial explanation of teenagers' conflicts. In addition to conflict theory, some explanation for the existence of juvenile cliques in the neighborhood as well as an account of why juveniles get involved in their elders' conflicts is still needed.[10] Strong juvenile cliques willing and able to confront other groups do not appear in every community, and even rarer do they commit themselves to the battles of their elders. More often they become absorbed in their competitions with other juvenile groups and ignore the broader conflicts of the community or society.[11] Thus, the domain of conflict theory as far as delinquency is concerned is limited. Conflict theory is more useful in explaining adult crime historically than juvenile delinquency.

Its domain is so narrow as far as delinquency is concerned that its scope is probably unmeasurable. Conflict theory accounts nicely for youthful anger and indignation during the 1960s, but the turmoil of that period was extraordinary. In normal times conflict theory has little application to delinquent behavior, and its scope is slight.

Its political implications, however, are noteworthy. Conservatives are suspicious of ideologies that defy tradition and established institutions. Conflict theory seeks out the structural flaws of the community and society and attributes the problems of the community—racial discrimination, labor unrest, poverty, vice, and delinquency—not to moral lapses, which many conservatives can appreciate, but to failures in these same traditions and institutions. Conservatives adhere to the opposite view that these same traditions and institutions could pull minorities out of their depressed condition, if only they were followed and accepted.

Conservatives could learn much from conflict theorists regarding problem areas in society that need attention. Often the main barrier is the conflict theorist's terminology itself—dialectical materialism, the ruling class, bourgeoisie, proletariat, surplus value, exploitation, class warfare, dictatorship of the proletariat, false consciousness—making conservatives grind their teeth. But conflict theorists have been resourceful and indefatigable in documenting their thesis that even conflict can be constructive, and their message could expand the vision of conservatives as they ponder ways to strengthen the community.

Progressives find the message of conflict theory more palatable. Progressives are not so sensitive regarding the destructive consequences of economic policies and institutions and are looking for ways to reform community structure so that delinquency can be prevented. Conflict theory points to basic problems with economic and political institutions and suggests ways of relieving these problems and easing community tensions. But

---

[10]The Schwendingers gave heavy emphasis to conflict theory in their own account of the conflict between socialite and street-corner groups. But they also paid considerable attention to these other issues as well. They must have realized that conflict theory is not a complete theory of delinquency.

[11]Only a few of Chicago's gang delinquents were drawn into the Black Panthers and their black power movement in the late 1960s. The juveniles were too busy in their internecine battles with other delinquent groups to give much heed to the black power movement (Short, 1980:298–301).

even progressives are cautious about endorsing class warfare as a reasonable means for redressing imbalances in community wealth and power.

CONCLUSIONS

Theories of conformity see delinquency primarily as an outgrowth of normative processes in the community. In control theory delinquency is viewed as an indirect result of inadequate social controls that fail to inhibit personal or social deviance. Control theorists look to ways of girding up the community in all its facets to reassert social dominance over youthful exuberance whether in the form of individual misbehavior or group delinquency. It is a broad theory with a wide domain, but it applies directly only to conforming behavior and can only recommend methods for extending the sway of community controls. It is a conservative theory, and attracts considerable interest in these conservative times. Since it does not deal directly with delinquency, it is not competitive with any other theory of delinquency.

Cultural deviance theory is regarded with some suspicion by many control theorists, even though it is a blood relative. It too sees delinquency as a product of social conformity, but here delinquency is a direct expression of forces rooted basically in juvenile cliques and gangs. In contrast to control theory, however, cultural deviance theory offers a broad explanation of the origins of juvenile cliques and gangs, explains their ability to shape and guide their members, and describes specific types of delinquency. Its domain, while somewhat narrower than control theory's, bears nonetheless on delinquency directly and embraces a substantial portion of all delinquents. It is probably the most powerful theory of delinquency in terms of its domain. But it has not attracted as much interest as control theory—perhaps because of its political neutrality—and its potential has not been fully exploited as yet. Its narrow scope leaves much room for theoretical development.

Theories of anomie—strain theory and conflict theory—view delinquency as an outgrowth of community disorganization. Social structure surrounds all socialized members with a tight web of prescribed and prohibited behaviors. But human nature is fractious, and substantial numbers find the normative guidelines of the community impossible to fulfill. Strain arising from the individual's awkwardness in living up to the community's commands is inherent in the match between human nature and social forces.

Similarly, complex communities must unify and coordinate their many distinct groups into a smoothly functioning system. But the interplay of institutions that fosters the integration and coordination of communal groups sometimes also gives advantages to some groups over others. These advantages may at times so alienate the victims of another group's strengths that they divorce themselves completely from these institutions and demand a restructuring of the fundamental processes of integration. At times these demands become irresistable and fundamental reform may result, either via revolution or more peaceful accommodation.

Strain theory seeks to explain both the strain that commonly arises in complex communities and the way in which this strain expresses itself in delinquency. Delinquency is not the only product of strain, but it is a common one. Conflict theory is basically interested in the complex integrating processes and institutions of society and how they ordain conflict among the community's basic groups. Conflict theory has only recently been utilized in explaining delinquency—in Schwendingers' writings—but even here other, more immediate forces are viewed as essential in explaining local gang delinquency.

Both strain theory and conflict theory see the individual's rejection by the community as the starting point for delinquency. In strain theory the individual attempts to deal with his rejection alone using whatever psychological resources he may have. The result is often closely dependent upon the psychological strengths and weaknesses of the youth. Strain theory has a special affinity for psychological theories that postulate complex interactions between human emotions, the self, and social demands. One such theory is neo-Freudian theory.

Conflict theory sees the individual as a member of a rejected group and, therefore, guided by this group in reacting to its rejection. The group may reject its rejector and abandon cooperation with the community and conformity to its rules. The outcome here depends heavily upon group dynamics as well as the relative strengths of the groups involved, and the individual's behavior under these conditions is best understood in terms of group decisions and policies, not by psychological theory. The outcome may involve violence, and during periods of extreme turmoil, otherwise talented and conventional juveniles may find themselves drawn into intense communal conflict and thereby into considerable delinquency. Nevertheless, since most juvenile gangs and cliques are normally removed from communal conflict at adult levels, conflict theory is not usually a general explanation of delinquency.

Neither strain theory nor conflict theory has generated a strong theoretical thrust since Merton's initial statement in the 1940s, but each has a domain that no other social theory can challenge and will probably attract broader interest as national politics shifts in a more progressive direction.

SUMMARY

It is useful to group social theories of delinquency into theories of conformity and theories of anomie. Theories of conformity explain delinquency as a result of the direct impact of group pressures on their members. In the case of social controls theory, pressures stemming from conventional groups in opposition to deviant behavior impinge upon adolescents and inhibit their delinquency, and in the case of cultural deviance theory, pressures stemming from deviant groups themselves prompt delinquency.

Despite the fact that several social controls theorists have denounced cultural deviance theory, it is nonetheless true that both theories use similar conceptual models in which both the absence of delinquency and its presence are explained in terms of cultural or structural features of immediate social groups. Even though social controls theorists have also been critical of differential association theory, it and social learning theory (its close relative) are useful in explaining the lasting impact of social groups on their members.

Theories of anomie, which include strain theory and conflict theory, also follow a common format. Initially, the individual in strain theory or the group in conflict theory devotes itself to the values and ideals of conventional groups in society and strives valiantly to find a comfortable and socially acceptable niche. But in the eyes of the individual or the group the larger group withholds rewards and social honors such that the individual or the group is denied an esteemed place in the broader group. Both the individual in strain theory and the group in conflict theory are condemned to disreputable positions in society, and their fall from grace is viewed by all as a direct attack on their legitimacy and worthiness.

In the case of strain theory the individual interprets this fall as a personal failure, and the guilt, resentment, and depression that result seriously interfere with his ability to fulfill conventional responsibilities. His illegitimacy undermines his adjustment to the rigors and pressures of conventional groups and opens the door to anomie and ultimately delinquency.

In the case of conflict theory, the group sees its fall from grace as one more indication of the immorality of conventional society and withdraws its allegiance as a result of its condemnation. In conflict theory the struggle is between two different conceptions of morality, and if the condemned group can discover some persuasive basis for establishing the immorality of the condemning group, it can defeat this group socially without resorting to civil war. In the United States the ability of labor groups, minorities, and particularly blacks to answer their critics with the Constitution has swayed responsible public opinion toward their cause and made an insurrection unnecessary. Where a moral victory can be achieved without violence, conflict among groups need not result in out-and-out warfare. But where no basis for compromise or moral reconciliation between the outgroup and society is possible, a civil war is likely.

Conflict theory is not especially relevant to delinquency in that most political conflicts among groups bearing upon social worth are settled without a strong participation from juveniles. But the fact remains that most deviant groups including delinquent gangs must face their denunciation and erect the same kinds of defense mechanisms against their critics that condemned political groups do. Like revolutionaries, delinquent gangs must also somehow deal with their outcast status. Conflict theory is relevant to delinquent gangs and cliques because it helps us understand why such gangs often launch denunciations toward conventional values and goals. They must condemn their condemners.

The point here is that both strain theory and conflict theory regard an estrangement from conventional values as a common outcome of moral conflict between conventional society and its constituents. Social anomie is the first step toward deviance, and since it is a wrenching step for both individual and group, it is taken only reluctantly with great soul searching and guilt.

Theories of personality that can interpret the significance of repeated social attacks on the moral worth of individuals and groups (neo-Freudian theory, for example) should prove of value. They are needed to explain how anomie arising from repeated condemnations is transmuted into either a diffuse, ambivalent ego-identity in the case of strain theory, or a focused, bitter counterattack in the case of conflict theory.

REFERENCES

Cloward, Richard A., and Lloyd E. Ohlin. 1960. *Delinquency and Opportunity: A Theory of Delinquent Gangs.* New York: The Free Press.

Cohen, Albert K. 1955. *Delinquent Boys: The Culture of the Gang.* New York: The Free Press.

Cohen, Albert K., and James F. Short, Jr. 1958. "Research in Delinquent Subcultures." *The Journal of Social Issues* 14:20–37.

Ferdinand, Theodore N. 1966. *Typologies of Delinquency.* New York: Random House.

Fyvel, T. R. 1964. *Troublemakers.* New York: Schocken Books.

Gove, Walter R., ed. 1975. *The Labeling of Deviance.* New York: John Wiley & Sons.

Hirschi, Travis. 1969. *Causes of Delinquency.* Berkeley: University of California Press.

Jensen, Gary F. 1972. "Parents, Peers and Delinquent Action: A Test of Differential Association Theory." *American Journal of Sociology* 78:562–575.

Kobrin, Solomon. 1951. "The Conflict of Values in Delinquency Areas." *American Sociological Review* 16 (October):653–661.

———. 1976. "The Labeling Approach, Problems and Limits." In *Delinquency, Crime, and Society.* Edited by James F. Short, Jr. Chicago: University of Chicago Press.

Kornhauser, Ruth Rosner. 1978. *Social Sources of Delinquency.* Chicago: University of Chicago Press.

Matsueda, Ross L. 1982. "Testing Control Theory and Differential Association." *American Sociological Review* 47, No. 4:489–504.

Matza, David. 1964. *Delinquency and Drift.* New York: John Wiley & Sons.

Merton, Robert K. 1957. "Social Structure and Anomie." In *Social Theory and Social Structure.* Revised and enlarged edition. Edited by Robert K. Merton. New York: The Free Press.

Miller, Walter B. 1958. "Lower Class Culture as a Generating Milieu of Gang Delinquency." *The Journal of Social Issues* 14, No. 3:5–19.

Parker, Howard J. 1974. *View from the Boys.* London: David and Charlers Publishers.

Polk, Kenneth. 1969. "Class, Strain, and Rebellion Among Adolescents." *Social Problems* 17, No. 2 (Fall):214–224.

Reiss, Albert J., Jr., and A. Lewis Rhodes. 1963. "Status Deprivation and Delinquent Behavior." *The Sociological Quarterly* 4 (Spring):135–149.

Scheler, Max. 1961. *Resentiment.* New York: The Free Press.

Schwendinger, Herman, and Julia R. Siegel Schwendinger. 1985. *Adolescent Subcultures and Delinquency.* New York: Praeger.

Short, James F., Jr. 1980. "Political Implications of Juvenile Delinquency: A Comparative Perspective." In *Critical Issues in Juvenile Delinquency.* Edited by David Shichor and Delos H. Kelly. Lexington, MA: Lexington Books: 297–316.

Suttles, Gerald. 1968. *The Social Order of the Slum.* Chicago: University of Chicago Press.

Sykes, Gresham M., and David Matza. 1957. "Techniques of Neutralization: A Theory of Delinquency." *The American Journal of Sociology* 22 (December):664–670.

Wellford, Charles. 1975. "Labeling Theory and Criminology: An Assessment." *Social Problems* 22, No. 3:332–345.

Chapter
13

Juvenile Justice at the Crossroads

*J*uvenile justice is at a crossroads. One path, defined by a just deserts perspective, views the juvenile justice system as an institution for meting out proportionate punishments to deserving offenders, and the other, hewing to a parens patriae doctrine, sees juvenile justice helping juveniles make a better life for themselves. The juvenile court and, indeed, the larger society are committed to both justice and rehabilitation for juveniles, but no one has found a way to harmonize the two within the juvenile court. Thus, the juvenile court is moving on a road leading toward due process, criminalization (making the juvenile court more like the criminal courts), and just punishments and away from parens patriae and treatment. The court is uneasy about the journey away from parens patriae, and yet it cannot forego the journey toward due process.

We will review this broad dilemma and describe how it arose within juvenile justice. In the final pages of this chapter we will propose some ways of resolving the dilemma.

A NEW STATUS: THE JUVENILE

During the Jacksonian era (roughly 1818 to 1837), as America began to industrialize, there was no such thing as a juvenile delinquent or juvenile law. Children under the age of 7 were regarded as "infants" who were not responsible for their actions nor subject to

Chapter 13 contains excerpts from "History Overtakes the Juvenile Justice System", *Crime and Delinquency* 37, No. 2, April 1991; 204–224, by Theodore N. Ferdinand. Copyright © 1991, Sage Publications, Inc. Reprinted by permission of the author.

the criminal law. In addition, since they were still dependent, their parents *were* responsible for them and their control. After 6 years children were regarded as partially responsible and, therefore, liable to criminal prosecution. If they were incorrigible within the family, for example, they could be punished severely, though few were. If they were independent and beyond the family's control, which occurred for boys around their fifteenth birthday, they were subject to the full rigor of the criminal law. Many boys between the ages of 12 and 15 both in America and in Europe were sentenced to adult punishments. Although such cases were not the rule, in 1827 the Walnut Street Prison in Philadelphia held a boy of just 12, and altogether about one-fifth of the inmates in several northeastern states were under 21 (Lewis, 1967: 293). When these children came before the criminal court, their prison sentences were routinely reported in the newspapers of the day.

By the 1820s things were beginning to change. As American cities absorbed growing numbers of impoverished migrants from nearby farms and villages as well as from Europe, many families were forced to abandon their children, with the result that throngs of homeless children wandered the city streets of Boston, Philadelphia, and New York both day and night.

Many of these children were simply looking for means of support. But others turned to crime, and growing numbers were being sentenced to adult prisons. Many juries refused to convict such children to spare them the agony of a prison sentence, but enough did to raise an alarm among concerned citizens. Many argued for more humane ways of dealing with young people who broke the law, especially for new custodial institutions that would segregate young people from adults.

In a related development the cities of the northeastern United States began also to establish secondary schools for children from 13 to 16 years of age. Boston, for example, built its first free public high school, Boston English High School, in 1821, and by 1826 the city enrolled in its schools a large majority of the children (4 to 15 years of age) who were eligible for a public education. The city fathers of that era were immensely proud of their accomplishment, but we are probably safe in saying that the children were not all equally pleased.

At least half of the delinquency committed by juveniles today takes place in, around, or against the schools. Teachers, school buildings and equipment, or classmates are regular targets of mischief, and it is no doubt true that children who were forced to go to school in the early nineteenth century faced many of the same frustrations as children today. Teachers and principals were skillful enough in controlling the children, but inevitably they failed with some. Children who were incapable of fitting into an organized classroom became a new problem for the city fathers.

To help these children, as well as the homeless and neglected children and those convicted of serious crimes, the northeastern cities began to build houses of refuge. New York opened the first house of refuge on January 1, 1825; Boston built a house of reformation in 1826; and Philadelphia established its house of refuge in 1828.

These early institutions were organized like the public schools they supported. Children between the ages of 12 and 16 (not 12 and 21, the age of majority) were placed in grades according to their needs and promoted according to their achievements. They were discharged when they had accomplished the goals set for them by the superintendent. The schools provided a regimen for the children of work, educational instruction, and religious devotions suffused with a kindly spirit of benevolence. The contrast between the houses of refuge and the state prisons was sharp.

The houses of refuge exerted an informal authority over the children, and at first no one questioned their right to take custody of juveniles. But in Philadelphia a complaint (*Ex parte Crouse,* 1838) challenged the right of the house of refuge to imprison Mary Ann Crouse without a jury trial (see Garlock, 1979: 364–367). Mary Ann had been committed to Philadelphia's house of refuge on her mother's complaint that she was beyond control. When Mary Ann's father learned of the girl's fate, he appealed her commitment to the Pennsylvania Supreme Court. The Court rejected his appeal, however, on the basis that Mary Ann had been sent to the house of refuge to be educated and reformed, not punished. Since her commitment was benevolent (i.e., for her own good), a jury trial was not necessary. The court's decision was based on parens patriae, a doctrine that had emerged during the eighteenth century in England's chancery court system (Ferdinand, 1980: 154–157).

As the common law evolved over the centuries, it inevitably lost some of its flexibility. Disputes were brought to the royal courts that did not fit the common law, and in some cases fairness was difficult to achieve. Appeals of such cases were brought not to the king nor the royal courts but to the king's religious advisor, the chancellor, and a whole new system of courts, the chancery courts, gradually took shape in England. By the eighteenth century these courts had defined a new kind of law, the equity law (known as the civil law in America), to deal with legal problems that were not well suited to the common law.

Infants and children presented particularly difficult problems to the courts. From time to time children with an interest in the estate of a recently deceased parent were forced into court to claim their inheritance. Similarly, children were regularly called into court to give testimony regarding custody arrangements when their parents were unable to care for them. Such children needed sound legal advice, and yet they often had no one to guide them in court (see Rendleman, 1971).

To safeguard their interests the chancery court devised the parens patriae doctrine, which in essense held that when a child lacked a guardian and was unable otherwise to safeguard his or her own interests, the court should enter the case and preserve the child's interests much as a responsible guardian would. The doctrine of parens patriae applied to adults as well as children, but it had a special significance for children, because they regularly found themselves in court without anyone to guide them.

Parens patriae was invented in England's chancery courts, but it became especially useful when cities in both England and the United States required children to attend public schools. Since children were sent to the public schools for their own good, and since the schools exercised broad authority over their pupils, their authority depended heavily upon parens patriae. Parens patriae became the cornerstone of the public school system.

As new educational institutions for adolescents were established, a new social status, the juvenile, was created midway between childhood and adulthood. Juveniles were required to cooperate with school authorities in preparing for adulthood. Most had little or no difficulty in accepting these new responsibilities, but some juveniles and their parents needed coercive help from the courts in the form of sanctions. Juveniles were neither children, whose responsibility was vested primarily in their parents, nor adults, who were responsible only to themselves. In school they had specific responsibilities that only they could fulfill, though at home they were still under the authority of their parents.

In support of this new status a new kind of institution, the house of refuge, was also required for children who could not adjust smoothly to school routines (Sutton, 1988: 107–115). It sought to instill greater discipline and ultimately restore them to their families. Large numbers of wayward children were also accepted by the house of refuge as well as a few children who had been convicted of serious crimes in the criminal courts. To provide a legal basis for all this the *civil* courts used their new doctrine, parens patriae, and incidentally established their primary jurisdiction over juvenile misbehavior. Since parens patriae assigned a benign, supportive role to the civil courts, juvenile justice from the very beginning followed a benevolent, rehabilitative philosophy vis-a-vis the juvenile. And the early juvenile institutions were mandated by parens patriae to fulfill this goal.

During this early period many juveniles who previously would have been left alone by the justice system were brought into the new houses of refuge, and the embryonic juvenile justice system widened the justice system's net of control. At the same time the advantages of the houses of refuge ought not to be denied. Many children who needed supervision and otherwise might have been completely undermined were given a second chance (see Ferdinand, 1989: 84–91).

The new laws and institutions provided needed services that elevated the lives of many, if not most, of the children they touched. Several studies suggest that upwards of 70 percent of their children made satisfactory adjustments in their communities after release, and there are many instances in which former inmates returned to their institution to renew friendships with children and staff (see Pickett, 1969: 91; Wines, 1880: 135; Mennel, 1973: 29–30; Peirce, 1969: 130, 143–149; Barnard, 1857: 354; Smith, 1989: 57, 62; but see Pisciotta, 1982).

A FORMATIVE PERIOD

Between 1830 and 1899 the states assembled piecemeal most of the elements of the juvenile justice system. Beginning in 1848 with the Industrial School for Boys at Westborough, Massachusetts, several states constructed custodial institutions patterned after the city-based houses of refuge. These state institutions generally served the same clientele, and in smaller states (e.g., Massachusetts) they also diverted a portion of the more receptive young people from the houses of refuge to their own programs. In addition, orphans' homes, homes for truants, homes for predelinquents, and homes for unmarried, pregnant girls were opened in many states, with the result that city and especially state institutions began increasingly to serve juveniles who were criminal offenders (Ferdinand, 1989).

With the expanding variety of institutions serving juveniles, children in the houses of refuge and industrial schools became increasingly antisocial, and the staffs lost much of their sympathy for their wards (Brenzel, 1983: 153). During the 1850s and 1860s strains began to appear, and critics of state institutions for delinquents gathered momentum. In Massachusetts, Samuel Gridley Howe strenuously opposed the construction in 1855 of the Industrial School for Girls at Lancaster, and Charles Loring Brace in New York fought equally hard against juvenile institutions in that state.[1] Howe observed regarding the girls' school at Lancaster that

> we might as well try to imitate within a house sunshine and rain, and clouds and dew and all the shifting scenery of nature, as initiate in a reformatory the ever varying influences of family life. The family must grow; it cannot be made in a day, nor be put together by rules and compass. . . . We have, at best, a make-believe society, a make-believe family, and, together a make-believe virtue. [Massachusetts Board of State Charities, 1866: xlvi–xlvii]

Institutions and their staffs were denounced as cruel and uncaring, bigoted and ineffective. Arson, typhoid and cholera epidemics, brutality by staff and children, and scandals were becoming common as the century drew to a close (Schlossman, 1977; Mennel, 1973: 73–77). No one had the answer, and by World War II juvenile training schools were seen by most observers as little more than juvenile prisons (Rothman, 1980; Deutsch, 1950). Their staffs were punitive, inmates were predatory, and judges were hesitant to commit any but the most delinquent children to their care. The parens patriae focus of the early institutions had long since vanished, and instead a cynical, punitive philosophy prevailed. Somehow child saving had grown much more difficult in these early institutions.

In addition to the institutions, homes, and asylums for juveniles that cities and states had built during this era, less custodial methods were also being tried. Charles Loring Brace and the New York Children's Aid Society developed the placing-out system in the 1850s whereby worthy children were transplanted from the streets of New York City to the farms of the Midwest. Young agents of Brace combed the streets of lower Manhattan for juveniles of both sexes to work on midwestern farms. When enough had been recruited, they boarded trains moving west, and when the trains reached hamlets in Ohio, Michigan, or Indiana, Brace or one of his followers greeted the townspeople to arrange placements for the children with local families. In this way hundreds, if not thousands, of young people were placed on midwestern farms before the Civil War (Trattner, 1979: 100–102).

After the Civil War, Massachusetts authorized in 1869 its Board of State Charities to send visiting agents to the families of delinquents to evaluate their social backgrounds and the suitability of their families for receiving them on parole, and in 1870 it empowered these same agents to commit worthy juveniles as indentured workers to benevolent employers or families in lieu of an institutional placement. In effect they were giving these juveniles an opportunity to prove themselves through probation. Other states did much the same, and probation quickly became a very useful alternative for the courts.

After the Civil War reform schools for juveniles were built in nearly every northern state. Most were state reform schools, but many were private institutions established by philanthropists or religious groups for misbehaving middle-class youths. Taken together they served a great variety of youths.

---

[1]Howe and Brace represented one branch of a three way schism among those interested in child-rearing practices. Romantics felt that children were naturally conforming and needed mainly supportive kindness to develop properly. Students of the Enlightenment believed that human problems (such as the condition of young people) could best be improved by rational, skeptical analysis, and Calvinists believed that children needed to be sternly taught the right path (see Sutton, 1988: 49–67).

According to a survey of 30 such reform schools taken in 1880 (Mennel, 1973: 49) 6 accepted only children who had been convicted of crimes punishable by imprisonment, and 14 took only children who had committed minor offenses (e.g., idleness) for which no penalty was prescribed in the penal law. Thirteen schools accepted children found guilty of determined rebellion against parental authority, seven took neglected or deserted children, and five accepted children committed by their parents without any reason. The maximum age for admission to these schools was 15, but the minimum age ranged from 7 to 11. Several schools had authority to transfer unmanageable children to prison, but most kept their inmates until the age of 21, if male, or 18, if female, or until they were reformed.

The juvenile justice system was becoming crowded with many different kinds of institutions and programs serving a bewildering variety of youths. A court that could classify these children according to their needs and send them to one of several specialized programs was badly needed by the more populous states.

THE JUVENILE COURT

Who was to define the guidelines, and who was to sort out the juveniles according to the guidelines? During this period while many states were moving toward separate courts for juveniles, both the number of public and private reform schools and the number of other placements were increasing rapidly (Sutton, 1990: 1369–1370). By 1890 the question of the appropriate placement for each child had become a complex issue requiring careful study not only of the children and their needs but also of the placement alternatives. An effective placement of these children, moreover, demanded a mastery of the relevant law.

Throughout the nineteenth century a civil court had been used—usually a probate court that was preoccupied with other matters and staffed by judges and lawyers whose expertise was neither in juvenile problems nor in treatment issues.

But as juveniles grew in numbers and their problems became more complex, the need for a full-time court devoted solely to juvenile issues was apparent. Fredrick Wines, a noted criminologist, commented in Chicago in 1898 that "an entirely separate system of courts [was needed] for children . . . who commit offenses which would be criminal in adults. We ought to have a 'children's court' in Chicago, and we ought to have a 'children's judge,' who should attend to no other business" (quoted in Mennel, 1973: 131).

In 1899 the Illinois legislature enacted the first juvenile code and established in Chicago the first juvenile court. Its jurisdiction extended to all juveniles—criminal offenders, status offenders, as well as neglected and dependent children. It embraced a much wider jurisdiction than the earlier juvenile justice system had.

During most of the nineteenth century serious juvenile offenders had been handled as adults in the criminal courts, while minor offenders along with status offenders and dependent and neglected children were handled by the probate courts and placed in juvenile facilities. The new juvenile court's jurisdiction included all youths from the most malevolent to the nearly benign, and its mandate was to deal with them all in terms of parens patriae.

Other industrial states quickly followed Illinois's lead with similar laws and courts, and the juvenile justice system was essentially complete. Parens patriae was the central pillar of the court, but its programs and facilities—probation, reform schools, and specialized homes for orphans, unmarried mothers, truants, and wayward, neglected, or dependent children—had been developed much earlier. In fact most of the key programs and facilities had been in place for decades when the court itself was established in 1899.

Since the early juvenile court viewed delinquency as largely a psychological problem, it turned to psychological theories and psychiatrists in search of solutions. The Chicago juvenile court established the first child guidance clinic in 1909 to help the court develop psychological diagnoses of children's problems and formulate effective placements, and it appointed William Healy, a psychiatrist, to run it. Similar child guidance clinics were set up in Ohio, Michigan, and Massachusetts, and together they spearheaded early research on delinquency.

The new court was hailed as a visionary institution that would bring intelligence, responsibility, and humanity to the emerging juvenile justice system. Few noted that the court had neither the authority nor the resources to mold juvenile institutions nor that it had only limited influence over treatment. No one asked How was the juvenile court supposed to reform juvenile justice with only meager resources and authority beyond its legal domain? But the public was willing to give it a chance, at least for a while.

The new juvenile court provided a base for the parens patriae approach, and juvenile judges were outspoken in advocating treatment and humane care for offenders. Judge Benjamin Lindsey of Denver, for example, was one of the first to argue from the bench on behalf of juveniles, and in 1904 he wrote that "the Juvenile Court rests upon the principle of love. Of course there is firmness and justice, for without this [sic] there would be danger in leniency. But there is no justice without love" (quoted in Mennel, 1973: 138).

The juvenile court, following informal procedures, gave its judges ample room to elaborate almost any perspective they wished. The early court was fortunate in that many of its judges shared Lindsey's deep sympathy for young delinquents. Judge Richard Tuthill, the first judge of the Chicago juvenile court, proclaimed that "I talk with the boy, give him a good talk, just as I would my own boy, and find myself as much interested in these boys as I would if they were my own" (quoted in Mennel, 1973: 135), and Judge George W. Stubbs of Indianapolis said, "It is the personal touch that does it. I have often observed that if . . . I could get close enough to [the boy] to put my hand on his head or shoulder, or my arm around him, in nearly every such case I could get his confidence" (quoted in Mennel, 1973: 135). In addition, most juvenile courts made heavy use of probation officers, who were also steadfast advocates of the parens patriae approach to juvenile delinquency. With the appearance of the juvenile court in many communities, vigorous and often eloquent spokesmen for a parens patriae point of view caught the public's attention.

World War I, the Great Depression, and World War II dominated the national scene during the first half of the twentieth century, and there was little change in juvenile justice between 1914 and 1945. After World War I scholars in sociology and psychology became interested in studying delinquency as a means of verifying their theoretical viewpoints. Freudian studies in both Europe and America appeared (see Aichorn, 1935; Alexander and Healy, 1936; Healy and Bronner, 1936); the social ecology of delinquency was analyzed by Shaw and McKay (1942); and Frederic Thrasher (1927) mapped the gang patterns of Chicago.

But little else changed in juvenile justice until the end of World War II, when Paul Tappan, a legally trained criminologist, pointed out (see Tappan, 1946) that the constitutional rights of juveniles were widely ignored in the parens patriae juvenile court. Several other criminologists in the late 1950s took up the same argument (see Allen, 1964 and Caldwell, 1961). They noted that therapeutic terms were used to describe punitive methods and techniques in institutions (solitary confinement was described, for example, as quiet time) and that therapeutic measures, even when sincerely applied, were often more severe than outright punishments.

Further, it was not unusual in the 1950s to learn that status offenders were punished more severely than all but the most serious delinquents. Creekmore (1976) found in a national sample of 400 juvenile courts that status offenders (26 percent) were less likely to be dismissed at intake by the juvenile court than misdemeanor (33 percent) and property (29 percent) offenders. Only youths charged with offenses against the person (16 percent) were less likely to be dismissed at intake.

With regard to gender bias, Yona Cohn (1963: 272–275) found in New York City that girls where much more likely to receive custodial placements than boys (see also chapter 8). Similarly, Terry (1967: 218) reported in a study of 9000 arrested youths in a midwestern city that 76.6 percent of the girls but only 59.7 percent of the boys were institutionalized after a court hearing. Racial bias, though reported in the juvenile court, was not so pervasive. Thornberry (1973) found in a study of nearly 3500 Philadelphia school boys that blacks were more likely to be arrested and referred to juvenile court for a hearing than white boys. But others (for example, Cohen, 1976; or Dungworth, 1977) found little racial bias in the juvenile courts.

Juvenile justice has no room for racial or gender bias, but most studies of bias in the juvenile court have ignored an important aspect of the problem. An officer's decision to make an arrest, or a court's decision to detain a juvenile, is strongly influenced by the attitude of the victim (Black and Reiss, 1970). When the victim is outraged and demands an arrest or court action, chances are strong that the police or the court will comply. A dismissal is much more difficult if a victim seeking punishment is close at hand. Thomas and Cage (1977), for example, found in a study of more than 1500 juveniles that sanctioning in the juvenile court was more severe if a parent or policeman had filed a complaint. Bias in the juvenile court reflects not only the attitudes of the judge but also the attitudes of the community. Studies of bias in the justice system should take into account community variability on this question.

To cope with the complexity and injustice of mingling status offenders and delinquents in the same system, New York passed its Family Court Act in 1962, which among other things distinguished status offenders from delinquents by renaming them PINS (Person in Need of Supervision). A decade later the New York Court of Appeals ruled in *In re Ellery C.* (1973) that confining PINS with delinquents in the same institution was unconstitutional. By 1980 many other states had enacted similar statutes defining MINS (Minor . . .), JINS (Juvenile . . .), and CHINS (Child . . .) and separating them from delinquents.

To deal with growing claims of ineffectiveness in juvenile justice the federal government teamed with the states and private philanthropy to find the "magic bullet" in delinquency prevention. Under the impetus of President Johnson's war on poverty during the mid-1960s, a nationwide effort was undertaken to prevent delinquency and rehabilitate delinquents. As a centerpiece, a massive preventive program, Mobilization for Youth, was mounted on the lower east side of Manhattan. Modeled after the Chicago Area Projects, it focused on preschool children, juveniles, gangs, schools, teachers, and community adults. More focused preventive programs were fielded in Boston, Chicago, and elsewhere. Research programs examining innovative juvenile programs were funded in Massachusetts, Michigan, and Utah, and community-based treatment programs in California were generously supported.

Sentiment for reforming juvenile justice was growing, but the direction of the reform was still in doubt. Should it focus on keeping predelinquents out of the juvenile justice system, or should it target the training schools and the courts? Much hinged on the outcome of the war on poverty programs, and millions were spent to insure sound methods and careful evaluations. But to nearly everyone's dismay, few of the innovative programs were effective.

Earlier, the Cambridge-Somerville study (Powers and Witmer, 1951) had foreshadowed the difficulties of treating predelinquents. Just before World War II researchers studied children with school behavioral problems and found that counseling by Harvard graduate students had little impact on their subsequent delinquency when compared with a control group of youth who had received no counseling. Detached worker programs investigated by Walter Miller (1962) in Boston and by Malcolm Klein (1971) in Los Angeles were worse than ineffective, since in Los Angeles the detached workers actually made delinquency worse. Gerald Robin (1969) studied the Neighborhood Youth Corps and its attempts to provide counseling, remedial education, and supervised work for juveniles in both Cincinnati and Detroit. He found no positive effect for either program on delinquency. In Provo, Utah, Lamar Empey (1972) designed a community-based program for delinquents that provided them daily group therapy for five or six months. He compared their delinquency with a comparison group of boys who had been placed on community probation and with a second group that had been sent to the state training school. Although the boys in the community-based program averaged about half as many arrests after release as those sent to the training school, there was little difference between them and the boys placed on probation. A similar program undertaken at Silverlake in Los Angeles by Empey got much the same results. Boys in a community-based treatment program at Silverlake showed after release only slightly lower delinquency rates than boys who were sent initially to an open institution for delinquents (Empey and Lubeck, 1971).

To be sure, successes were sprinkled among the delinquency treatment and prevention projects (see Lipsey, 1990; Quay, 1987: Chapter 9; Gendreau and Ross, 1979; Andrews et al., 1990). Probation, for example, has been thoroughly studied, and the results indicate that despite superficial supervision a large majority of probationers complete their probation without further incident and go on to crime-free adult lives as well. Diana (1955) found that 84 percent of 280 juveniles who had been placed on probation in the juvenile court in Pittsburgh in 1940 avoided further convictions, and Scarpitti and Stephenson (1968) found much the same in a study of 1210 male delinquents in New Jersey. Although contacts with the probation officer were brief and infrequent, 72 percent of this group completed their probation without revocation.

Marguerite Warren (1976) and Ted Palmer (1974) reported strong positive results in treating specific types of delinquents in the community when compared with similar youngsters sent to juvenile institutions in California (but see Lerman, 1975: chapter 4). In addition, the studies of Street, Vinter, and Perrow (1966) in Michigan found that benign institutions with a supportive staff were much more effective in changing youthful attitudes than custodial institutions and a punitive staff. The former were especially successful in instilling a prosocial climate among the bulk of their inmates. Finally, the world renowned Chicago Area Projects initiated by Henry McKay and Clifford Shaw in the 1930s were probably successful in preventing delinquency, even though a controlled research design was not used and a definitive assessment of its impact is impossible.

Each of these studies has been examined critically, and reservations have been lodged regarding their findings. But these criticisms have not shaken the overall conclusion that many juveniles respond to treatment programs when they are intelligently designed (i.e., tailored to the needs of the child and the strengths of the staff) and carefully administered (i.e., via a trained and experienced staff that has a stake in its success).

Despite these encouraging results, the view has taken hold that treatment, whether in an institution or in the community, does not work in preventing or reducing delinquency (Martinson, 1974).

THE CRISIS IN JUVENILE JUSTICE

The conclusion that treatment is ineffective seemed to strike a chord in the nation at large, and the advantage swung quickly to those who favor a due process, retributive approach to the problem, spearheaded by a criminalized juvenile court. Criminologists have argued for decades as to the causes of delinquency and the preferred methods of treatment. But this quarrel ran much deeper. The evidence by no means supported a wholesale shift away from treatment and prevention, but the fact that it was so quickly and so widely endorsed suggests something basic was at work. No doubt some of the disillusionment and pessimism of the Vietnam era as well as the conservative administrations of Nixon and Reagan were factors.

Keep in mind that the juvenile justice system had been founded in the nineteenth century on the premise that the juvenile court should assume the role of a responsible parent and when necessary provide guidance, supervision, and support to children. If the juvenile court could not provide effective treatment for juveniles, it meant that the parens patriae doctrine and the court itself were failures.

It was argued that if the juvenile court could not insure a child's successful treatment, it not only defeated the whole purpose of parens patriae but also made a mockery of justice. The child was asked to forego due process so that the court could help him control his delinquency. The parens patriae doctrine was still a noble idea, but if the juvenile court could not act effectively as a responsible parent, the least it could do was act effectively as a court. But in reality the juvenile court and its parens patriae doctrine were held hostage to the apparent ineffectiveness of community and institutional programs in treating delinquency.

No one remembered that the court and its parens patriae doctrine had never had great influence over treatment programs. The one program the court did control, probation, was generally well run and effective in helping delinquents regain social balance. In effect the juvenile court and its commitment to parens patriae were being evaluated not only in terms of their relevance to the needs of juveniles, but also in terms of their ability to guide the *rest of the juvenile justice system* in the path of parens patriae.

The critics of the parens patriae court expected it to find ways of carrying out its rehabilitative responsibilities despite its inability to shape community-based therapeutic programs or custodial institutions within its jurisdiction. The parens patriae court was doomed from the very beginning by its limited authority.

In fact it was the state that failed, because it established a parens patriae court without providing the resources that would enable it to provide effective parens patriae programs in the community. To be sure, many treatment centers and programs were developed with the help of private philanthropy, religious organizations, social welfare agencies, and even the federal government. But few if any public authorities enjoyed a permanent mandate to carry out parens patriae aims, and all depended on individual and, therefore, ad hoc initiatives. Well-meaning philanthropists, criminologists, and federal agencies, however, have not been able to supply what is needed: a balanced, continuing effort to treat and prevent delinquency. As a result the court's parens patriae efforts have fallen short, and now it is in danger of being abandoned all together (see Feld, 1991: 723).

Some have argued it would be better to send serious juvenile offenders into the criminal court, where their due process rights will be protected, and to give minor offenders including status offenders to nonlegal social agencies, as in many European countries. But if the problem lies with the structure of juvenile justice, the solution is not the dissolution of the parens patriae juvenile court. What is needed is a public authority with continuing responsibility for treatment programs in the community as well as in juvenile institutions.[2] This treatment authority would parallel the juvenile correctional system, and although it would provide treatment programs for the correctional system, it would be independent of that system. In short, the treatment authority would be the court's rehabilitative arm, just as juvenile corrections is the court's custodial arm.

Juvenile treatment programs in progressive societies are as essential as unemployment insurance for adults. Many delinquents need wise, supportive counsel in making sound adjustments in adolescence. Unfortunately, many cannot get such counsel from their families, and to deny them by abandoning treatment is cruel and socially self-defeating.

Treatment has worked only occasionally up to now, because it has not been championed consistently by a permanent state agency with roots in regional communities and continuing support by a state legislature. Where such agencies have emerged (e.g., in Massachusetts [1972] in the Department of Youth Services and in Utah [1981] in the

---

[2]We might call this authority the Department of Youth Services. Many states have departments of children and family services that serve nondelinquent children, and the Department of Youth Services would offer many of the same programs for delinquents and children at risk of delinquency. It would adjust its efforts to the needs of the juvenile courts, just as juvenile corrections does. Three statewide agencies, therefore, would provide social services to adolescents: juvenile corrections, which manages custodial institutions for juveniles; the Department of Youth Services, which manages the treatment effort for juvenile delinquents; and the Department of Children and Family Services, which manages the treatment function for nondelinquent youth. Further consolidation of these three agencies would not necessarily be ruled out.

Division of Youth Corrections), the results have been just, humane, and socially useful in that delinquency has been controlled.

Massachusetts, under the Department of Youth Services (DYS), has been using a system of community-based treatment programs for its delinquents since 1972 with excellent results (see Loughran, 1987). On any given day its youthful clients number about 1700. Some 1000 youths live at home and participate in a wide variety of treatment and educational programs. The remaining children, about 700, are divided between foster homes (30), nonsecure residential programs (500), and secure facilities (170). Serious offenders are screened for violent tendencies, emotional stability, threat to the community, and social needs, and given assignments in programming especially designed for them.

The results in Massachusetts have been remarkable (Miller and Ohlin, 1985; Krisberg, Austin, and Steele, 1989). In the beginning, budgetary costs of caring for children via a system of community-based treatment centers were slightly higher than with a network of custodial institutions. But with experience the system has grown more efficient, and in 1989 the annual cost per child in the Massachusetts Department of Youth Services was about $23,000, compared with $35,000 to $40,000 reported by many other states using more traditional juvenile justice systems (Krisberg, Austin, and Steele, 1989: 32–37).

The results in terms of human development have been outstanding. Despite the fact that the vast bulk of the children who have come into the system since 1972 have been dealt with via nonsecure living arrangements, the level of delinquency arraignments in Massachusetts by 1986 had dropped 24 percent from their 1980 level (Loughran, 1987). Delinquency arraignments for released offenders including violent or chronic offenders were about one-half their preadmission level; the number of adult inmates in Massachusetts who had previously been clients of its juvenile justice system dropped from 35 percent in 1972 to 15 percent in 1985. Finally, since 1974 postrelease recidivism rates among DYS youths have dropped sharply, from 74 percent in 1974 (Coates, Miller, and Ohlin, 1976) to about 51 percent in 1985 (Krisberg, Austin, and Steele, 1989: 24–25). In comparison with other states where recidivism is measured comparably, DYS youths have equaled or bettered the recidivism rates of all other state juvenile systems. These results all point to the same conclusion: Many juveniles in the Massachusetts Department of Youth Services are significantly helped by their experiences in the system.

In Utah a new Division of Youth Corrections modeled after the Massachusetts Department of Youth Services was inaugurated in 1981, with full responsibility for secure and community-based treatment programs for delinquents. Although the system is still too new to offer firm evidence of its effectiveness, its architects are well pleased with the results so far.

Treatment need not substitute for, nor interfere with, justice in the juvenile court. Juveniles need to be assured no less than adults that fairness and justice await them in the justice system. But neither should treatment be eliminated in dispositions informed mainly by an emphasis upon justice. The juvenile court should follow adversarial, due process rules in its adjudicatory phase as mandated by the Supreme Court, but when it moves to the dispositional phase, the court should adjust its recommendations to the treatment needs of the child. In many states sentencing minima and maxima have been established for a range of juvenile offenses, and *within these limits* each child's treatment needs should be addressed. By following due process in its adjudicatory phase and treatment goals in its dispositional phase, both goals can be met without seriously compromising either.

The twin aims of justice and rehabilitation can be blended effectively in the juvenile court. And if diagnostic and treatment programs are made conveniently available to juvenile judges via a state treatment authority, justice in adjudication can be balanced with humane, effective treatment in disposition.

Bifurcation: A Stumbling Block?

Still, a difficult problem confronting juvenile justice is the likelihood that its more secure facilities will become punitive and malevolent as they age. Juvenile institutions since the houses of refuge (see Ferdinand, 1989; Pisciotta, 1982) have shown a distinct tendency to become punitive, conflict ridden, and calloused toward their inmates, that is, to undergo custodial drift. As Stanley Cohen has noted (1985), institutions and programs tend to separate themselves into segregative, custodial, stigmatizing, and punitive centers (which he labels exclusionary programs), and community-based, rehabilitative, benign centers (which he describes as inclusionary programs).

Cohen (1985) saw this bifurcation of programs as paralleling an analogous bifurcation of clientele coming into juvenile justice. On the one hand, we have a small stream of embittered, dangerous offenders who are committed to an antisocial way of life; and on the other, we have a much larger stream of prosocial but disoriented offenders who wish to live as honorable citizens but have not yet discovered how to fulfill that goal. Exclusionary programs tend to transform their stigmatized and shunned inmates into predatory criminals, while inclusionary programs are designed to help prosocial offenders find a way back into mainstream society.

Cohen (1985) argues that most new inclusionary programs tend to become segregated and punitive exclusionary programs by virtue of the fact that new, benign programs tend to draw off the cream of the clientele and staff from older programs, leaving the latter to deal with a less tractable clientele by means of a less effective staff. As the older programs adapt to their worsening inmates, they become more like total institutions: punitive, criminalizing, and stigmatizing. Slowly, inclusionary programs are transformed into exclusionary centers. A recurrent cycle of reform and decay asserts itself as the system repeatedly attempts to improve itself by reaching for new and more tractable segments of the offender spectrum.

Before long the correctional system evolves into a hierarchical system (see Steele and Jacobs, 1975) of punitive exclusionary centers at the deep end serving predatory, antisocial inmates, and inclusionary centers at the shallow end serving socially normal clientele but with focused problems. As each new program comes along, it attracts the most responsive clientele and the most effective staff, while the rest adapt as best they can to the ensuing realignments. Correctional reform carries the seeds of its own destruction.

The answer to this problem of reform and decay is not difficult to imagine. New programs need not concentrate solely on the shallow end, responsive clientele. Rather they should focus on a problematic group—serious, predatory offenders, for example—and apply their treatment skills effectively to that group. In this case the older programs would give up some of their *least* responsive inmates, and their tone would no doubt improve. Steele and Jacobs (1975) regard these kinds of focused treatment centers, when organized into a system, as a differentiated system.

This policy would avoid draining the more tractable inmates from the older centers, but even more to the point it would provide the kind of small, focused treatment settings that are most consistent with a prosocial inmate climate (see Street, Vinter, and Perrow, 1966). Small programs permit more personal relationships among staff and children and provide more opportunity for a benevolent staff to influence the kids in positive ways. Small programs are easier to manage and supervise, and treatment policies can be implemented more effectively over the long haul.

This policy has been followed by Massachusetts since 1972—small, treatment-oriented centers for virtually all juveniles in the Department of Youth Services (the *largest* is only 36 beds)—and no doubt some of its success can be attributed to the positive attitudinal climate small centers generate (see Krisberg, Austin, and Steele, 1989: 4). If this analysis is correct, a policy of small centers would slow down the punitive drift of custodial centers by inhibiting their transformation into total institutions.

Still, a system of small treatment facilities must be closely monitored lest some centers stray from their assigned path. The likelihood is strong that a center, if left to itself, will develop punitive policies and practices based on local philosophy. To avoid such missteps it is essential that each treatment center be held closely accountable to reputable standards of performance. It is desirable that each center regularly justify its policies with verifiable data. How many children have or have attempted to run away during the last six months? How many suicides or attempts? How many fights? How is morale among the children? What is their attitude toward the staff? Are the children prosocial in word and deed? Do any children return to the center for visits with the staff? How many children return to delinquency once they are released?

Overall, punitive centers do much worse by these standards than treatment facilities, and responsible program directors must gather information systematically on a variety of issues to insure that each center is performing its mission well. Our Department of Youth Services must develop a research arm that can reliably identify effective or ineffective treatment centers and provide them guidance.

CONCLUSIONS

Few would argue that juvenile justice in the United States has lived up to its promise, though many would dispute the idea that its future lies with humane treatment programs for youth. On the other hand, if treatment and rehabilitation were abandoned in favor of a just deserts policy in which serious delinquents were punished by lengthy terms in large, custodial institutions, several untoward consequences would follow. Delinquency would deepen in seriousness and expand its sway, laying the foundation for a worsening problem among adult criminals in the years ahead. Second, an important voice for humane programs in the justice system would be stilled, with the result that a monolithic custodial system and its programs would prevail not only in delinquency programs but also in the criminal justice system.

Those who are pessimistic, however, need not despair. The problems of treating juveniles effectively are not insoluble. A differentiated system of small treatment facilities in Massachusetts has shown that programs for treating juveniles can be effective. Such systems, when left to the local community, tend to be haphazardly managed and though some are very effective, many fall short. The state is a more responsible manager, and if as in Massachusetts and Utah the state accepts its responsibility to manage juvenile justice with a benevolent hand, it does work.

State departments of youth services need research arms that can evaluate the effectiveness of each center with an eye to weeding out those that do not work. Departments of youth services must also represent a rehabilitative philosophy to the rest of state government and the media so that a balanced perspective in juvenile justice and policies can make itself felt. The people of a state must ultimately, through their elected representatives, choose the direction of their correctional system, but they must be aware of the alternatives. The just deserts perspective is already well represented by the courts and adult corrections. The rehabilitative path has not been presented well and the department of youth services must step into the void.

Were such a department available in the states, it would remove an immense burden from the juvenile court. The juvenile court has long pursued parens patriae in the community but with uncertain success and, lately, with waning confidence in rehabilitation. A department of youth services could provide the variety in community programming that the court needs to carry out its parens patriae goals effectively. The juvenile court cannot be both official classification agent and unofficial programs agent. It was neither intended nor designed to do both jobs. It is effective as a classification center, but it needs a rehabilitative counterpart at the state level creating treatment programs throughout the state for local courts to use. Local juvenile courts working hand in glove with a state department of youth services could finally get a grip on the problem of delinquency.

SUMMARY

When America began to industrialize around the turn of the eighteenth century many migrants including many wayward children were drawn to eastern population centers in search of a better life. Around this time compulsory education for children through the age of fifteen was adopted in these same cities, and one result was a growing pattern of misbehavior and truancy among adolescents. To curb these particular forms of childish delinquency and to provide a place for juveniles who committed minor criminal offenses, houses of refuge and then training schools were built in many eastern states based on the novel doctrine of parens patriae. This was the beginning of juvenile justice in the United States.

Over the next 74 years from 1825 to 1899 the elements of a juvenile justice system—probation, group homes for orphans, truants, and pre-delinquents, and custodial schools for criminal delinquents and incorrigible children—were assembled, and the whole was served by the civil court and its doctrine of parens patriae. But during and after the Civil War juvenile caseloads grew to sizable proportions, and the deficiences of a civil court expert in family law but insensitive to juvenile psychology or treatment became glaring.

A special court devoted to juveniles and their problems and using parens patriae as its doctrine was introduced in Illinois in 1899 with great confidence and enthusiasm.

But by 1950 several contradictions in juvenile justice could no longer be ignored. Mixing status offenders and serious delinquents in institutions was not a sound policy, because it subjected very minor offenders and very serious offenders to the same kinds of treatment, and often gave minor offenders more lengthy "treatment" than serious delinquents. In 1951 the first study of the impact of treatment on pre-delinquents (the Cambridge-Somerville Youth Study) reported that counseling had no positive effect on pre-delinquents. In the next several years a whole host of studies focusing on treatment in juvenile training schools, in group homes, in diversion programs, and in community-based programs reported a lack of improvement over untreated control groups. By the early 1970s it appeared that nothing worked in the treatment of delinquency, and training schools themselves became the focus of recurrent epidemics, brutalities between staff and inmates, and illegal punishments. Something was wrong with parens patriae and the juvenile justice system.

The U.S. Supreme Court in a series of landmark decisions decreed that the juvenile court could at least provide fundamental due process protections for juveniles, and it set in motion a series of reforms in juvenile justice. Status offenders were separated from delinquents, and some states decriminalized them altogether. The apparent failure of treatment both in the community and in training schools persuaded many states to de-emphasize rehabilitation for delinquents, leaving juvenile institutions as penal centers primarily for retribution and deterrence.

Massachusetts, however, pioneered in using small treatment centers for the bulk of its delinquent population and in the 1980s began to achieve remarkable successes. Other states adopted the Massachusetts system, and evidence for the benefits of treatment for delinquents began to mount.

A solution to the problems of juvenile justice seemed to require the following steps. First, a state-level agency is needed to sponsor the treatment of delinquents in the community and institutions much as the Department of Youth Services does in Massachusetts. Second, this state-level agency should work closely with juvenile judges in developing appropriate treatment programs for distinctive types of delinquents. Third, it should evaluate these novel programs for their effectiveness and continue only the most successful beyond a probationary period. Fourth, it should advise state-level political leaders, judges, and agencies on the advantages of treatment for offenders, and in this way offer counter-arguments to those advanced by other elements of criminal or juvenile justice in favor of punishment.

The state expected the juvenile court to lead juvenile justice along a rehabilitative path, but it provided few resources that would enable the court to accomplish this task. If a state-level agency were backed by the resources of the state and given a mandate to develop treatment programs for delinquents, the evidence is strong that parens patriae could be realized for most delinquents.

The failure lies not with the idea of parens patriae but with the manner in which the states implemented the idea. The juvenile court was asked to champion treatment via its parens patriae doctrine, but no one was given ultimate responsibility for treatment in institutions or in the community. The institutions themselves, which were usually funded at the state-level, were nevertheless left free to develop in any direction that was convenient, and in most cases they simply developed in a punitive direction. Had their development been guided firmly toward treatment, their expertise would have unfolded in that broad area, and parens patriae would have been much closer to fulfillment.

REFERENCES

Aichorn, August. 1935. *Wayward Youth.* New York: Viking Press.

Alexander, Franz, and William Healy. 1936. *Roots of Crime.* New York: Knopf.

Allen, Francis A. 1964. *The Borderland of Criminal Justice.* Chicago: University of Chicago Press.

Andrews, D. A., Ivan Zinger, Robert D. Hoge, James Bonta, Paul Gendreau, and Francis T. Cullen. 1990. "Does Correctional Treatment Work? A Clinically Relevant and Psychologically Informed Meta-Analysis." *Criminology* 28, No. 3:369–404.

Barnard, Henry. 1857. *Preventive, Correctional, and Reformatory Institutions and Agencies.* Hartford, Conn.: F.C. Brownell.

Black, Donald J., and Albert J. Reiss, Jr. 1970. "Police Control of Juveniles." *American Sociological Review* 15 (February):63–77.

Brenzel, Barbara M. 1983. *Daughters of the State.* Cambridge, Mass.: M.I.T. Press.

Caldwell, R. G. 1961. "The Juvenile Court: Its Development and Some Major Problems." *Journal of Criminal Law, Criminology, and Police Science* 51:493–511.

Coates, Robert B., Alden D. Miller, and Lloyd E. Ohlin. 1976. *Diversity in a Youth Correctional System.* Cambridge: Ballinger Publishing.

Cohen, Lawrence E. 1976. *Delinquency Dispositions: An Empirical Analysis of Processing Decisions in Three Juvenile Courts.* National Criminal Justice Information and Statistics Service, Law Enforcement Assistance Administration. Washington, D.C.: Government Printing Office.

Cohen, Stanley. 1985. *Visions of Social Control.* Cambridge: Polity Press.

Cohn, Yona. 1963. "Criteria for Probation Officers' Recommendations to the Juvenile Court." *Crime and Delinquency* 1:267–275.

Creekmore, Mark. 1976. "Case Processing: Intake, Adjudication, and Disposition." In *Brought to Justice? Juveniles, the Courts and the Law.* Edited by Rosemary Sarri and Yeheskel Hasenfeld. Ann Arbor, Mich.: University of Michigan Press.

Deutsch, Albert. 1950. *Our Rejected Children.* Boston: Little, Brown and Company.

Diana, Lewis. 1955. "Is Casework in Probation Necessary?" *Focus* 34, No. 1 (January):1–8.

Dungworth, Terence. 1977. "Discretion in the Juvenile Justice System: The Impact of Case Characteristics on Prehearing Detention." In *Little Brother Grows Up.* Edited by Theodore Ferdinand. Beverly Hills: Sage Publications.

Empey, Lamar, and Steven G. Lubeck. 1971. *Silverlake Experiment: Testing Delinquency Theory and Community Intervention.* Chicago: Aldine Press.

Empey, Lamar, and Maynard Erickson. 1972. *The Provo Experiment: Evaluating Community Control of Delinquency.* Lexington, Mass.: Lexington Books.

Feld, Barry. 1991. "The Transformation of the Juvenile Court." *Minnesota Law Review* 75, No. 3:691–725.

Ferdinand, Theodore N. 1980. "History and Policy in Juvenile Justice." In *History and Crime.* Edited by James A. Inciardi and Charles E. Faupel. Beverly Hills: Sage Publications.

————. 1989. "Juvenile Delinquency or Juvenile Justice: Which Came First?" *Criminology* 27, No. 1:79–106.

Garlock, Peter D. 1979. " 'Wayward' Children and the Law, 1820–1900: The Genesis of the Status Offense Jurisdiction of the Juvenile Court." *Georgia Law Review* 13, No. 2:340–447.

Gendreau, Paul, and R. R. Ross. 1979. "Effectiveness of Correctional Treatment: Bibliotherapy for Cynics." *Crime & Delinquency* 25:463–489.

Healy, William, and Augusta Bronner. 1926. *Delinquents and Criminals, Their Making and Unmaking.* New York: Macmillan.

————. 1936. *New Light on Delinquency and Its Treatment.* New Haven: Yale University Press.

Klein, Malcolm. 1971. *Street Gangs and Street Workers.* Englewood Cliffs, N.J.: Prentice-Hall.

Krisberg, Barry, James Austin, and Patricia A. Steele. 1989. *Unlocking Juvenile Corrections: Evaluating the Massachusetts Department of Youth Services.* San Francisco: The National Council of Crime and Delinquency.

Lerman, Paul. 1975. *Community Treatment and Control.* Chicago: University of Chicago Press.

Lewis, Orlando F. 1967. *The Development of American Prisons and Prison Customs, 1776–1845.* Monclair, N.J.: Patterson Smith.

Lipsey, Mark W. 1990. "Juvenile Delinquency Treatment: A Meta-Analytic Inquiry into the Variability of Effects." A Report to the Research Synthesis Committee of the Russell Sage Foundation. New York.

Loughran, Edward J. 1987. "Juvenile Corrections: The Massachusetts Experience." In *Reinvesting in Youth Corrections Resources: A Tale of Three States.* Edited by Lee Eddison. Ann Arbor: School of Social Work, University of Michigan.

Martinson, Robert. 1974. "What Works—Questions and Answers About Prison Reform." *Public Interest* 32:22–54.

Massachusetts Board of State Charities. 1866. *Second Annual Report.* Boston: State Printers.

Mennel, Robert M. 1973. *Thorns & Thistles.* Hanover, N.H.: University Press of New England.

Miller, Alden D., and Lloyd E. Ohlin. 1985. *Delinquency and Community.* Beverly Hills: Sage Publications.

Miller, Walter. 1962. "The Impact of a 'Total-Community' Delinquency Control Project." *Social Problems* 10, No. 2 (Fall):168–191.

Palmer, Ted. 1974. "The Youth Authority Community Treatment Project." *Federal Probation* 38:3–14.

Peirce, Bradford Kinney. 1969. *A Half Century with Juvenile Delinquents.* Montclair, N.J.: Patterson Smith.

Pickett, Robert S. 1969. *House of Refuge.* Syracuse: Syracuse University Press.

Pisciotta, A. 1982. "Saving the Children: The Promise and Practice of Parens Patriae." *Crime & Delinquency* 28 (3):410–425.

Powers, Edwin and Helen Witmer. 1951. *An Experiment in the Prevention of Juvenile Delinquency: The Cambridge-Somerville Youth Study.* New York: Columbia University Press.

Quay, Herbert, ed. 1987. *Handbook of Juvenile Delinquency.* New York: Wiley-Interscience Publications.

Rendleman, D. R. 1971. "Parens Patriae: From Chancery to the Juvenile Court." *South Carolina Law Review* 23:205–230.

Rothman, David J. 1980. *Conscience and Convenience.* Boston: Little, Brown and Company.

Sarnecki, Jerzy. 1989. *Juvenile Delinquency in Sweden.* Stockholm: National Council for Crime Prevention, Information Division.

Scarpitti, Frank R., and Richard M. Stephenson. 1968. "A Study of Probation Effectiveness." *Journal of Criminal Law, Criminology, and Police Science* 3 (September):361–369.

Schlossman, Steven L. 1977. *Love and the American Delinquent.* Chicago: University of Chicago Press.

Shaw, Clifford R. and Henry D. McKay. 1942. *Juvenile Delinquency and Urban Areas.* Chicago: The University of Chicago Press.

Smith, Beverly A. 1989. "Female Admissions and Paroles of the Western House of Refuge in the 1880s: An Historical Example of Community Corrections." *Journal of Research in Crime and Delinquency* 26, No. 1:36–66.

Steele, Eric H., and James B. Jacobs. 1975. "A Theory of Prison Systems." *Crime and Delinquency* 21:149–162.

Street, David, Robert D. Vinter, and Charles Perrow. 1966. *Organization for Treatment.* New York: The Free Press.

Sutton, John R. 1988. *Stubborn Children.* Berkeley: University of California Press.

———. 1990. "Bureaucrats and Entrepreneurs: Institutional Responses to Children, 1890–1920s." *American Journal of Sociology* 95, No. 6:1367–1400.

Tappan, Paul. 1946. "Treatment Without Trial?" *Social Problems* 24 (March):306–311.

Terry, Robert. 1967. "Discrimination in the Police Handling of Juvenile Offenders by Social Control Agencies." *Journal of Research in Crime and Delinquency* 14:212–220.

Thomas, Charles W., and Robin J. Cage. 1977. "The Effects of Social Characteristics on Juvenile Court Dispositions." *The Sociological Quarterly* 18, No. 2 (Spring):237–252.

Thornberry, Terence P. 1973. "Race, Socioeconomic Status and Sentencing in the Juvenile Justice System." *Journal of Criminal Law and Criminology* 64, (March):90–98.

Thrasher, Frederic M. 1927. *The Gang: A Study of 1,313 Gangs in Chicago.* Chicago: University of Chicago Press.

Trattner, Walter I. 1979. *From Poor Law to Welfare State.* 2nd Edition. New York: The Free Press.

Warren, Marguerite. 1976. "Intervention with Juvenile Delinquents." In *Pursuing Justice for the Child.* Edited by Margaret K. Rosenheim. Chicago: University of Chicago Press.

Wines, E. C. 1880. *The State of Prisons and of Child-Saving Institutions in the Civilized World.* Cambridge: University Press.

Name Index

Subject Index